ACCA 13 P.S.

NATSUME

CONTENTS

Chapter 6	The Watchman on a Perch in the Broad Sky (Part One)	003
Chapter 7	The Watchman on a Perch in the Broad Sky (Part Two)	038
Chapter 8	Sentry Days, Together Days	080
Chapter 9	To the Land of Flowers, as Guided	098
Chapter 10	Tonight, Pray for Tomorrow's Sky	140
Final Chapter	The Dinner Party	164

ACCA 13 P.S.

TERRITORY INSPECTION DEPARTMENT

NATSUME ONO

パチ
PACHI (CRACKLE)
PACHI
パチ
PACHI
パチ
CHAPTER 6
The Watchman on a Perch in the Broad Sky (Part One)

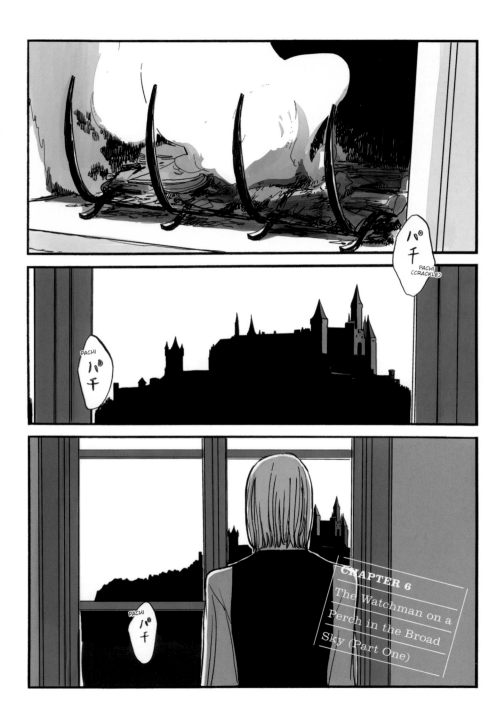

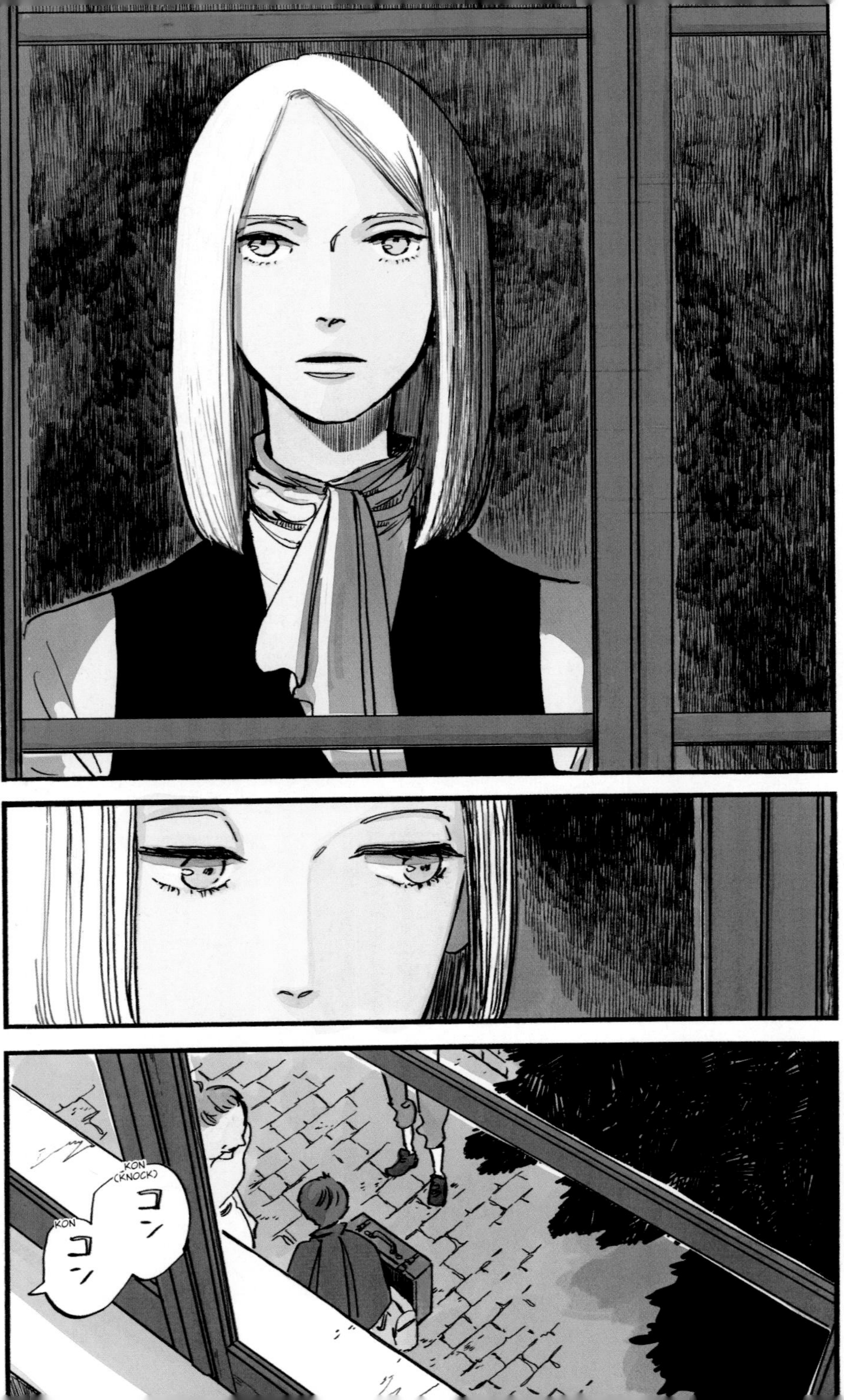
KON (KNOCK)
コン
KON
コン

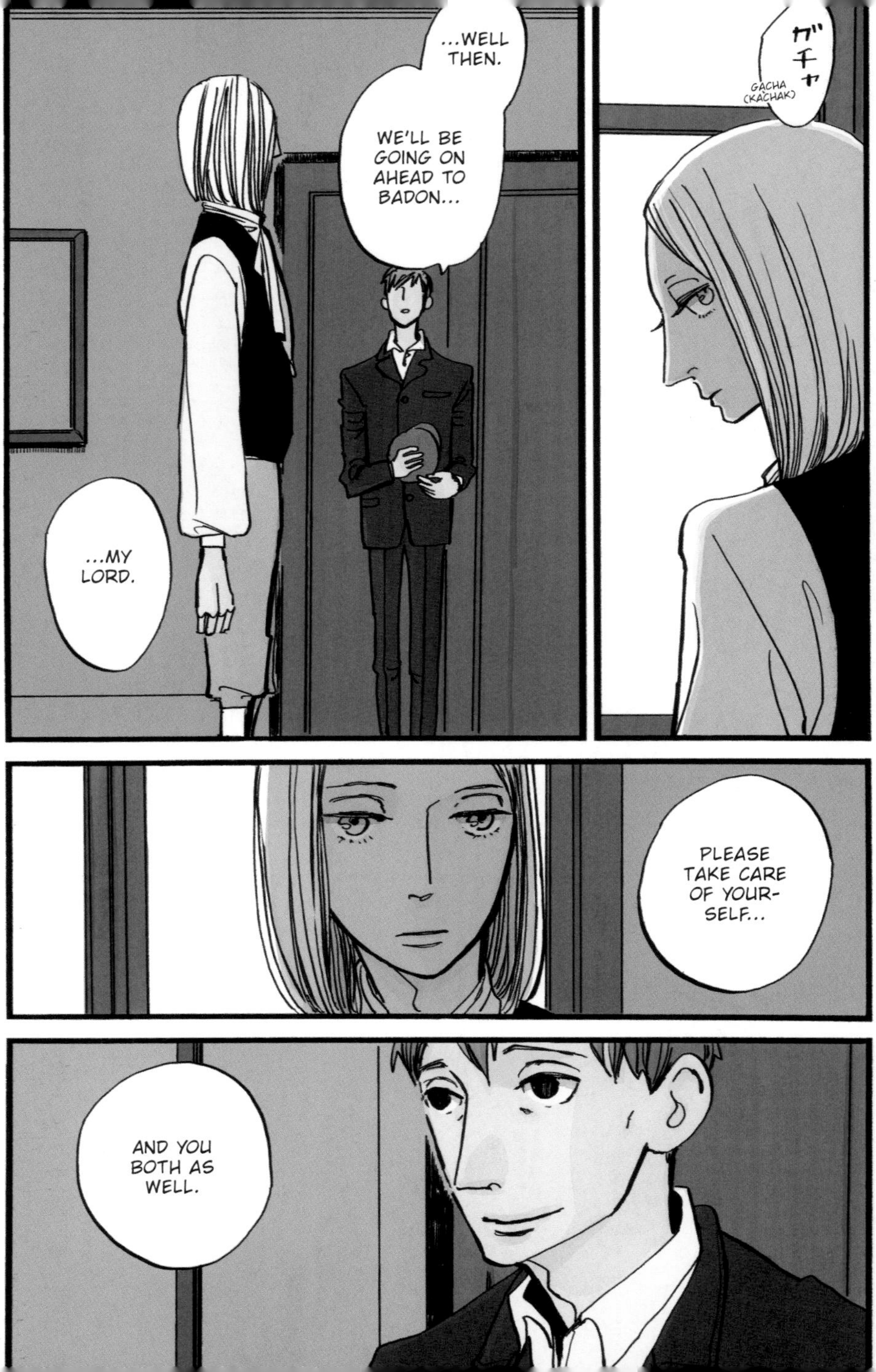
ガチャ
GACHA (KACHAK)
...WELL THEN.
WE'LL BE GOING ON AHEAD TO BADON...
...MY LORD.
PLEASE TAKE CARE OF YOUR-SELF...
AND YOU BOTH AS WELL.

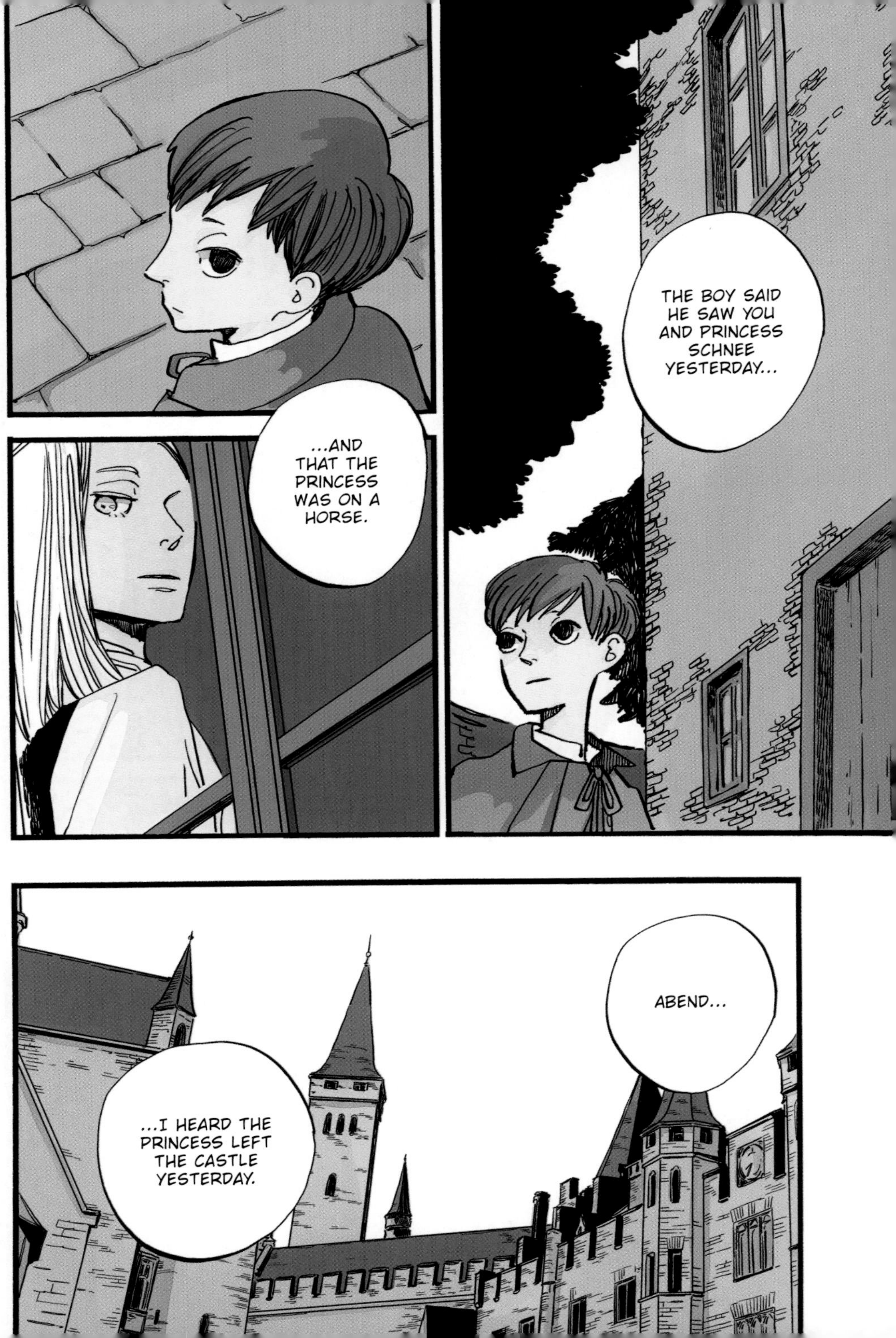
THE BOY SAID HE SAW YOU AND PRINCESS SCHNEE YESTERDAY...
...AND THAT THE PRINCESS WAS ON A HORSE.
ABEND...
...I HEARD THE PRINCESS LEFT THE CASTLE YESTERDAY.

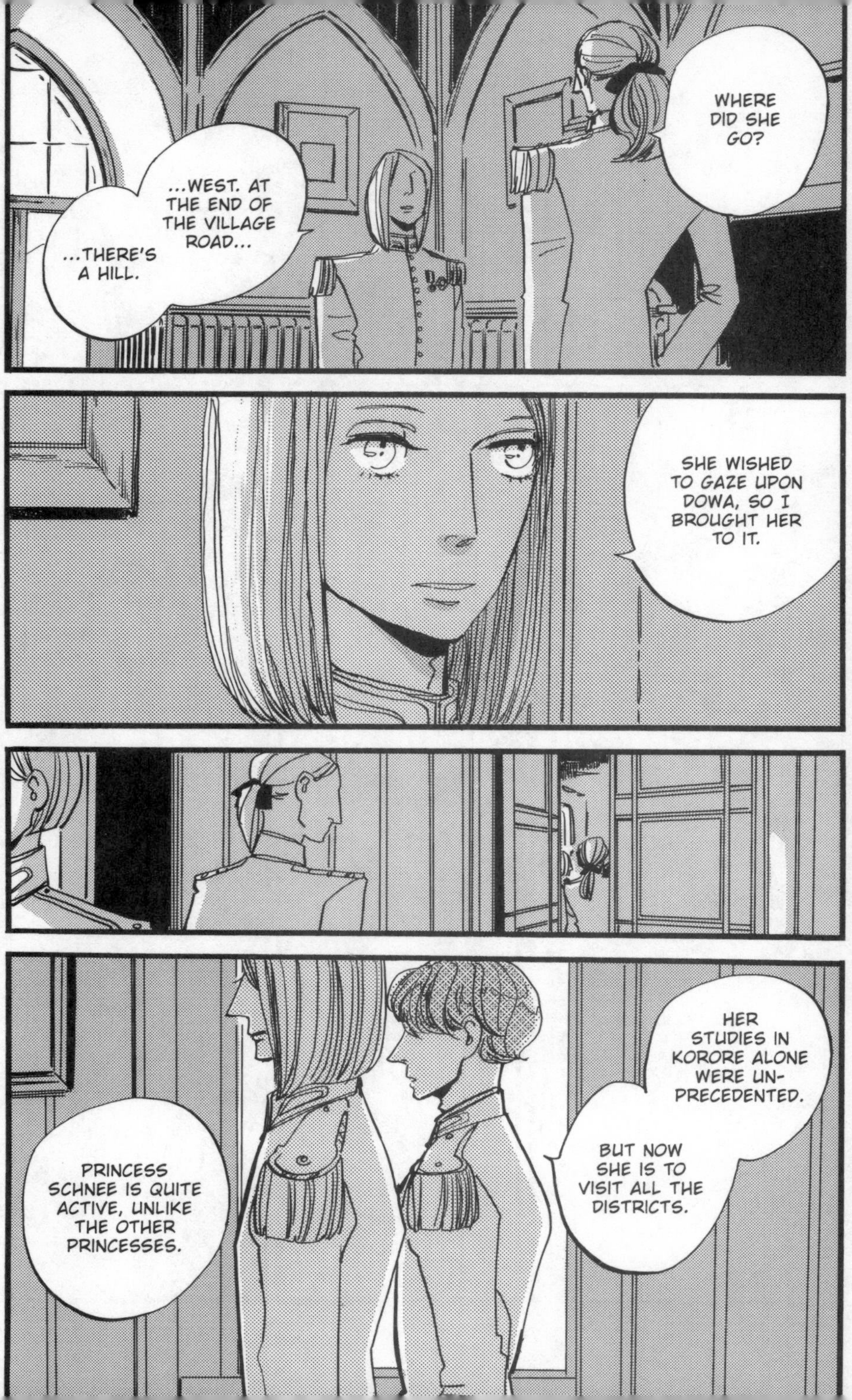

WHERE DID SHE GO?
...WEST. AT THE END OF THE VILLAGE ROAD...
...THERE'S A HILL.
SHE WISHED TO GAZE UPON DOWA, SO I BROUGHT HER TO IT.
HER STUDIES IN KORORE ALONE WERE UN-PRECEDENTED.
BUT NOW SHE IS TO VISIT ALL THE DISTRICTS.
PRINCESS SCHNEE IS QUITE ACTIVE, UNLIKE THE OTHER PRINCESSES.

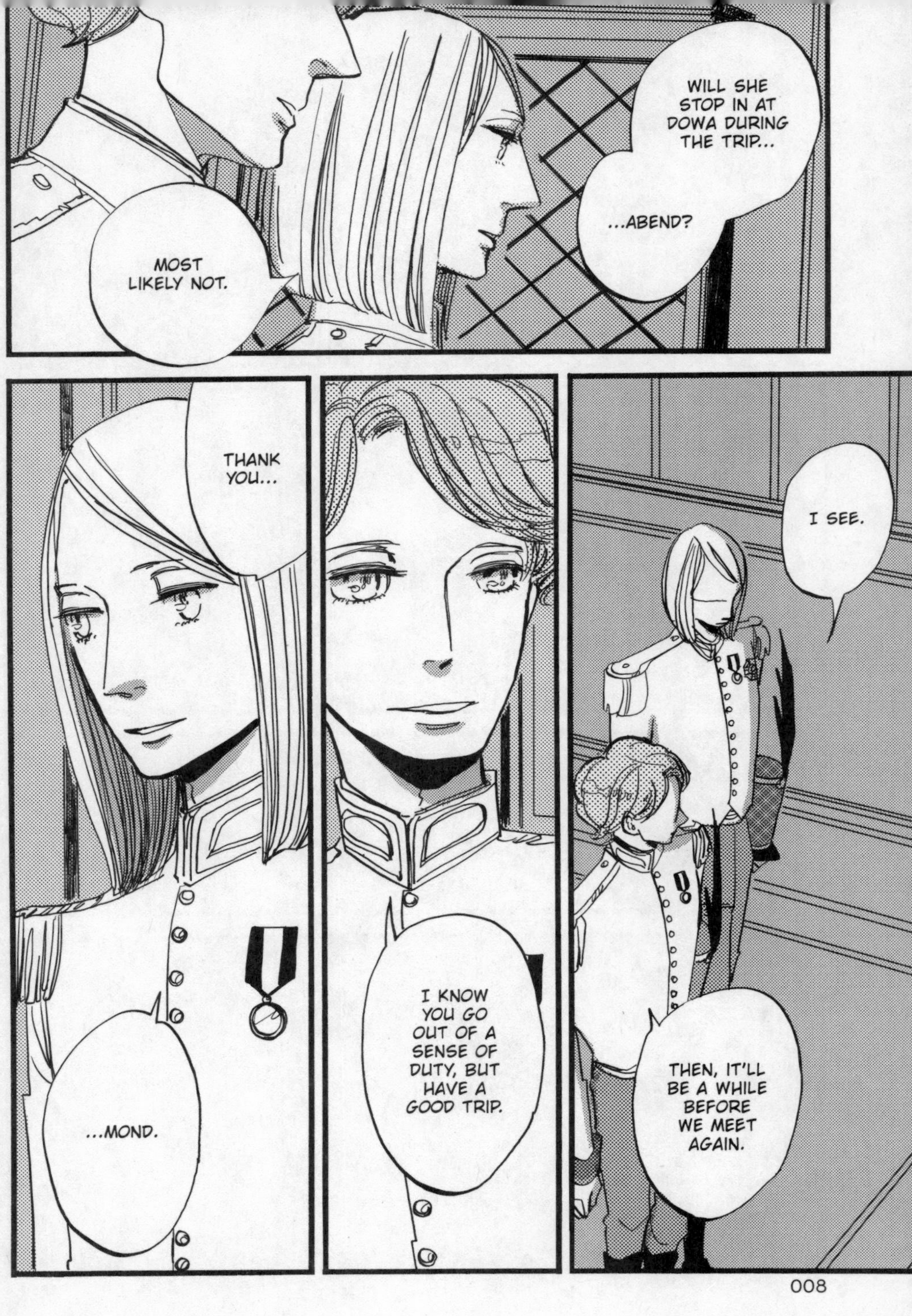
WILL SHE STOP IN AT DOWA DURING THE TRIP...
...ABEND?
MOST LIKELY NOT.
I SEE.
THEN, IT'LL BE A WHILE BEFORE WE MEET AGAIN.
I KNOW YOU GO OUT OF A SENSE OF DUTY, BUT HAVE A GOOD TRIP.
THANK YOU...
...MOND.

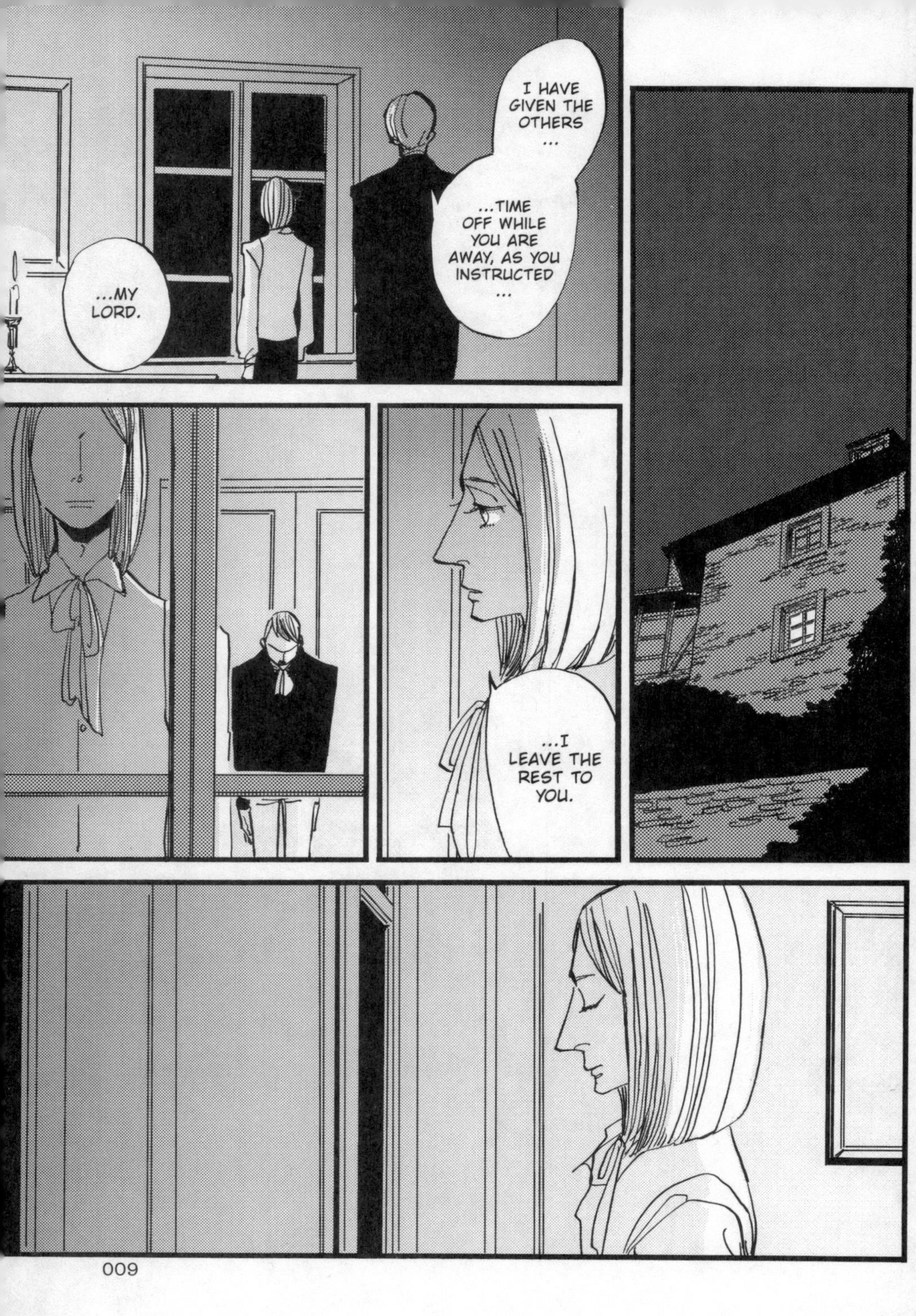
I HAVE GIVEN THE OTHERS ...
...TIME OFF WHILE YOU ARE AWAY, AS YOU INSTRUCTED ...
...MY LORD.
...I LEAVE THE REST TO YOU.

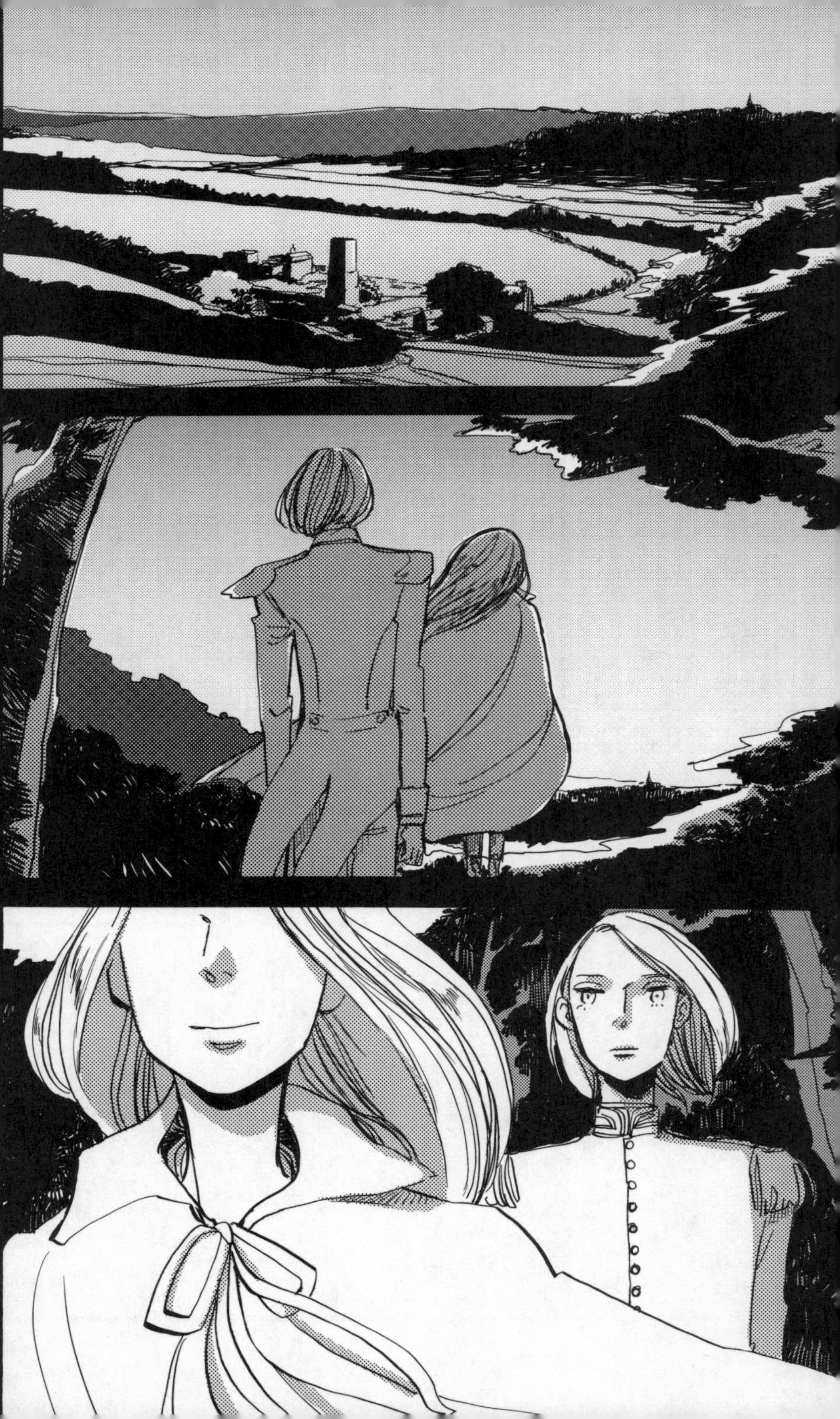

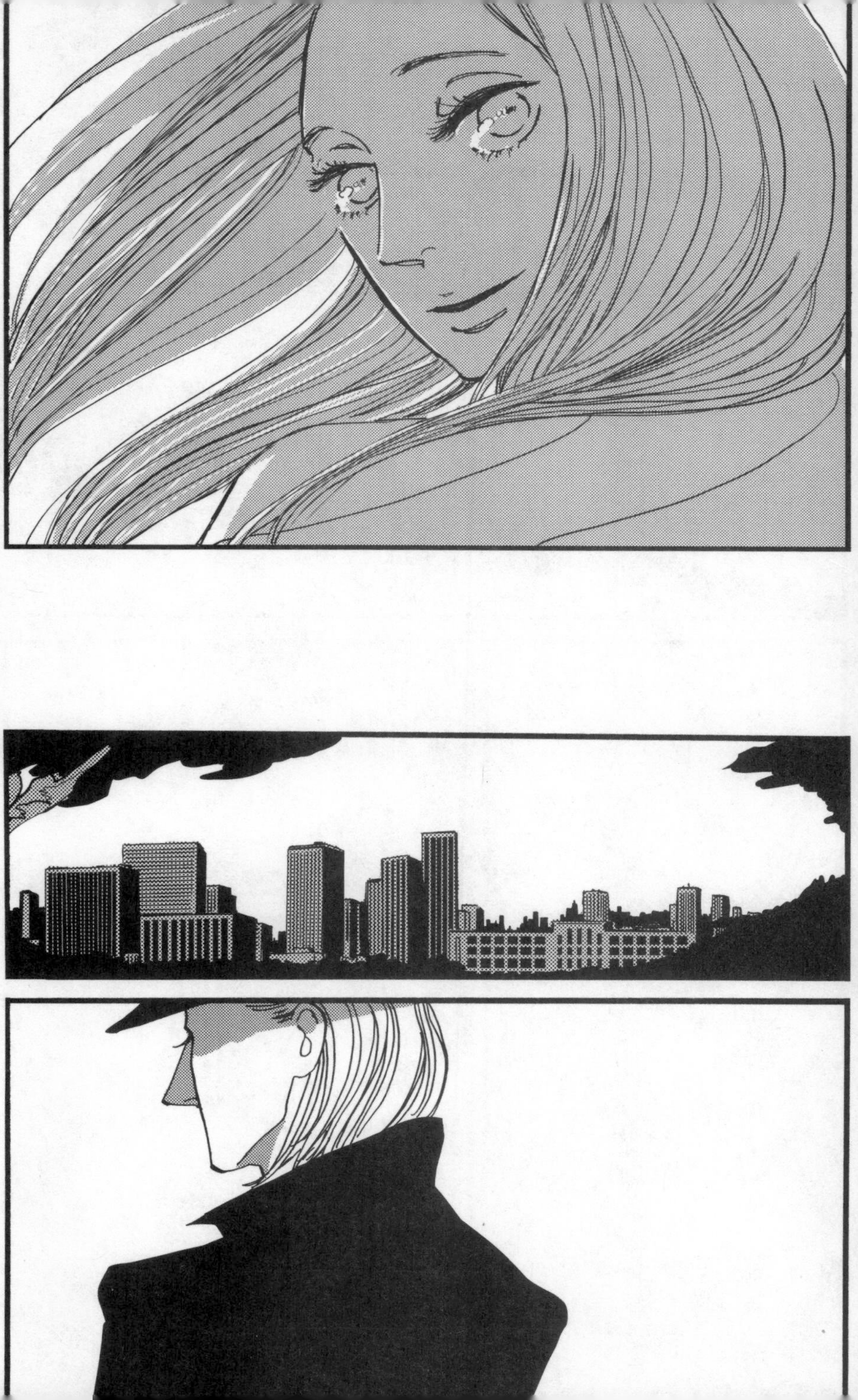

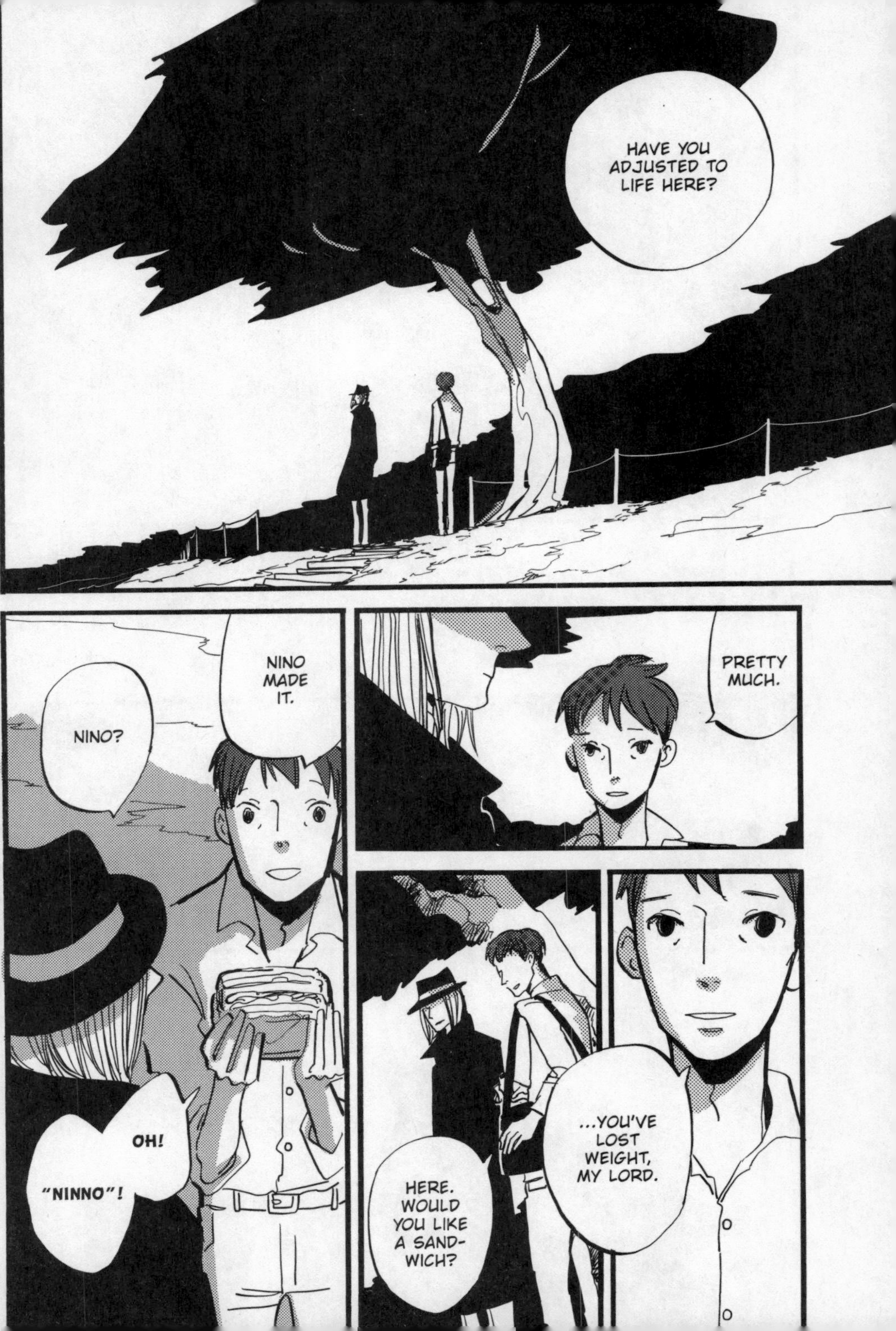
HAVE YOU ADJUSTED TO LIFE HERE?
PRETTY MUCH.
...YOU'VE LOST WEIGHT, MY LORD.
HERE. WOULD YOU LIKE A SAND-WICH?
NINO MADE IT.
NINO?
OH!
"NINNO"!

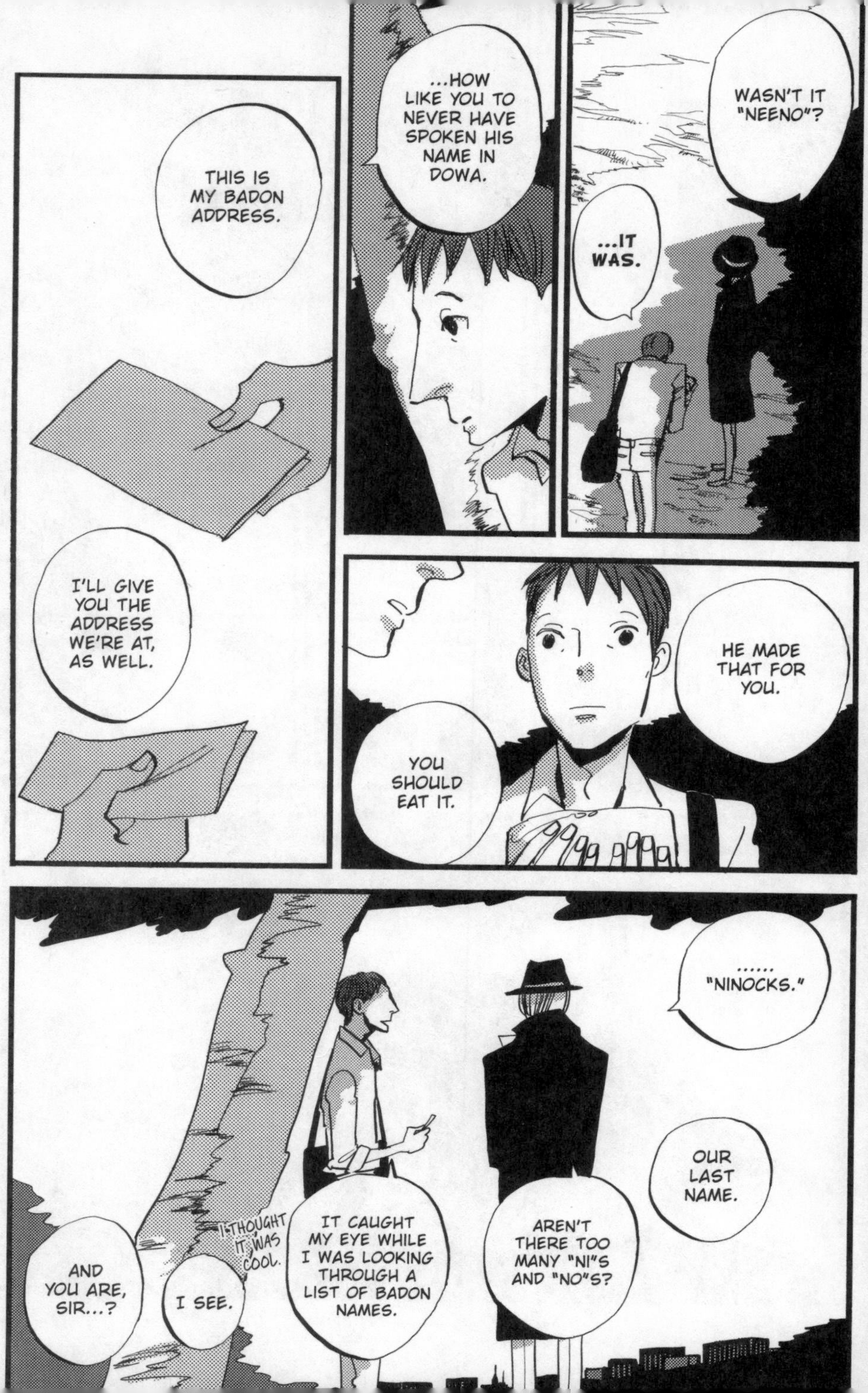

WASN'T IT "NEENO"?
...IT WAS.
...HOW LIKE YOU TO NEVER HAVE SPOKEN HIS NAME IN DOWA.
HE MADE THAT FOR YOU.
YOU SHOULD EAT IT.
THIS IS MY BADON ADDRESS.
I'LL GIVE YOU THE ADDRESS WE'RE AT, AS WELL.
...... "NINOCKS."
OUR LAST NAME.
AREN'T THERE TOO MANY "NI"S AND "NO"S?
IT CAUGHT MY EYE WHILE I WAS LOOKING THROUGH A LIST OF BADON NAMES.
I THOUGHT IT WAS COOL.
I SEE.
AND YOU ARE, SIR...?

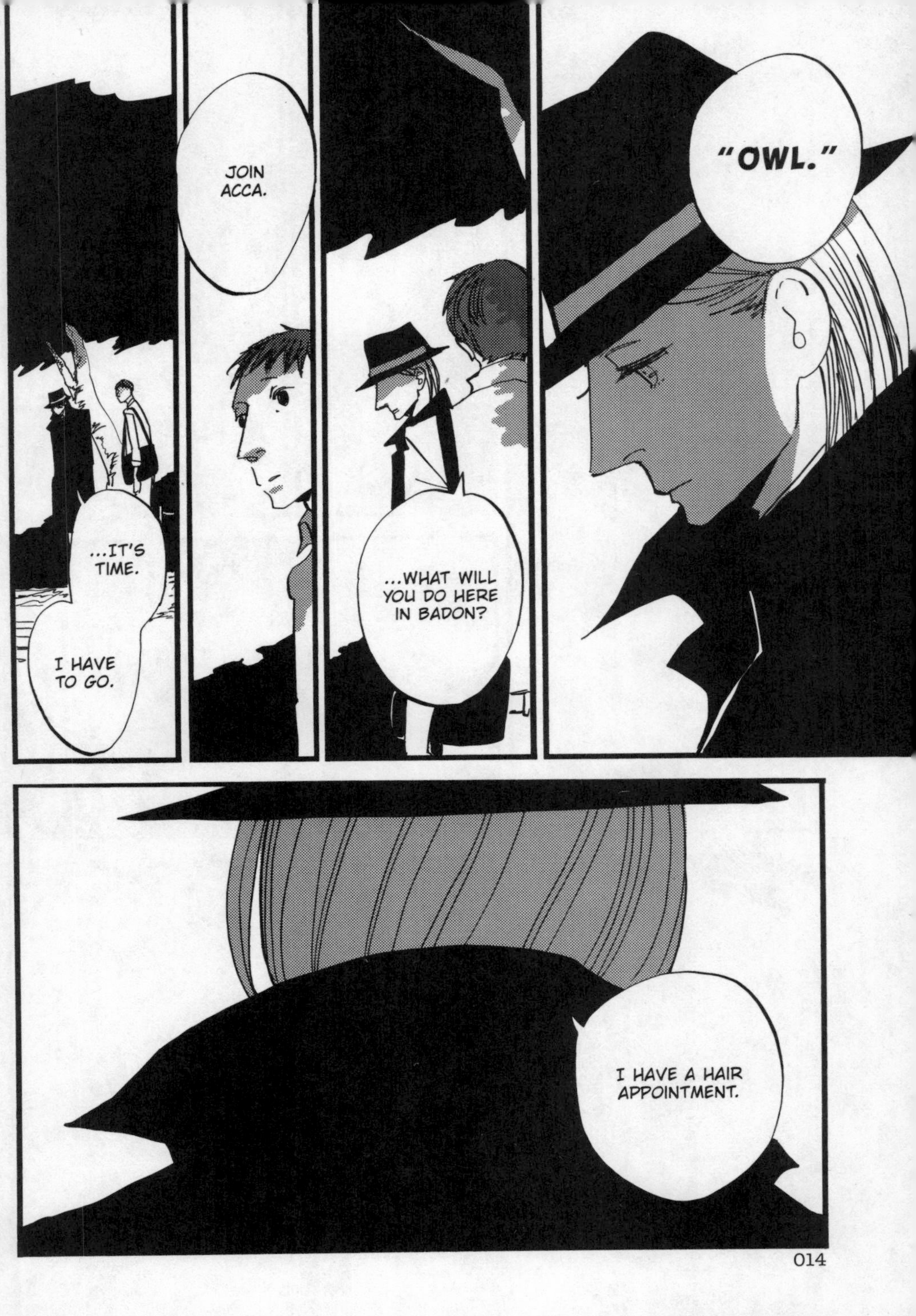
"OWL."
...WHAT WILL YOU DO HERE IN BADON?
JOIN ACCA.
...IT'S TIME.
I HAVE TO GO.
I HAVE A HAIR APPOINTMENT.

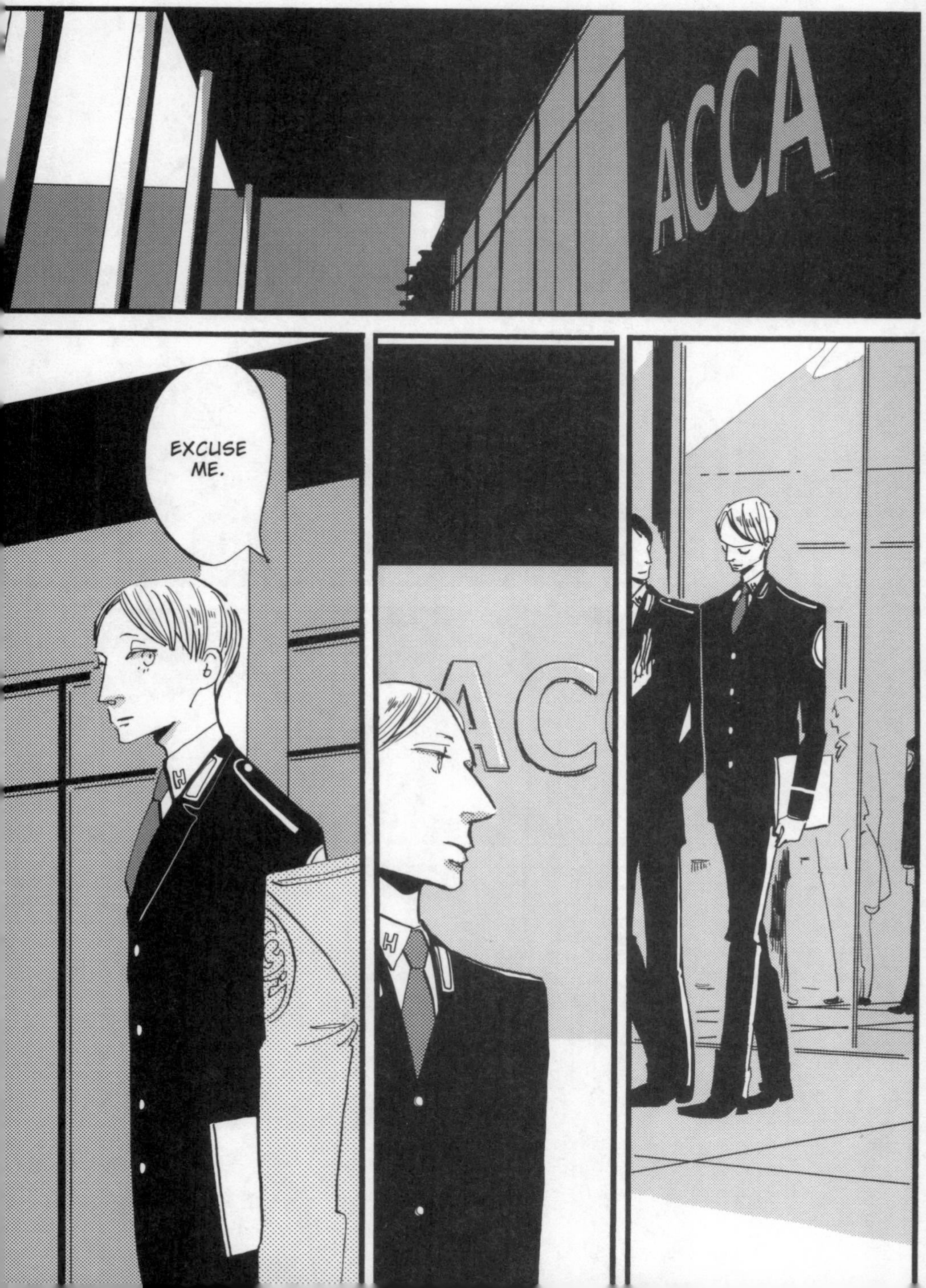
ACCA
EXCUSE ME.
ACC

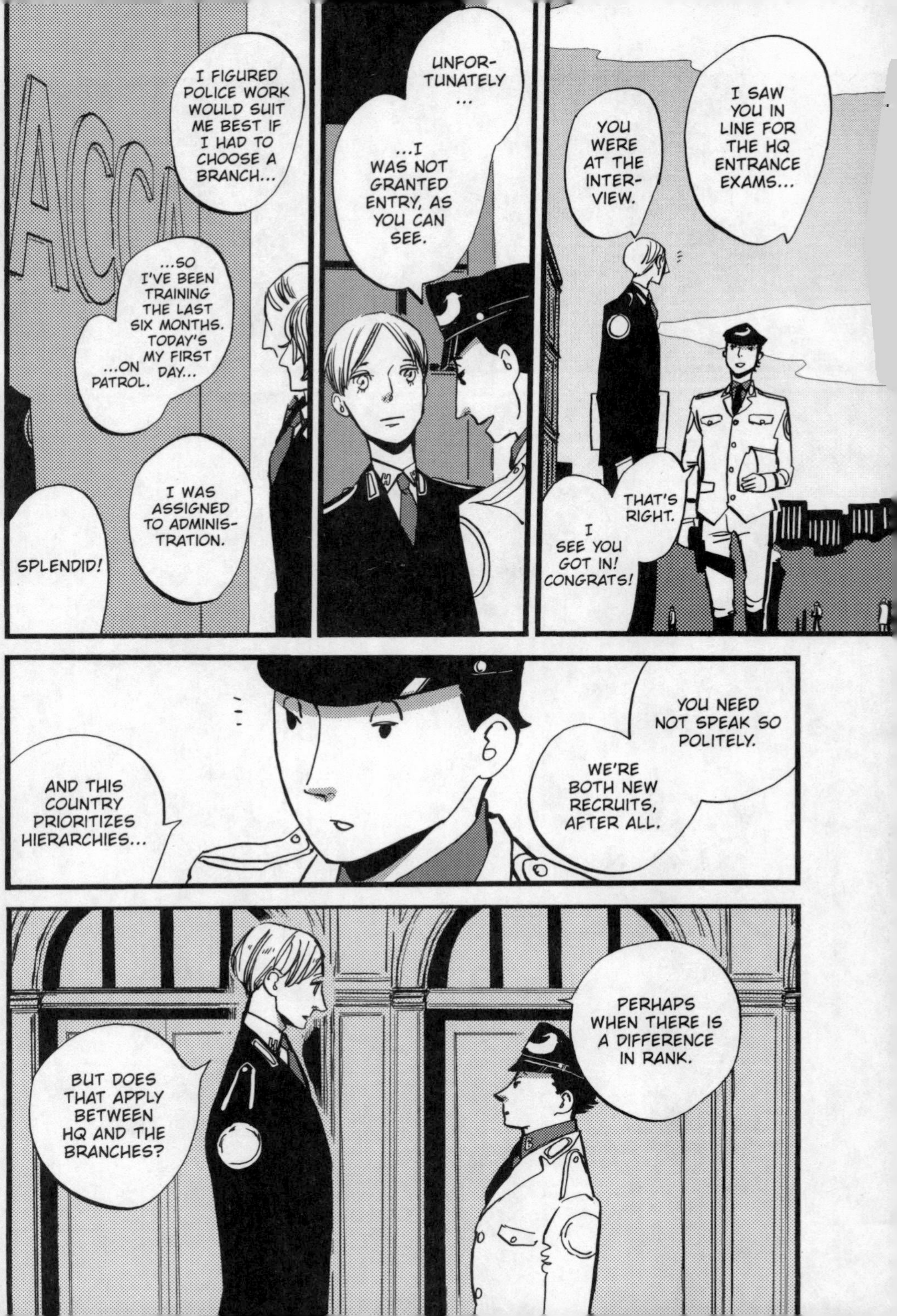
I SAW YOU IN LINE FOR THE HQ ENTRANCE EXAMS...
YOU WERE AT THE INTER-VIEW.
THAT'S RIGHT.
I SEE YOU GOT IN! CONGRATS!
UNFOR-TUNATELY...
...I WAS NOT GRANTED ENTRY, AS YOU CAN SEE.
ACCA
I FIGURED POLICE WORK WOULD SUIT ME BEST IF I HAD TO CHOOSE A BRANCH...
...SO I'VE BEEN TRAINING THE LAST SIX MONTHS. TODAY'S MY FIRST DAY... ...ON PATROL.
I WAS ASSIGNED TO ADMINIS-TRATION.
SPLENDID!
YOU NEED NOT SPEAK SO POLITELY.
WE'RE BOTH NEW RECRUITS, AFTER ALL.
AND THIS COUNTRY PRIORITIZES HIERARCHIES...
PERHAPS WHEN THERE IS A DIFFERENCE IN RANK.
BUT DOES THAT APPLY BETWEEN HQ AND THE BRANCHES?

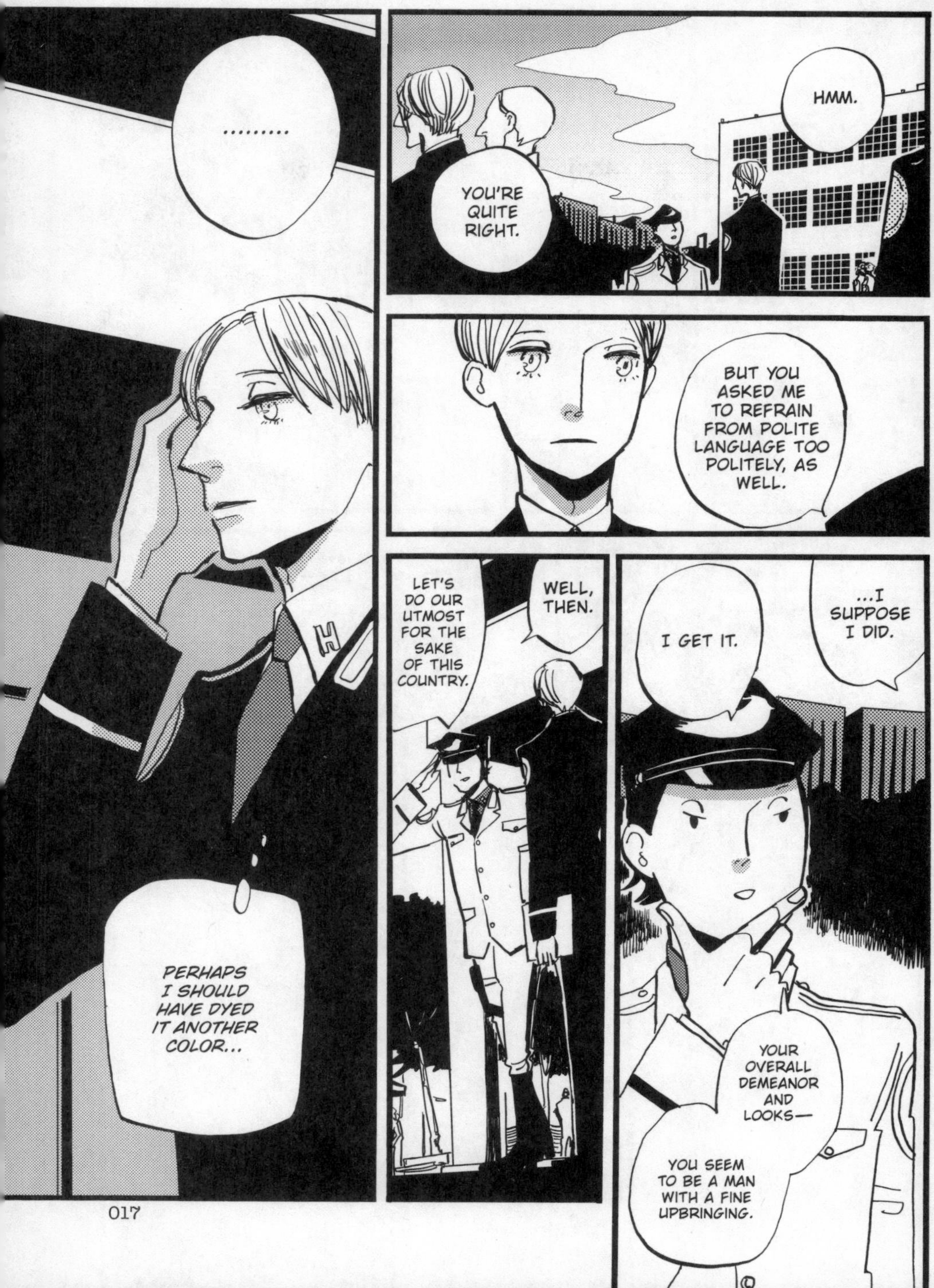
HMM.
YOU'RE QUITE RIGHT.
BUT YOU ASKED ME TO REFRAIN FROM POLITE LANGUAGE TOO POLITELY, AS WELL.
...I SUPPOSE I DID.
I GET IT.
YOUR OVERALL DEMEANOR AND LOOKS—
YOU SEEM TO BE A MAN WITH A FINE UPBRINGING.
WELL, THEN.
LET'S DO OUR UTMOST FOR THE SAKE OF THIS COUNTRY.
....
PERHAPS I SHOULD HAVE DYED IT ANOTHER COLOR...

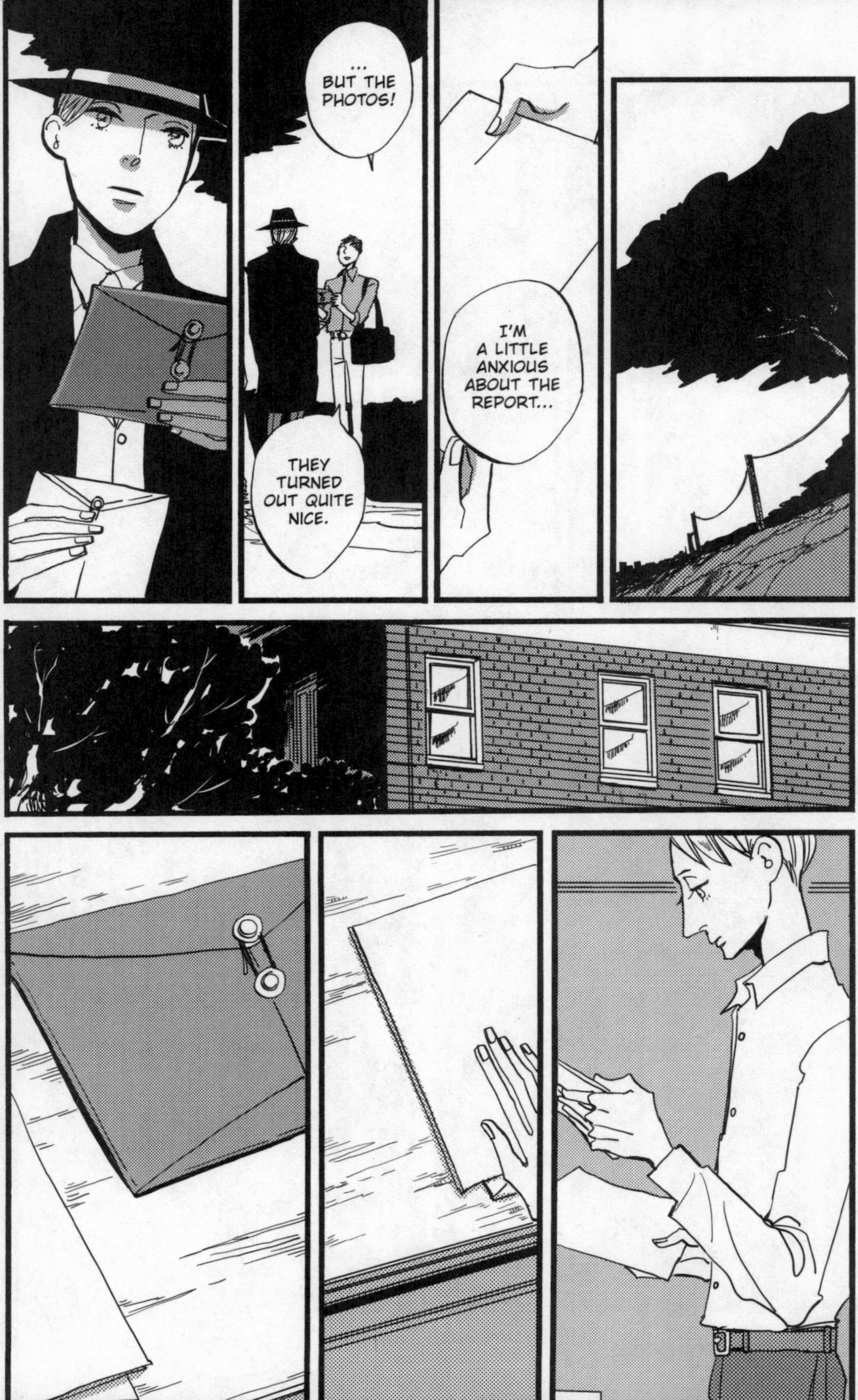
I'M A LITTLE ANXIOUS ABOUT THE REPORT...
... BUT THE PHOTOS!
THEY TURNED OUT QUITE NICE.

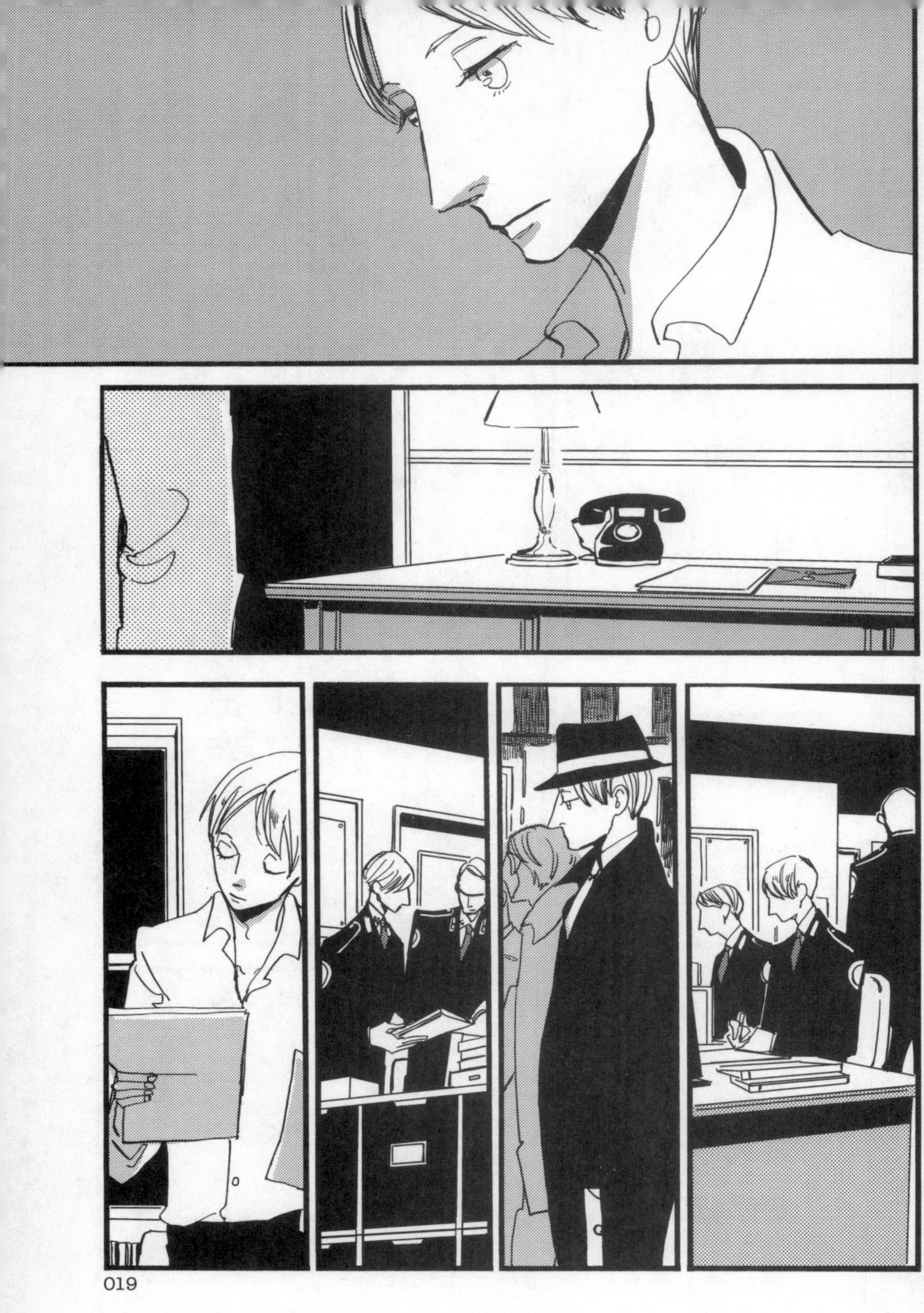

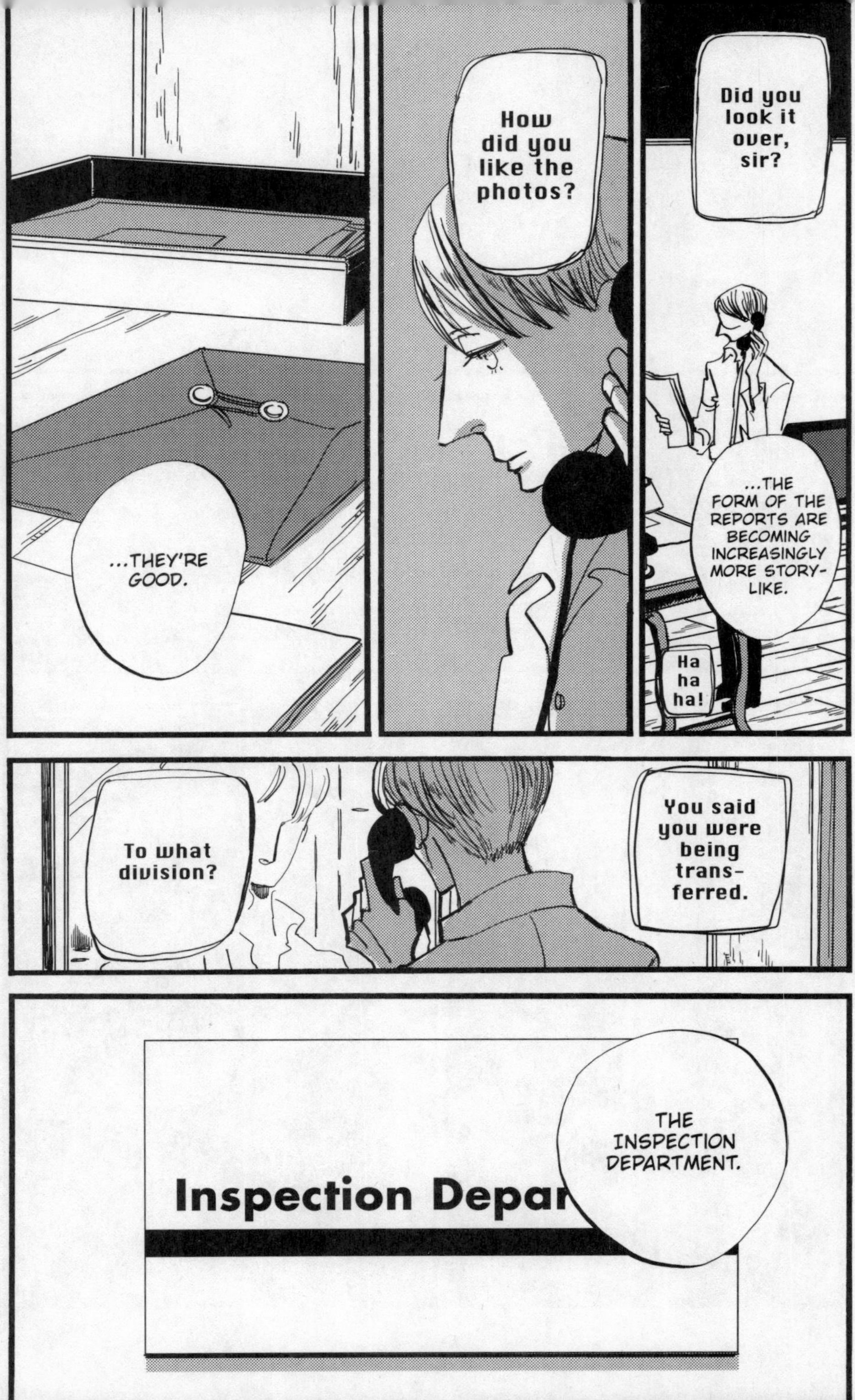
Did you look it over, sir?
...THE FORM OF THE REPORTS ARE BECOMING INCREASINGLY MORE STORY-LIKE.
Ha ha ha!
How did you like the photos?
...THEY'RE GOOD.
You said you were being transferred.
To what division?
THE INSPECTION DEPARTMENT.
Inspection Depar

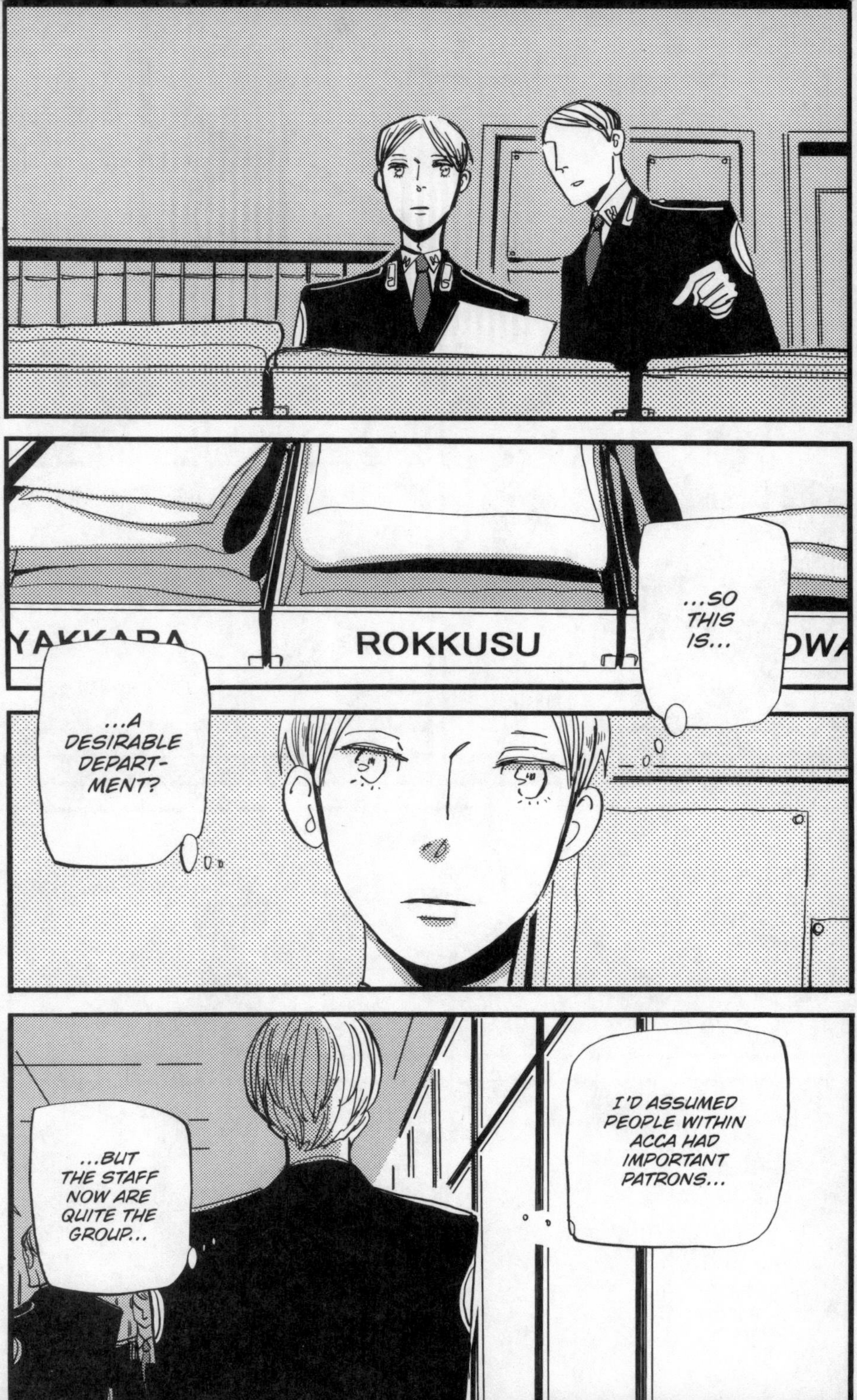

...SO THIS IS...
ROKKUSU
YAKKARA
...A DESIRABLE DEPART-MENT?
I'D ASSUMED PEOPLE WITHIN ACCA HAD IMPORTANT PATRONS...
...BUT THE STAFF NOW ARE QUITE THE GROUP...

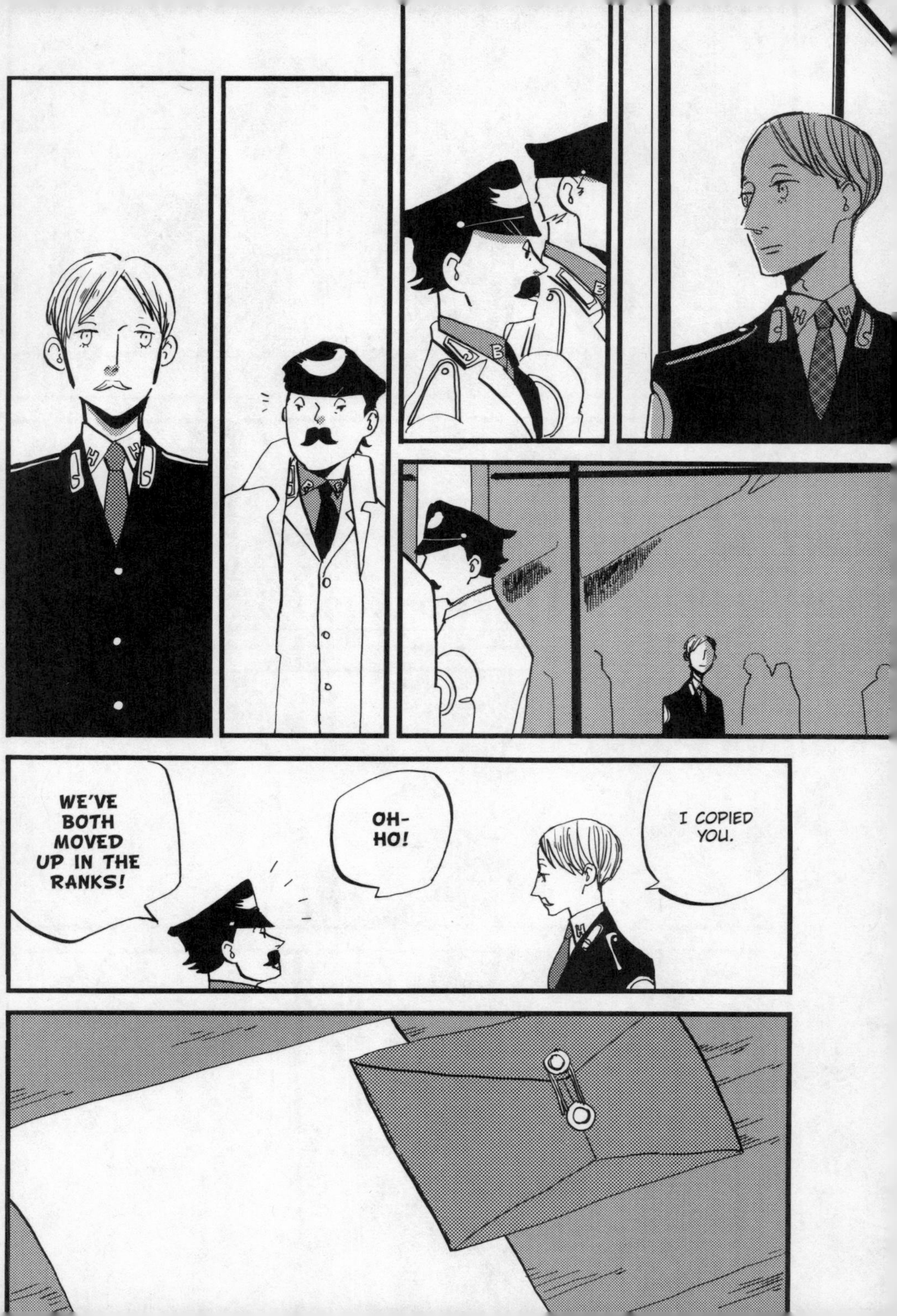
I COPIED YOU.
OH-HO!
WE'VE BOTH MOVED UP IN THE RANKS!

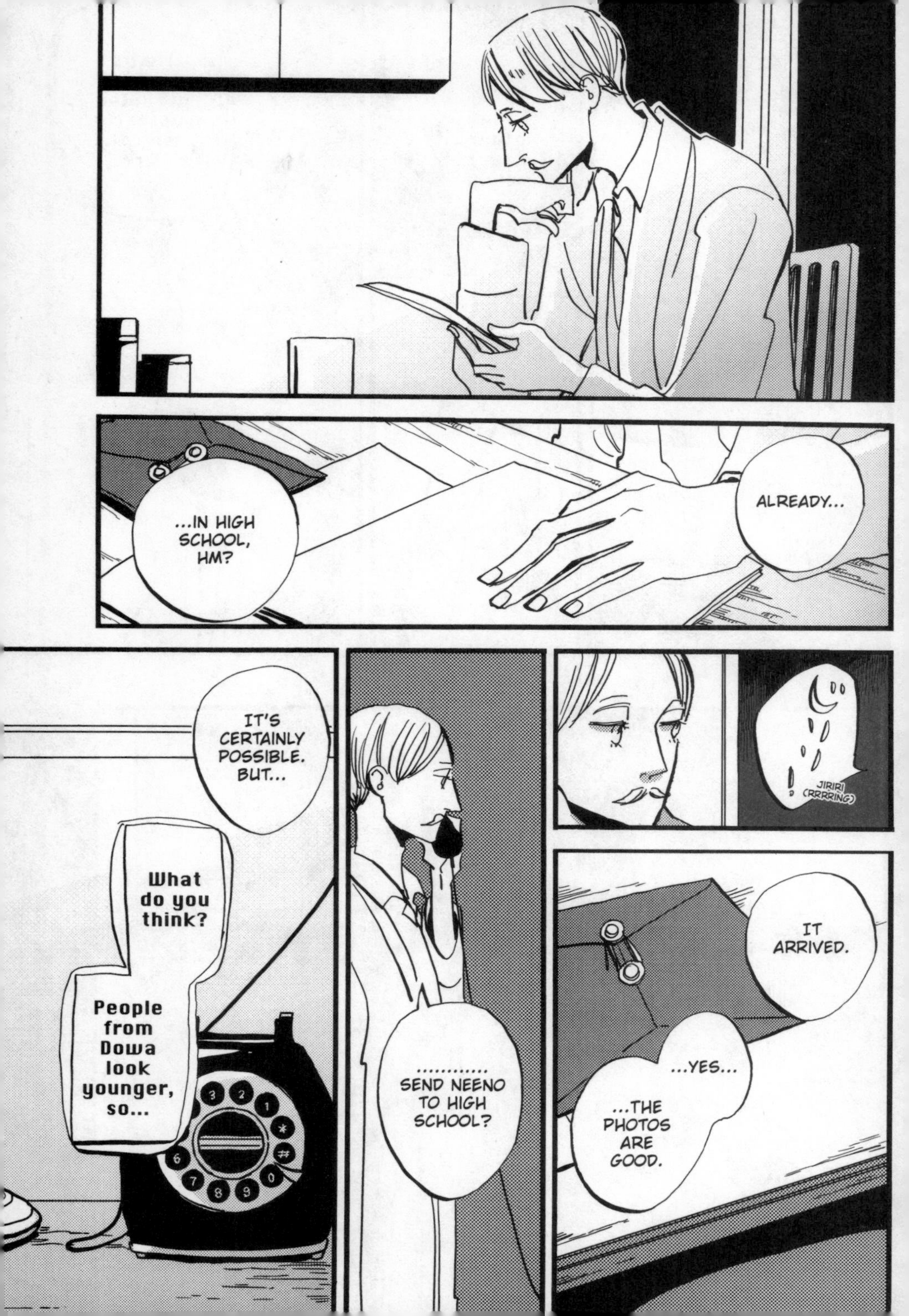
ALREADY...
...IN HIGH SCHOOL, HM?
JIRIRI (RRRRING)
IT ARRIVED.
...YES...
...THE PHOTOS ARE GOOD.
.... SEND NEENO TO HIGH SCHOOL?
IT'S CERTAINLY POSSIBLE. BUT...
What do you think?
People from Dowa look younger, so...

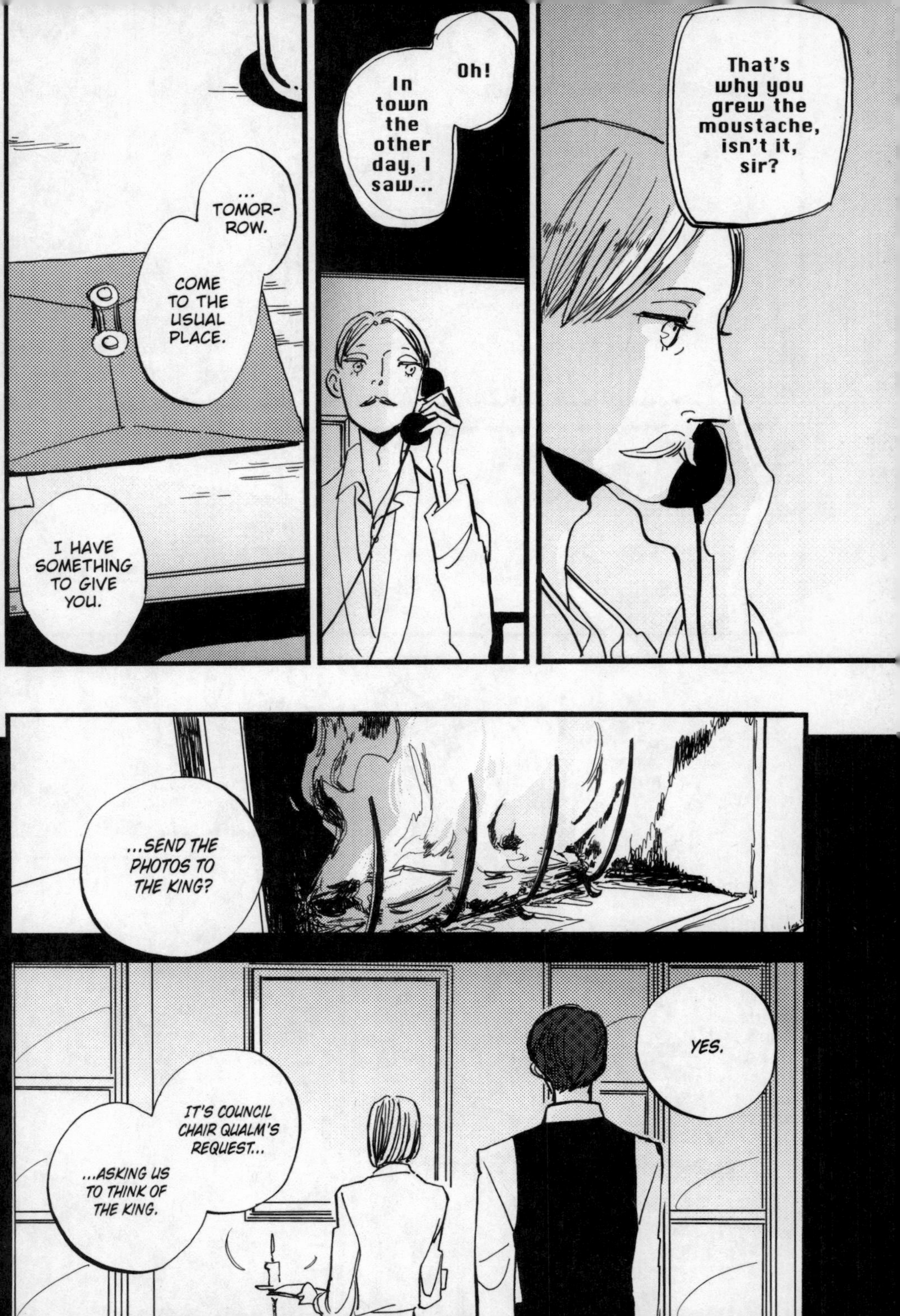
That's why you grew the moustache, isn't it, sir?
Oh!
In town the other day, I saw...
...TOMORROW.
COME TO THE USUAL PLACE.
I HAVE SOMETHING TO GIVE YOU.
...SEND THE PHOTOS TO THE KING?
YES.
IT'S COUNCIL CHAIR QUALM'S REQUEST...
...ASKING US TO THINK OF THE KING.

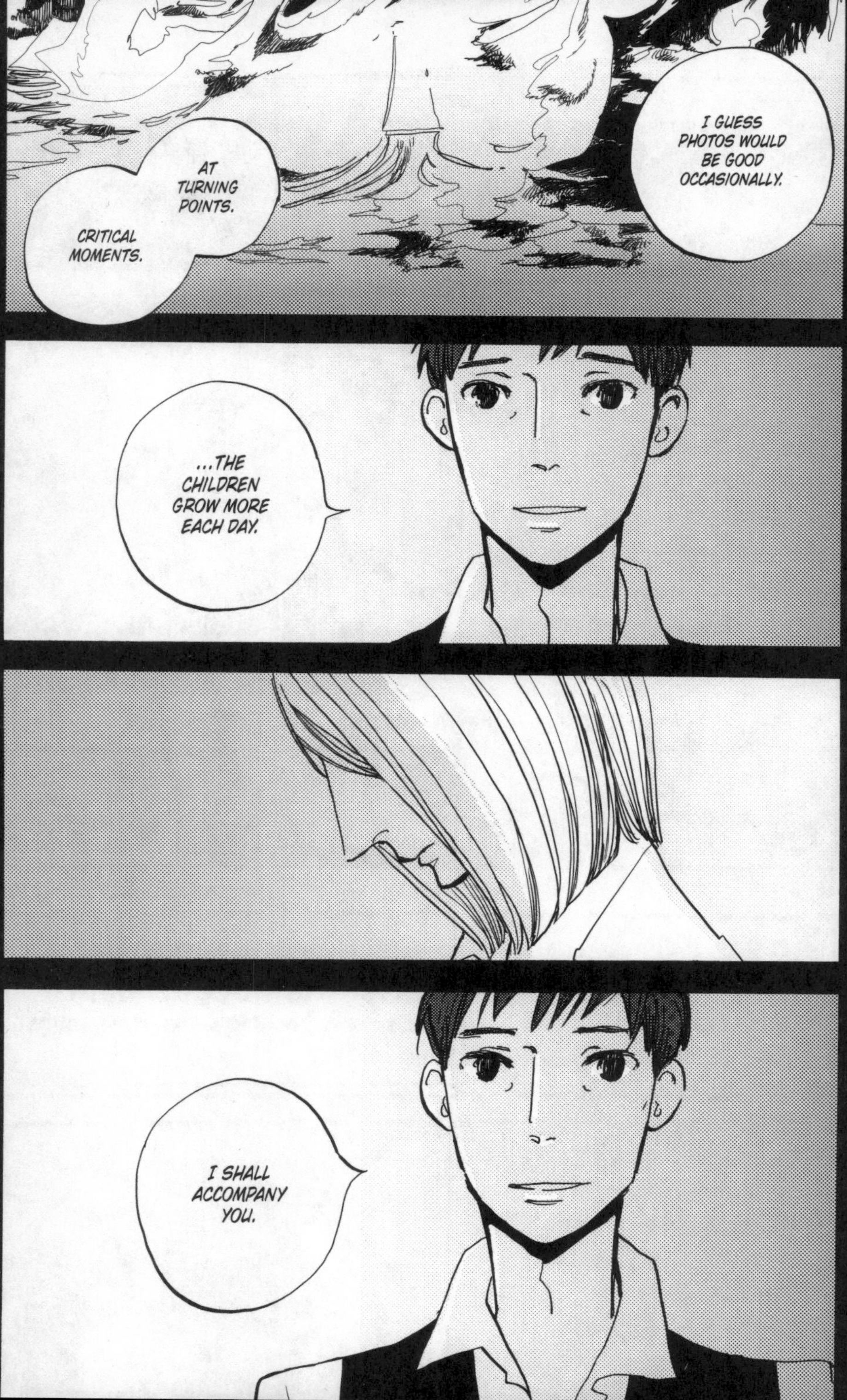
I GUESS PHOTOS WOULD BE GOOD OCCASIONALLY.
AT TURNING POINTS.
CRITICAL MOMENTS.
...THE CHILDREN GROW MORE EACH DAY.
I SHALL ACCOMPANY YOU.

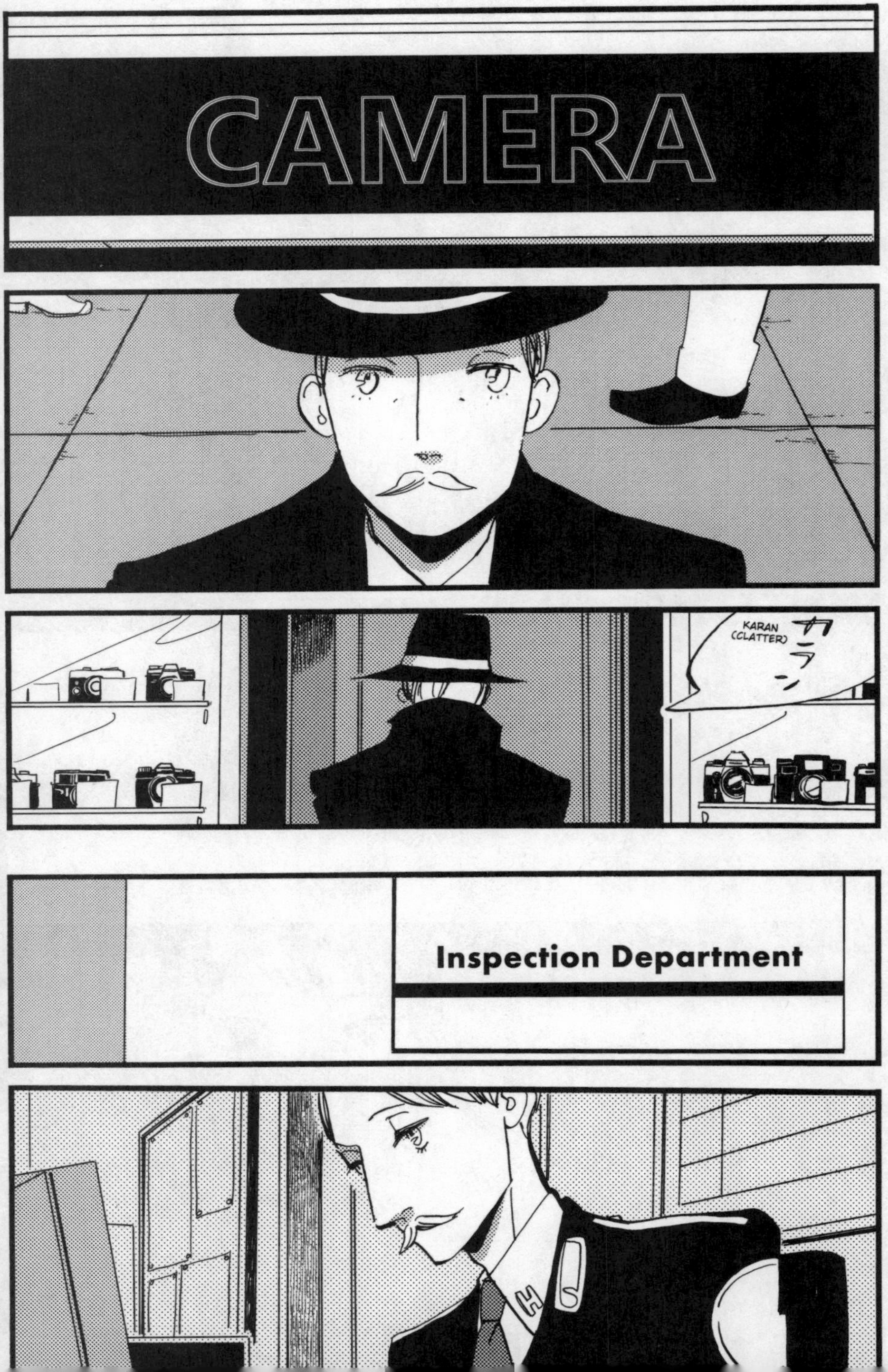
CAMERA
KARAN (CLATTER)
カラン
Inspection Department

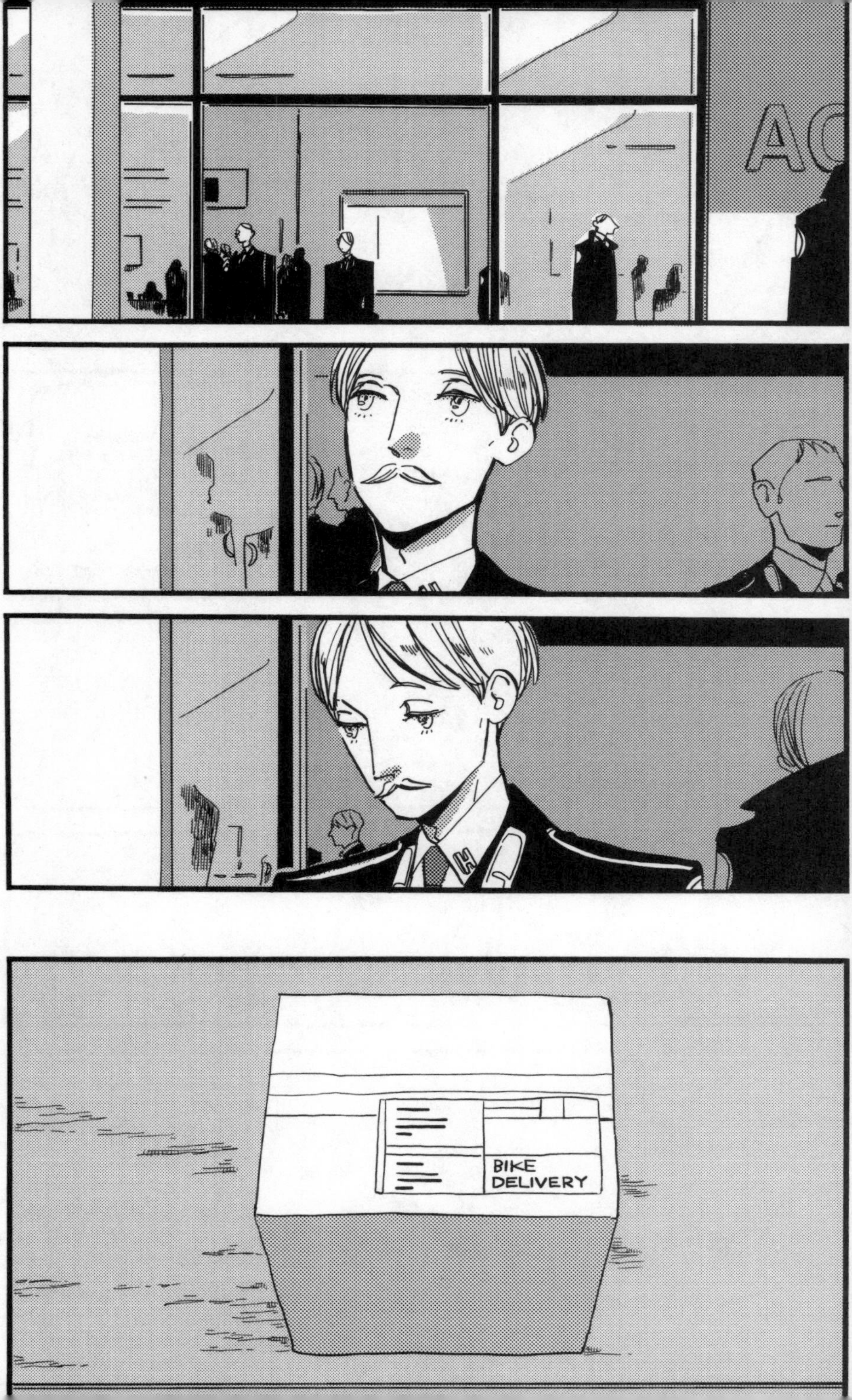
BIKE
DELIVERY

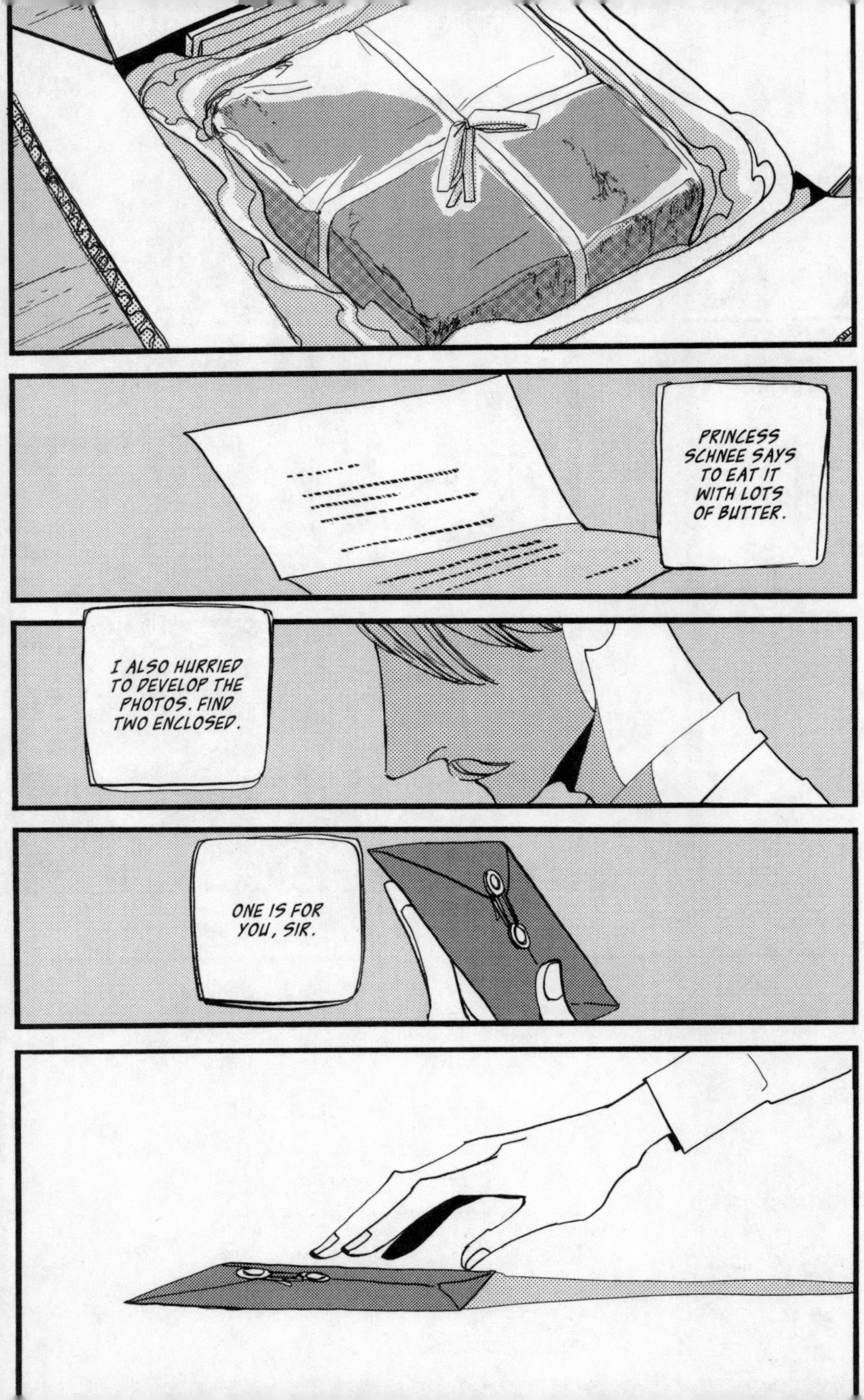
PRINCESS SCHNEE SAYS TO EAT IT WITH LOTS OF BUTTER.
I ALSO HURRIED TO DEVELOP THE PHOTOS. FIND TWO ENCLOSED.
ONE IS FOR YOU, SIR.

HAS PRINCESS SCHNEE CAUGHT ONTO US?

PROBABLY.

THEN, I SUPPOSE SHE BAKED THAT BREAD FOR HIS LORDSHIP?

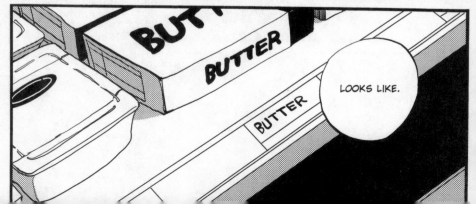

LOOKS LIKE.

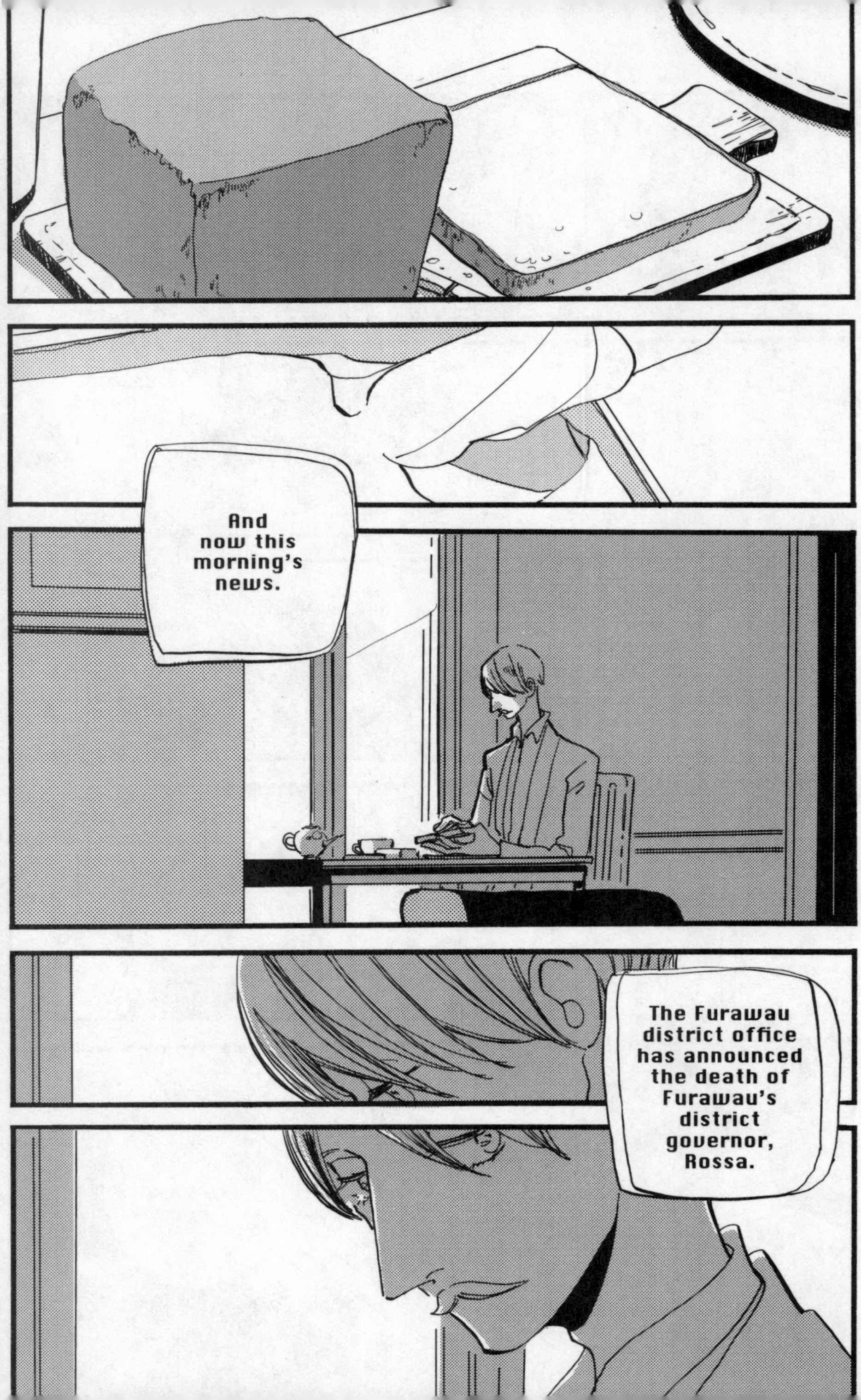
And now this morning's news.
The Furawau district office has announced the death of Furawau's district governor, Rossa.

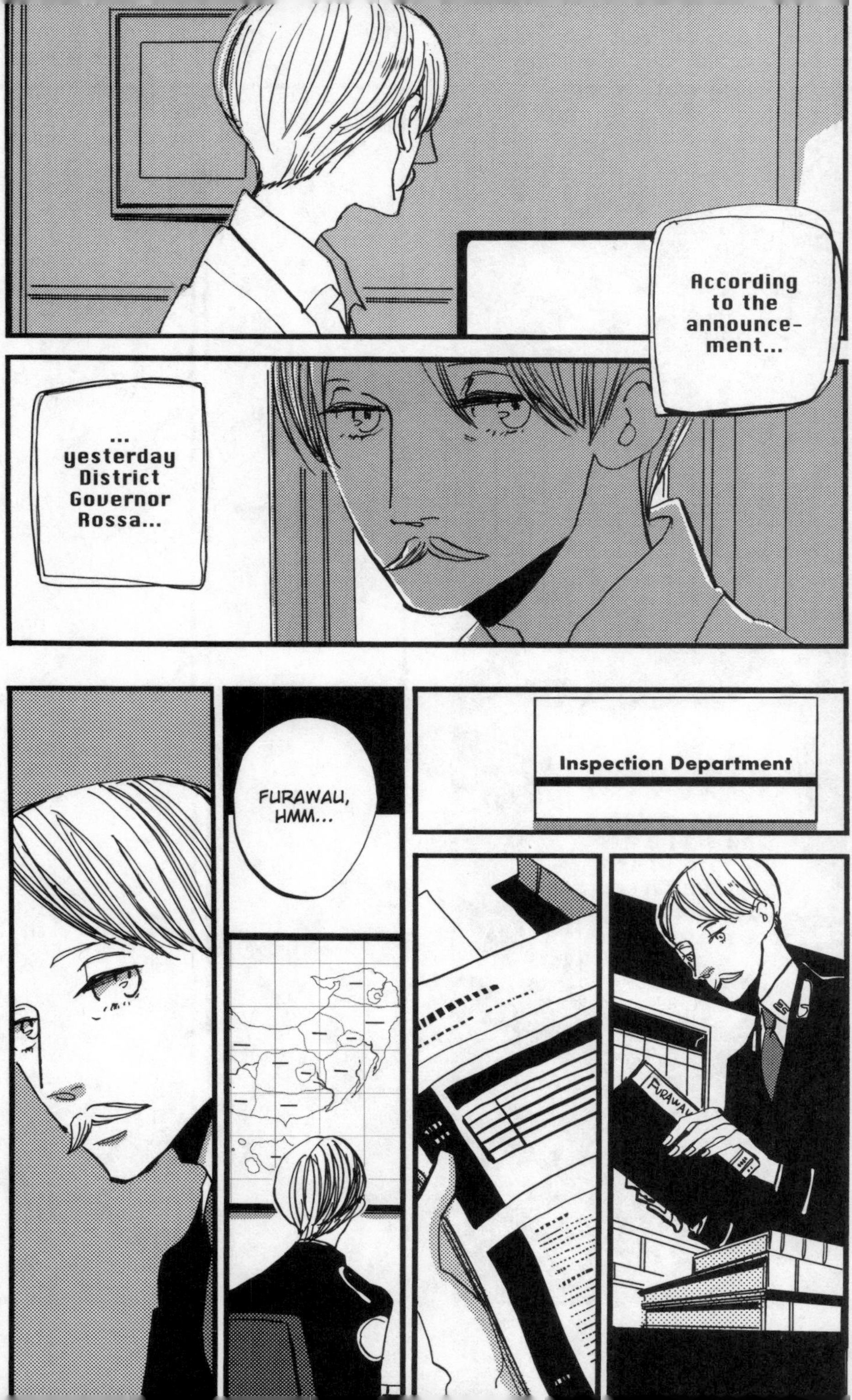
According to the announcement...
...yesterday District Governor Rossa...
Inspection Department
FURAWAU
FURAWAU, HMM...

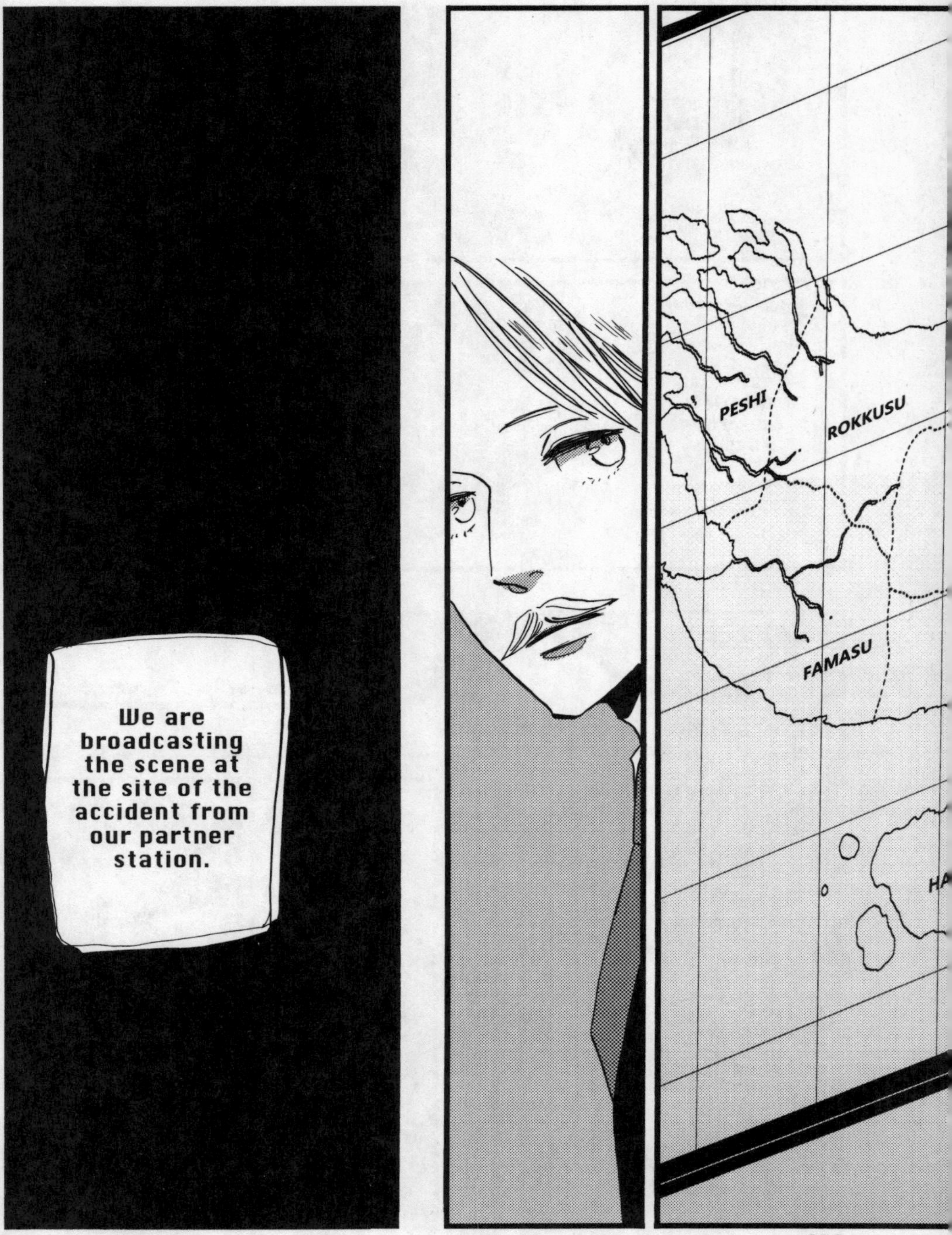
PESHI
ROKKUSU
FAMASU
We are broadcasting the scene at the site of the accident from our partner station.

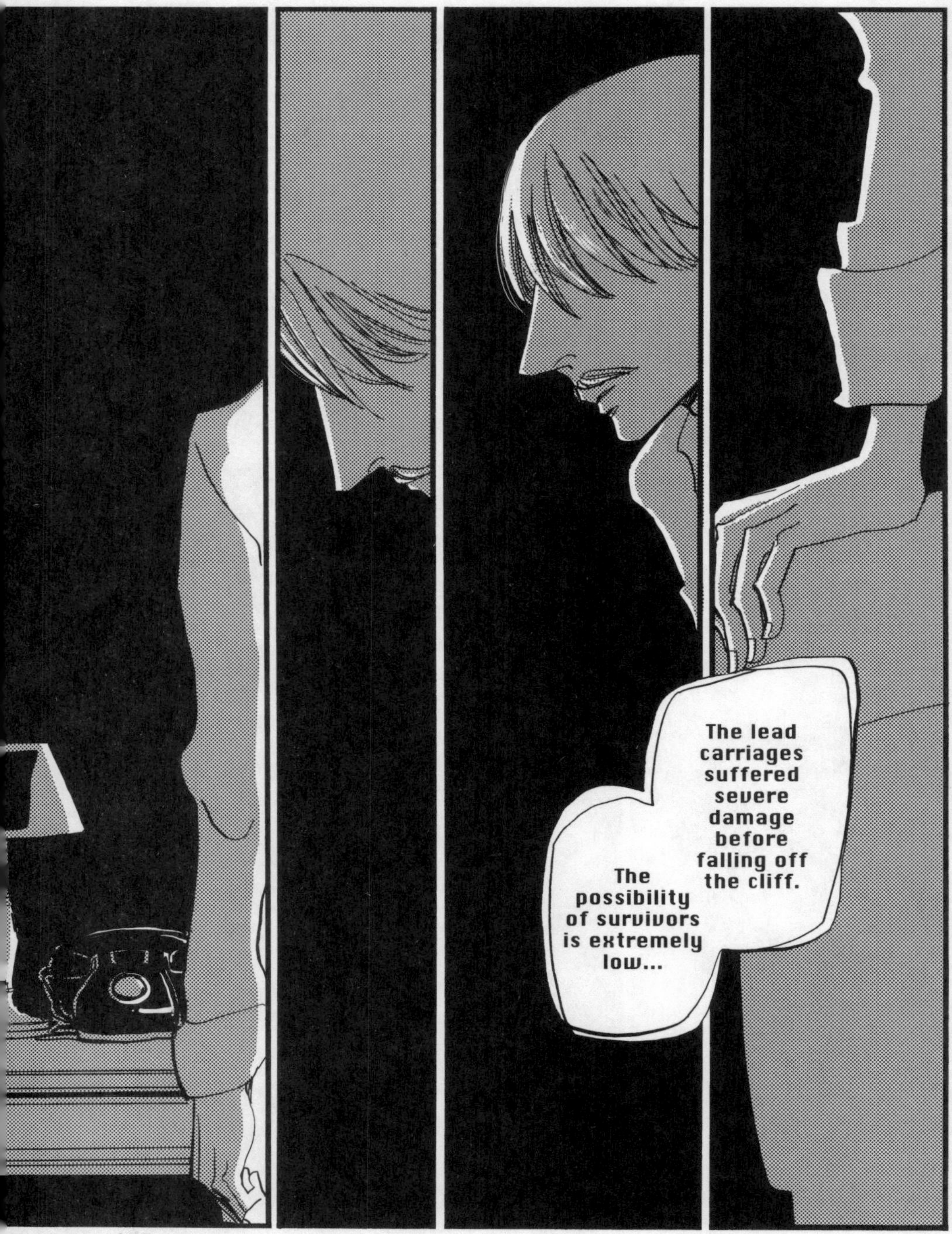
The lead carriages suffered severe damage before falling off the cliff.
The possibility of survivors is extremely low...

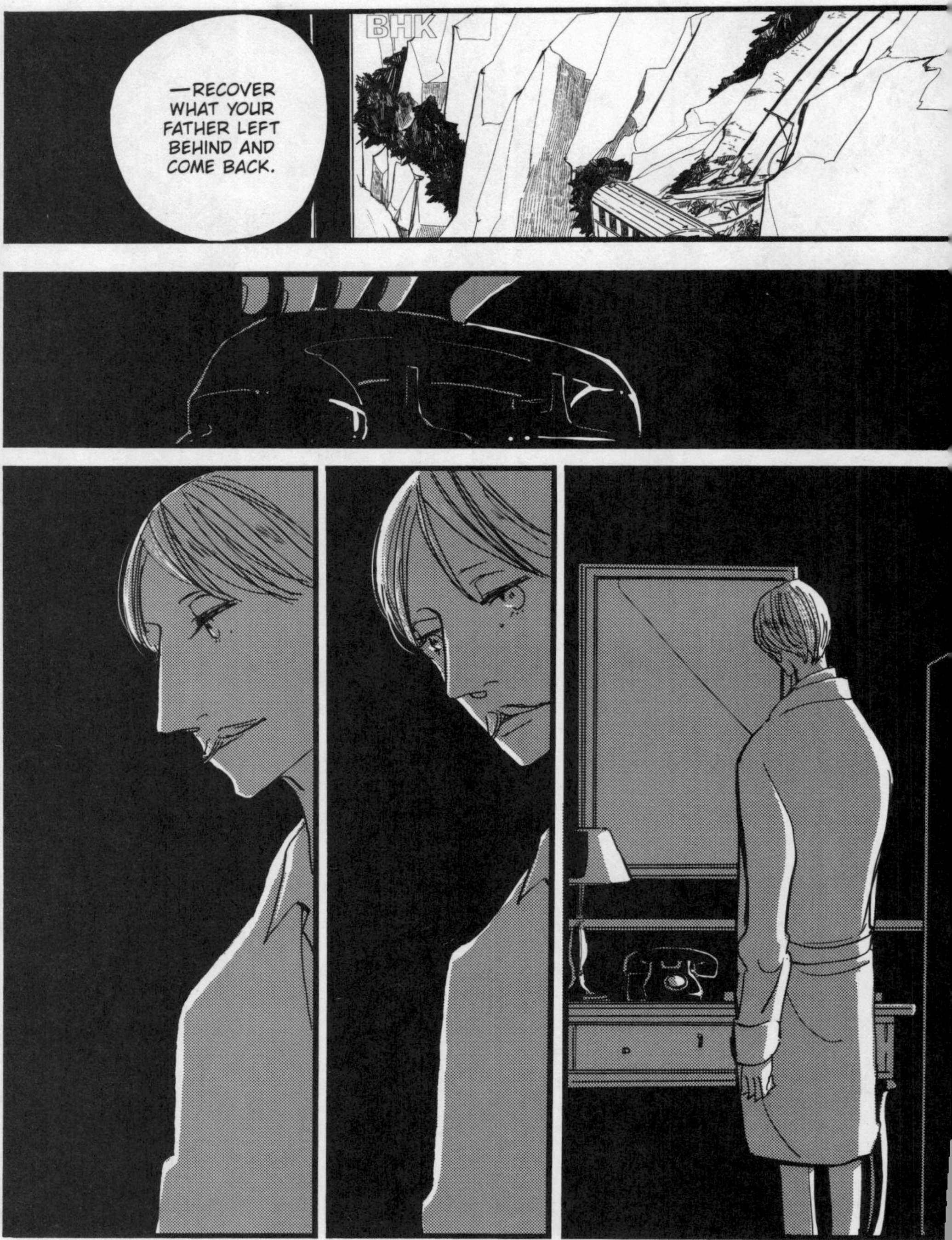
BHK
—RECOVER WHAT YOUR FATHER LEFT BEHIND AND COME BACK.

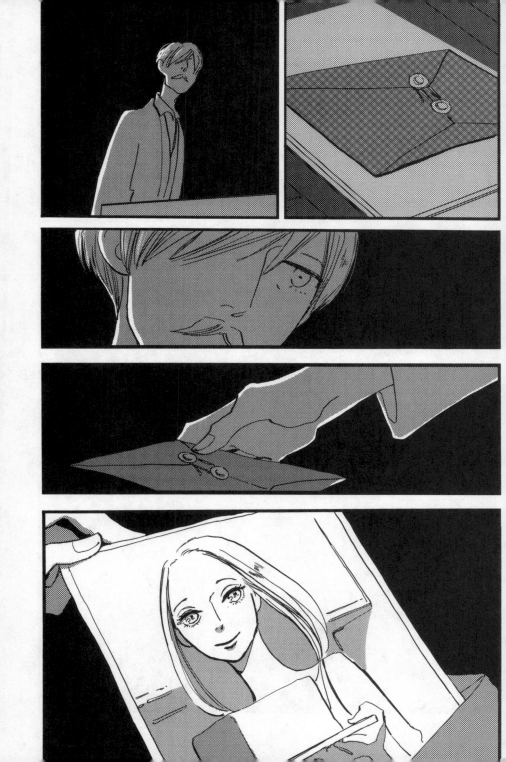

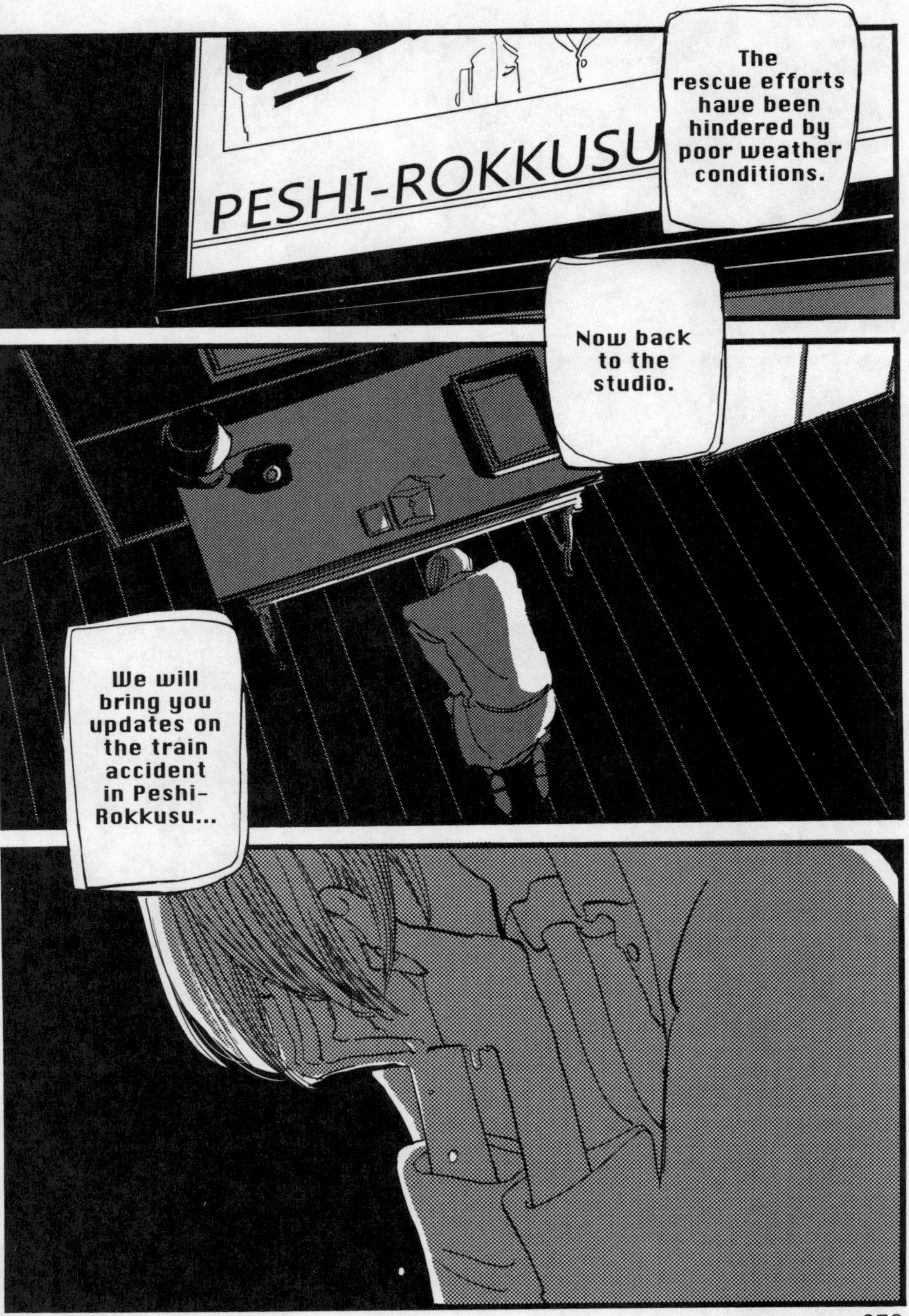
PESHI-ROKKUSU
The rescue efforts have been hindered by poor weather conditions.
Now back to the studio.
We will bring you updates on the train accident in Peshi-Rokkusu...

CHAPTER 6

The Watchman on a Perch in the Broad Sky (Part One)

PASS

INSPECTION DEPT. ACCA 13 TERRITORY

P.S.

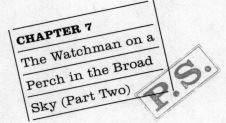

CHAPTER 7

The Watchman on a

Perch in the Broad

Sky (Part Two)

P.S.

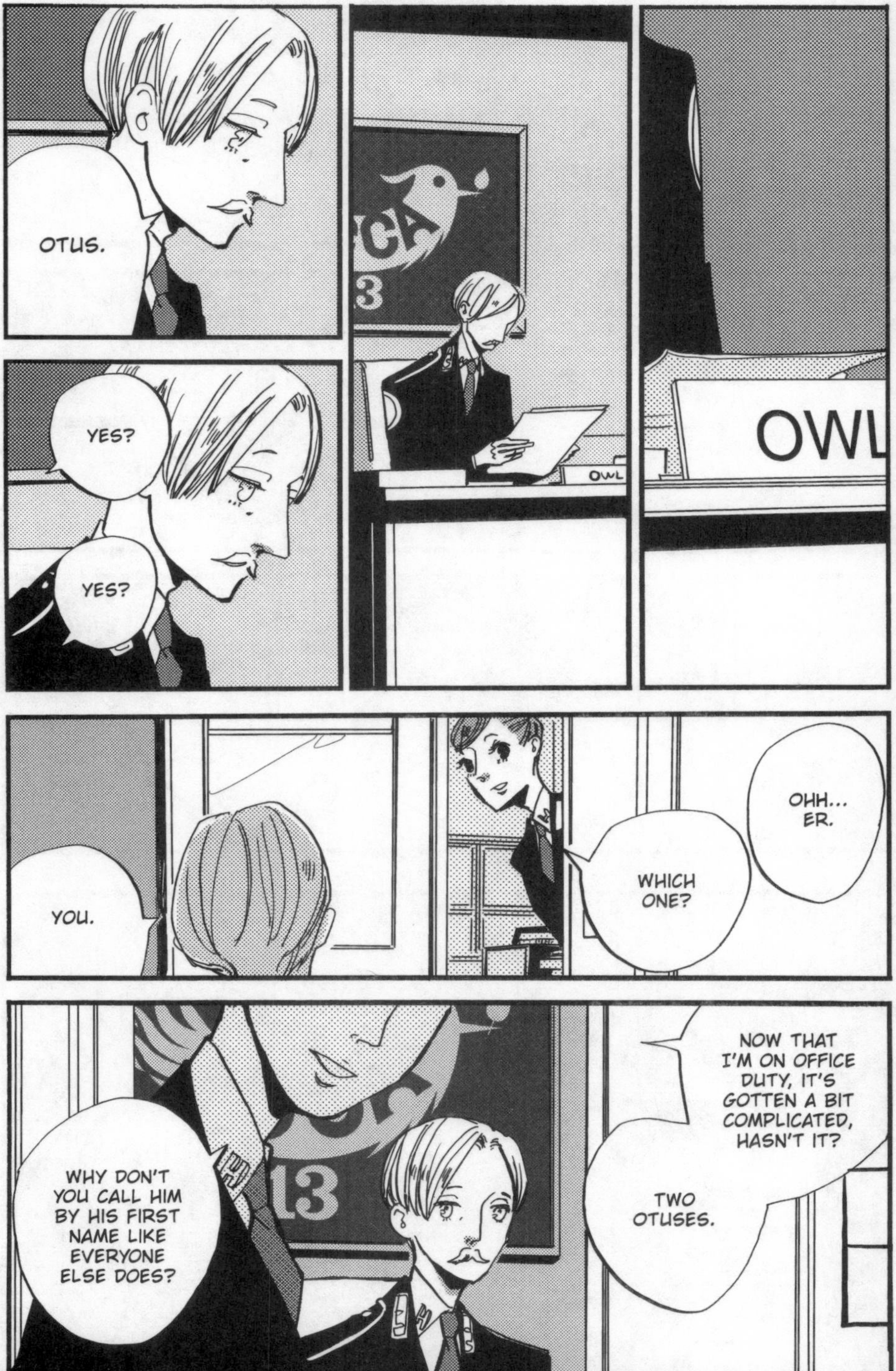
OWL
OWL
OTUS.
YES?
YES?
OHH... ER.
WHICH ONE?
YOU.
NOW THAT I'M ON OFFICE DUTY, IT'S GOTTEN A BIT COMPLICATED, HASN'T IT?
TWO OTUSES.
WHY DON'T YOU CALL HIM BY HIS FIRST NAME LIKE EVERYONE ELSE DOES?

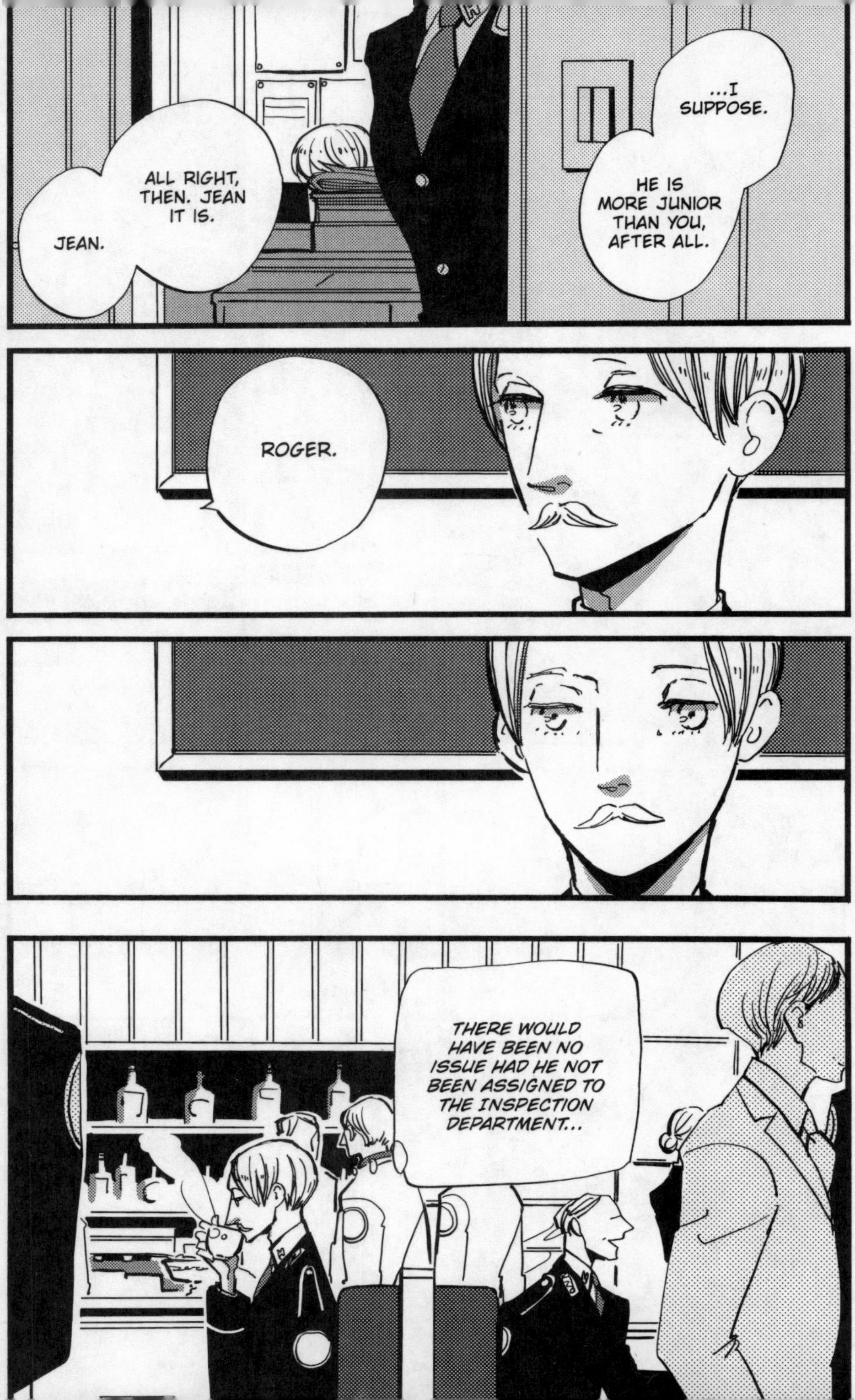
...I SUPPOSE.
HE IS MORE JUNIOR THAN YOU, AFTER ALL.
ALL RIGHT, THEN. JEAN IT IS.
JEAN.
ROGER.
THERE WOULD HAVE BEEN NO ISSUE HAD HE NOT BEEN ASSIGNED TO THE INSPECTION DEPARTMENT...

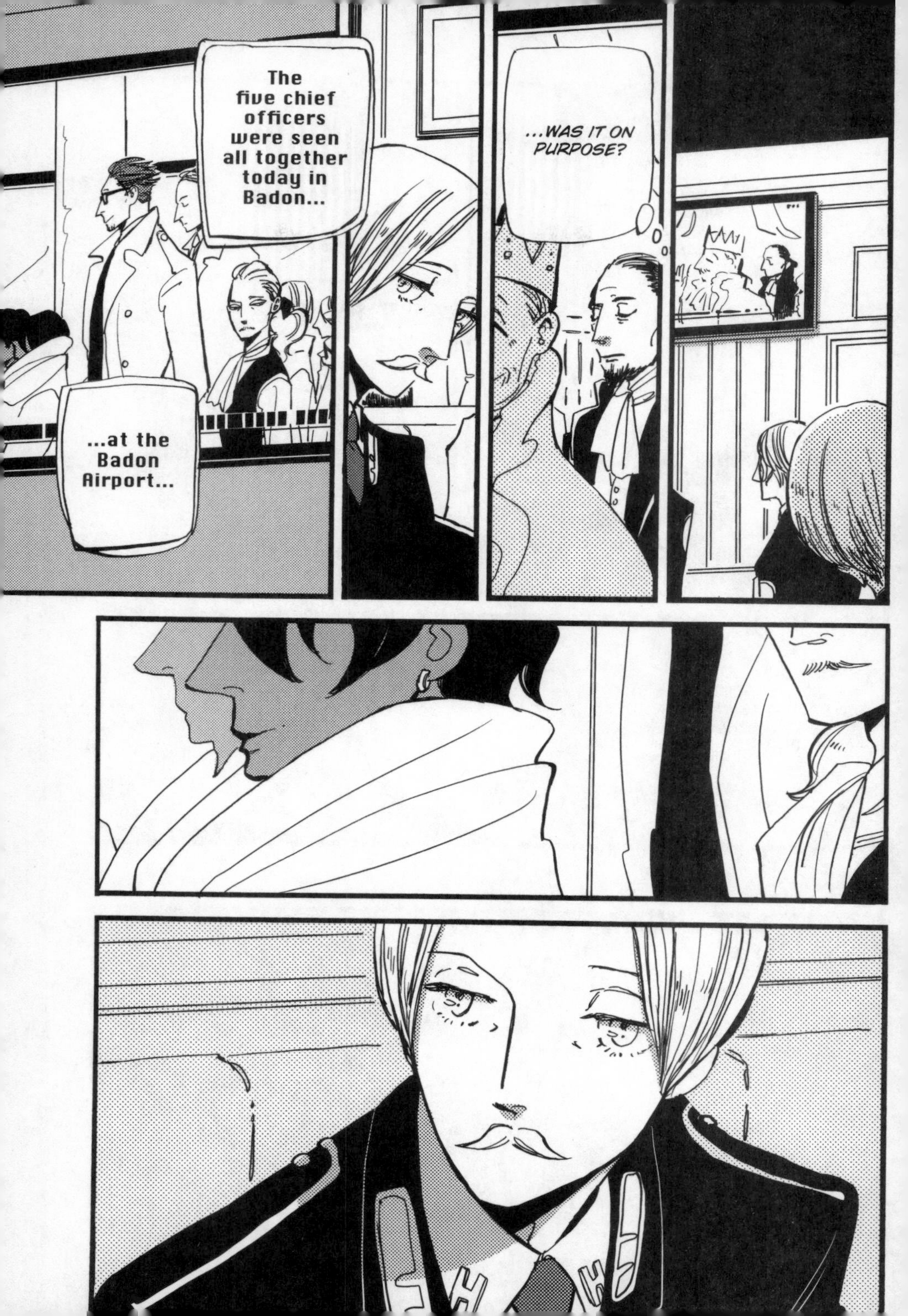
...WAS IT ON PURPOSE?
The five chief officers were seen all together today in Badon...
...at the Badon Airport...

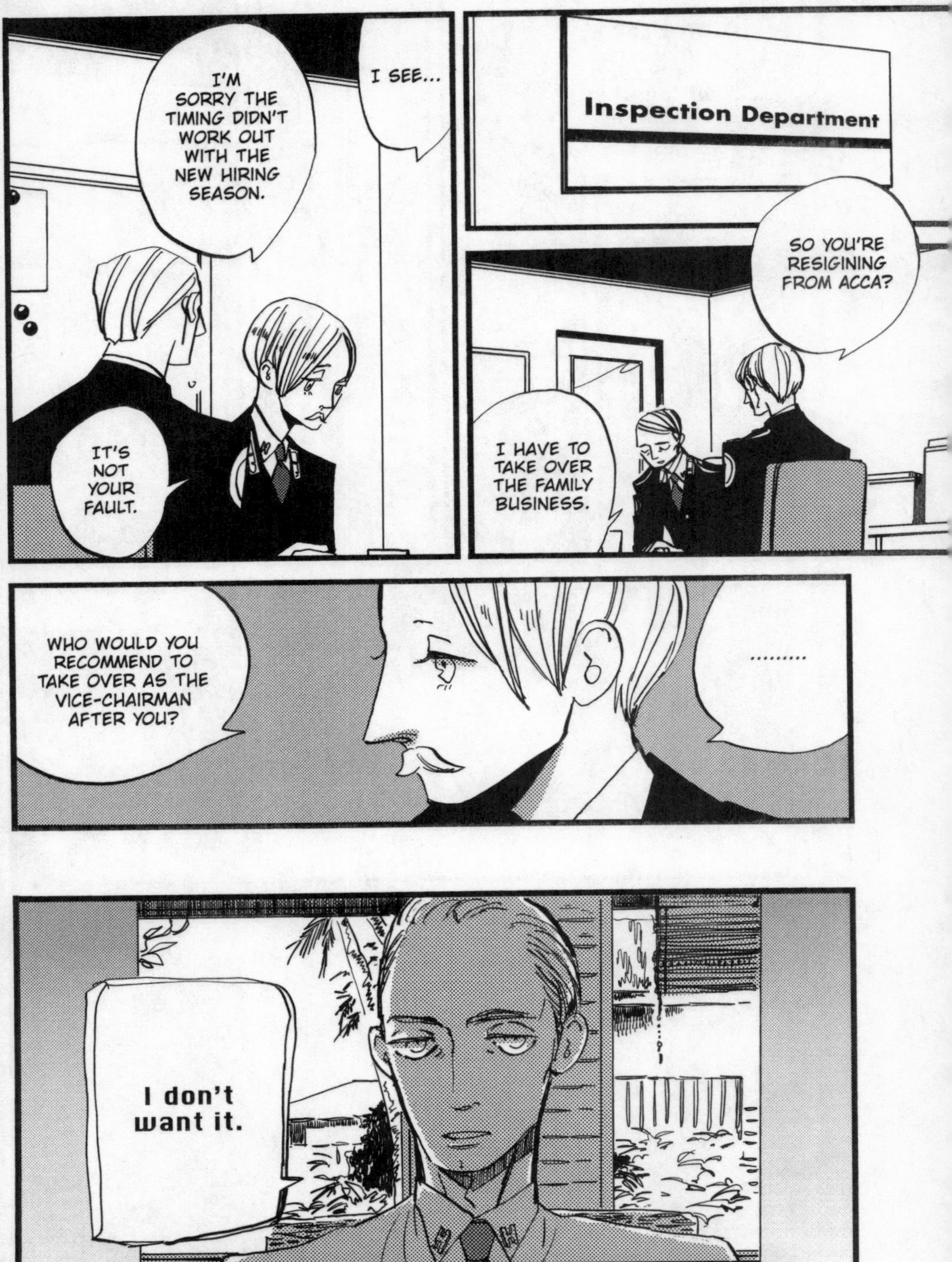
Inspection Department
SO YOU'RE RESIGINING FROM ACCA?
I HAVE TO TAKE OVER THE FAMILY BUSINESS.
I SEE...
I'M SORRY THE TIMING DIDN'T WORK OUT WITH THE NEW HIRING SEASON.
IT'S NOT YOUR FAULT.
....
WHO WOULD YOU RECOMMEND TO TAKE OVER AS THE VICE-CHAIRMAN AFTER YOU?
I don't want it.
HQ <......> HARE • | INSPECTION DEPT. | 04:13 |

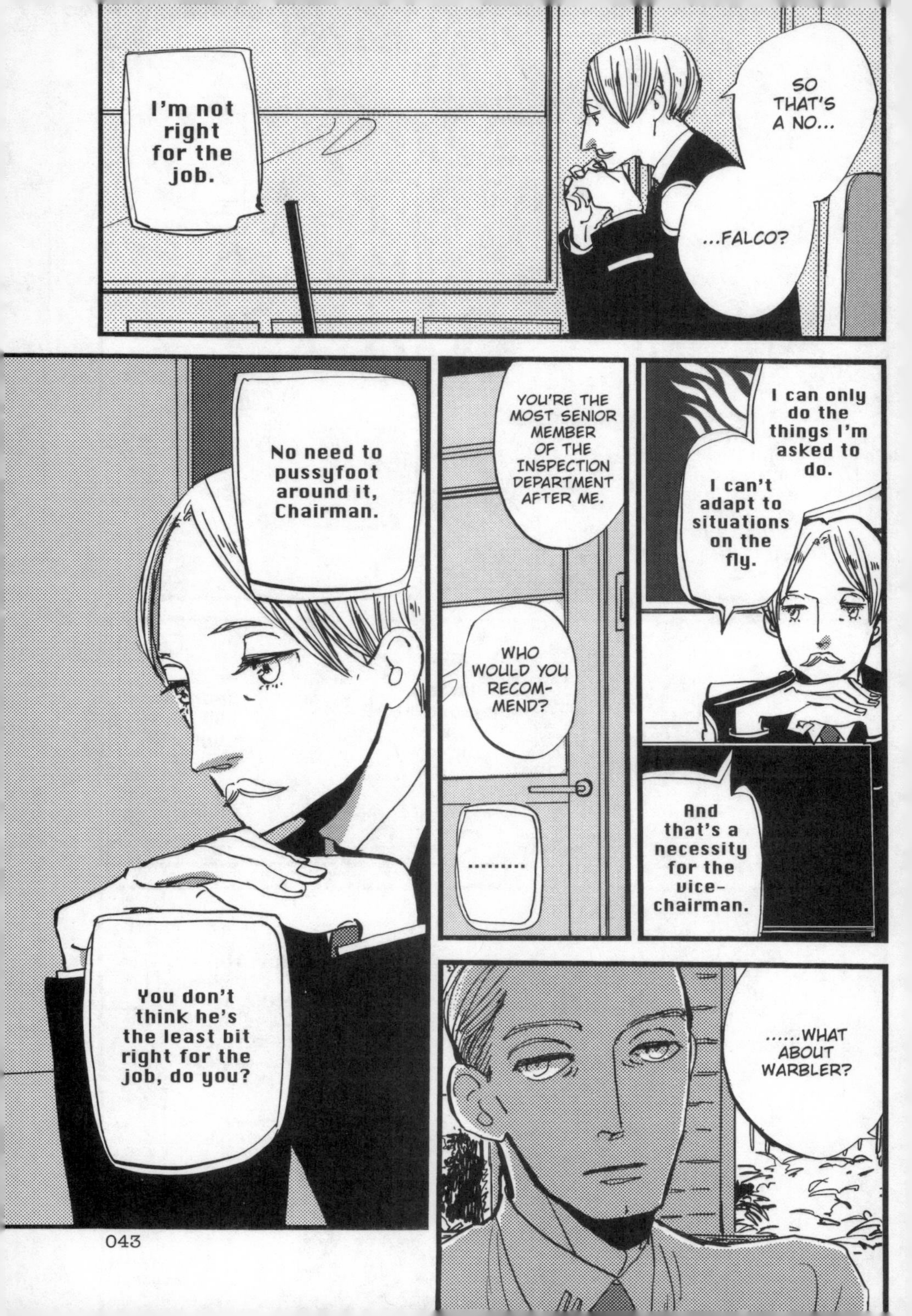
SO THAT'S A NO...
...FALCO?
I'm not right for the job.
I can only do the things I'm asked to do.
I can't adapt to situations on the fly.
And that's a necessity for the vice-chairman.
YOU'RE THE MOST SENIOR MEMBER OF THE INSPECTION DEPARTMENT AFTER ME.
WHO WOULD YOU RECOMMEND?
....
......WHAT ABOUT WARBLER?
No need to pussyfoot around it, Chairman.
You don't think he's the least bit right for the job, do you?

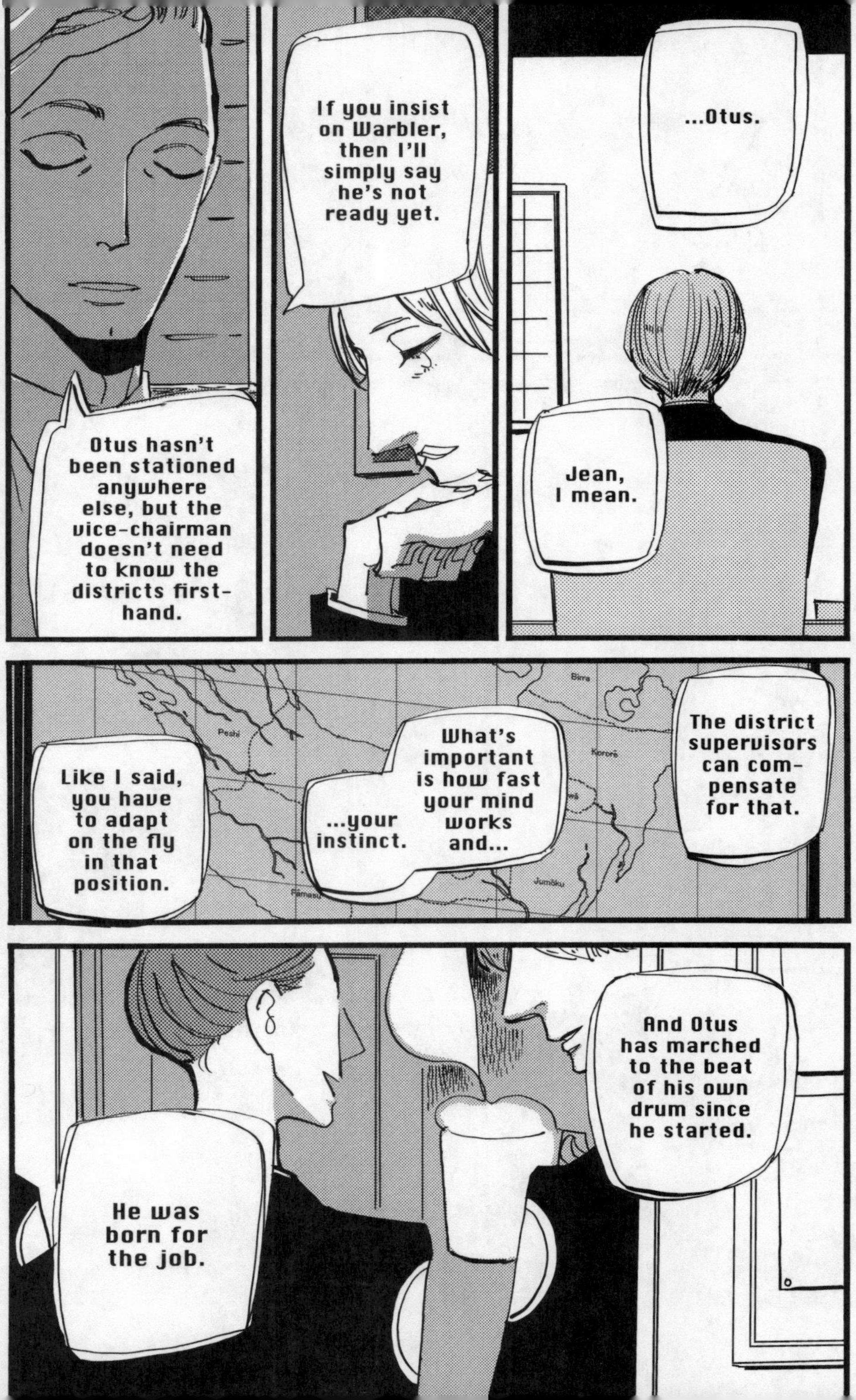
...Otus.
Jean, I mean.
If you insist on Warbler, then I'll simply say he's not ready yet.
Otus hasn't been stationed anywhere else, but the vice-chairman doesn't need to know the districts first-hand.
The district supervisors can compensate for that.
What's important is how fast your mind works and...
...your instinct.
Like I said, you have to adapt on the fly in that position.
And Otus has marched to the beat of his own drum since he started.
He was born for the job.

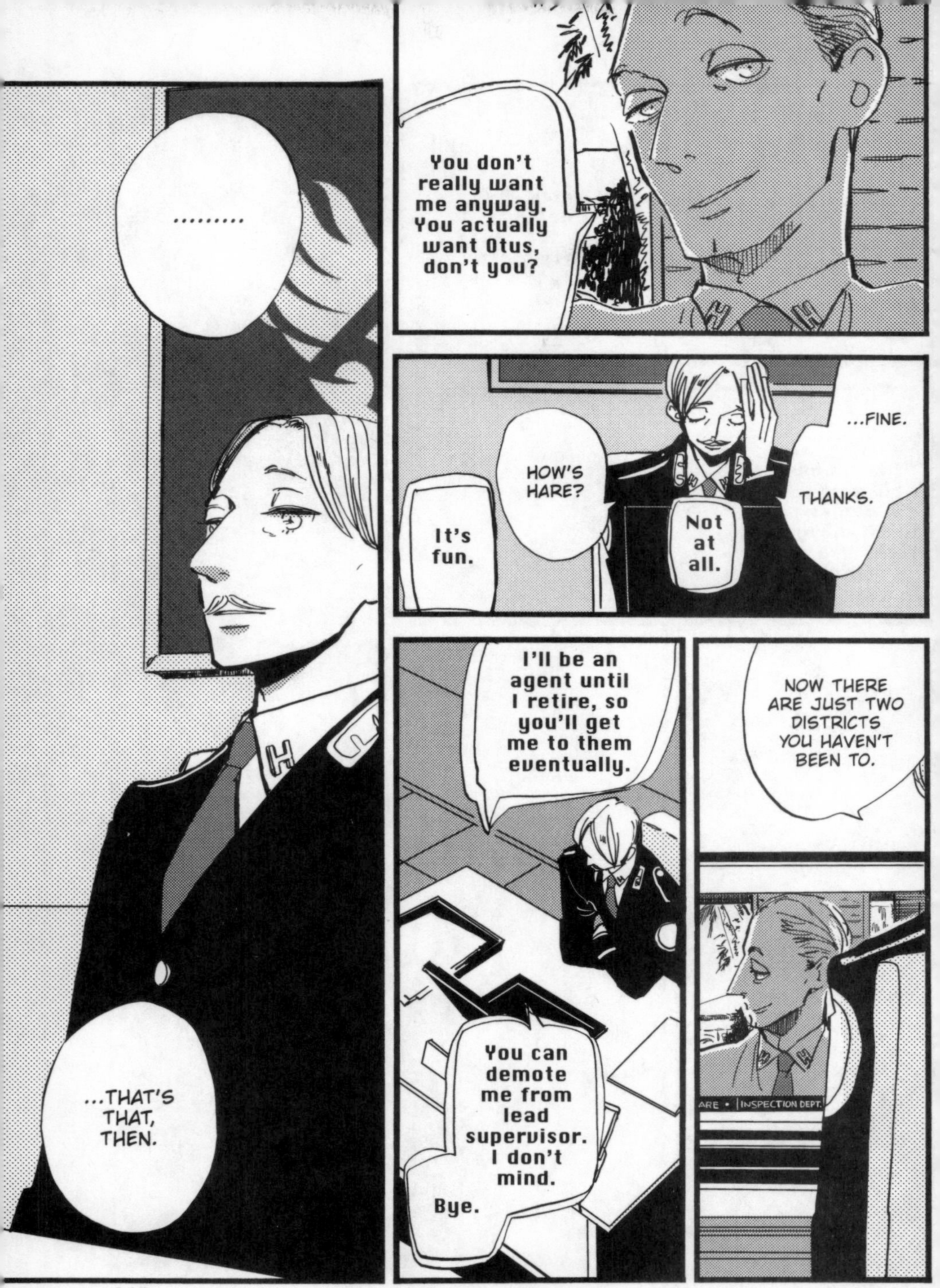
You don't really want me anyway. You actually want Otus, don't you?
...FINE.
THANKS.
Not at all.
HOW'S HARE?
It's fun.
NOW THERE ARE JUST TWO DISTRICTS YOU HAVEN'T BEEN TO.
ARE • INSPECTION DEPT.
I'll be an agent until I retire, so you'll get me to them eventually.
You can demote me from lead supervisor. I don't mind.
Bye.
....
...THAT'S THAT, THEN.

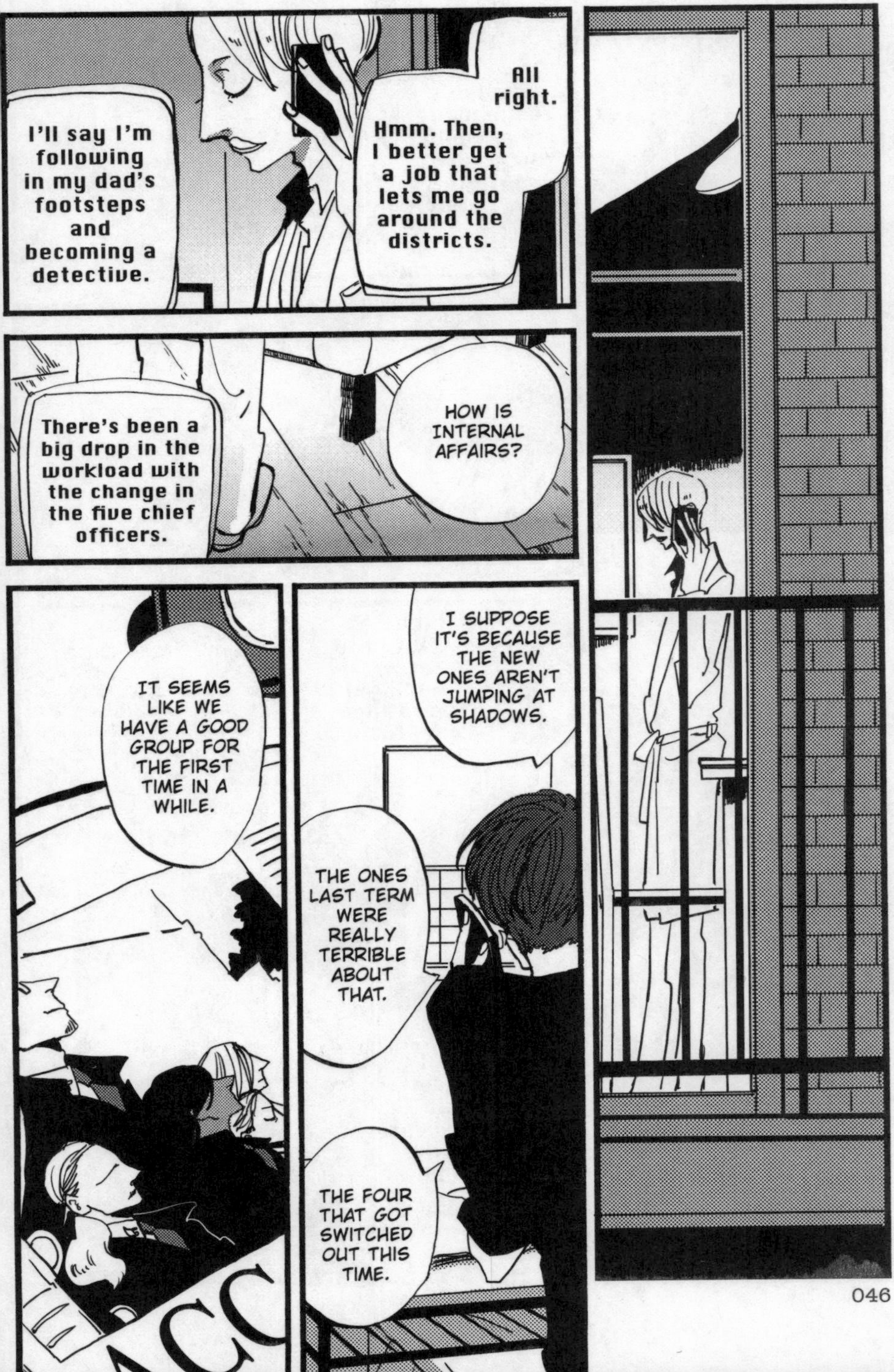
All right.
Hmm. Then, I better get a job that lets me go around the districts.
I'll say I'm following in my dad's footsteps and becoming a detective.
HOW IS INTERNAL AFFAIRS?
There's been a big drop in the workload with the change in the five chief officers.
I SUPPOSE IT'S BECAUSE THE NEW ONES AREN'T JUMPING AT SHADOWS.
THE ONES LAST TERM WERE REALLY TERRIBLE ABOUT THAT.
THE FOUR THAT GOT SWITCHED OUT THIS TIME.
IT SEEMS LIKE WE HAVE A GOOD GROUP FOR THE FIRST TIME IN A WHILE.

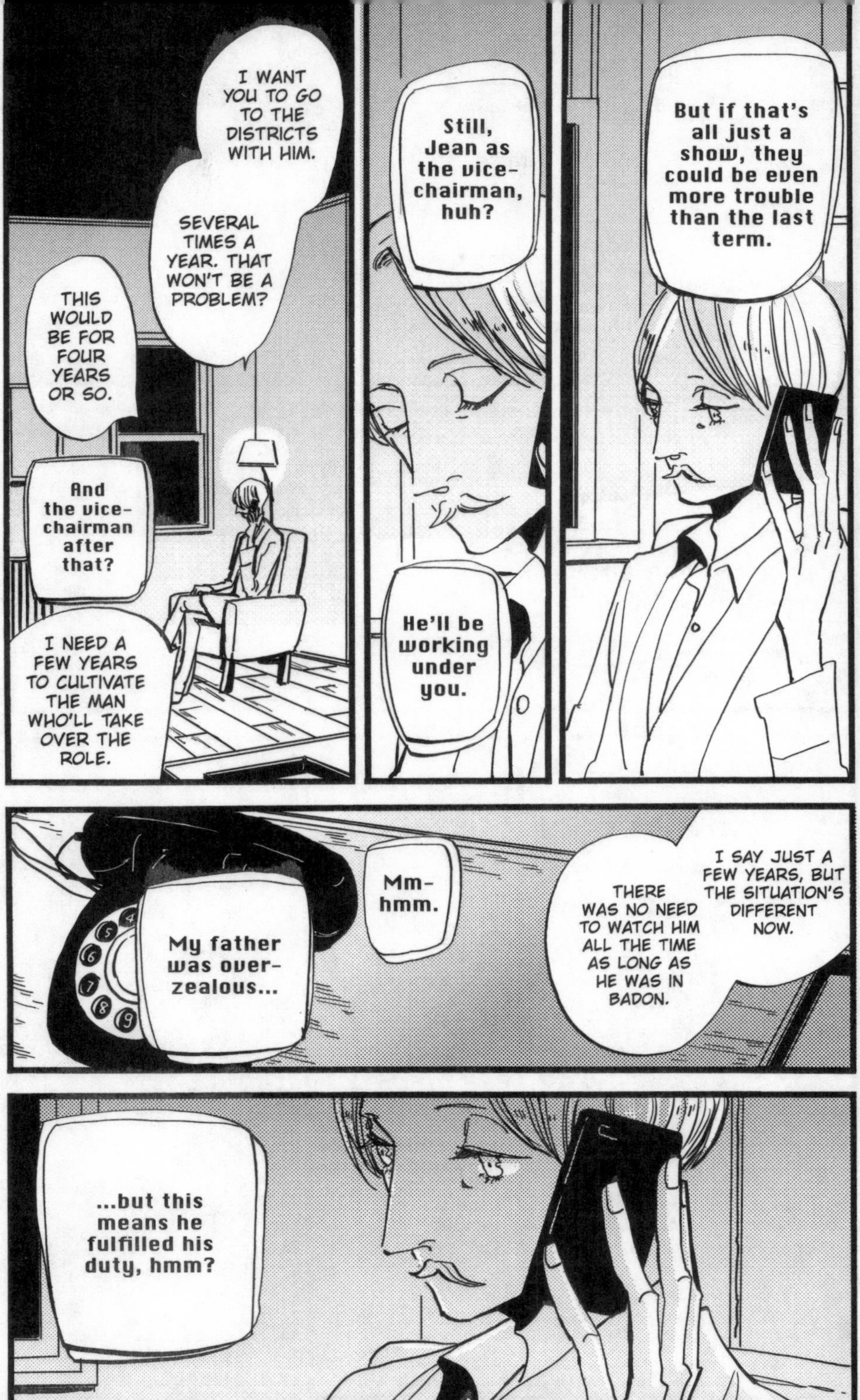
But if that's all just a show, they could be even more trouble than the last term.
Still, Jean as the vice-chairman, huh?
He'll be working under you.
I WANT YOU TO GO TO THE DISTRICTS WITH HIM.
SEVERAL TIMES A YEAR. THAT WON'T BE A PROBLEM?
THIS WOULD BE FOR FOUR YEARS OR SO.
And the vice-chairman after that?
I NEED A FEW YEARS TO CULTIVATE THE MAN WHO'LL TAKE OVER THE ROLE.
I SAY JUST A FEW YEARS, BUT THE SITUATION'S DIFFERENT NOW.
THERE WAS NO NEED TO WATCH HIM ALL THE TIME AS LONG AS HE WAS IN BADON.
Mm-hmm.
My father was over-zealous...
...but this means he fulfilled his duty, hmm?

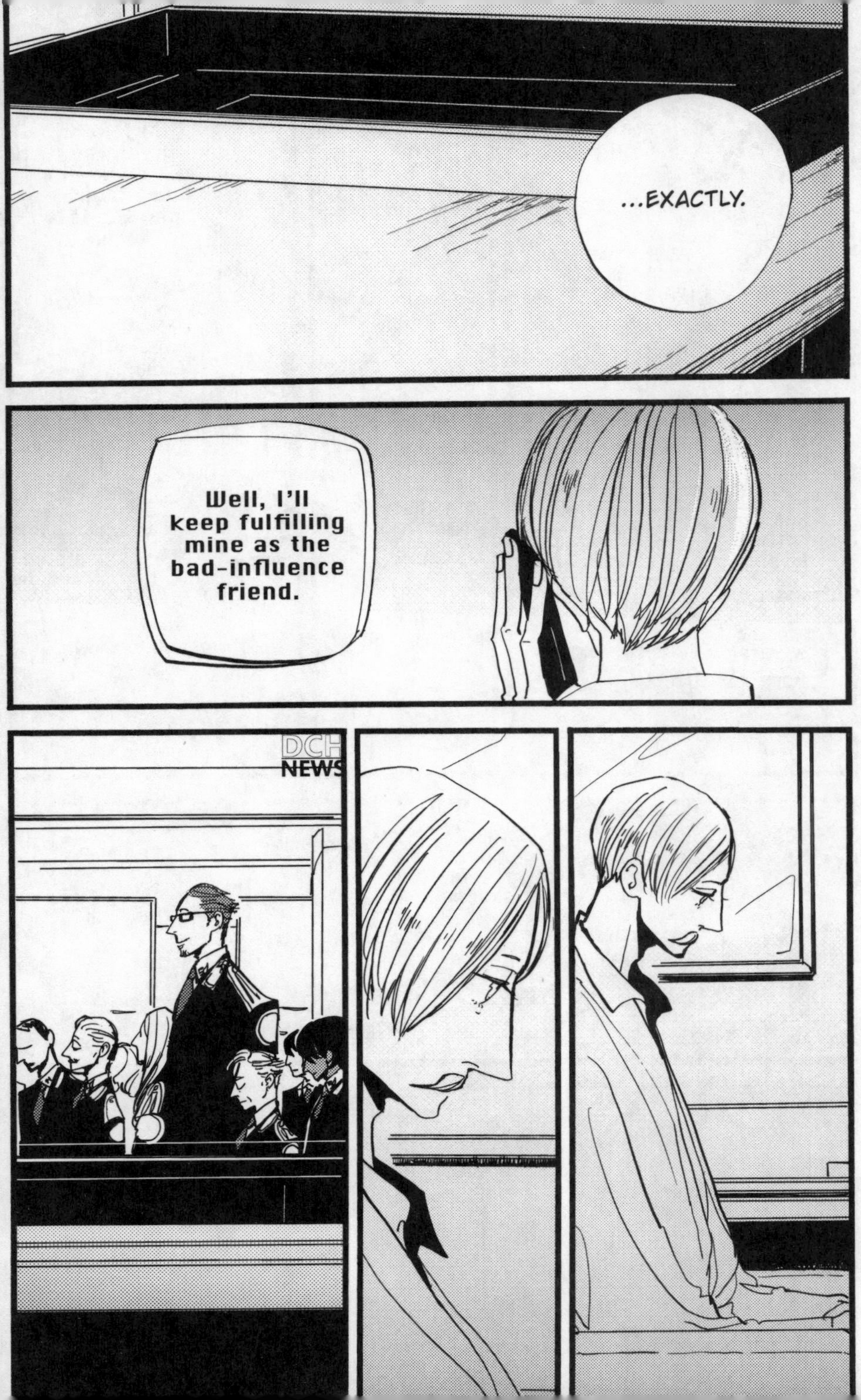
...EXACTLY.
Well, I'll keep fulfilling mine as the bad-influence friend.
DCH NEWS

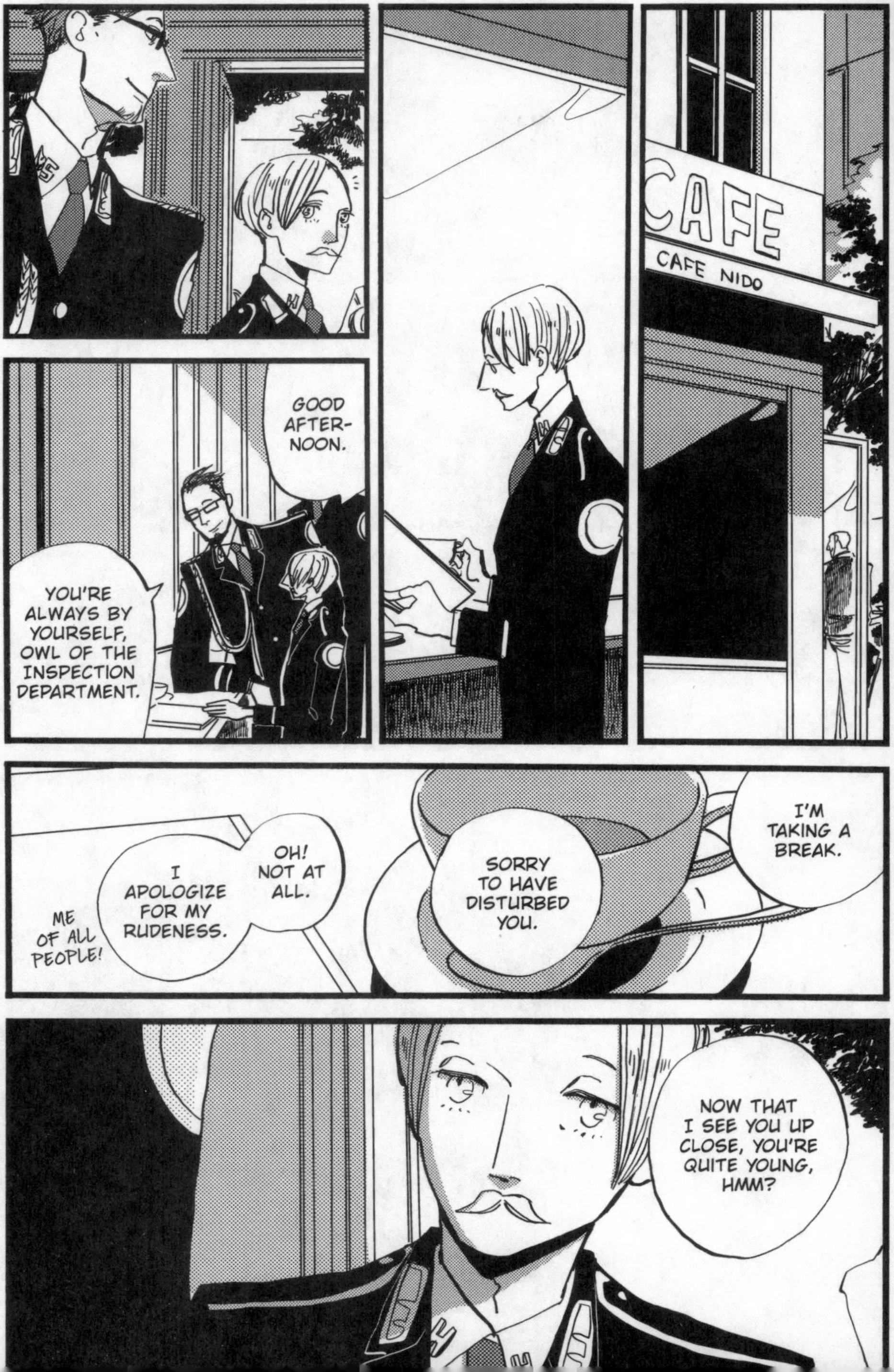
CAFE
CAFE NIDO
GOOD AFTER-NOON.
YOU'RE ALWAYS BY YOURSELF, OWL OF THE INSPECTION DEPARTMENT.
I'M TAKING A BREAK.
SORRY TO HAVE DISTURBED YOU.
OH! NOT AT ALL.
I APOLOGIZE FOR MY RUDENESS.
ME OF ALL PEOPLE!
NOW THAT I SEE YOU UP CLOSE, YOU'RE QUITE YOUNG, HMM?

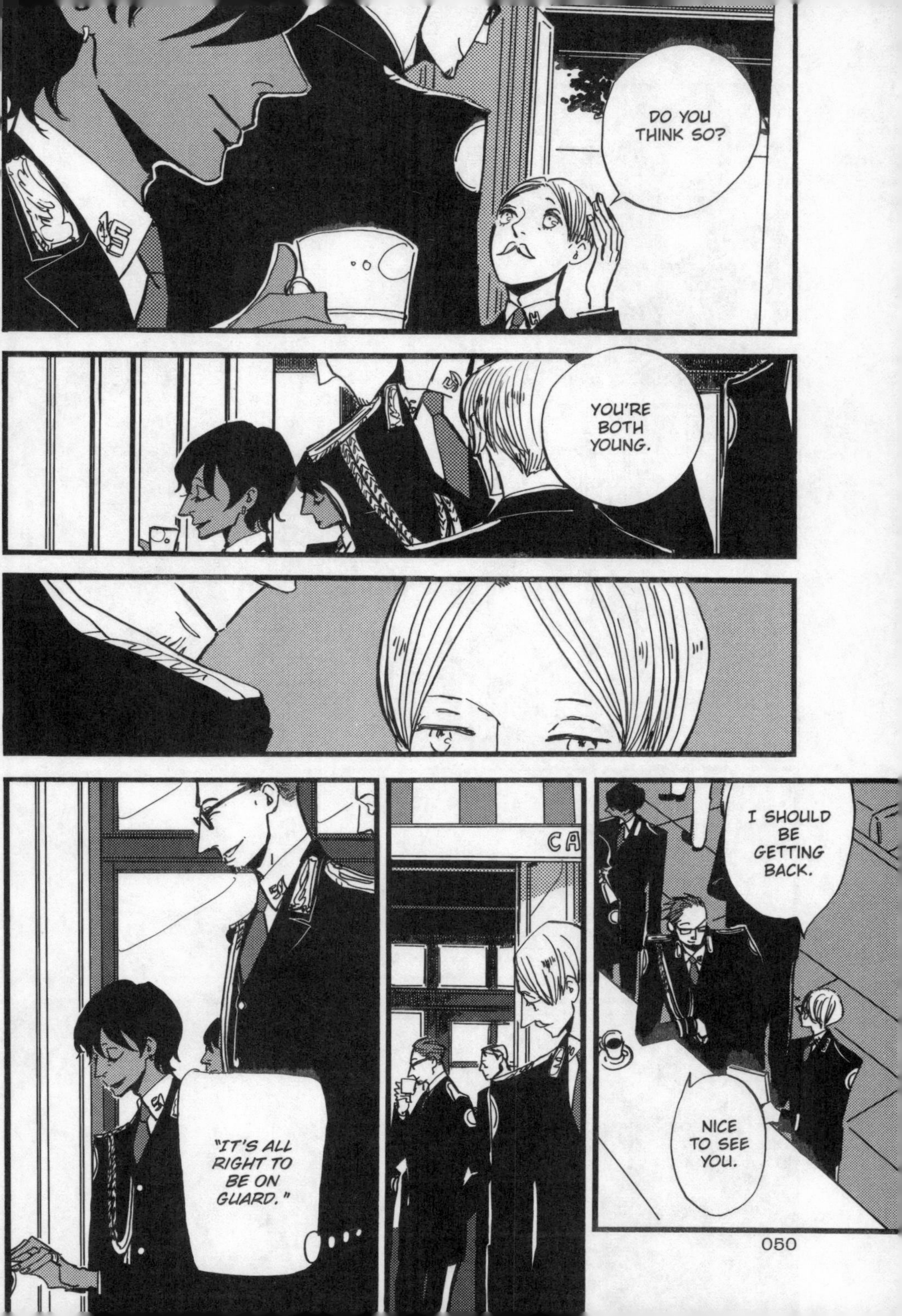
DO YOU THINK SO?
YOU'RE BOTH YOUNG.
I SHOULD BE GETTING BACK.
NICE TO SEE YOU.
CA
"IT'S ALL RIGHT TO BE ON GUARD."

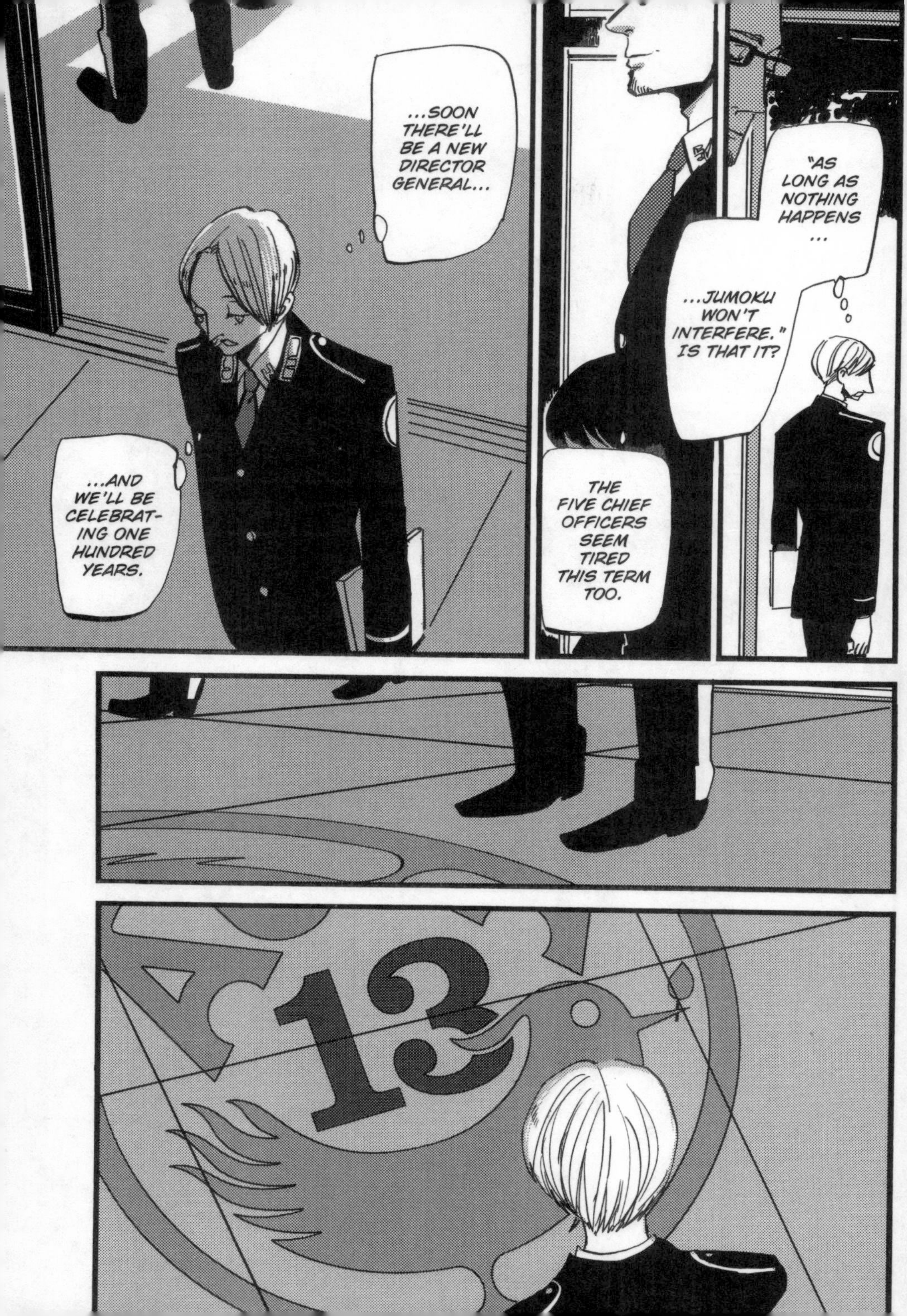
"AS LONG AS NOTHING HAPPENS ...
...JUMOKU WON'T INTERFERE." IS THAT IT?
THE FIVE CHIEF OFFICERS SEEM TIRED THIS TERM TOO.
...SOON THERE'LL BE A NEW DIRECTOR GENERAL...
...AND WE'LL BE CELEBRATING ONE HUNDRED YEARS.

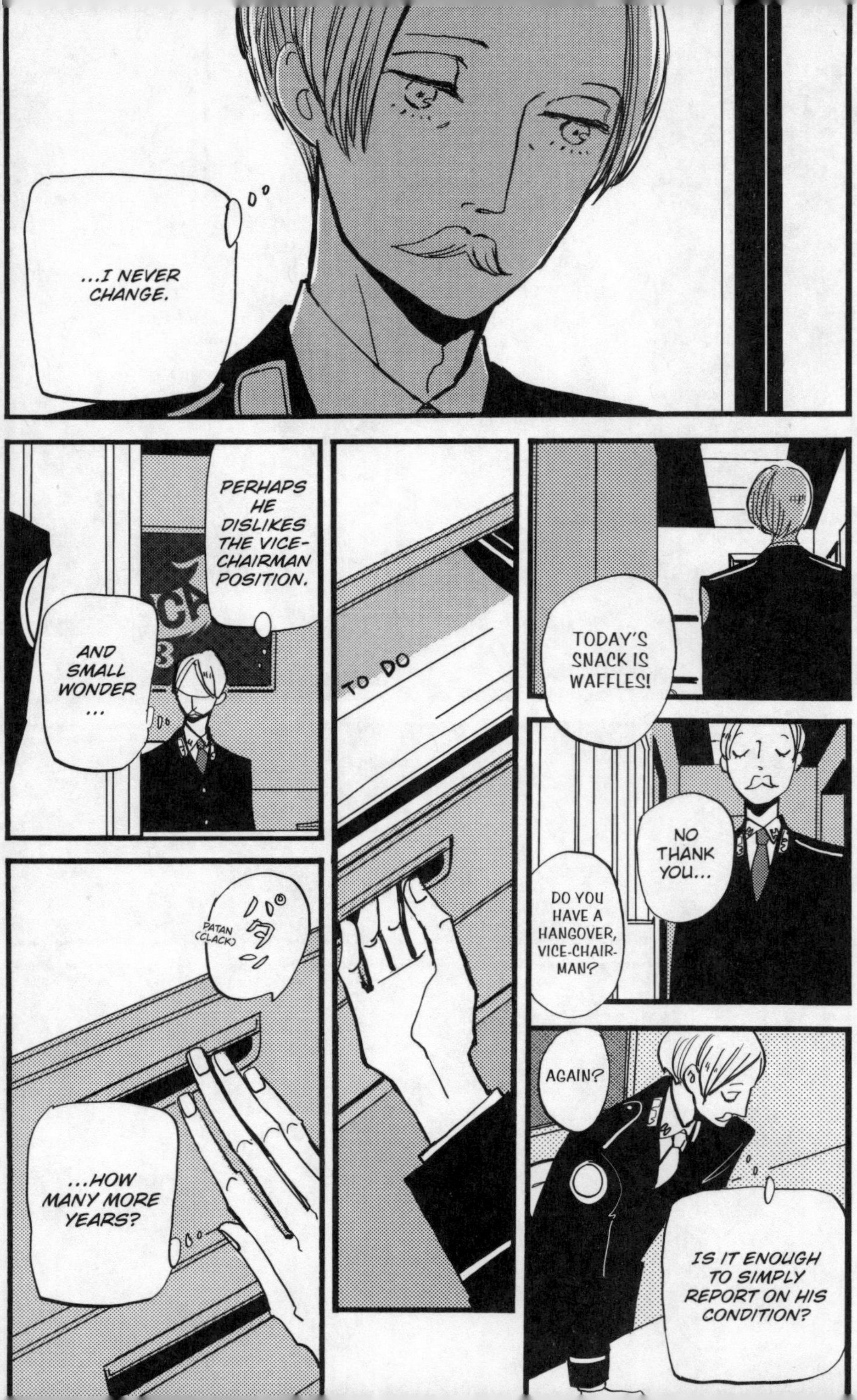
...I NEVER CHANGE.
TODAY'S SNACK IS WAFFLES!
NO THANK YOU...
DO YOU HAVE A HANGOVER, VICE-CHAIRMAN?
AGAIN?
IS IT ENOUGH TO SIMPLY REPORT ON HIS CONDITION?
TO DO
PERHAPS HE DISLIKES THE VICE-CHAIRMAN POSITION.
AND SMALL WONDER ...
PATAN (CLACK)
...HOW MANY MORE YEARS?

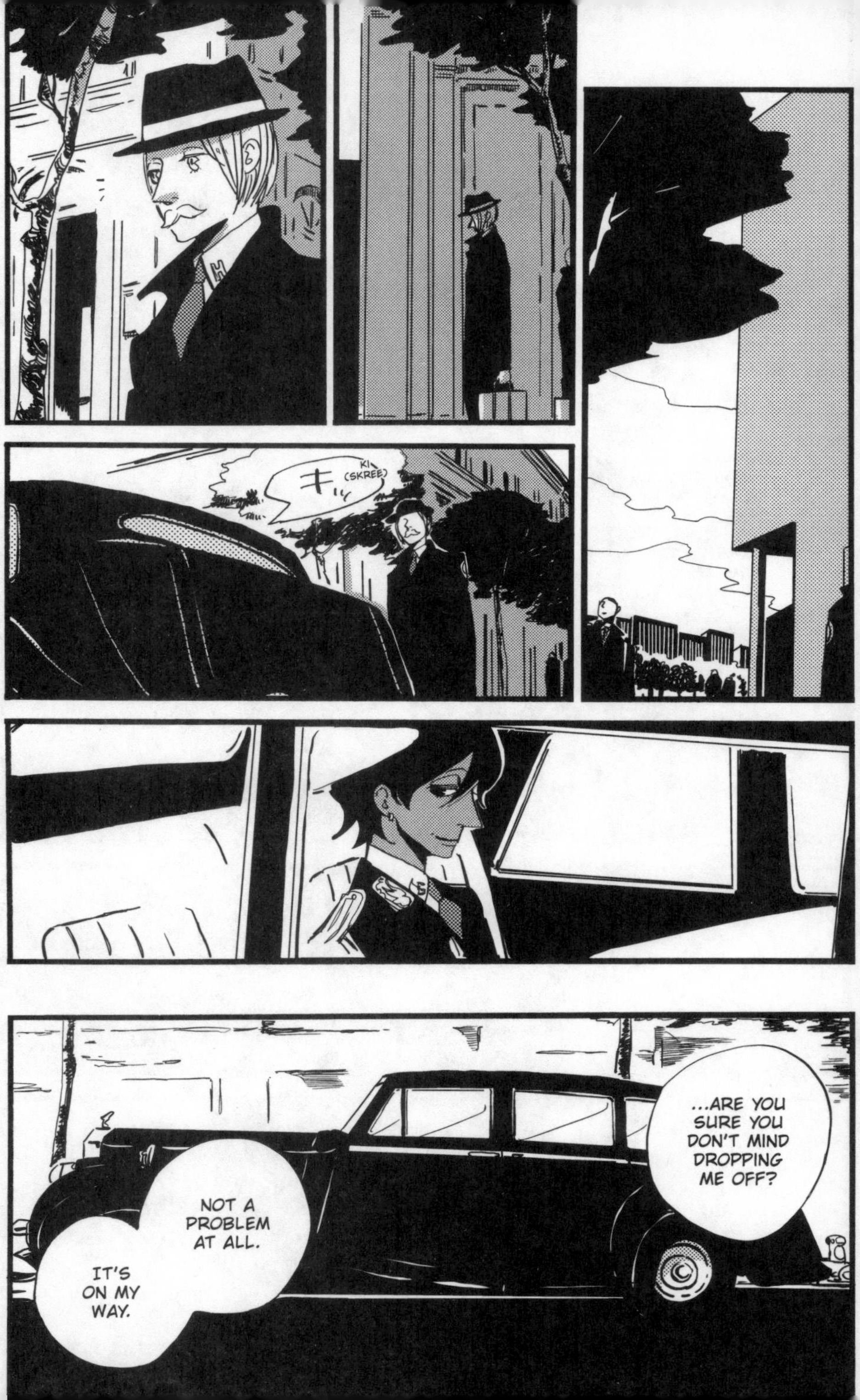
キ
KI
(SKREE)
...ARE YOU SURE YOU DON'T MIND DROPPING ME OFF?
NOT A PROBLEM AT ALL.
IT'S ON MY WAY.

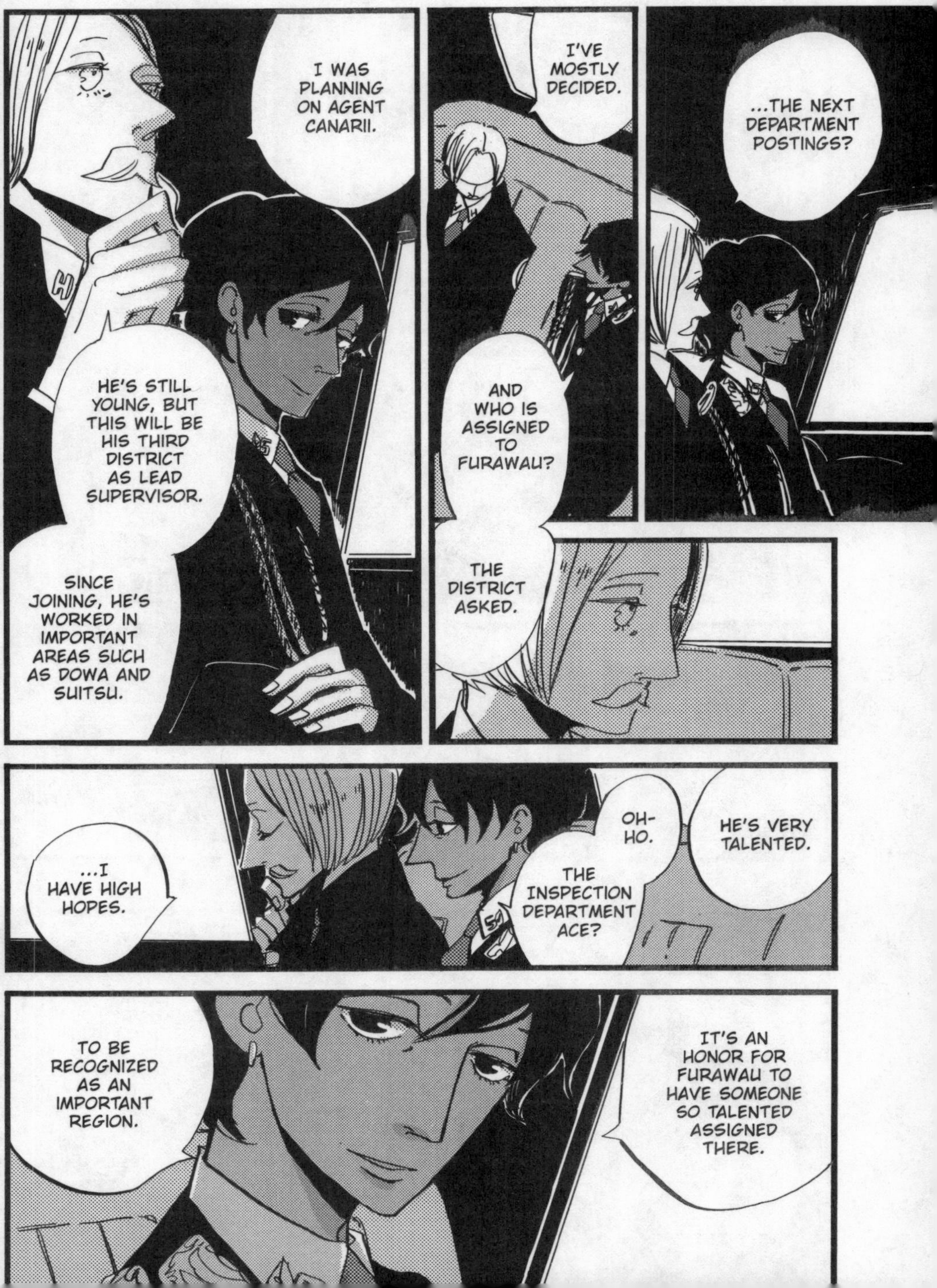
...THE NEXT DEPARTMENT POSTINGS?
I'VE MOSTLY DECIDED.
AND WHO IS ASSIGNED TO FURAWAU?
THE DISTRICT ASKED.
I WAS PLANNING ON AGENT CANARII.
HE'S STILL YOUNG, BUT THIS WILL BE HIS THIRD DISTRICT AS LEAD SUPERVISOR.
SINCE JOINING, HE'S WORKED IN IMPORTANT AREAS SUCH AS DOWA AND SUITSU.
HE'S VERY TALENTED.
OH-HO.
THE INSPECTION DEPARTMENT ACE?
...I HAVE HIGH HOPES.
IT'S AN HONOR FOR FURAWAU TO HAVE SOMEONE SO TALENTED ASSIGNED THERE.
TO BE RECOGNIZED AS AN IMPORTANT REGION.

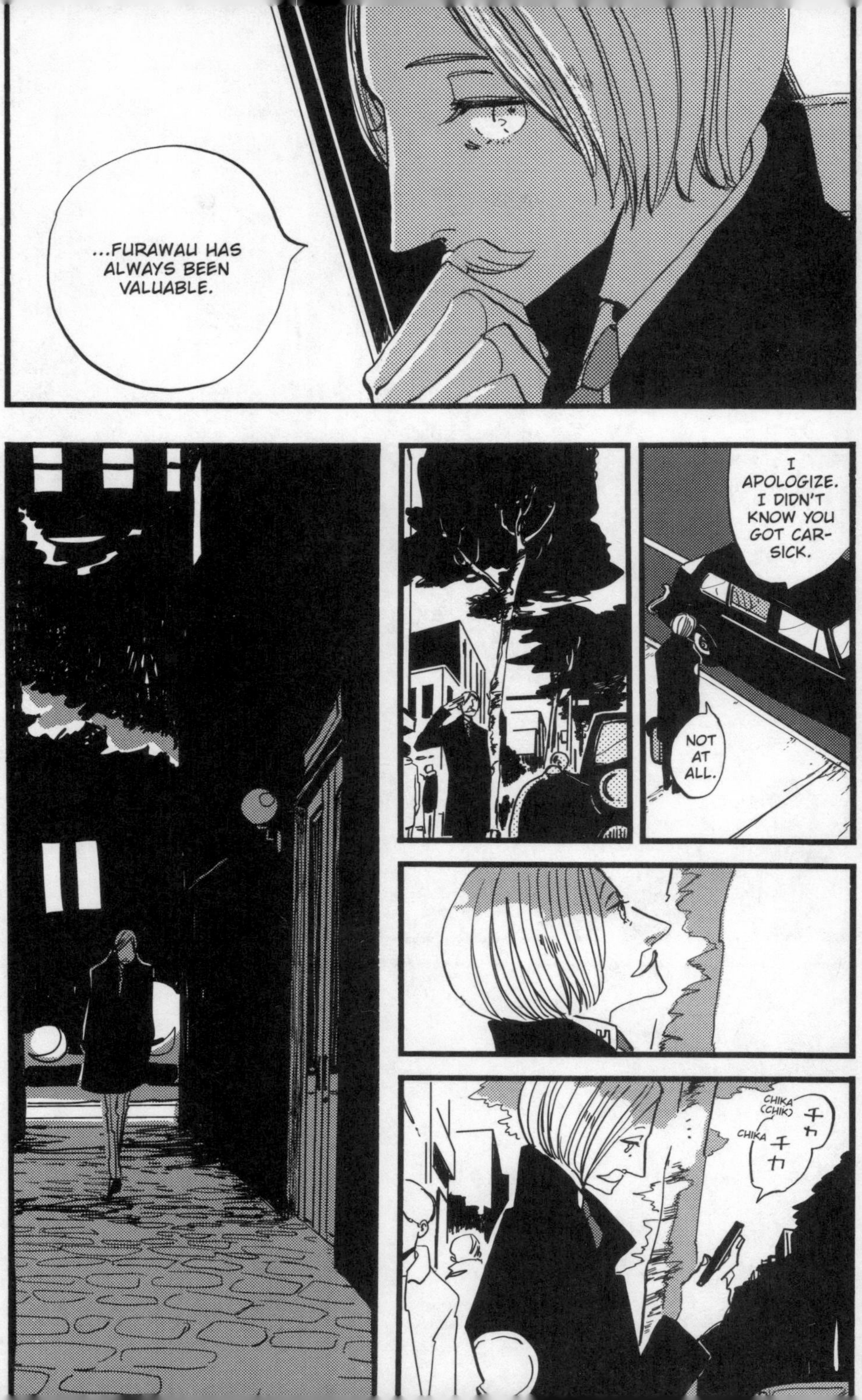
...FURAWAU HAS ALWAYS BEEN VALUABLE.
I APOLOGIZE. I DIDN'T KNOW YOU GOT CAR-SICK.
NOT AT ALL.
CHIKA (CHIK)
チカ
CHIKA
チカ

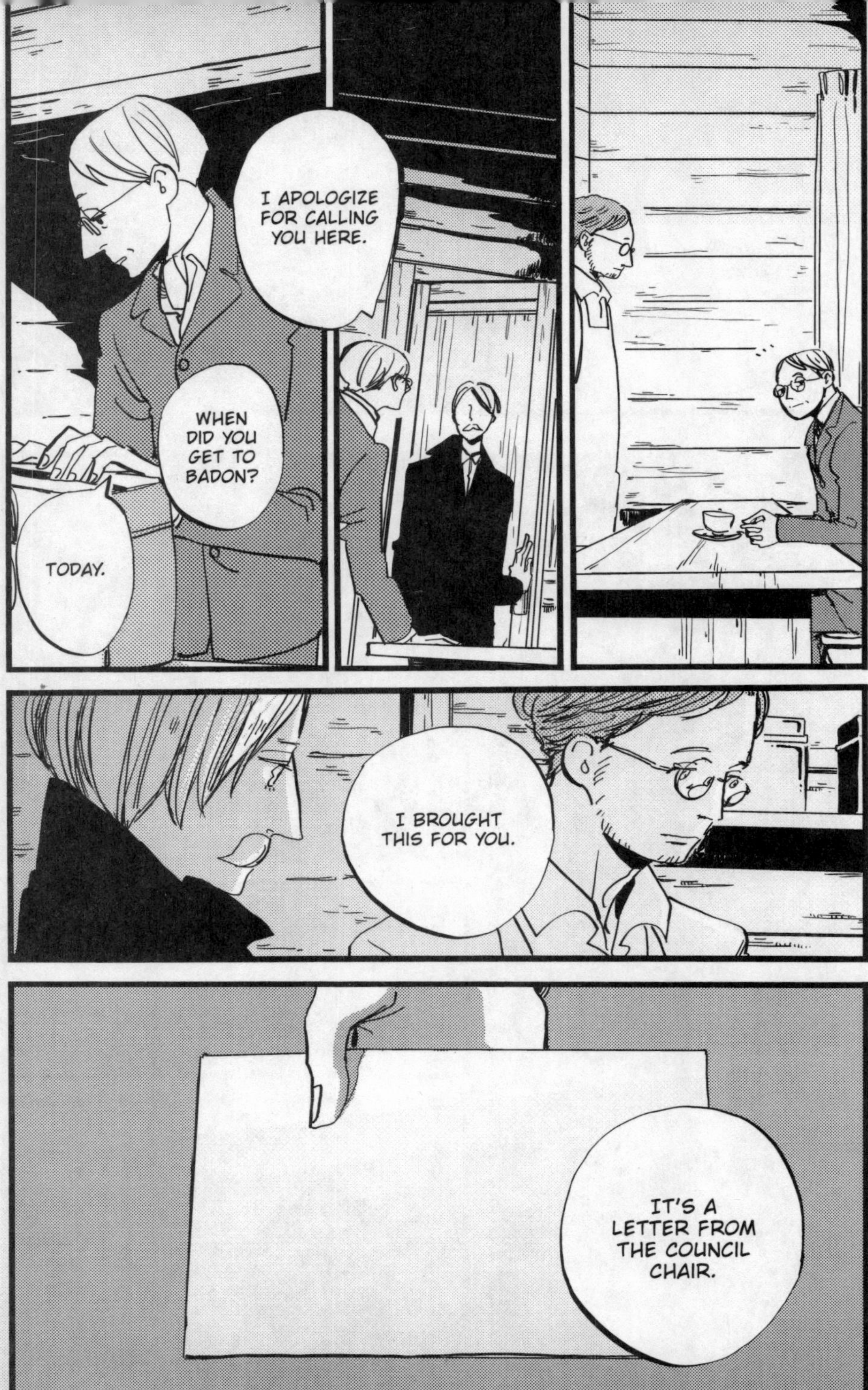
I APOLOGIZE FOR CALLING YOU HERE.
WHEN DID YOU GET TO BADON?
TODAY.
I BROUGHT THIS FOR YOU.
IT'S A LETTER FROM THE COUNCIL CHAIR.

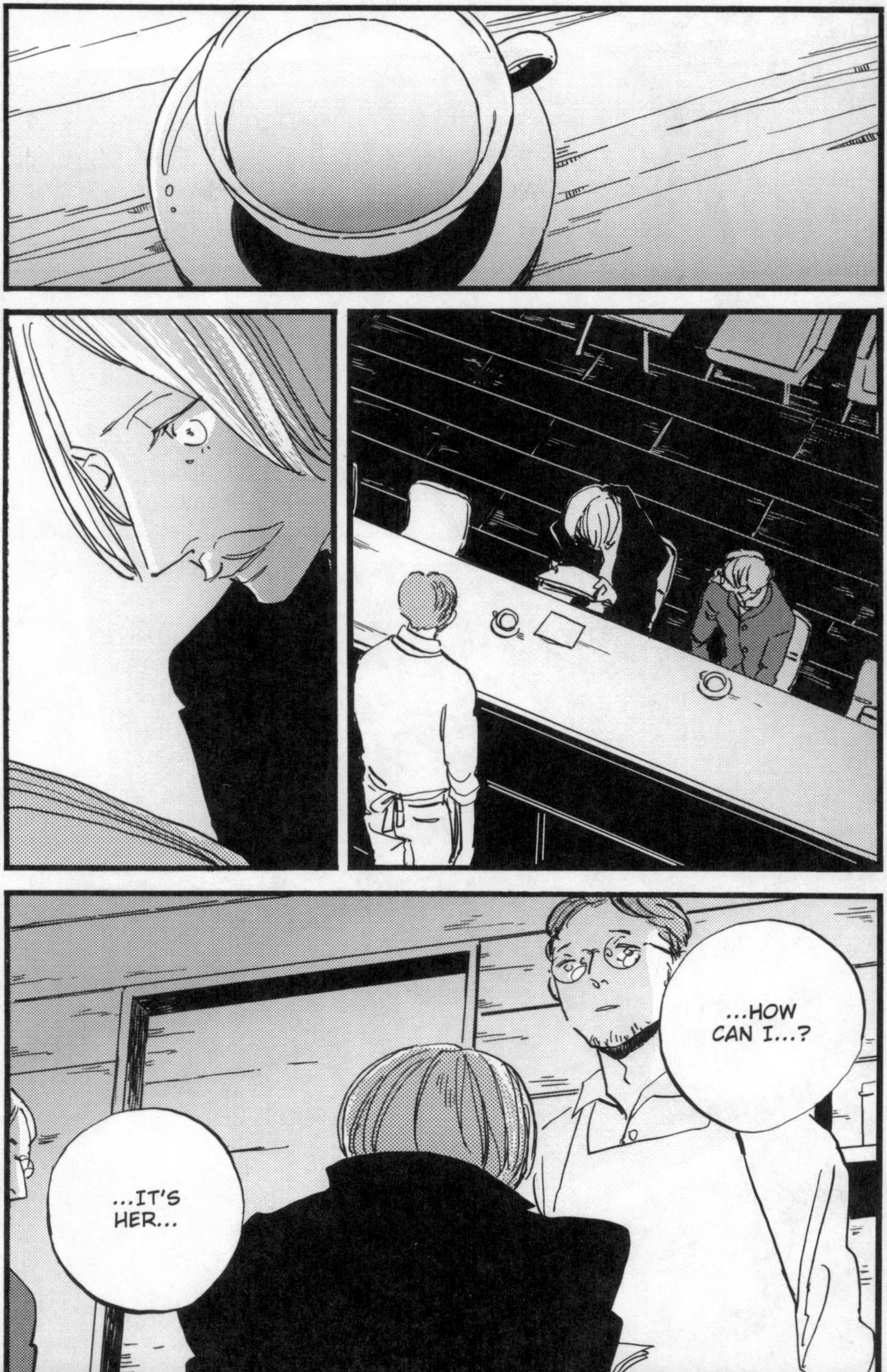
...HOW CAN I...?
...IT'S HER...

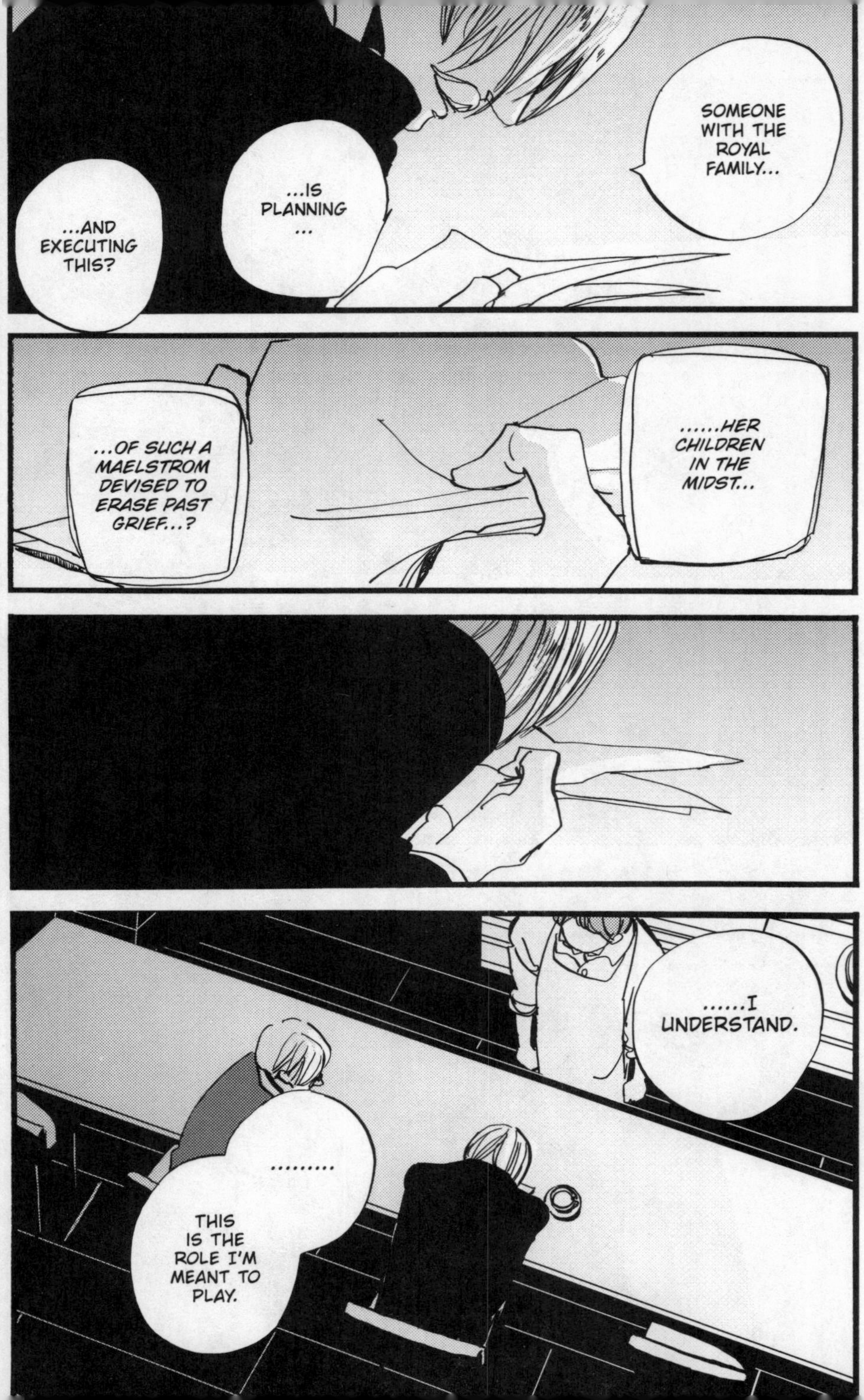
SOMEONE WITH THE ROYAL FAMILY...
...IS PLANNING ...
...AND EXECUTING THIS?
......HER CHILDREN IN THE MIDST...
...OF SUCH A MAELSTROM DEVISED TO ERASE PAST GRIEF...?
......I UNDERSTAND.
....
THIS IS THE ROLE I'M MEANT TO PLAY.

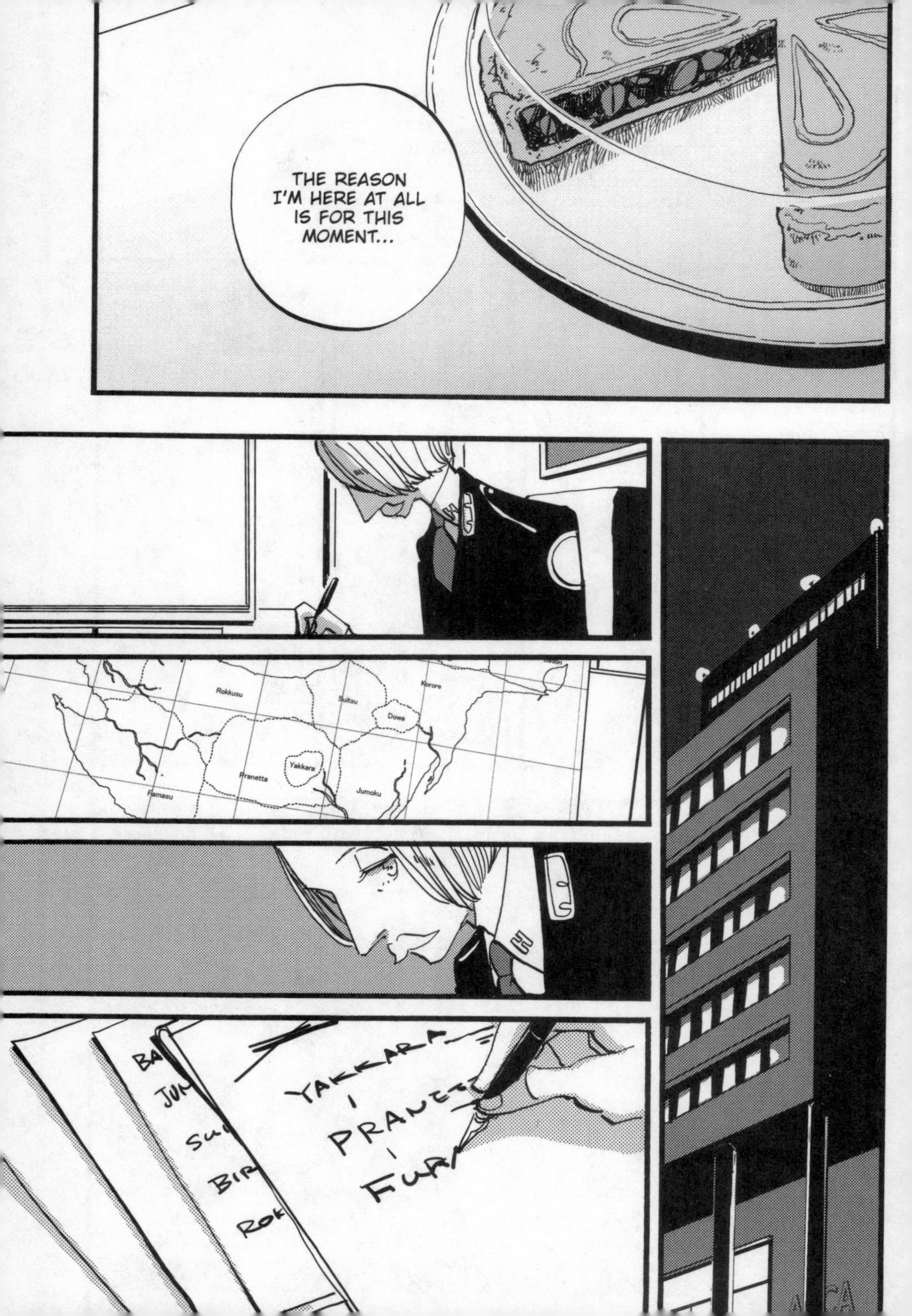
THE REASON I'M HERE AT ALL IS FOR THIS MOMENT...
Rokkusu
Suitsu
Korore
Dowa
Yakkara
Pranetta
Jumoku
Famasu
YAKKARA

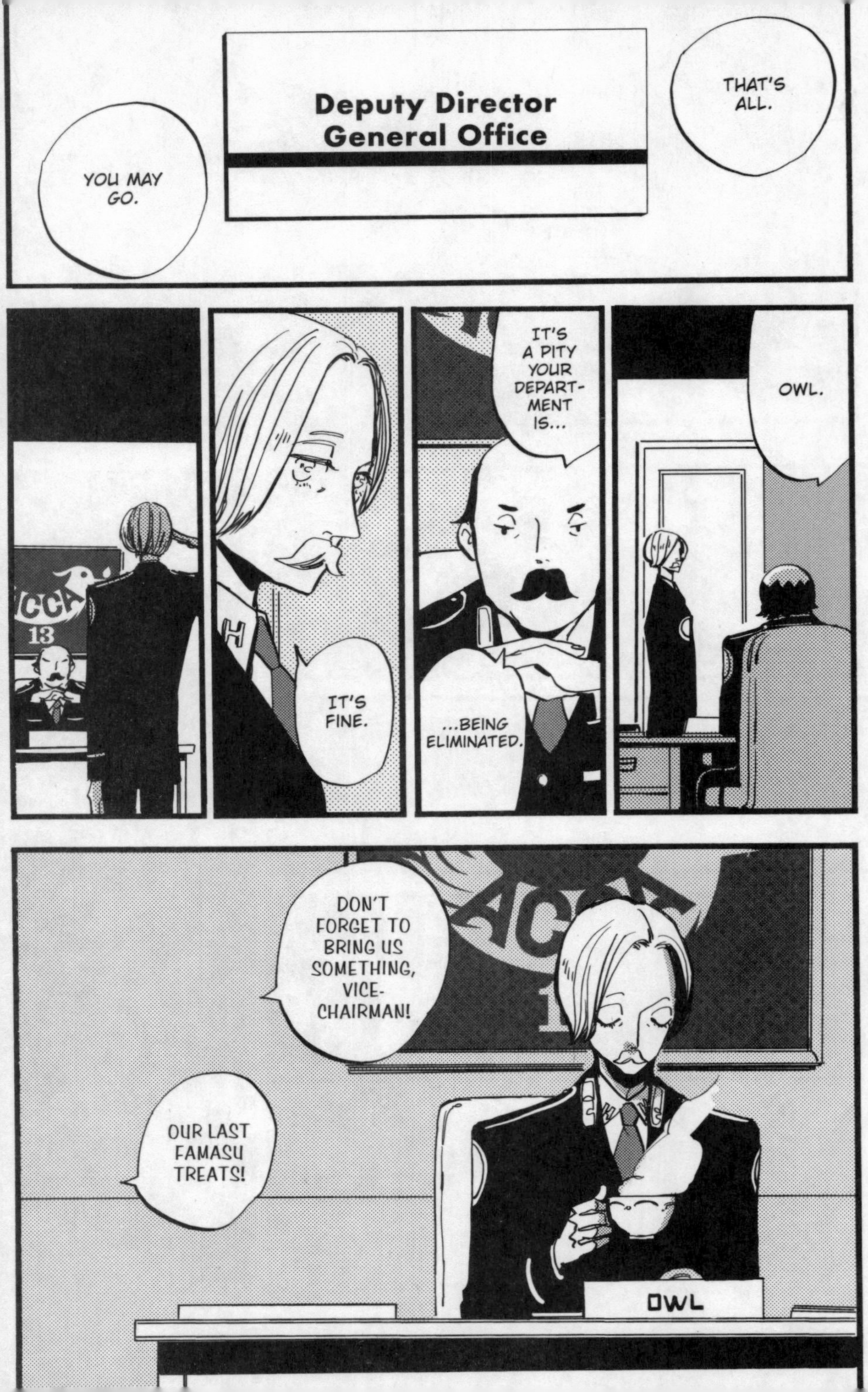
THAT'S ALL.
Deputy Director General Office
YOU MAY GO.
OWL.
IT'S A PITY YOUR DEPART-MENT IS...
...BEING ELIMINATED.
IT'S FINE.
DON'T FORGET TO BRING US SOMETHING, VICE-CHAIRMAN!
OUR LAST FAMASU TREATS!
OWL

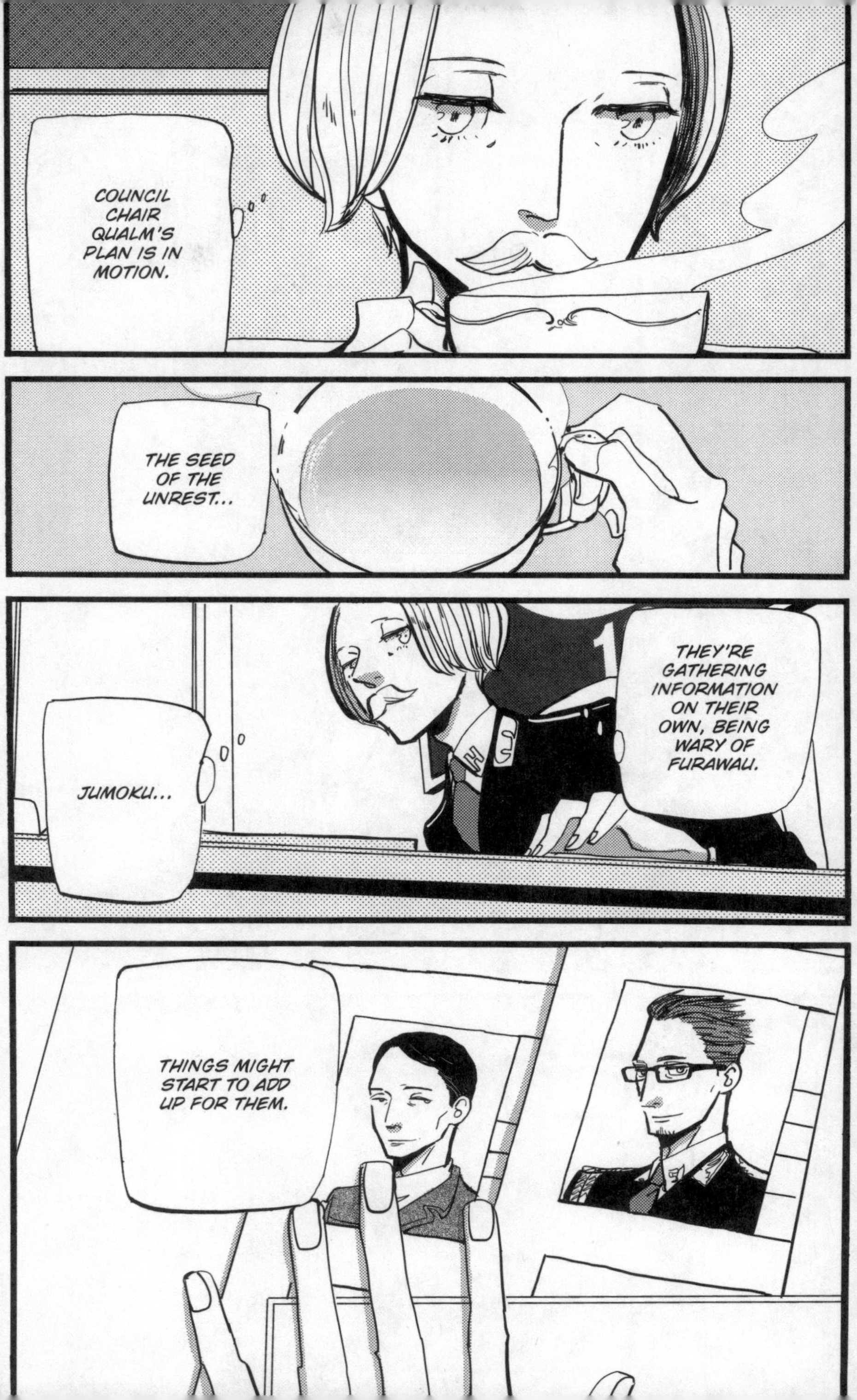
COUNCIL CHAIR QUALM'S PLAN IS IN MOTION.
THE SEED OF THE UNREST...
THEY'RE GATHERING INFORMATION ON THEIR OWN, BEING WARY OF FURAWAU.
JUMOKU...
THINGS MIGHT START TO ADD UP FOR THEM.

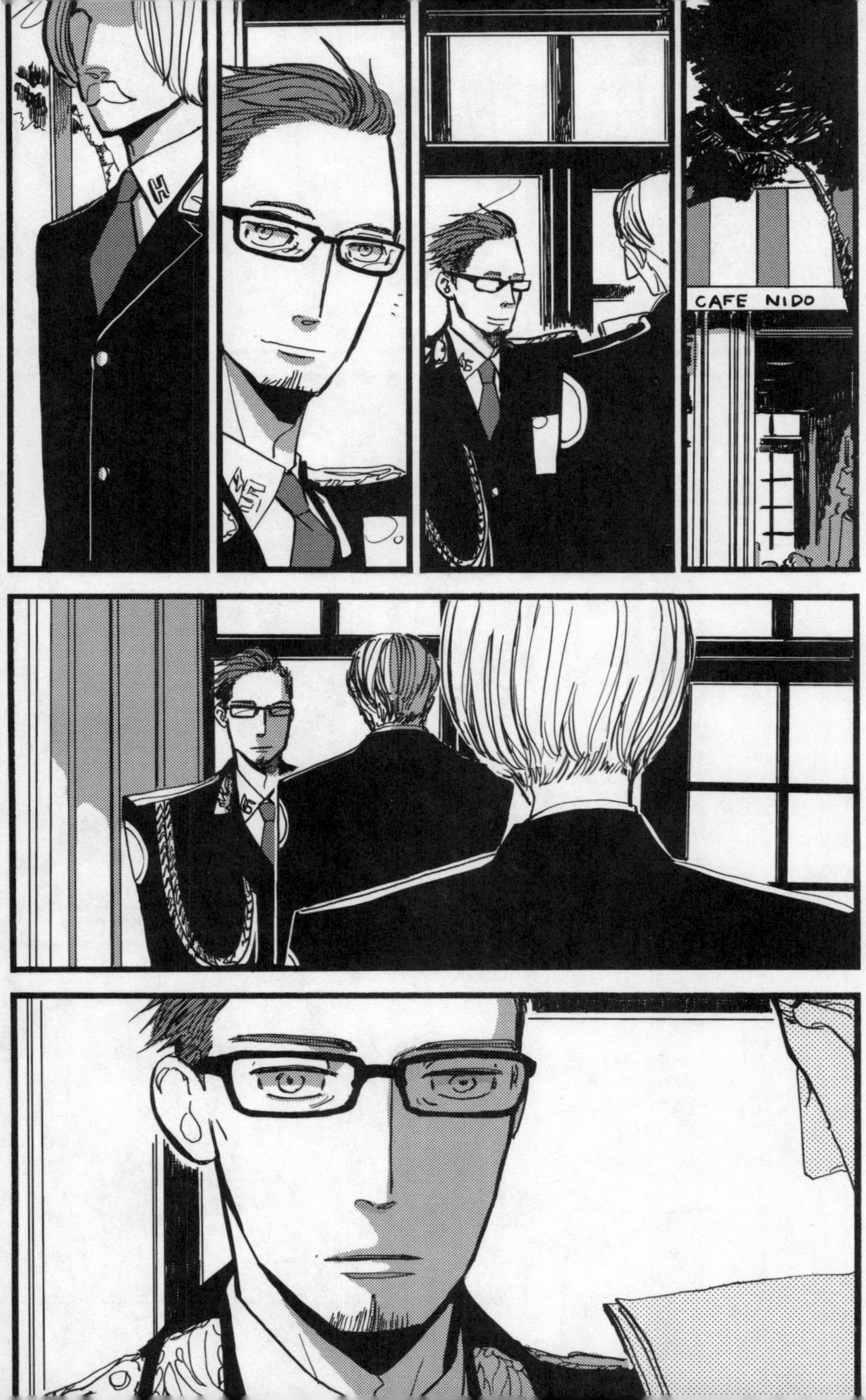
CAFE NIDO

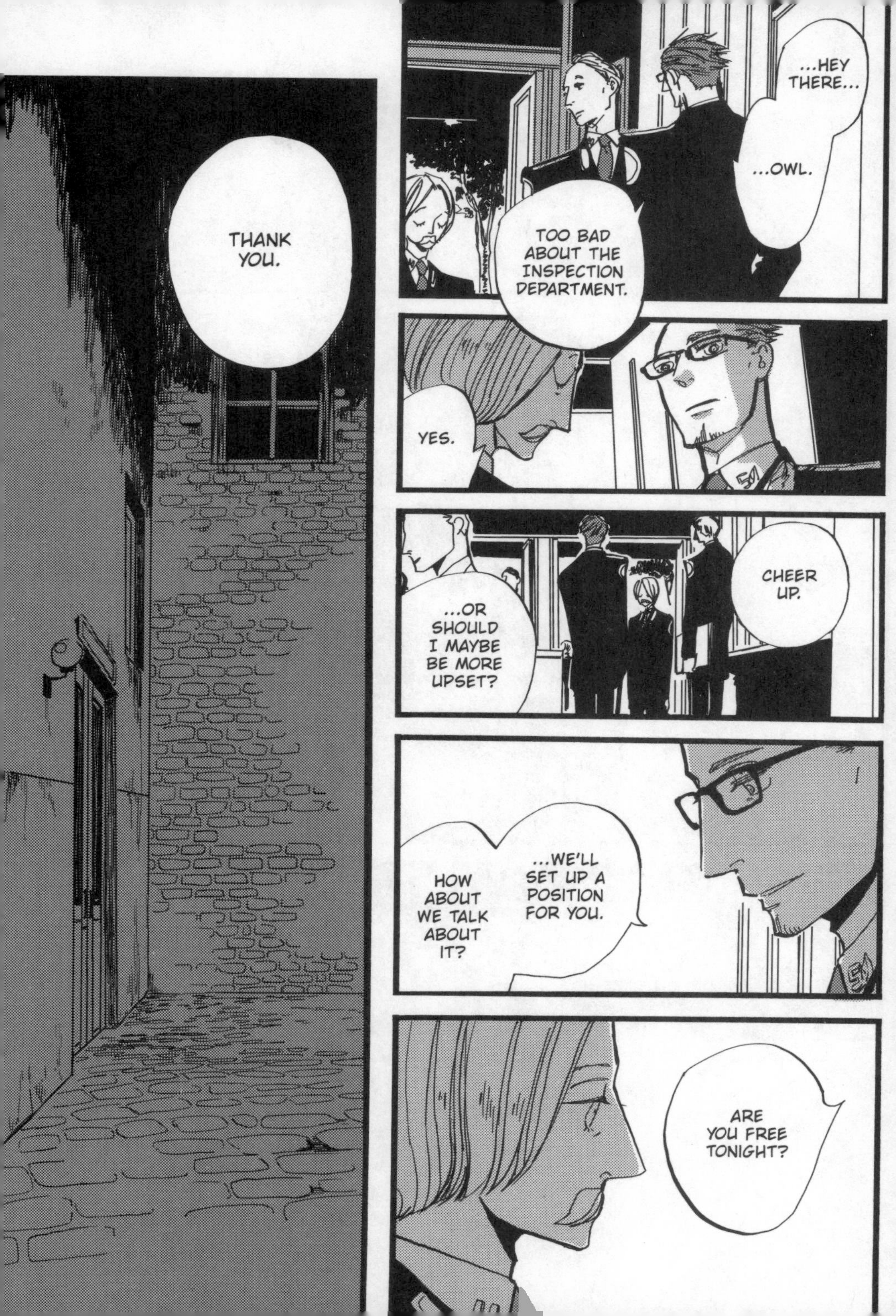
...HEY THERE...
...OWL.
TOO BAD ABOUT THE INSPECTION DEPARTMENT.
YES.
CHEER UP.
...OR SHOULD I MAYBE BE MORE UPSET?
...WE'LL SET UP A POSITION FOR YOU.
HOW ABOUT WE TALK ABOUT IT?
ARE YOU FREE TONIGHT?
THANK YOU.

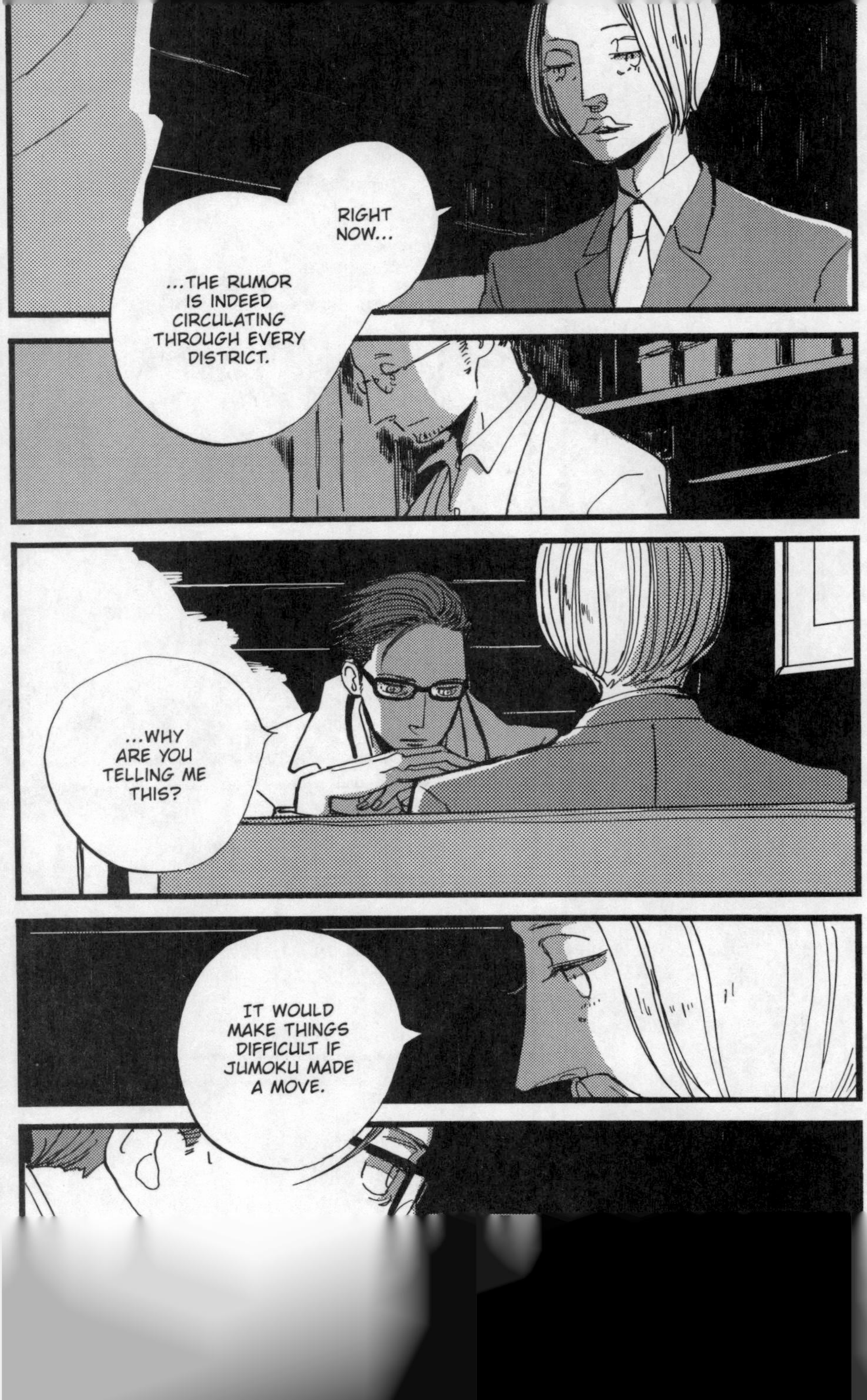
RIGHT NOW...
...THE RUMOR IS INDEED CIRCULATING THROUGH EVERY DISTRICT.
...WHY ARE YOU TELLING ME THIS?
IT WOULD MAKE THINGS DIFFICULT IF JUMOKU MADE A MOVE.

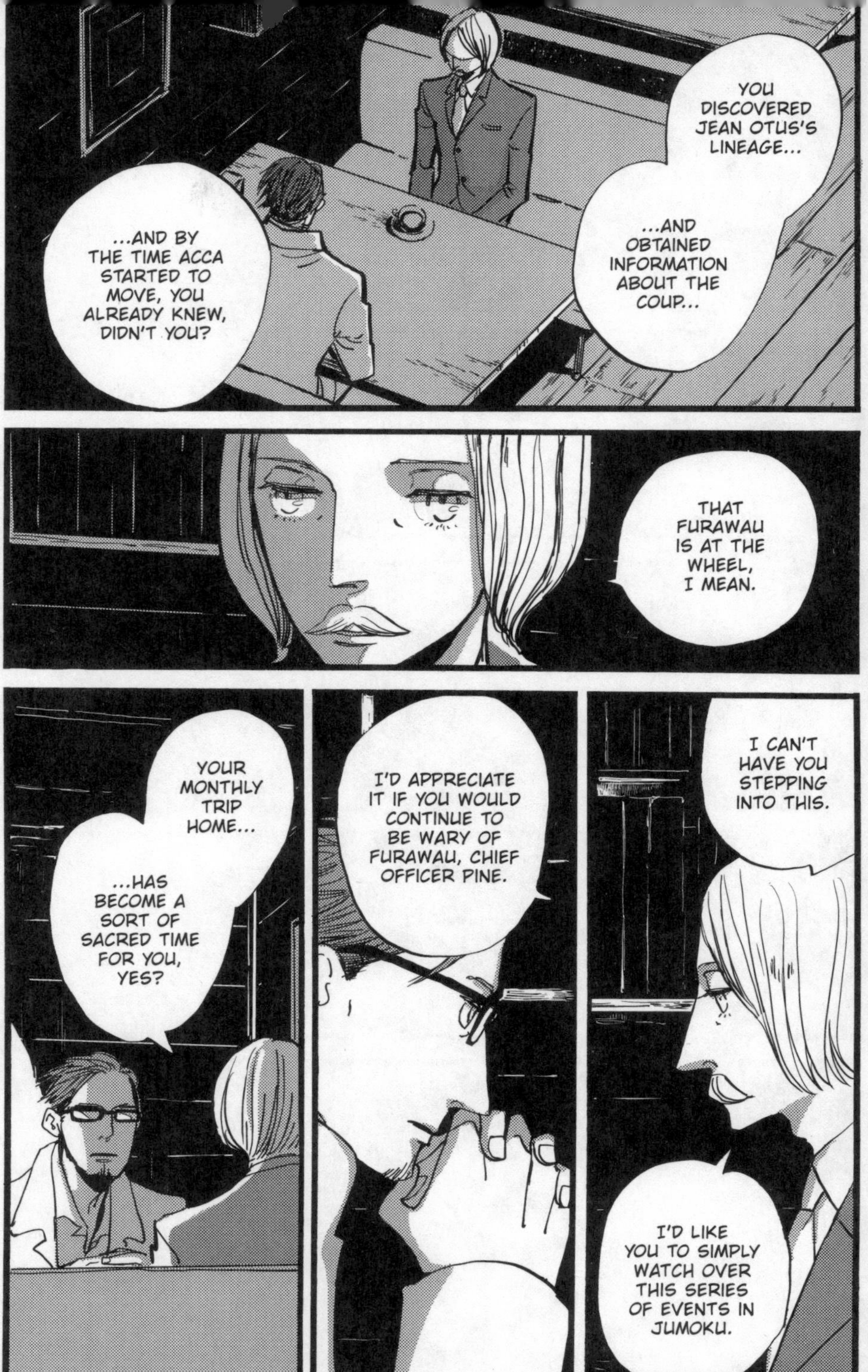
YOU DISCOVERED JEAN OTUS'S LINEAGE...
...AND OBTAINED INFORMATION ABOUT THE COUP...
...AND BY THE TIME ACCA STARTED TO MOVE, YOU ALREADY KNEW, DIDN'T YOU?
THAT FURAWAU IS AT THE WHEEL, I MEAN.
I CAN'T HAVE YOU STEPPING INTO THIS.
I'D LIKE YOU TO SIMPLY WATCH OVER THIS SERIES OF EVENTS IN JUMOKU.
I'D APPRECIATE IT IF YOU WOULD CONTINUE TO BE WARY OF FURAWAU, CHIEF OFFICER PINE.
YOUR MONTHLY TRIP HOME...
...HAS BECOME A SORT OF SACRED TIME FOR YOU, YES?

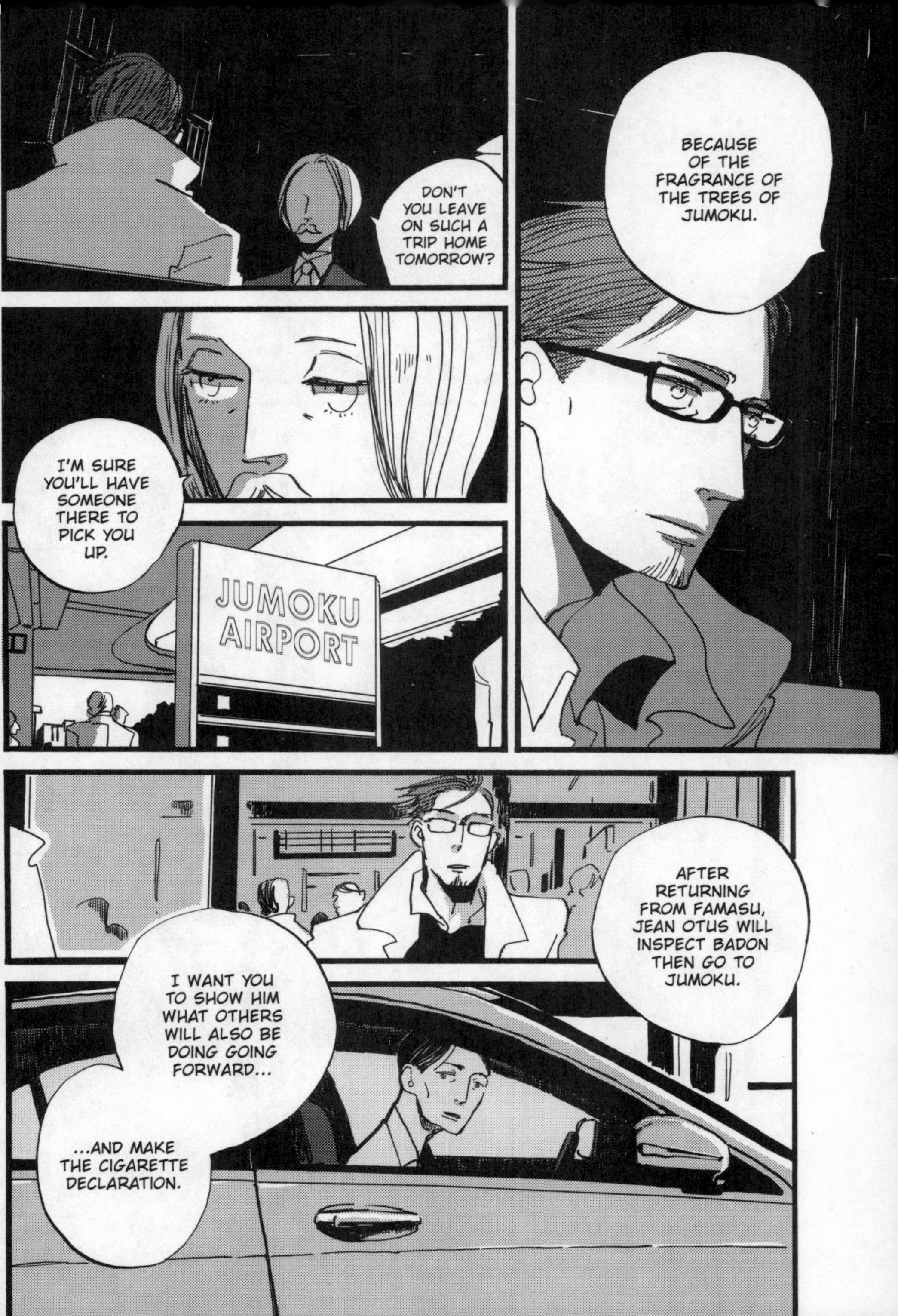
BECAUSE OF THE FRAGRANCE OF THE TREES OF JUMOKU.
DON'T YOU LEAVE ON SUCH A TRIP HOME TOMORROW?
I'M SURE YOU'LL HAVE SOMEONE THERE TO PICK YOU UP.
JUMOKU AIRPORT
AFTER RETURNING FROM FAMASU, JEAN OTUS WILL INSPECT BADON THEN GO TO JUMOKU.
I WANT YOU TO SHOW HIM WHAT OTHERS WILL ALSO BE DOING GOING FORWARD...
...AND MAKE THE CIGARETTE DECLARATION.

PINE...

I KNOW...

...THE RUMOR.

WE DON'T NEED TO DO ANYTHING.

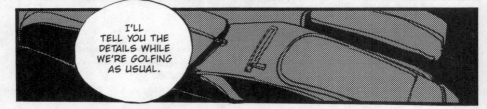

I'LL TELL YOU THE DETAILS WHILE WE'RE GOLFING AS USUAL.

TO BE HONEST, IT'S A LOAD OFF MY SHOULDERS.

ALL WE HAVE TO DO FROM HERE ON OUT IS NOTHING.

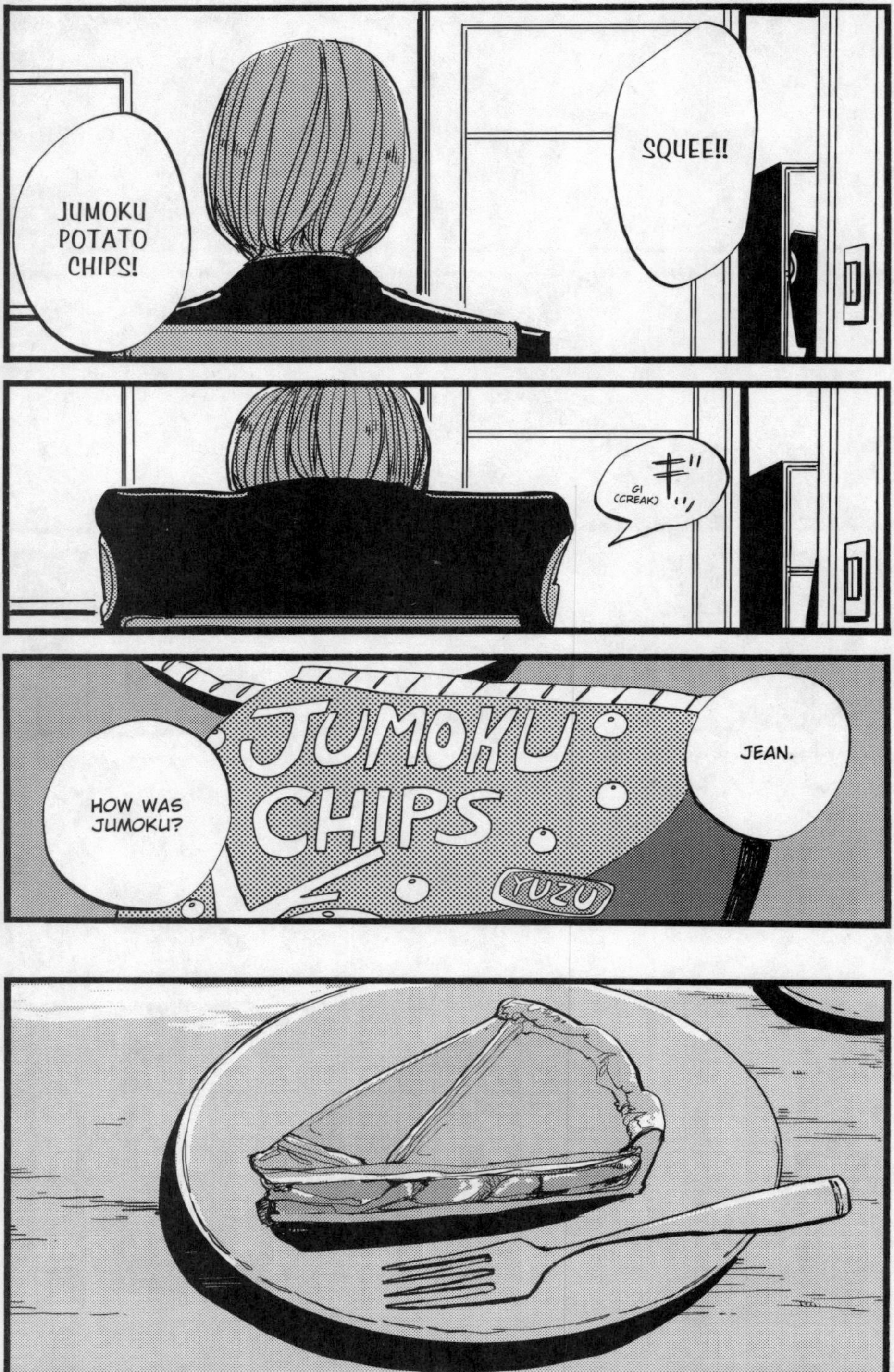
SQUEE!!
JUMOKU POTATO CHIPS!
ギ GI (CREAK)
JEAN.
HOW WAS JUMOKU?
JUMOKU CHIPS
YUZU

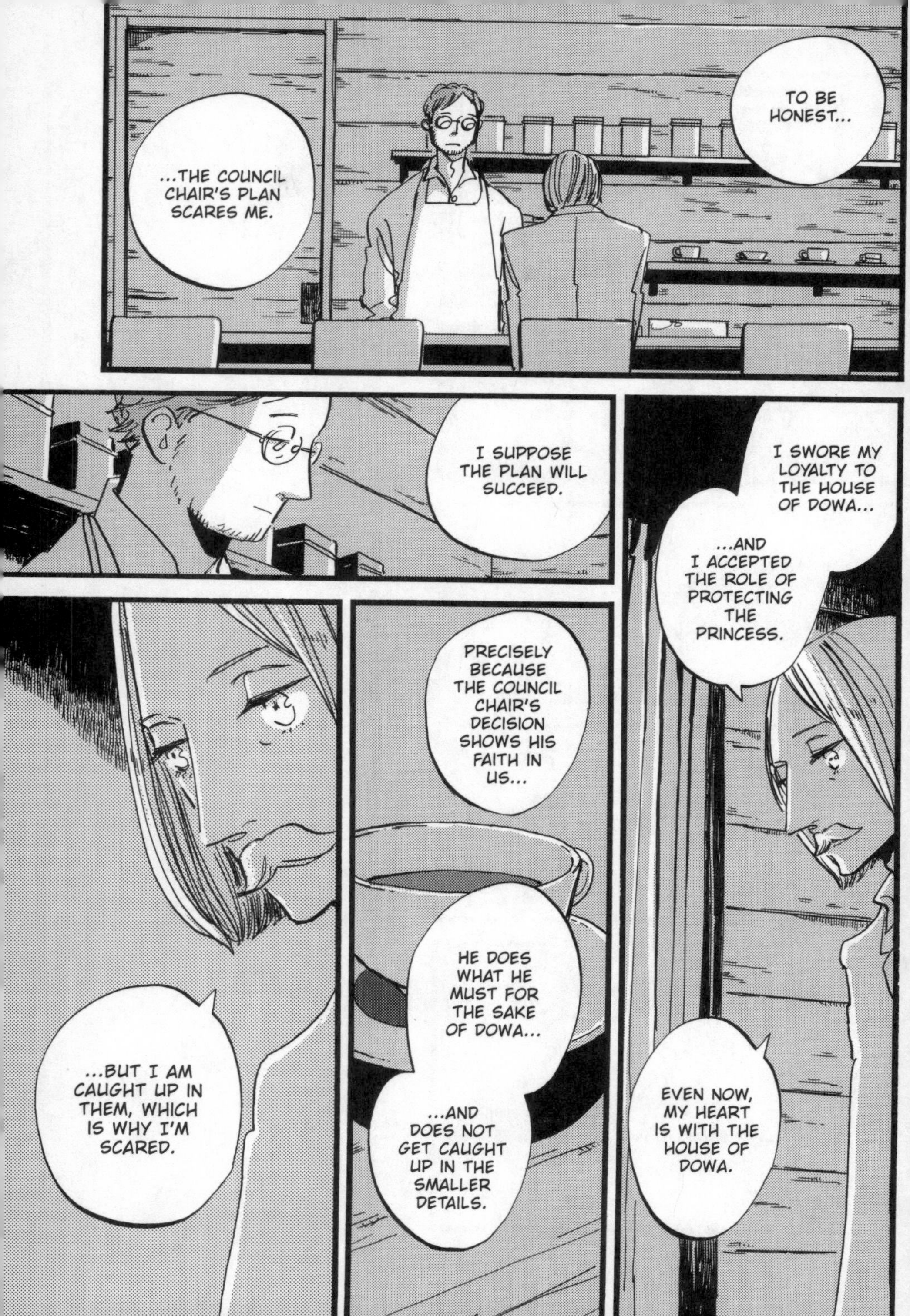
TO BE HONEST...
...THE COUNCIL CHAIR'S PLAN SCARES ME.
I SWORE MY LOYALTY TO THE HOUSE OF DOWA...
...AND I ACCEPTED THE ROLE OF PROTECTING THE PRINCESS.
EVEN NOW, MY HEART IS WITH THE HOUSE OF DOWA.
I SUPPOSE THE PLAN WILL SUCCEED.
PRECISELY BECAUSE THE COUNCIL CHAIR'S DECISION SHOWS HIS FAITH IN US...
HE DOES WHAT HE MUST FOR THE SAKE OF DOWA...
...AND DOES NOT GET CAUGHT UP IN THE SMALLER DETAILS.
...BUT I AM CAUGHT UP IN THEM, WHICH IS WHY I'M SCARED.

OUR EXISTENCE ...
...AND THE WAY WE'VE LIVED...
...WHAT WILL WE DO IF IT'S ALL TURNED TO NOTHING?
Today is the coming-of-age ceremony for Prince Schwan in Dowa...
DOWA
Suitsu
Birra
Rokkusu

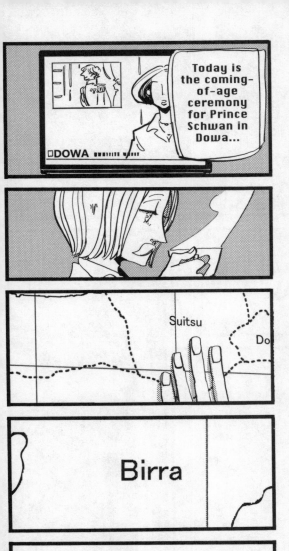

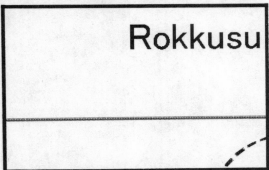

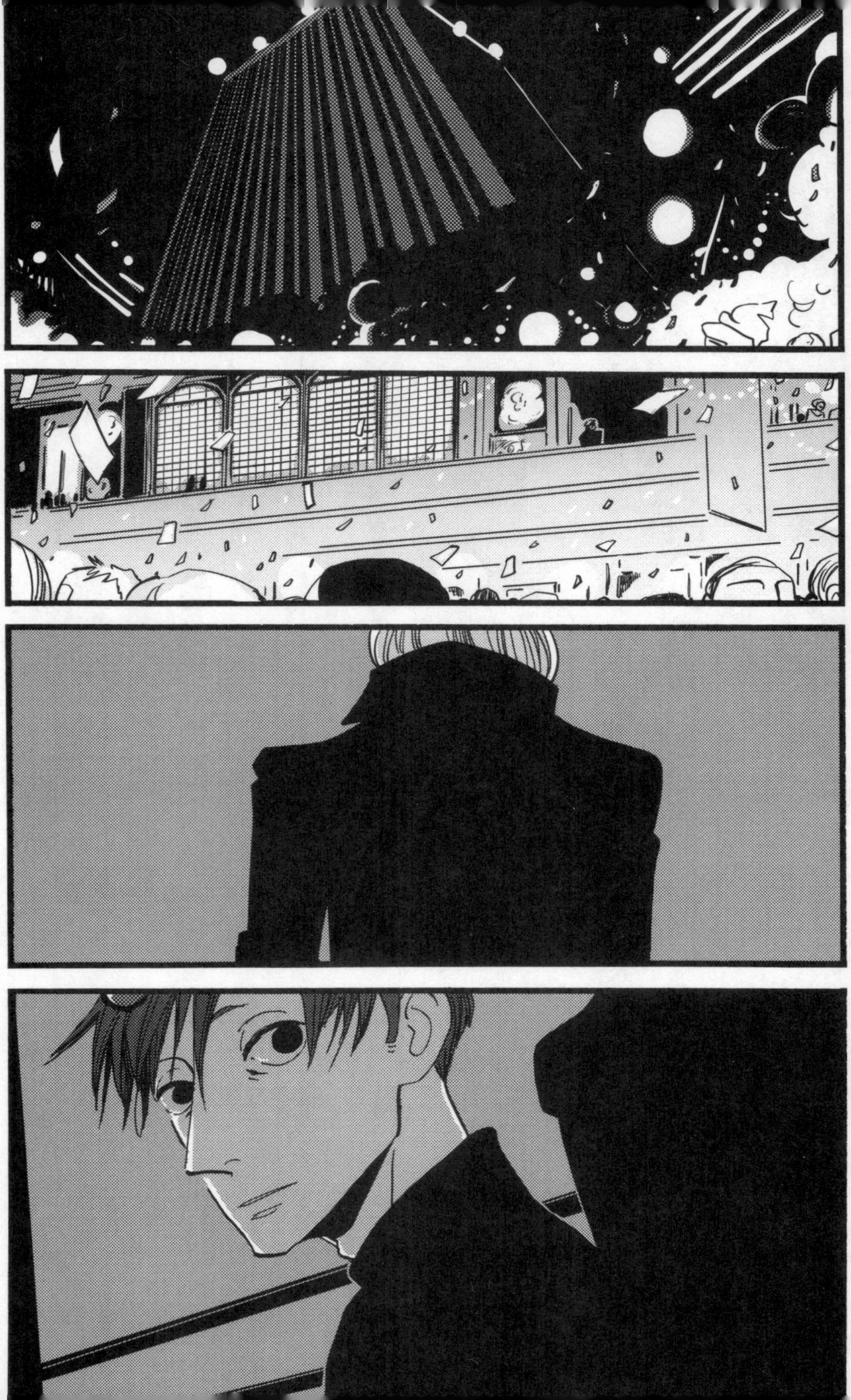

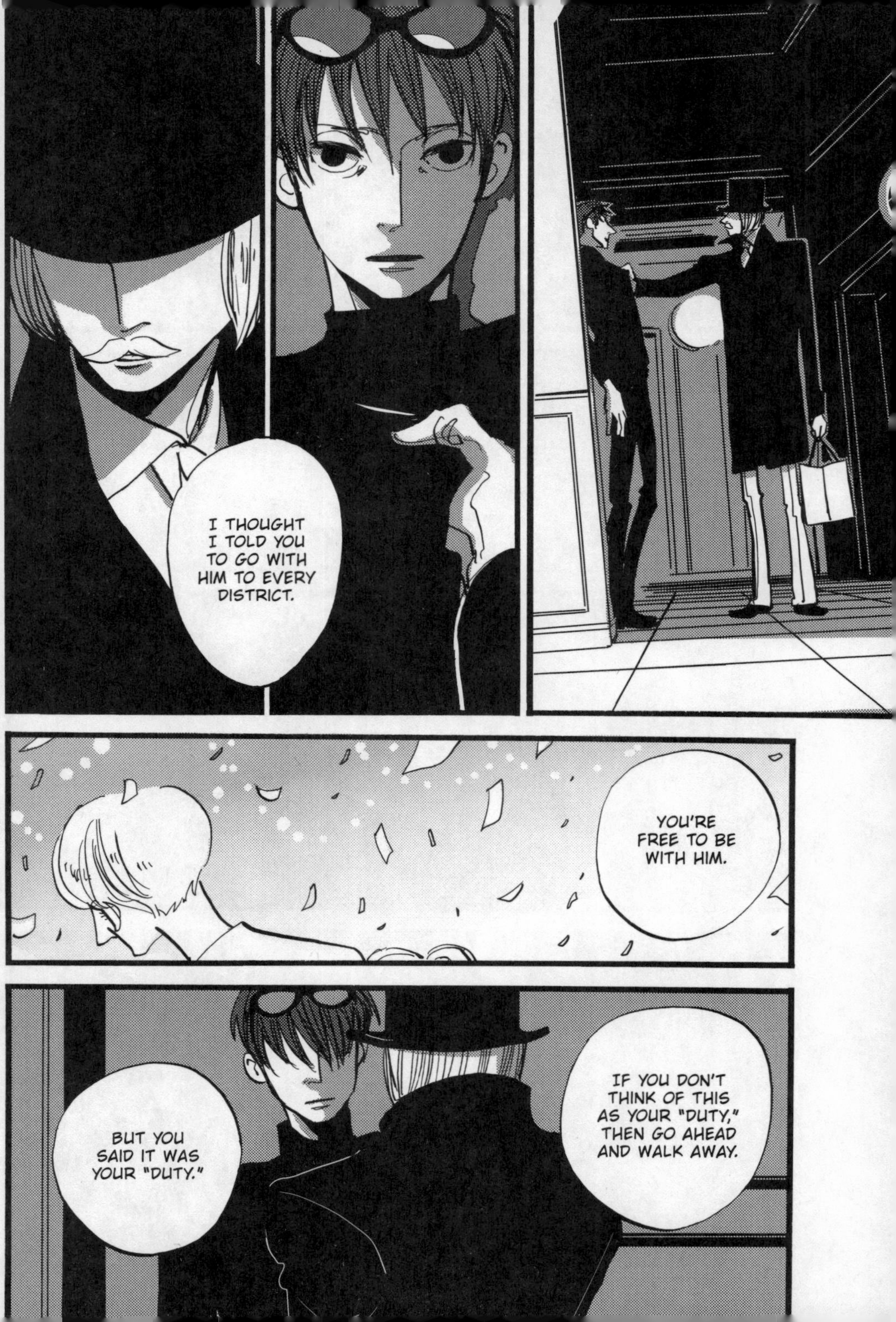
I THOUGHT I TOLD YOU TO GO WITH HIM TO EVERY DISTRICT.
YOU'RE FREE TO BE WITH HIM.
IF YOU DON'T THINK OF THIS AS YOUR "DUTY," THEN GO AHEAD AND WALK AWAY.
BUT YOU SAID IT WAS YOUR "DUTY."

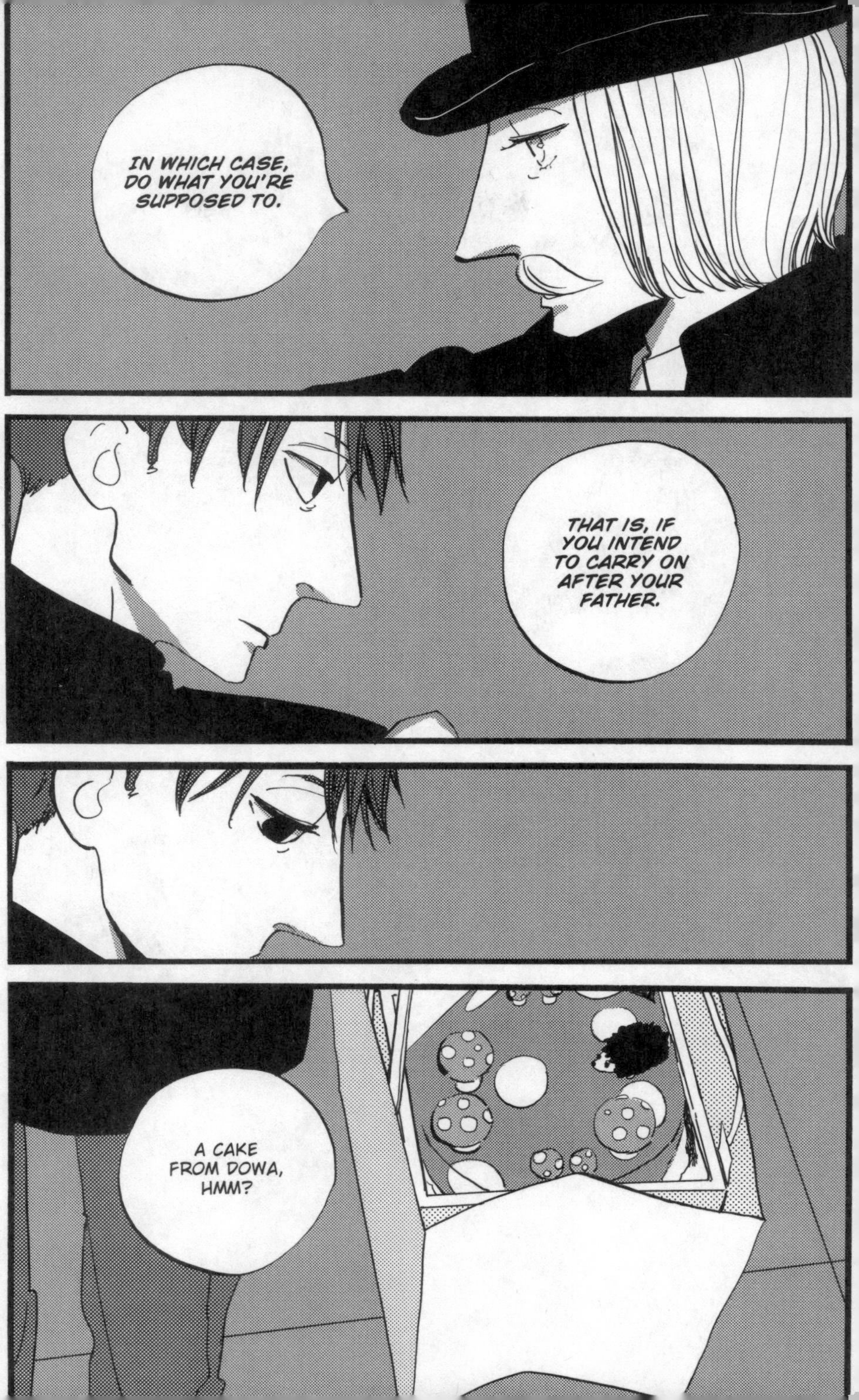
IN WHICH CASE, DO WHAT YOU'RE SUPPOSED TO.
THAT IS, IF YOU INTEND TO CARRY ON AFTER YOUR FATHER.
A CAKE FROM DOWA, HMM?

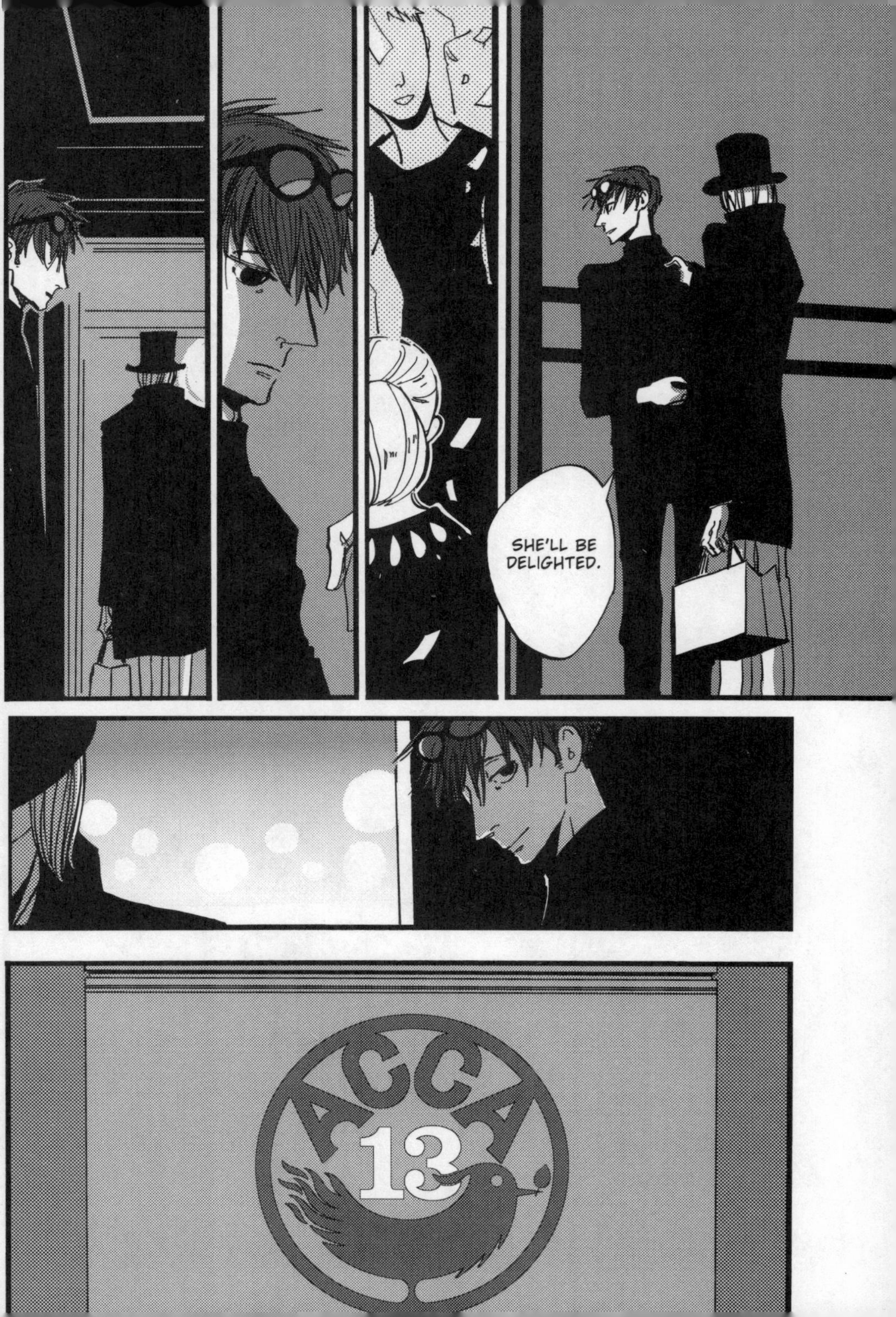
SHE'LL BE DELIGHTED.
ACCA
13

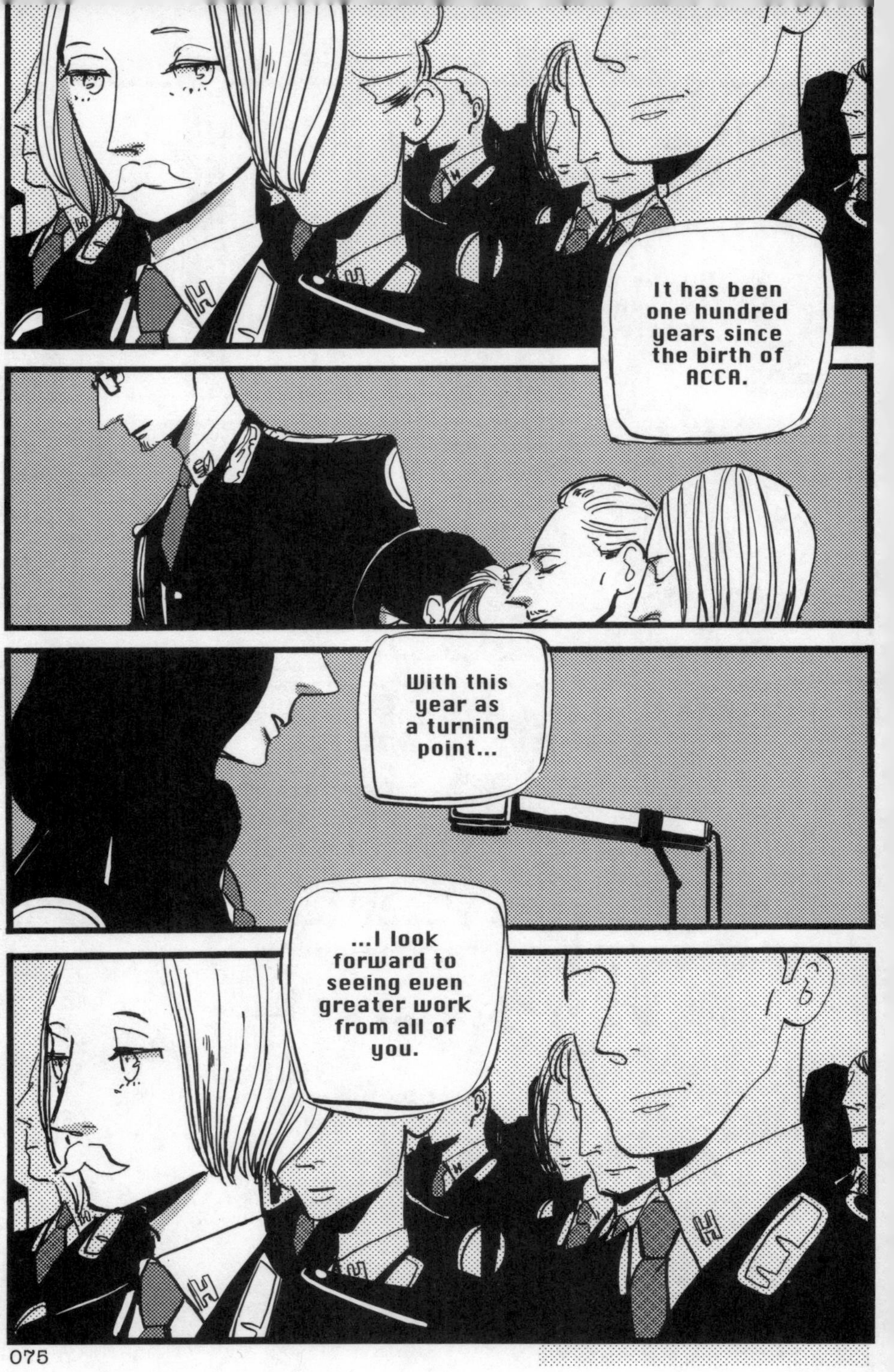
It has been one hundred years since the birth of ACCA.
With this year as a turning point...
...I look forward to seeing even greater work from all of you.

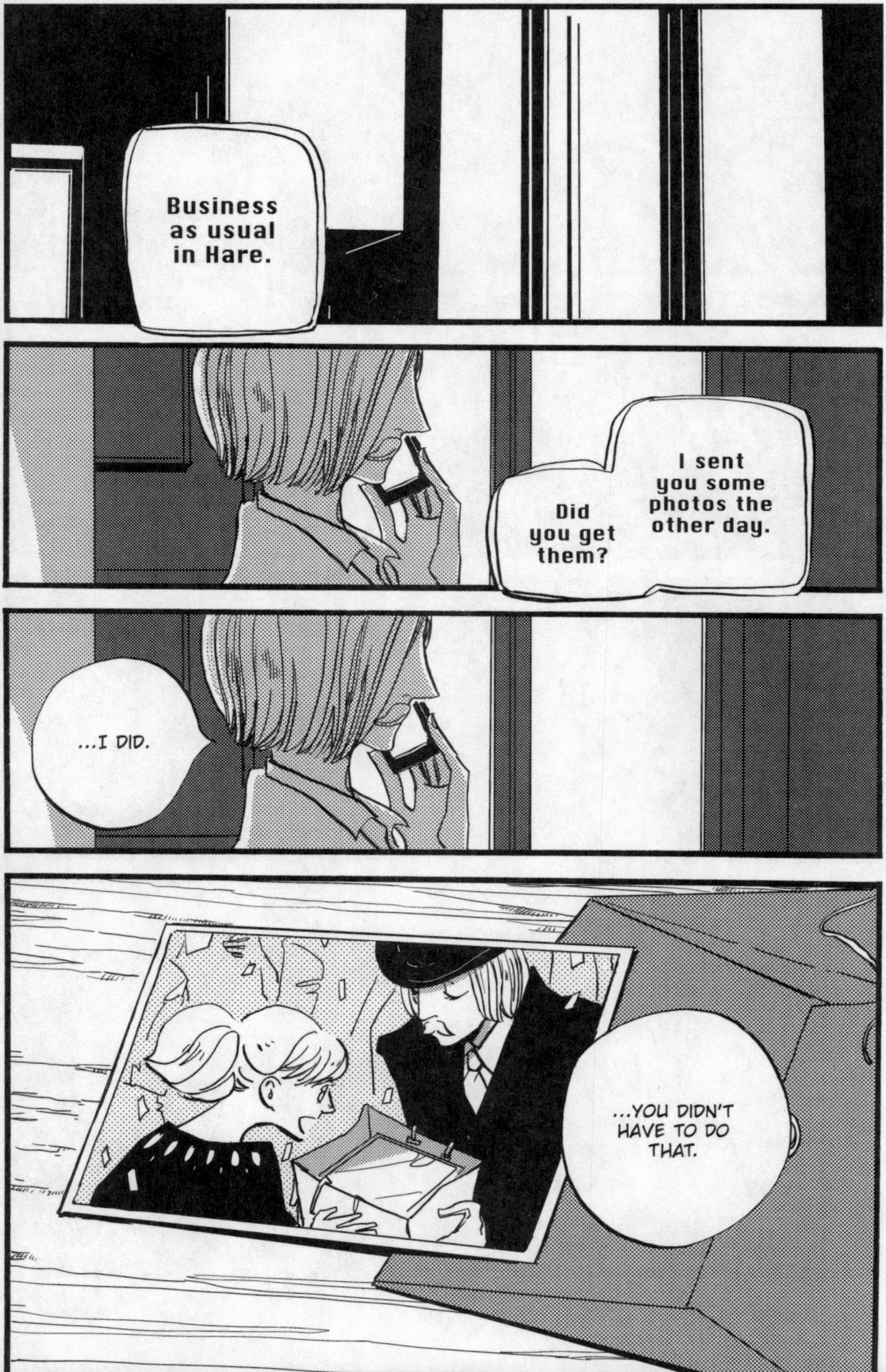
Business as usual in Hare.
I sent you some photos the other day.
Did you get them?
...I DID.
...YOU DIDN'T HAVE TO DO THAT.

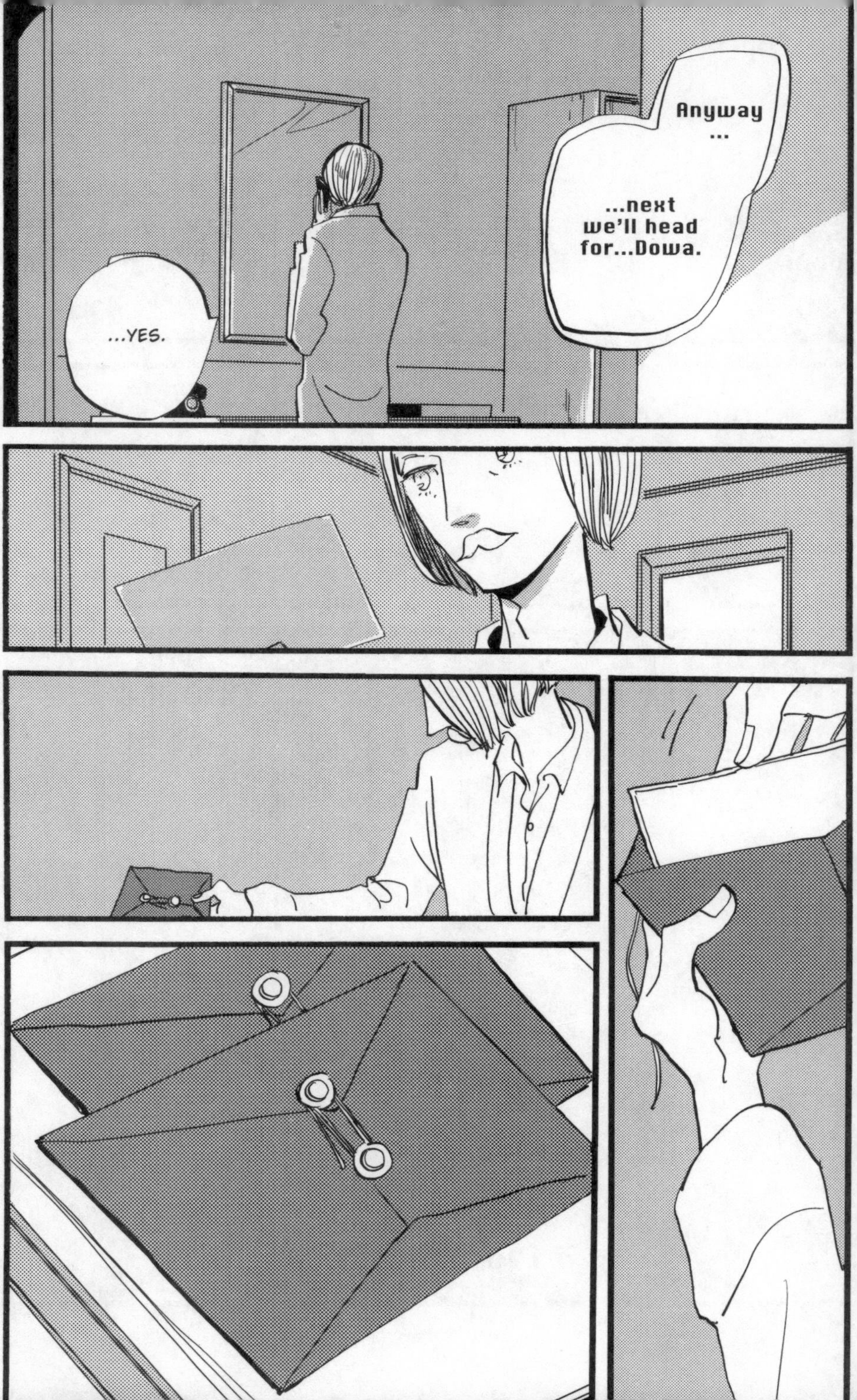
Anyway... ...next we'll head for...Dowa.
...YES.

MUGIMAKI
SAKU (CRUNCH)
サク

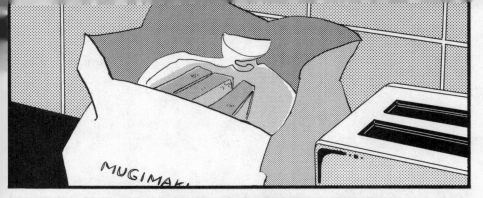

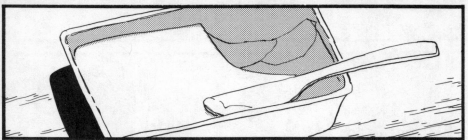

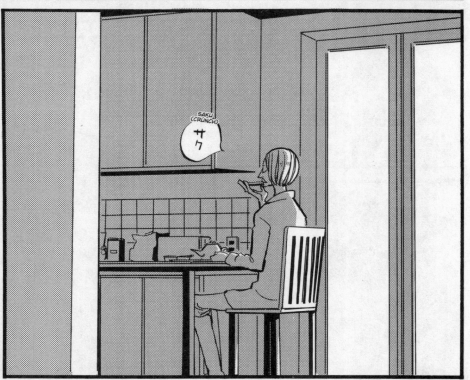

P.S.

DEPT. ACCA 13 TERRITORY INSPECTION

PASS

CHAPTER 7

The Watchman on a Perch in the Broad Sky (Part Two)

CHAPTER 8

Sentry Days,
Together Days

P.S.

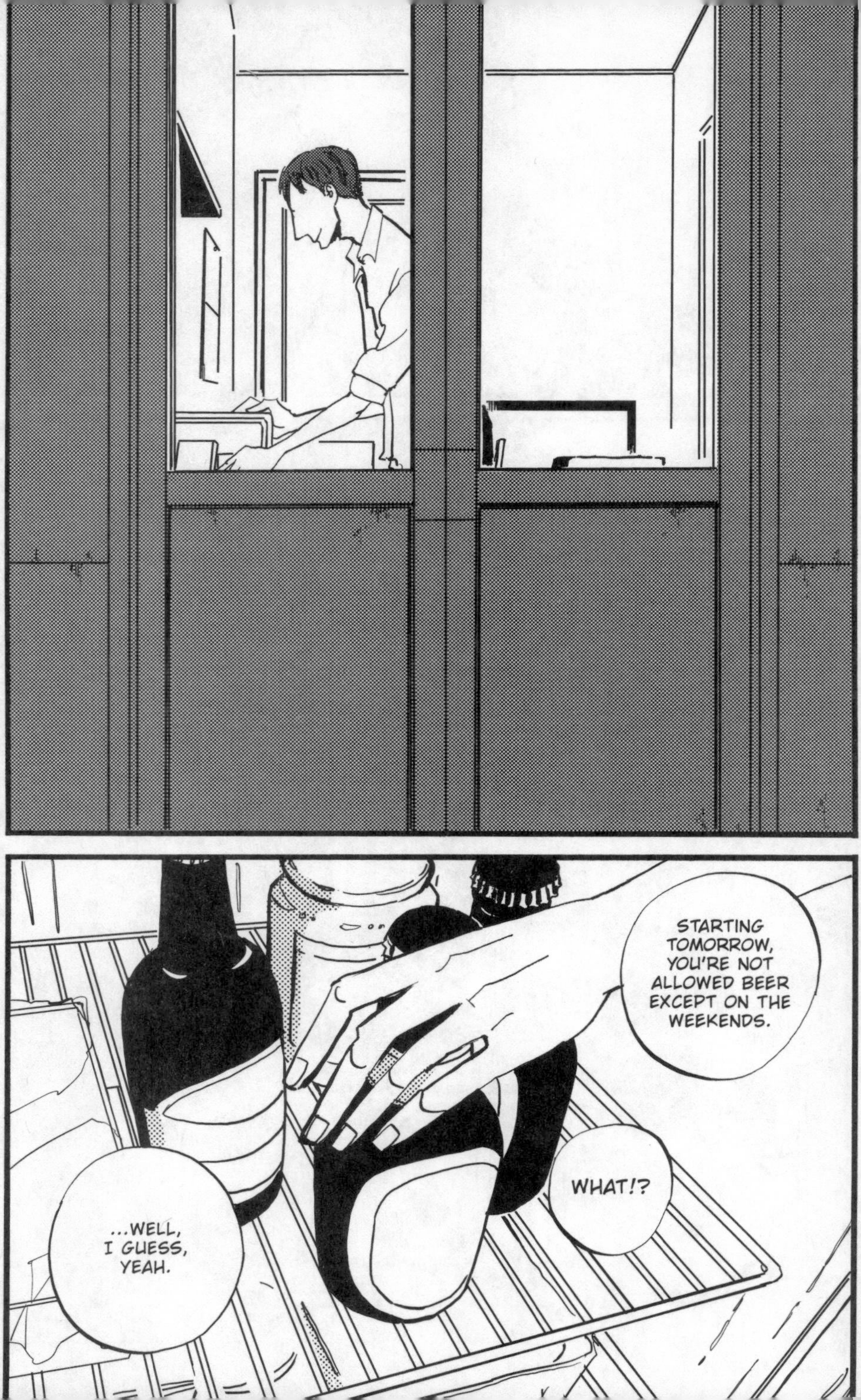
STARTING TOMORROW, YOU'RE NOT ALLOWED BEER EXCEPT ON THE WEEKENDS.
WHAT!?
...WELL, I GUESS, YEAH.

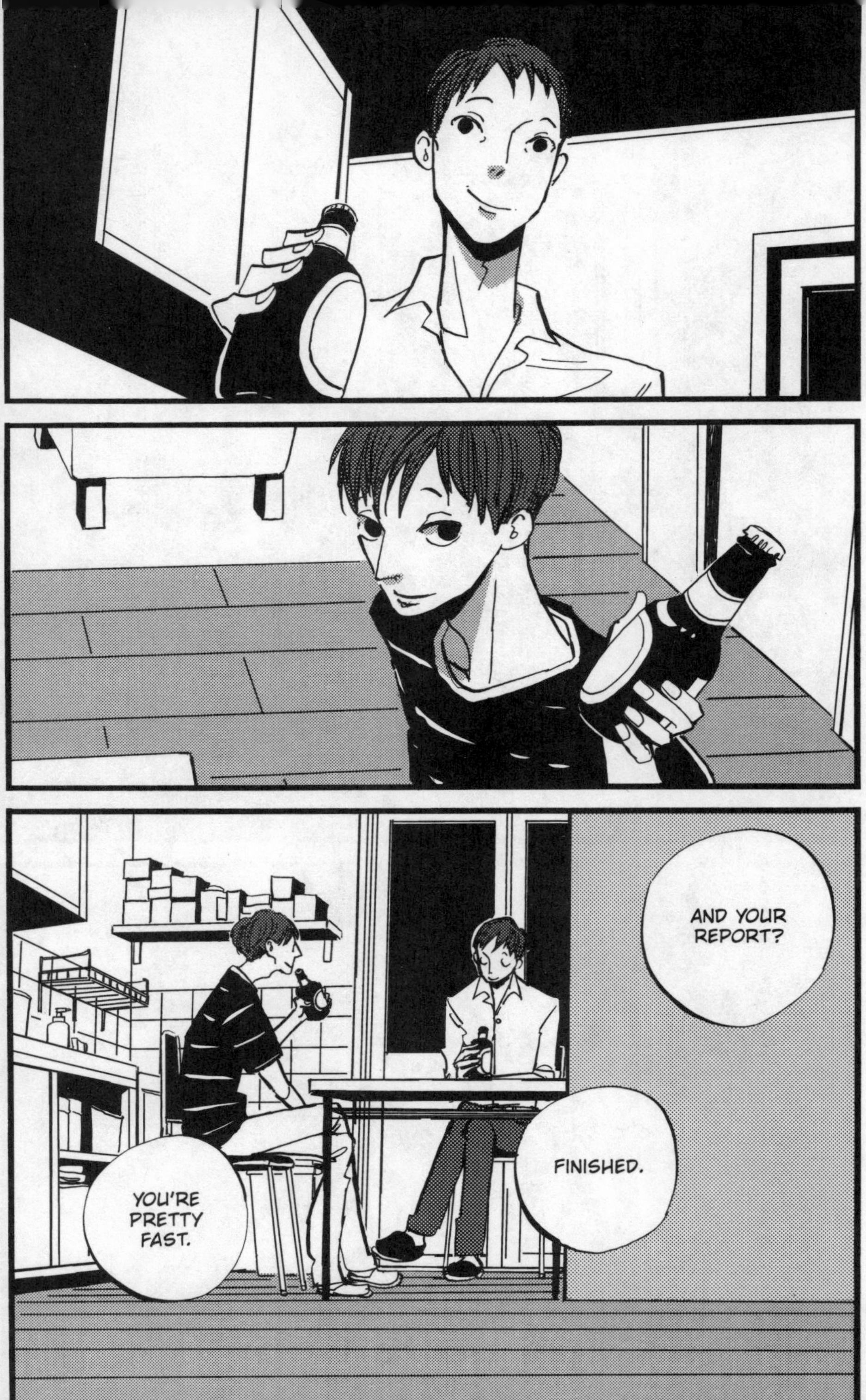
AND YOUR REPORT?
FINISHED.
YOU'RE PRETTY FAST.

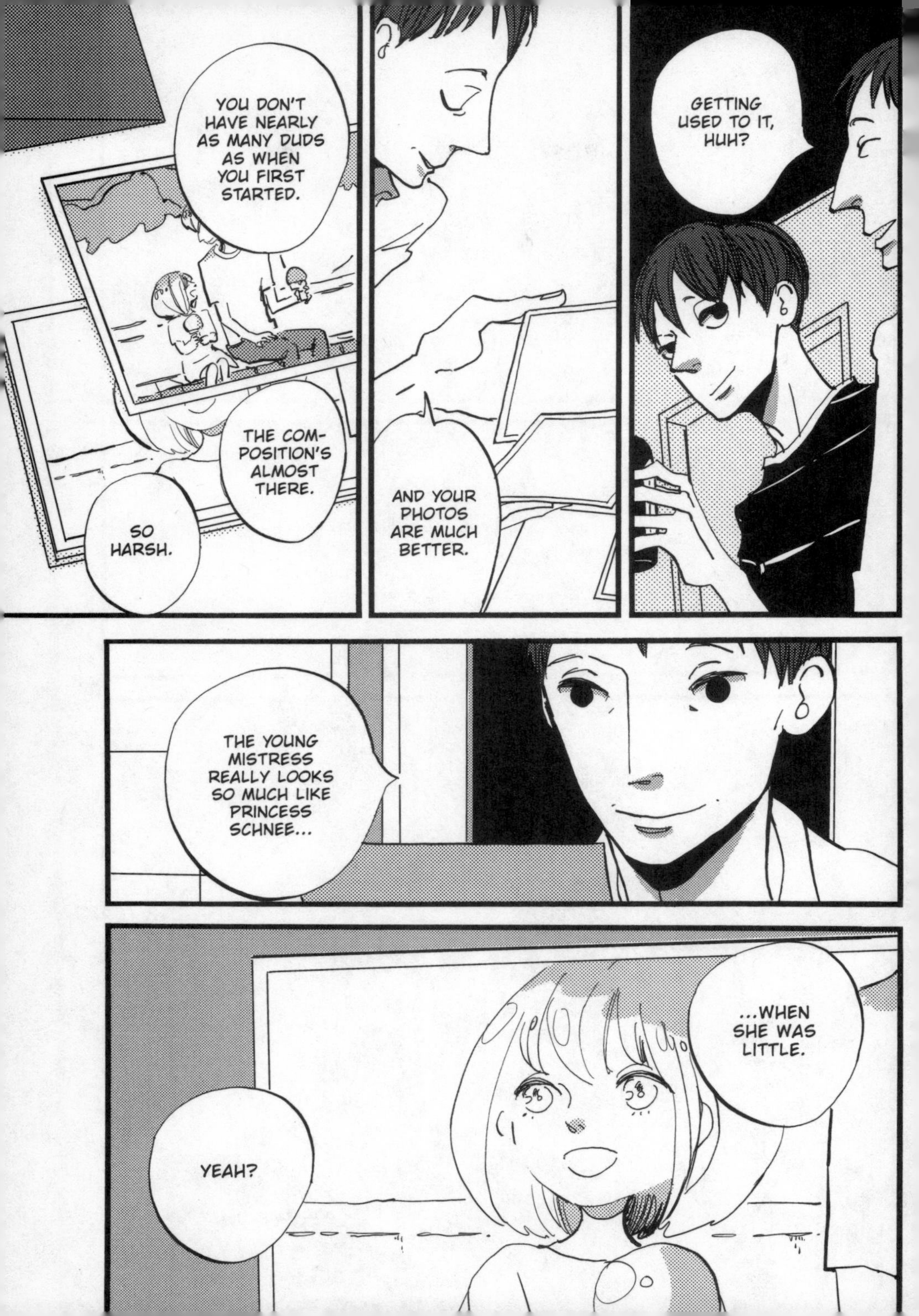
GETTING USED TO IT, HUH?
AND YOUR PHOTOS ARE MUCH BETTER.
YOU DON'T HAVE NEARLY AS MANY DUDS AS WHEN YOU FIRST STARTED.
THE COMPOSITION'S ALMOST THERE.
SO HARSH.
THE YOUNG MISTRESS REALLY LOOKS SO MUCH LIKE PRINCESS SCHNEE...
...WHEN SHE WAS LITTLE.
YEAH?

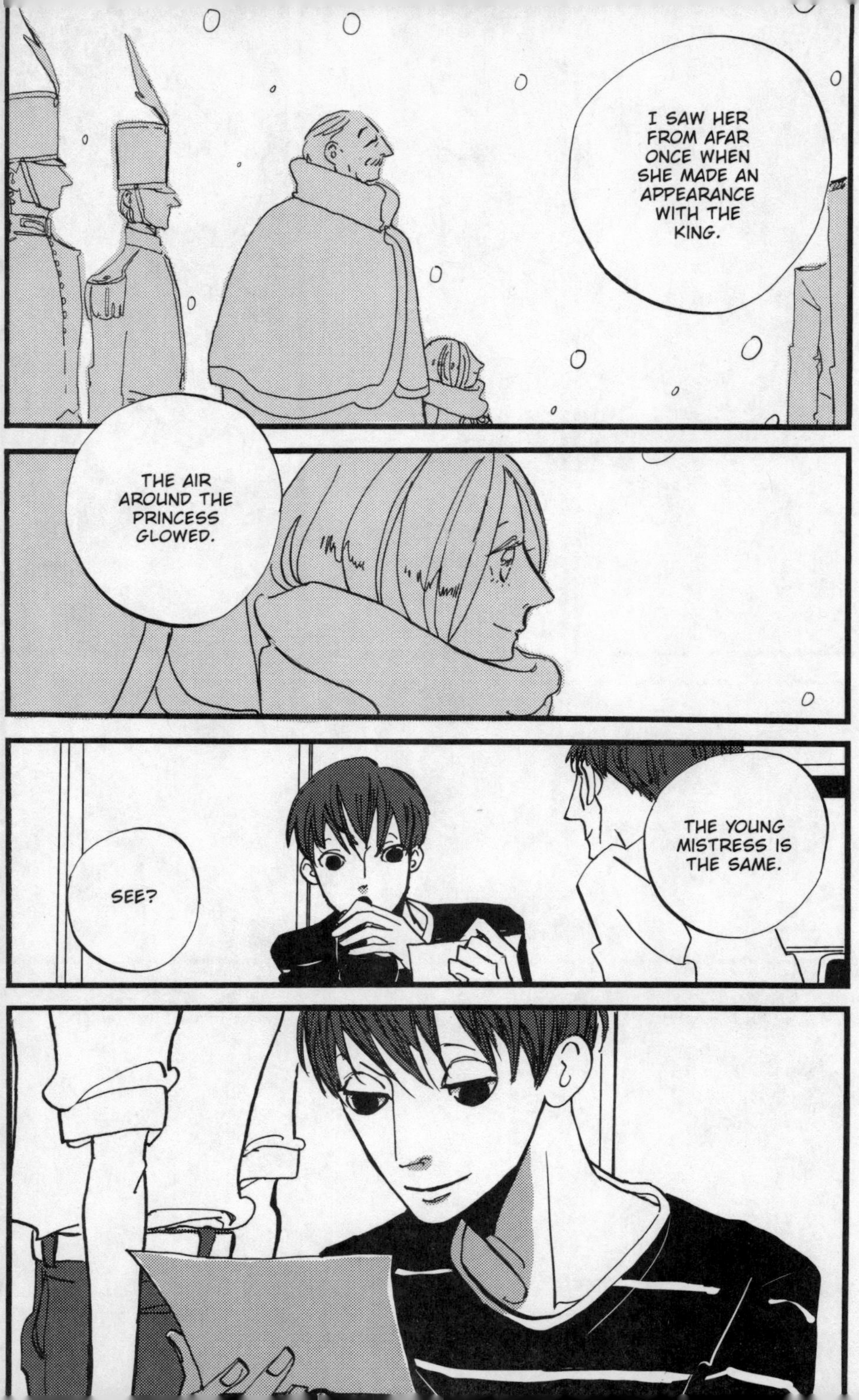
I SAW HER FROM AFAR ONCE WHEN SHE MADE AN APPEARANCE WITH THE KING.
THE AIR AROUND THE PRINCESS GLOWED.
THE YOUNG MISTRESS IS THE SAME.
SEE?

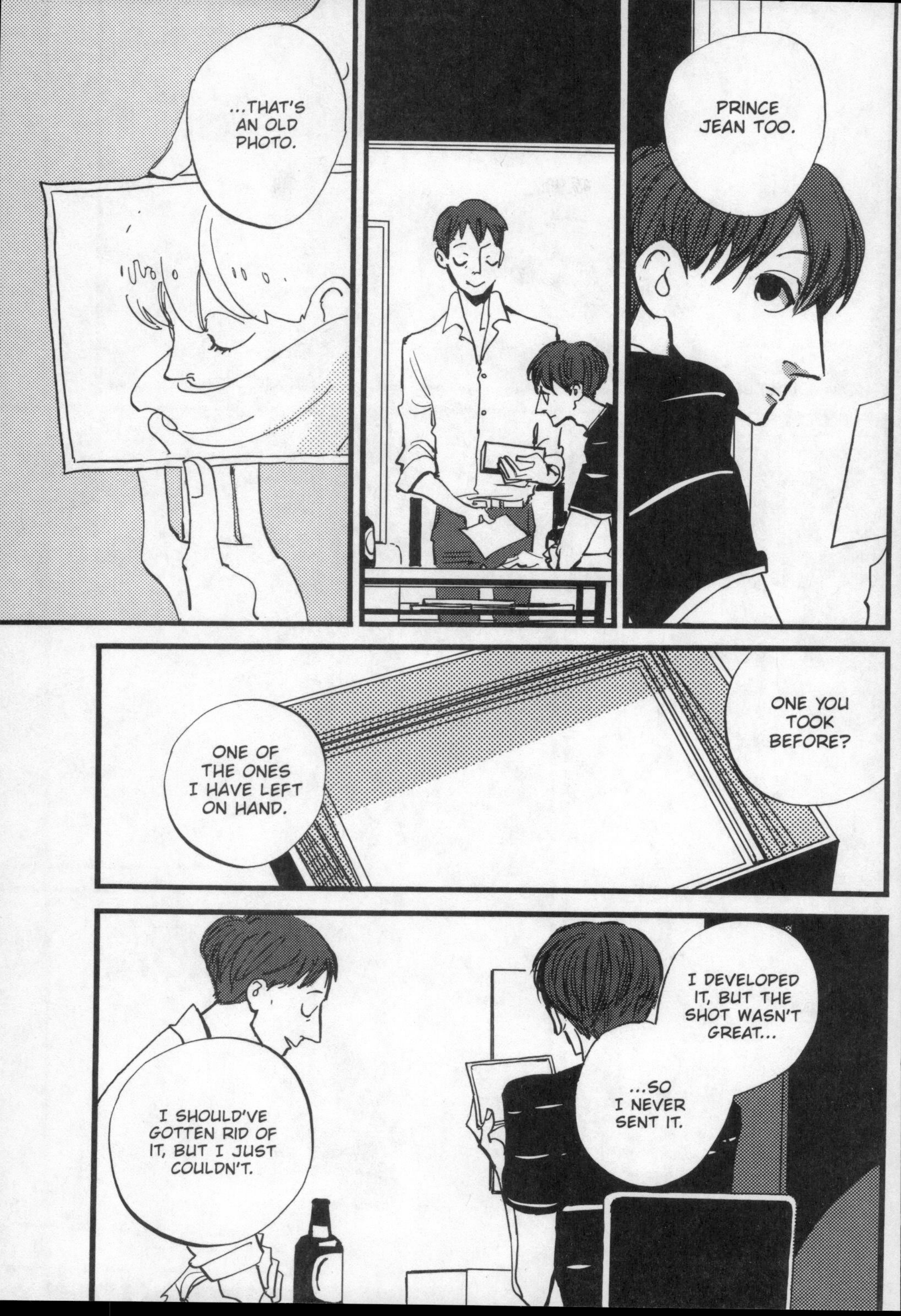
PRINCE JEAN TOO.
...THAT'S AN OLD PHOTO.
ONE YOU TOOK BEFORE?
ONE OF THE ONES I HAVE LEFT ON HAND.
I DEVELOPED IT, BUT THE SHOT WASN'T GREAT...
...SO I NEVER SENT IT.
I SHOULD'VE GOTTEN RID OF IT, BUT I JUST COULDN'T.

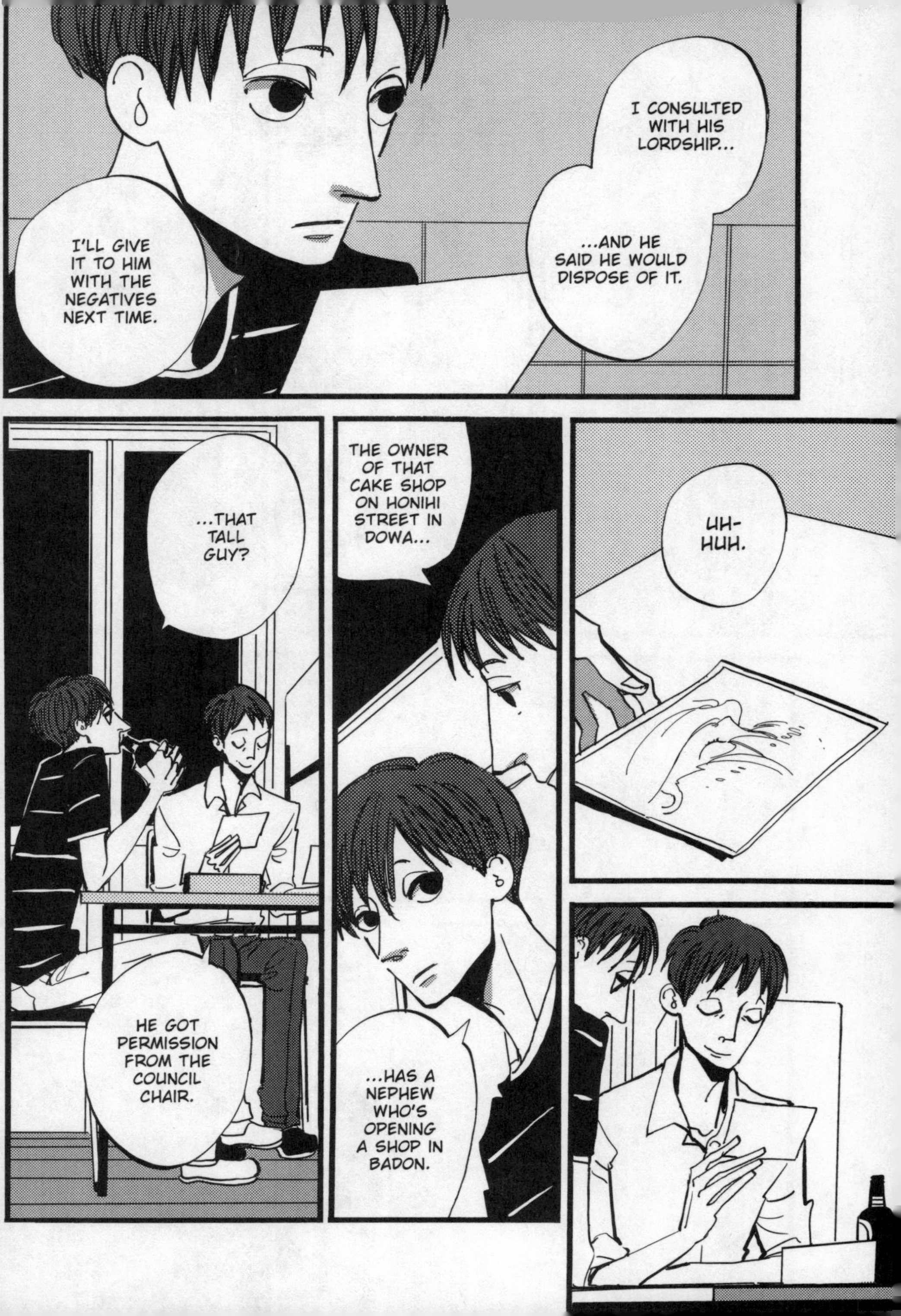
I CONSULTED WITH HIS LORDSHIP...
...AND HE SAID HE WOULD DISPOSE OF IT.
I'LL GIVE IT TO HIM WITH THE NEGATIVES NEXT TIME.
UH-HUH.
THE OWNER OF THAT CAKE SHOP ON HONIHI STREET IN DOWA...
...HAS A NEPHEW WHO'S OPENING A SHOP IN BADON.
...THAT TALL GUY?
HE GOT PERMISSION FROM THE COUNCIL CHAIR.

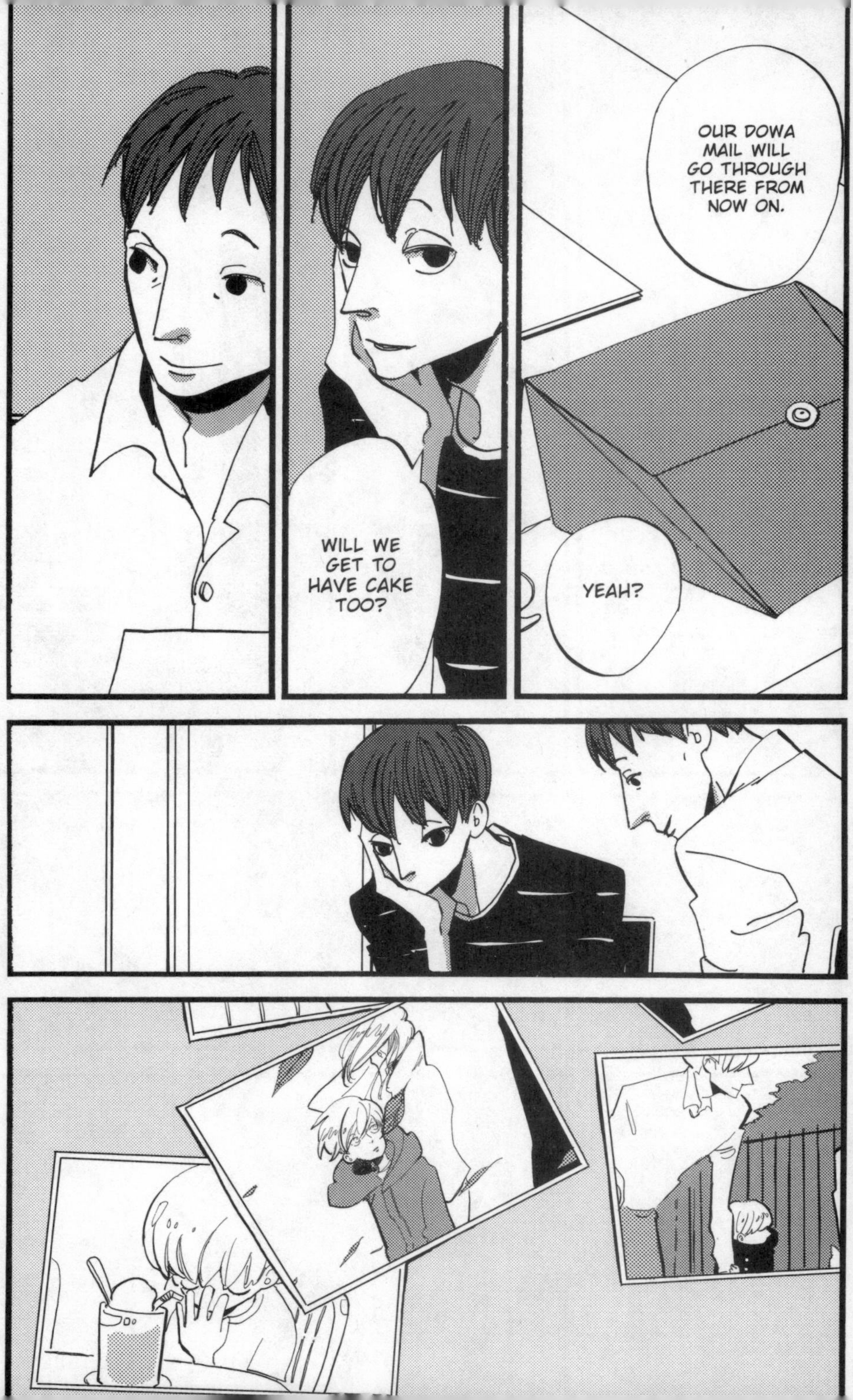
OUR DOWA MAIL WILL GO THROUGH THERE FROM NOW ON.
YEAH?
WILL WE GET TO HAVE CAKE TOO?

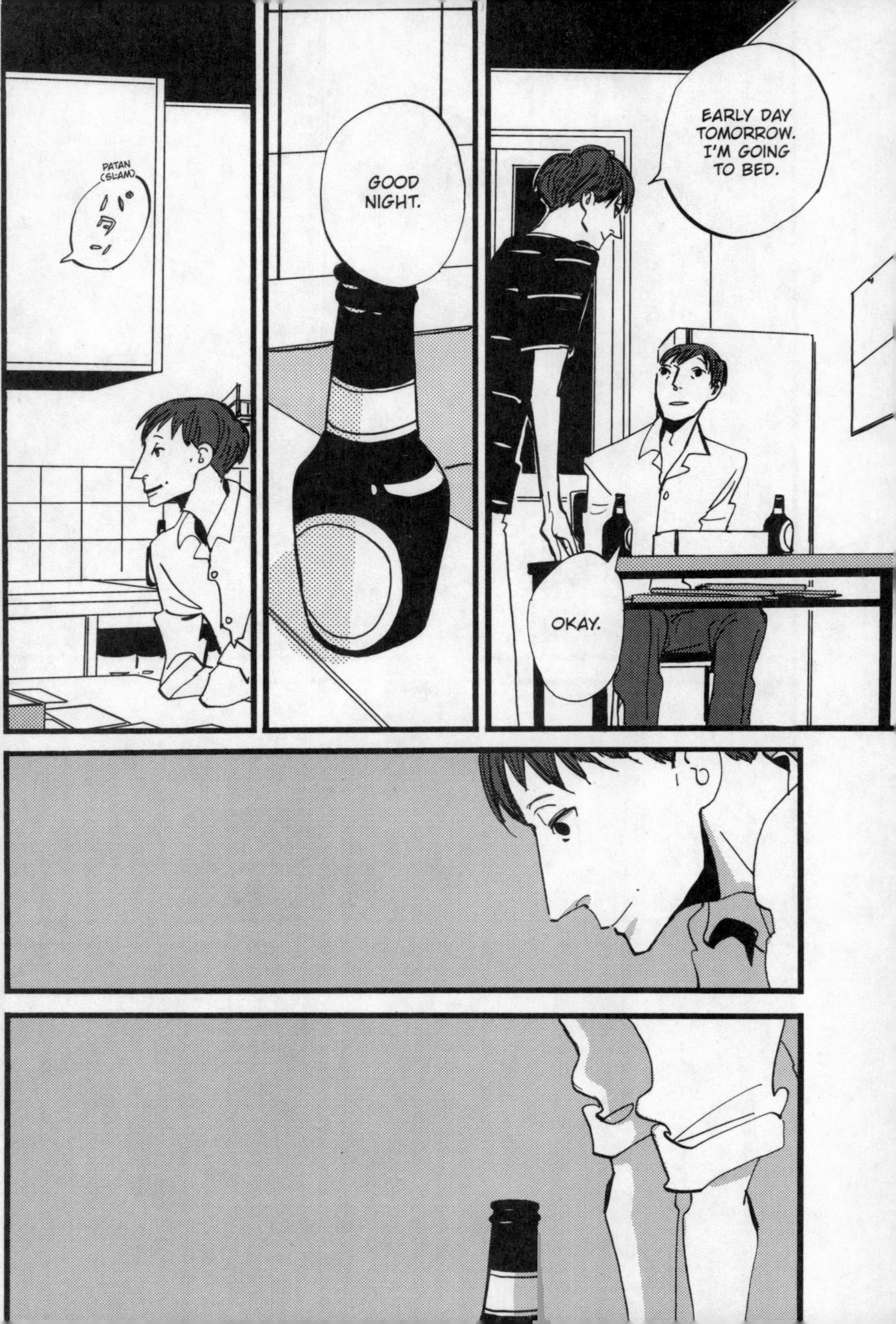
EARLY DAY TOMORROW. I'M GOING TO BED.
OKAY.
GOOD NIGHT.
パタン
PATAN (SLAM)

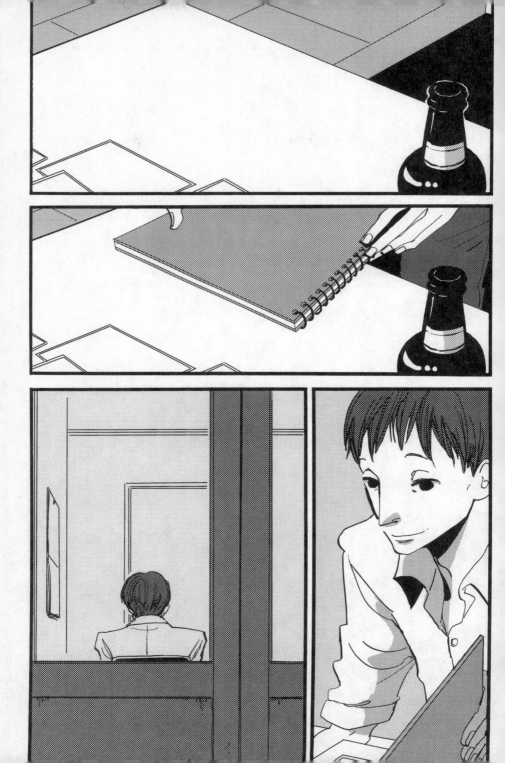

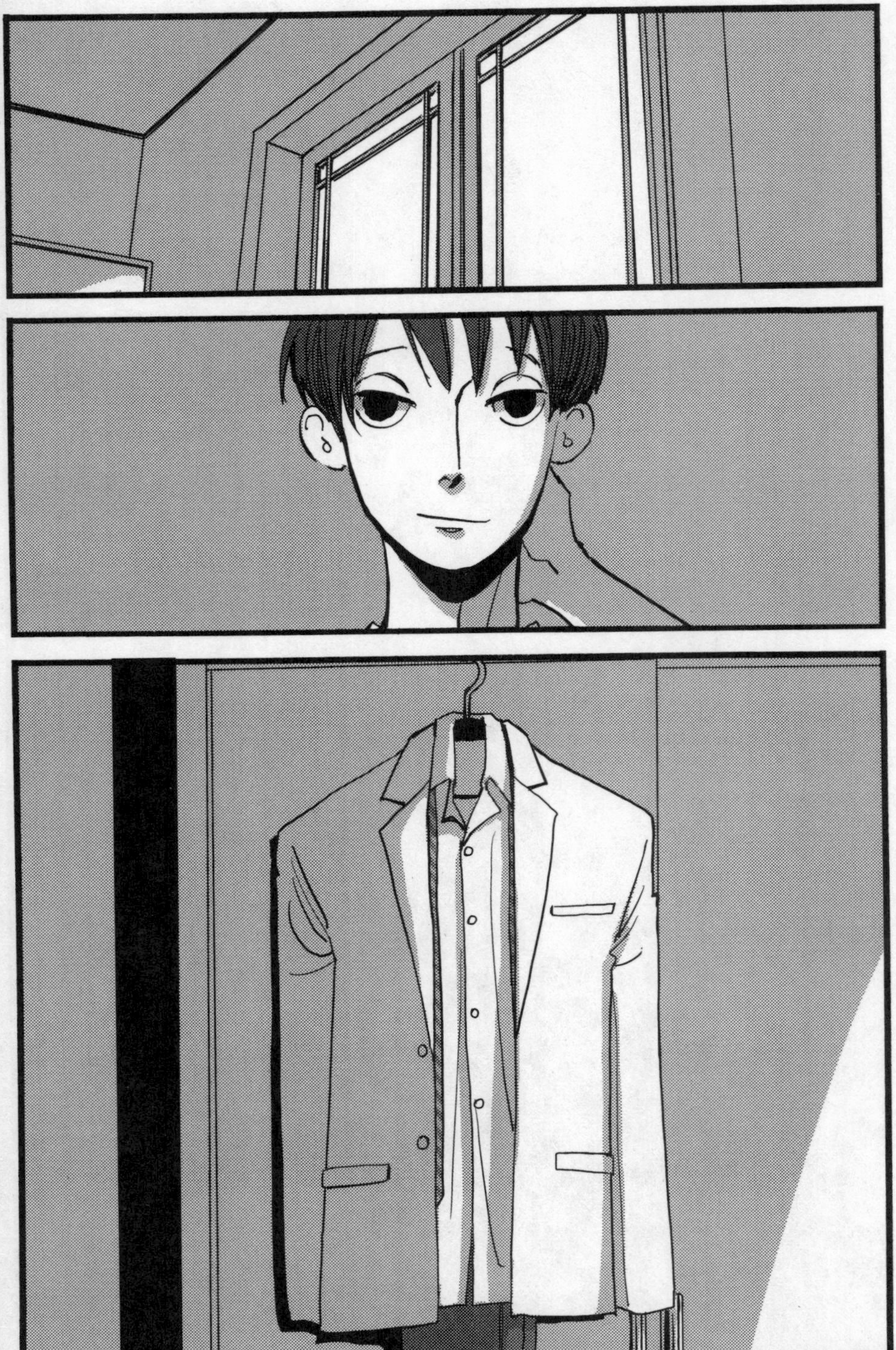

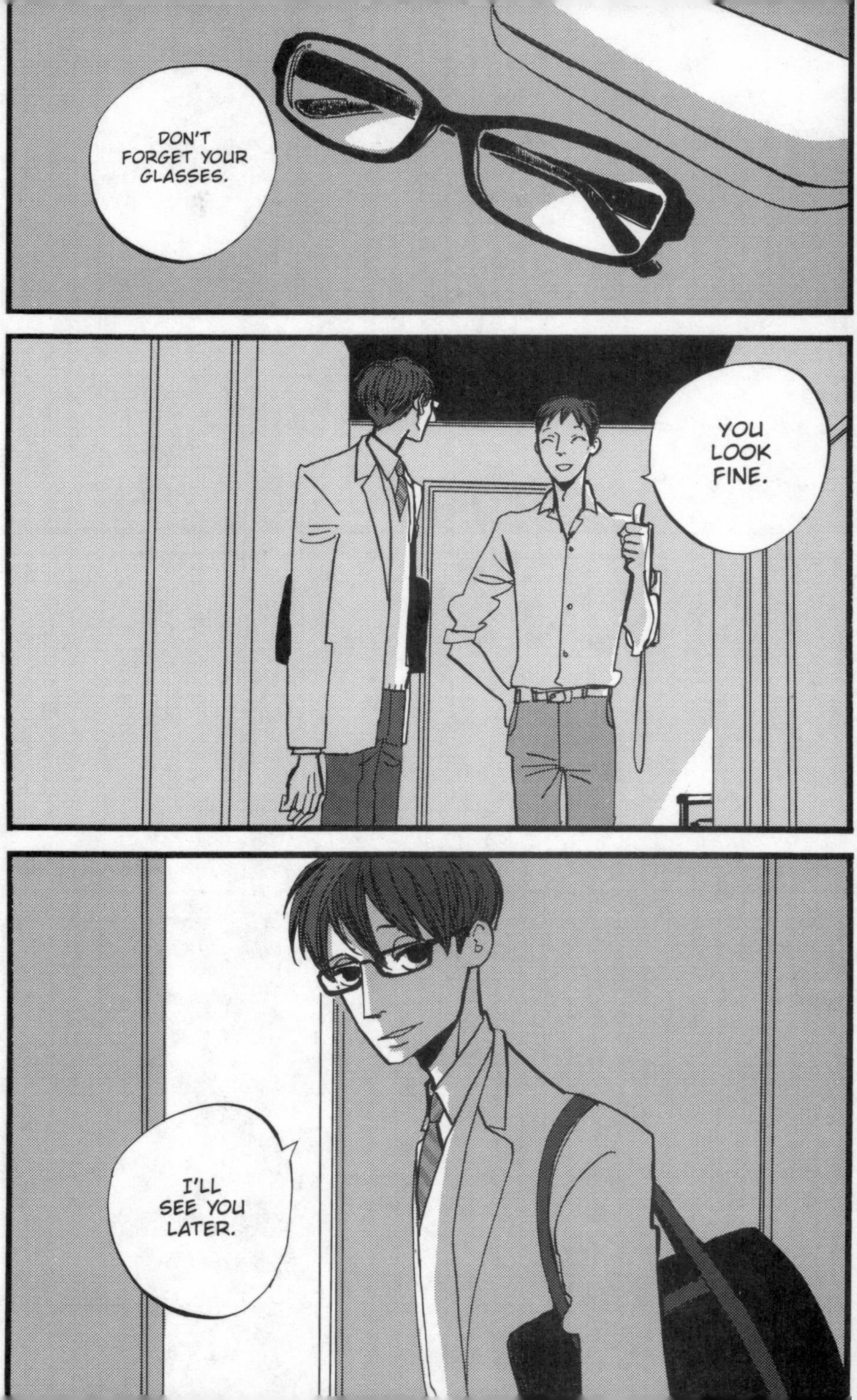
DON'T FORGET YOUR GLASSES.
YOU LOOK FINE.
I'LL SEE YOU LATER.

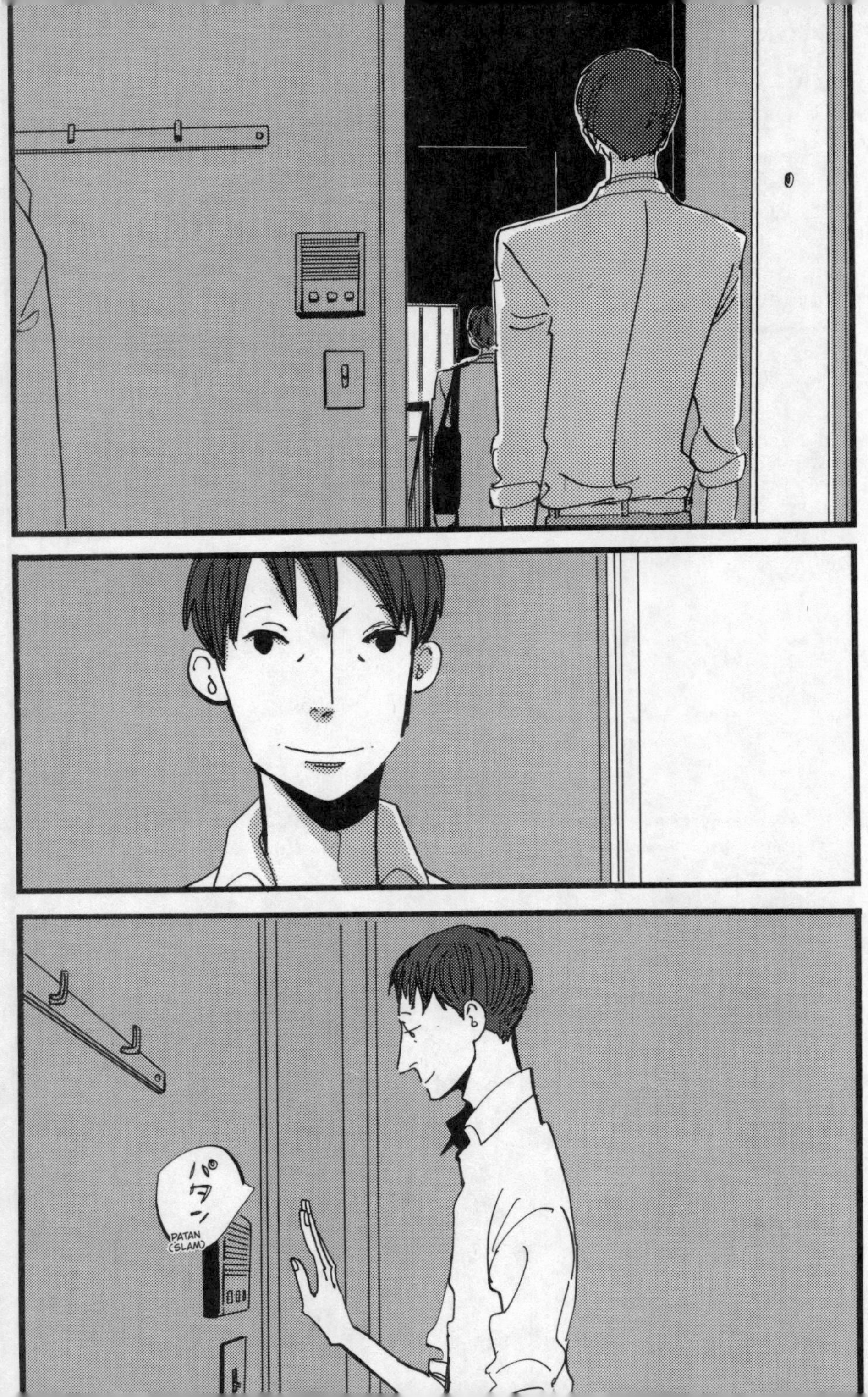
パタン
PATAN (SLAM)

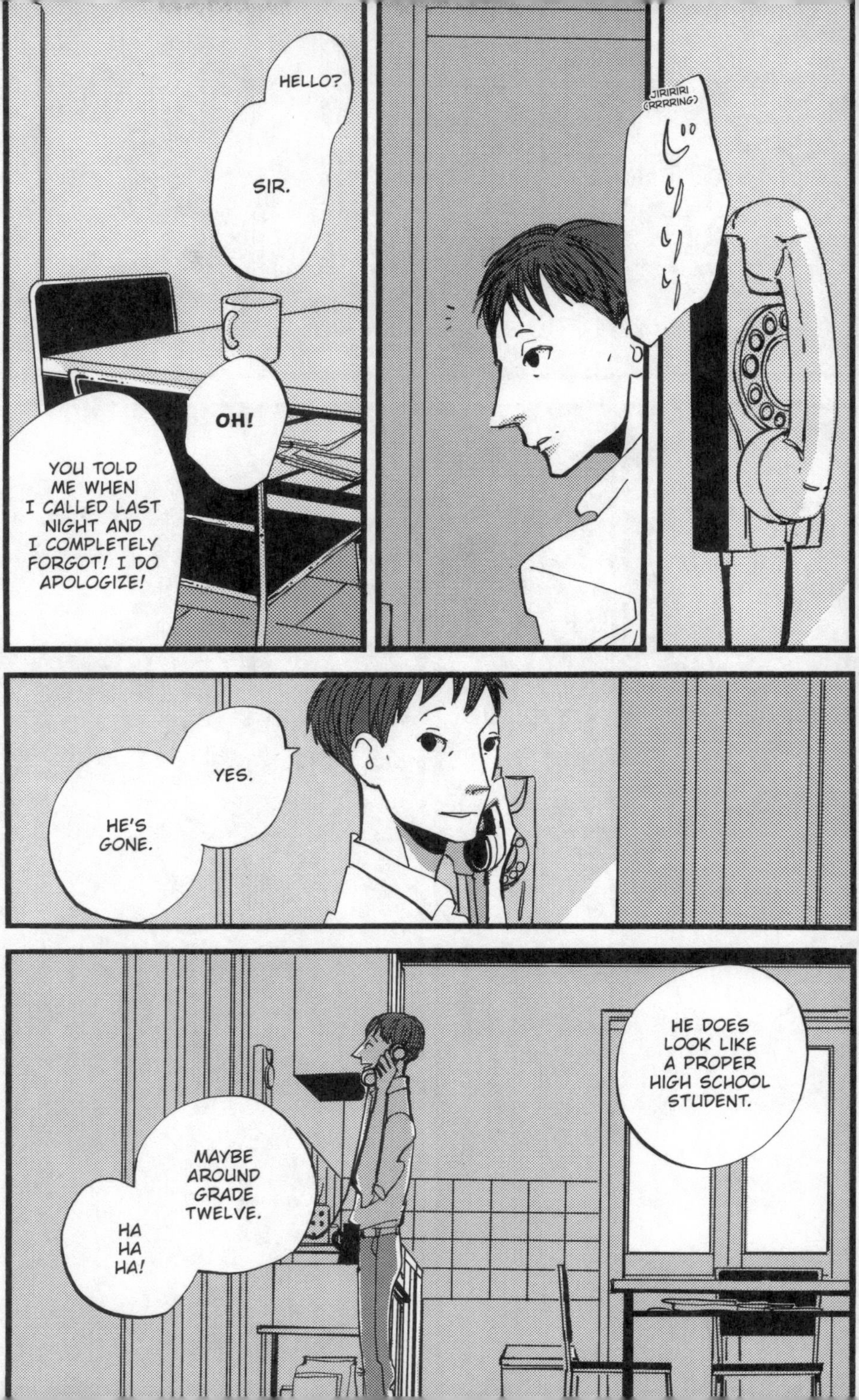
JIRIRIRI (RRRRING)
HELLO?
SIR.
OH!
YOU TOLD ME WHEN I CALLED LAST NIGHT AND I COMPLETELY FORGOT! I DO APOLOGIZE!
YES.
HE'S GONE.
HE DOES LOOK LIKE A PROPER HIGH SCHOOL STUDENT.
MAYBE AROUND GRADE TWELVE.
HA HA HA!

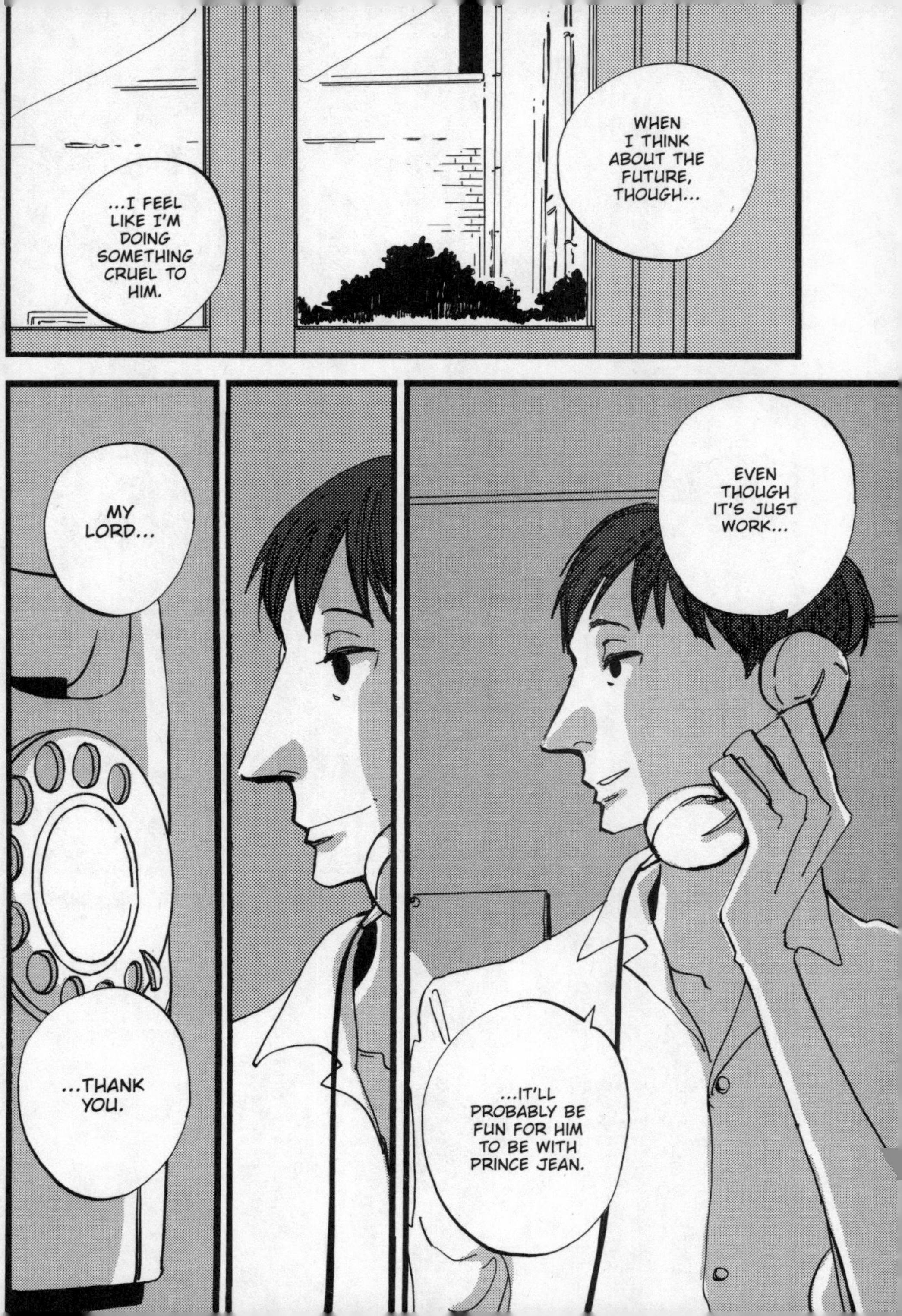
WHEN I THINK ABOUT THE FUTURE, THOUGH...
...I FEEL LIKE I'M DOING SOMETHING CRUEL TO HIM.
EVEN THOUGH IT'S JUST WORK...
...IT'LL PROBABLY BE FUN FOR HIM TO BE WITH PRINCE JEAN.
MY LORD...
...THANK YOU.

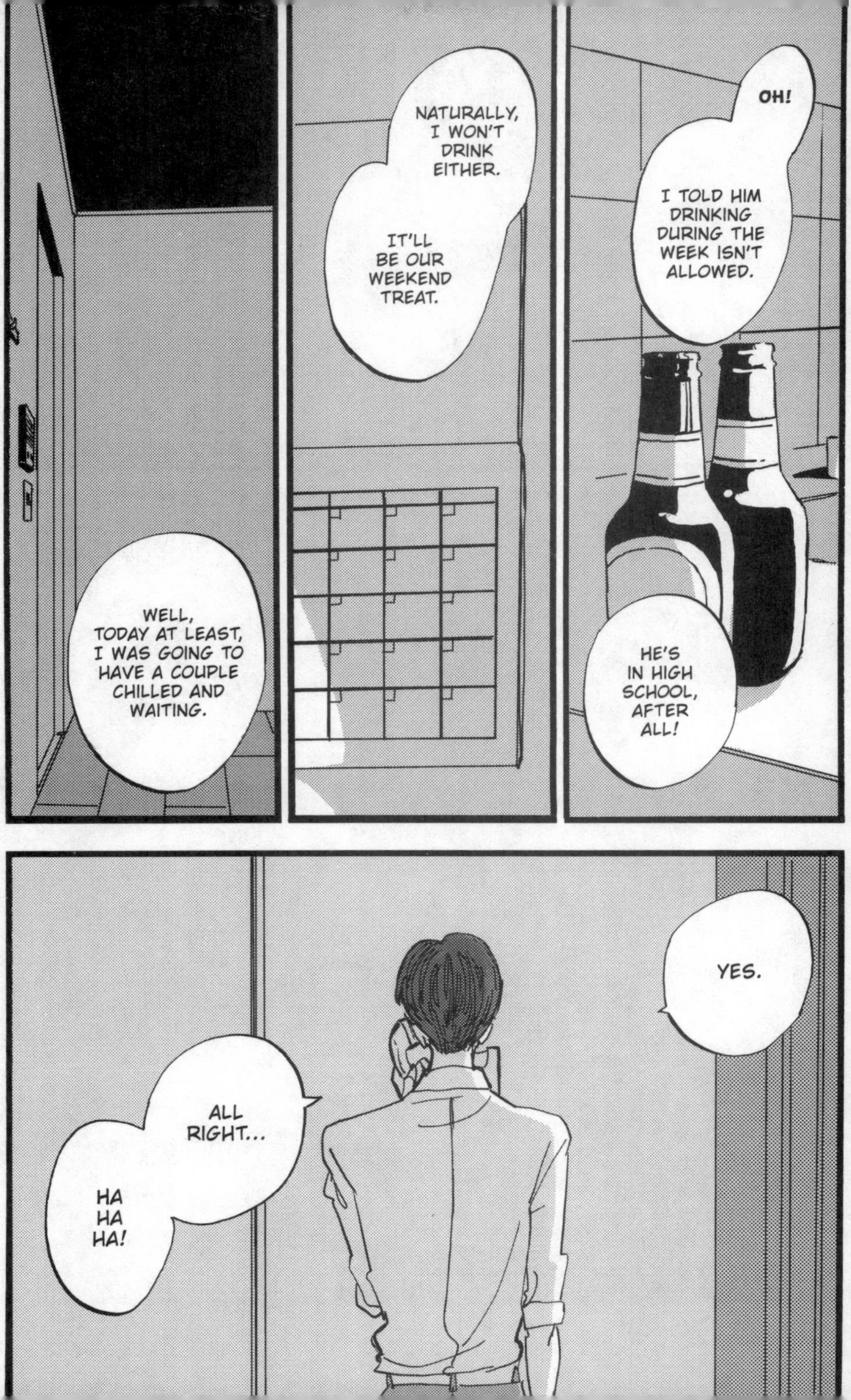
OH!
I TOLD HIM DRINKING DURING THE WEEK ISN'T ALLOWED.
HE'S IN HIGH SCHOOL, AFTER ALL!
NATURALLY, I WON'T DRINK EITHER.
IT'LL BE OUR WEEKEND TREAT.
WELL, TODAY AT LEAST, I WAS GOING TO HAVE A COUPLE CHILLED AND WAITING.
YES.
ALL RIGHT...
HA HA HA!

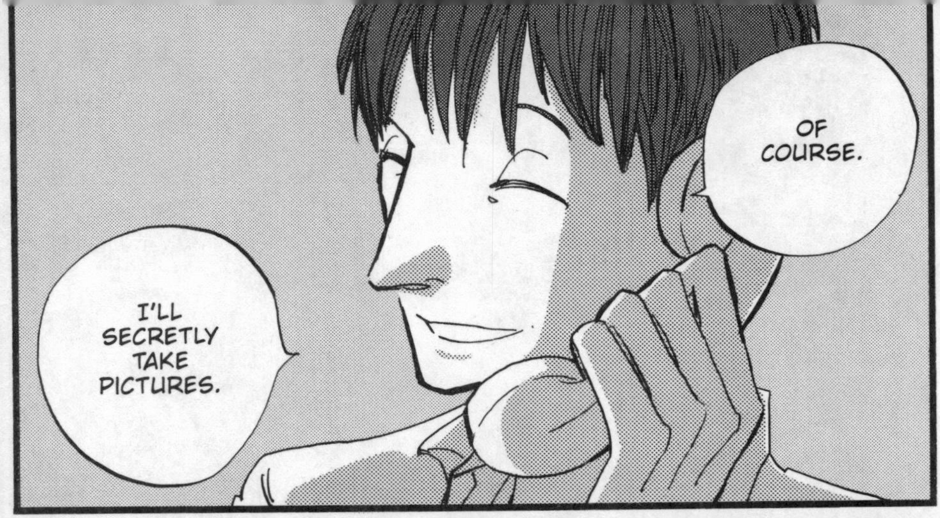
OF COURSE.
I'LL SECRETLY TAKE PICTURES.

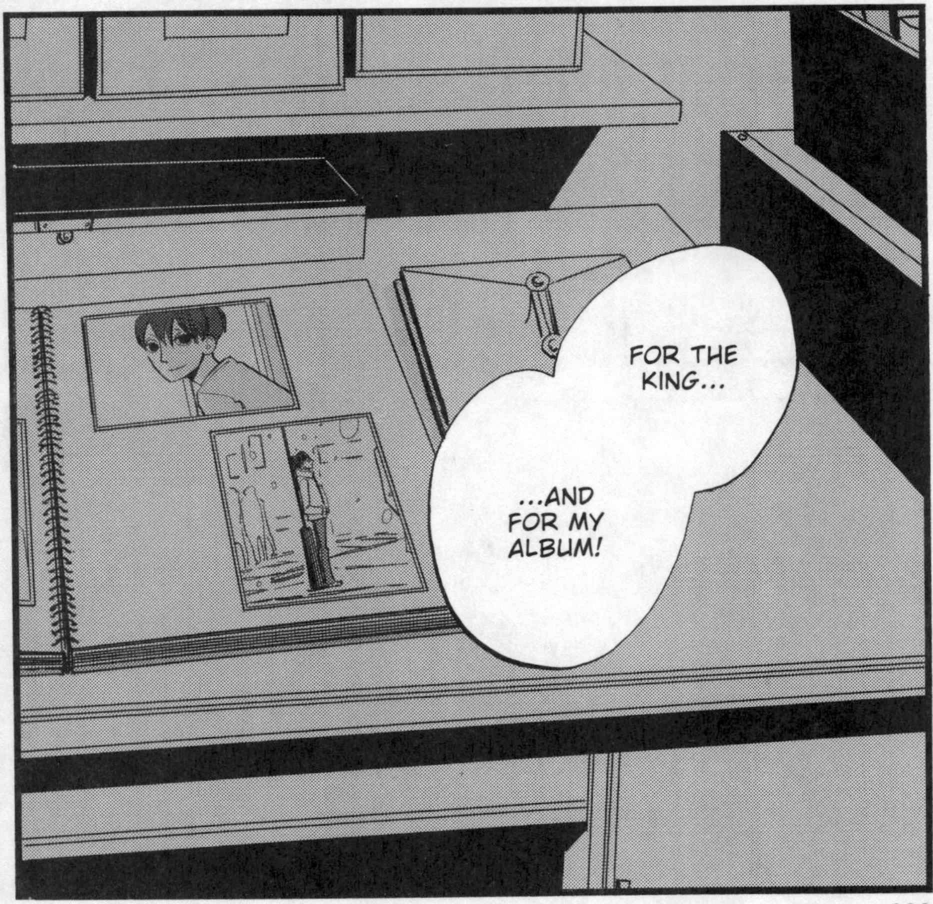
FOR THE KING...
...AND FOR MY ALBUM!

CHAPTER 8

Sentry Days, Together Days

P.S.

DEPT. ACCA 13 TERRITORY INSPECTION

PASS

CHAPTER 9

To the Land of

Flowers, as Guided

P.S.

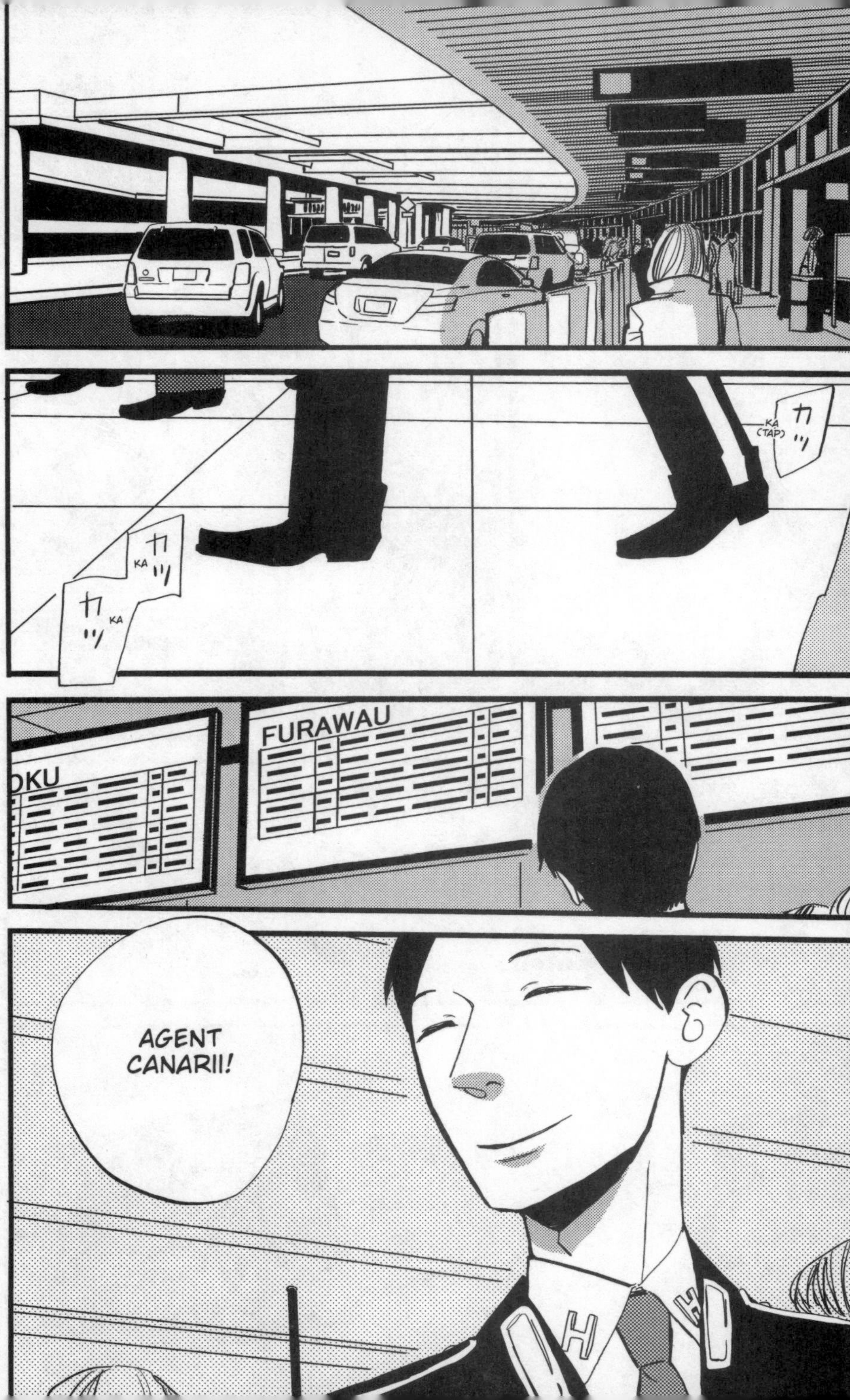
カッ
KA (TAP)
カッ
KA
カッ
KA
FURAWAU
AGENT CANARII!

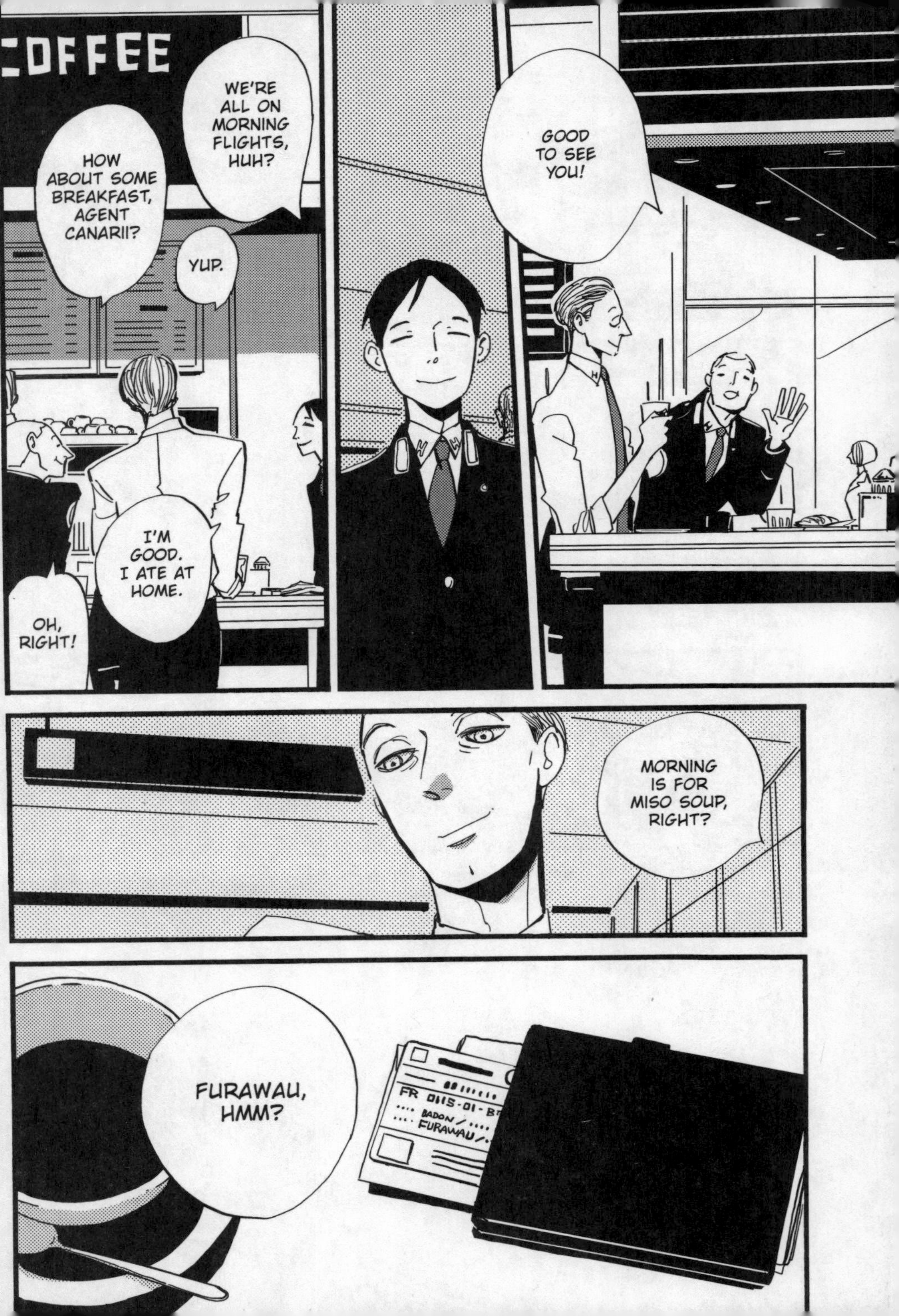
GOOD TO SEE YOU!
WE'RE ALL ON MORNING FLIGHTS, HUH?
HOW ABOUT SOME BREAKFAST, AGENT CANARII?
YUP.
I'M GOOD. I ATE AT HOME.
OH, RIGHT!
MORNING IS FOR MISO SOUP, RIGHT?
FURAWAU, HMM?
BADON /
FURAWAU /

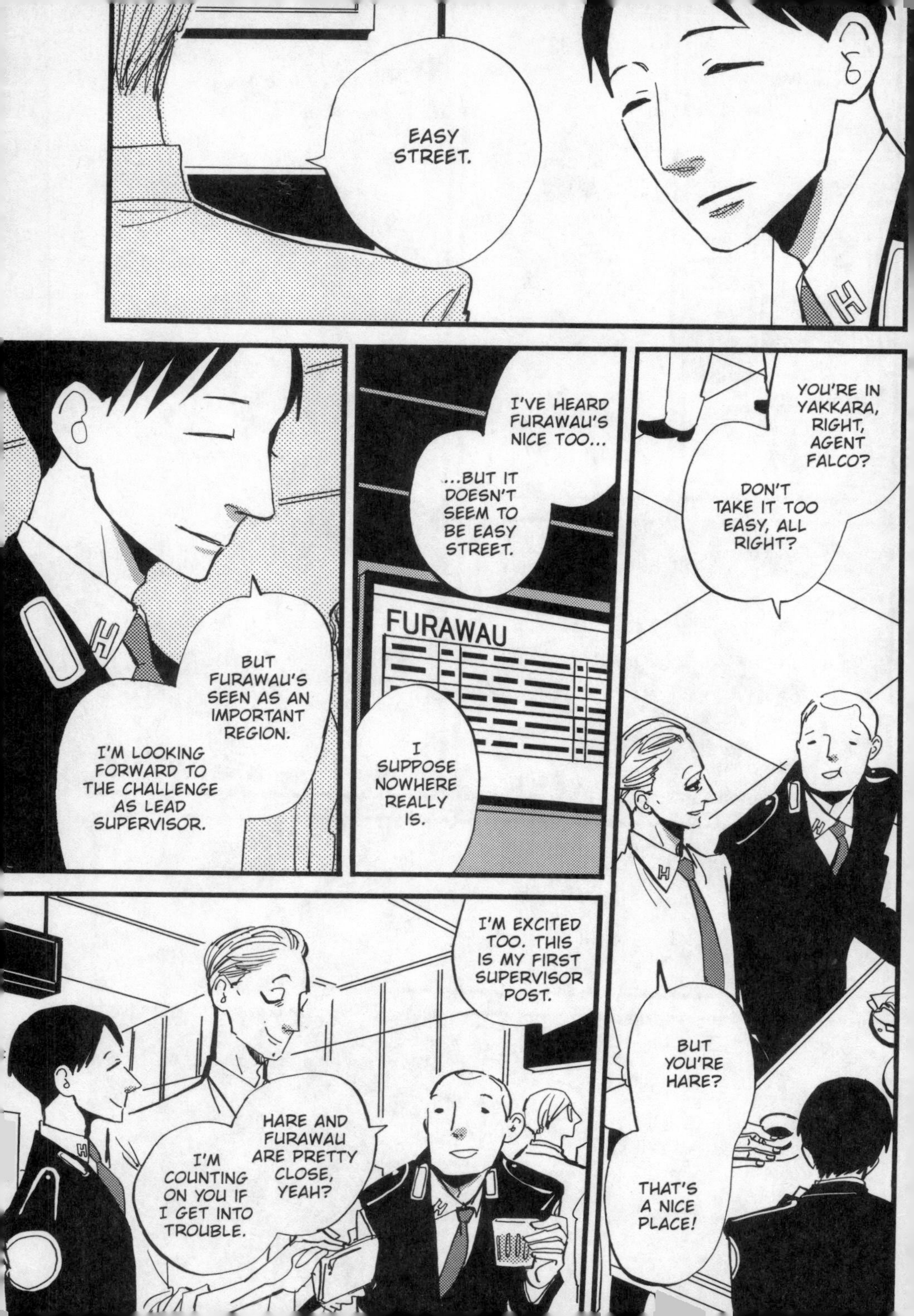
EASY STREET.
YOU'RE IN YAKKARA, RIGHT, AGENT FALCO?
DON'T TAKE IT TOO EASY, ALL RIGHT?
BUT YOU'RE HARE?
THAT'S A NICE PLACE!
I'VE HEARD FURAWAU'S NICE TOO...
...BUT IT DOESN'T SEEM TO BE EASY STREET.
FURAWAU
I SUPPOSE NOWHERE REALLY IS.
BUT FURAWAU'S SEEN AS AN IMPORTANT REGION.
I'M LOOKING FORWARD TO THE CHALLENGE AS LEAD SUPERVISOR.
I'M EXCITED TOO. THIS IS MY FIRST SUPERVISOR POST.
HARE AND FURAWAU ARE PRETTY CLOSE, YEAH?
I'M COUNTING ON YOU IF I GET INTO TROUBLE.

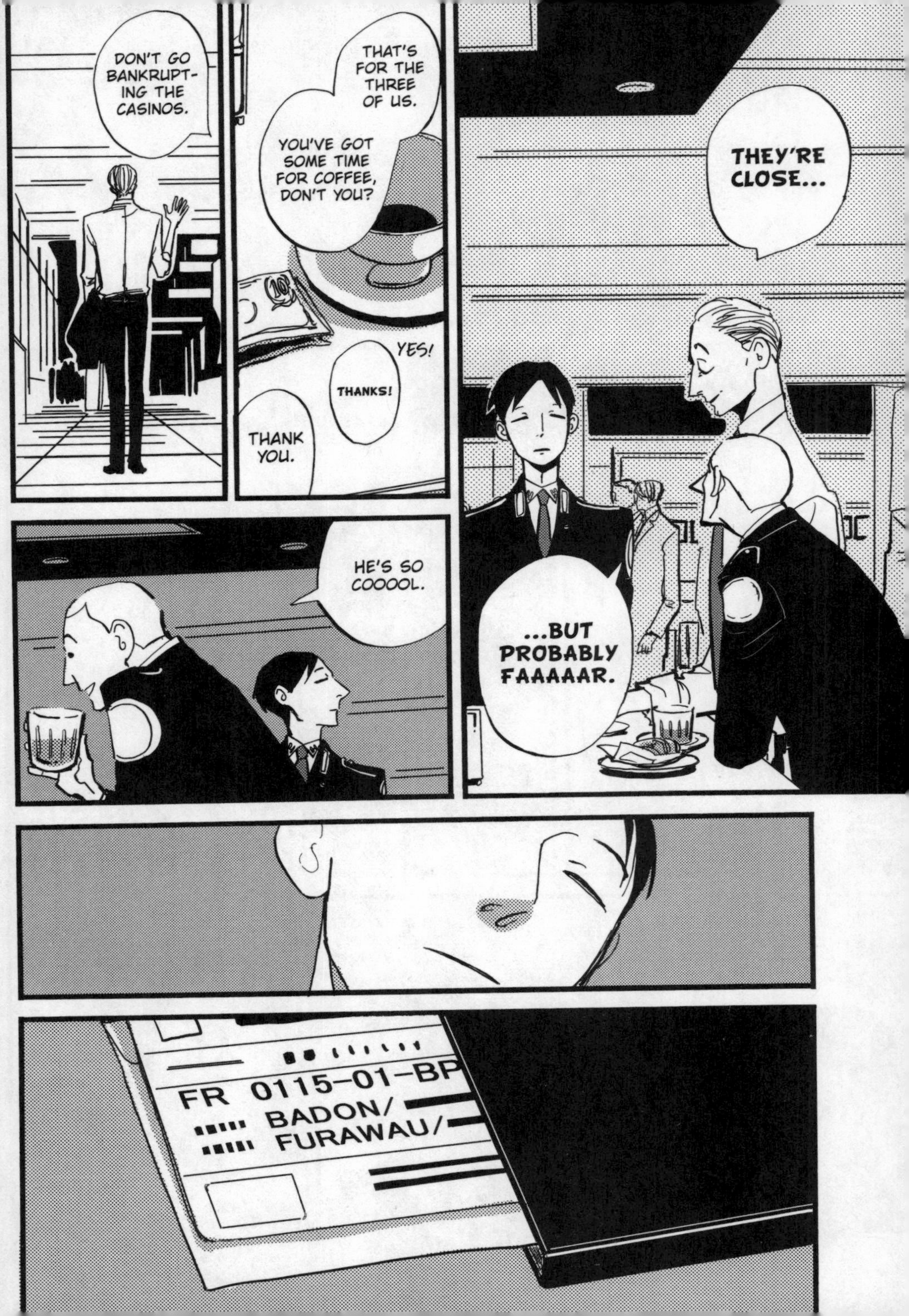
THEY'RE CLOSE...
...BUT PROBABLY FAAAAAR.
THAT'S FOR THE THREE OF US.
YOU'VE GOT SOME TIME FOR COFFEE, DON'T YOU?
YES!
THANKS!
THANK YOU.
DON'T GO BANKRUPTING THE CASINOS.
HE'S SO COOOOL.
FR 0115-01-BP
BADON/
FURAWAU/

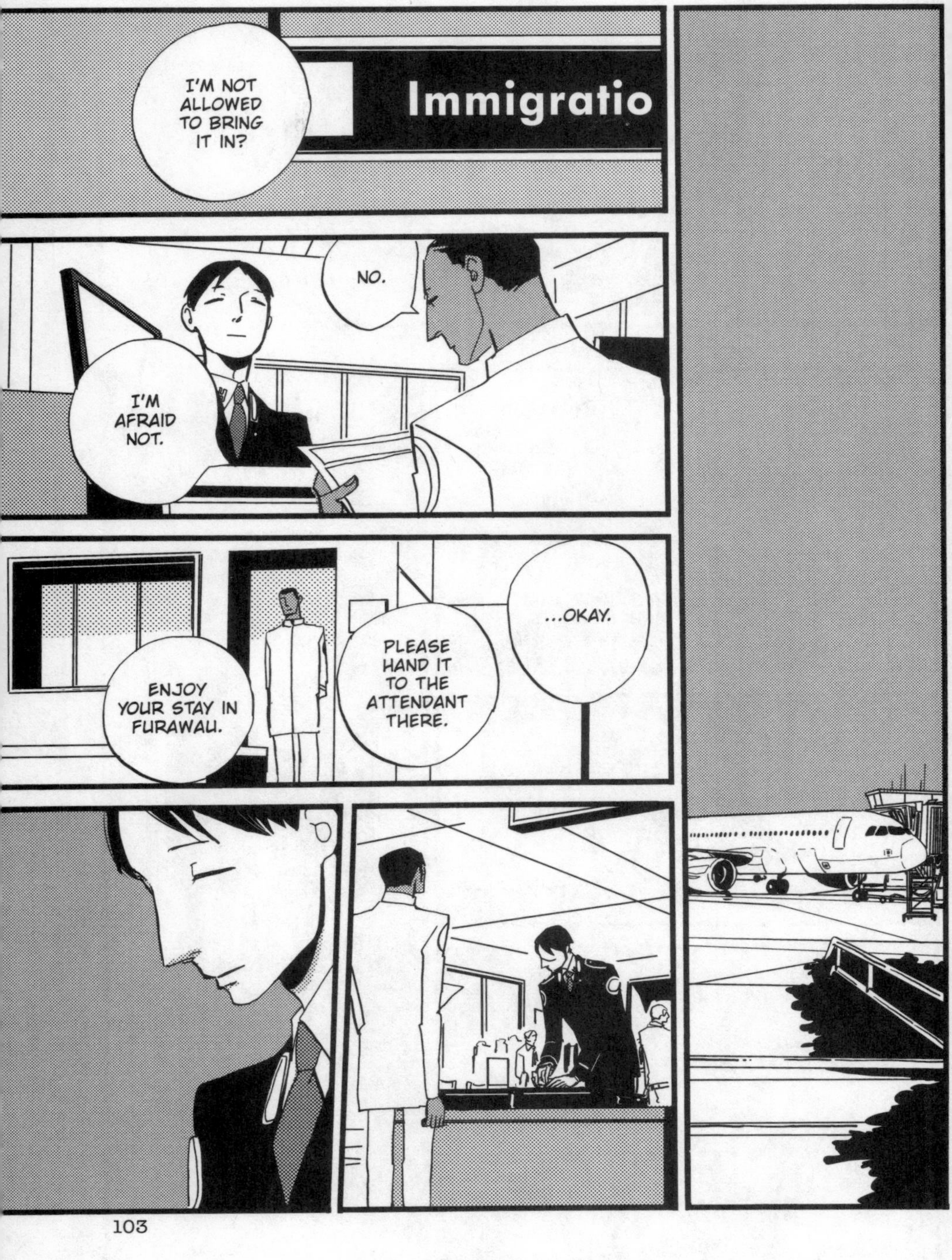
Immigratio
I'M NOT ALLOWED TO BRING IT IN?
NO.
I'M AFRAID NOT.
...OKAY.
PLEASE HAND IT TO THE ATTENDANT THERE.
ENJOY YOUR STAY IN FURAWAU.

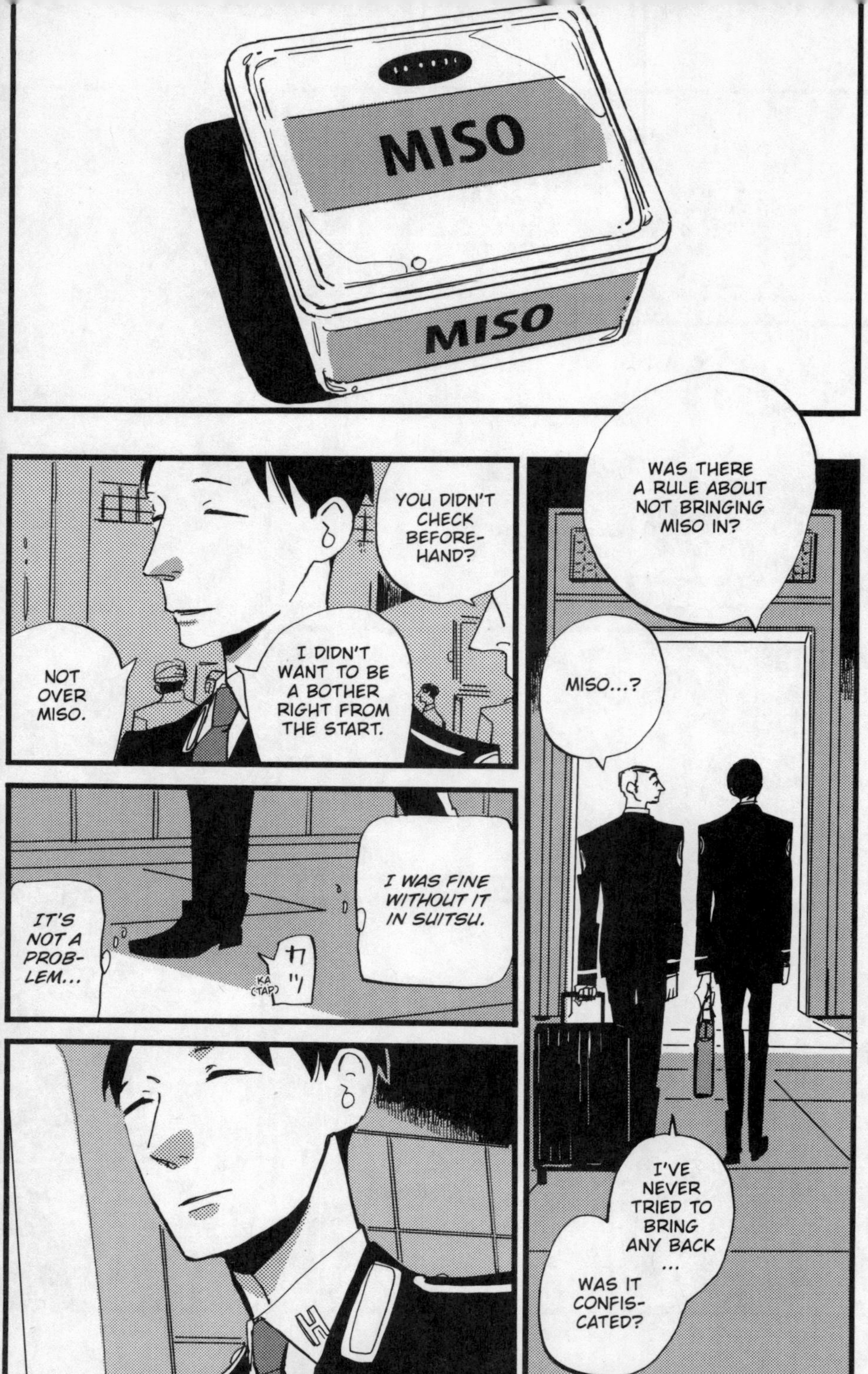
MISO
MISO
WAS THERE A RULE ABOUT NOT BRINGING MISO IN?
MISO...?
I'VE NEVER TRIED TO BRING ANY BACK ...
WAS IT CONFISCATED?
YOU DIDN'T CHECK BEFORE-HAND?
I DIDN'T WANT TO BE A BOTHER RIGHT FROM THE START.
NOT OVER MISO.
I WAS FINE WITHOUT IT IN SUITSU.
カッ
KA (TAP)
IT'S NOT A PROB-LEM...

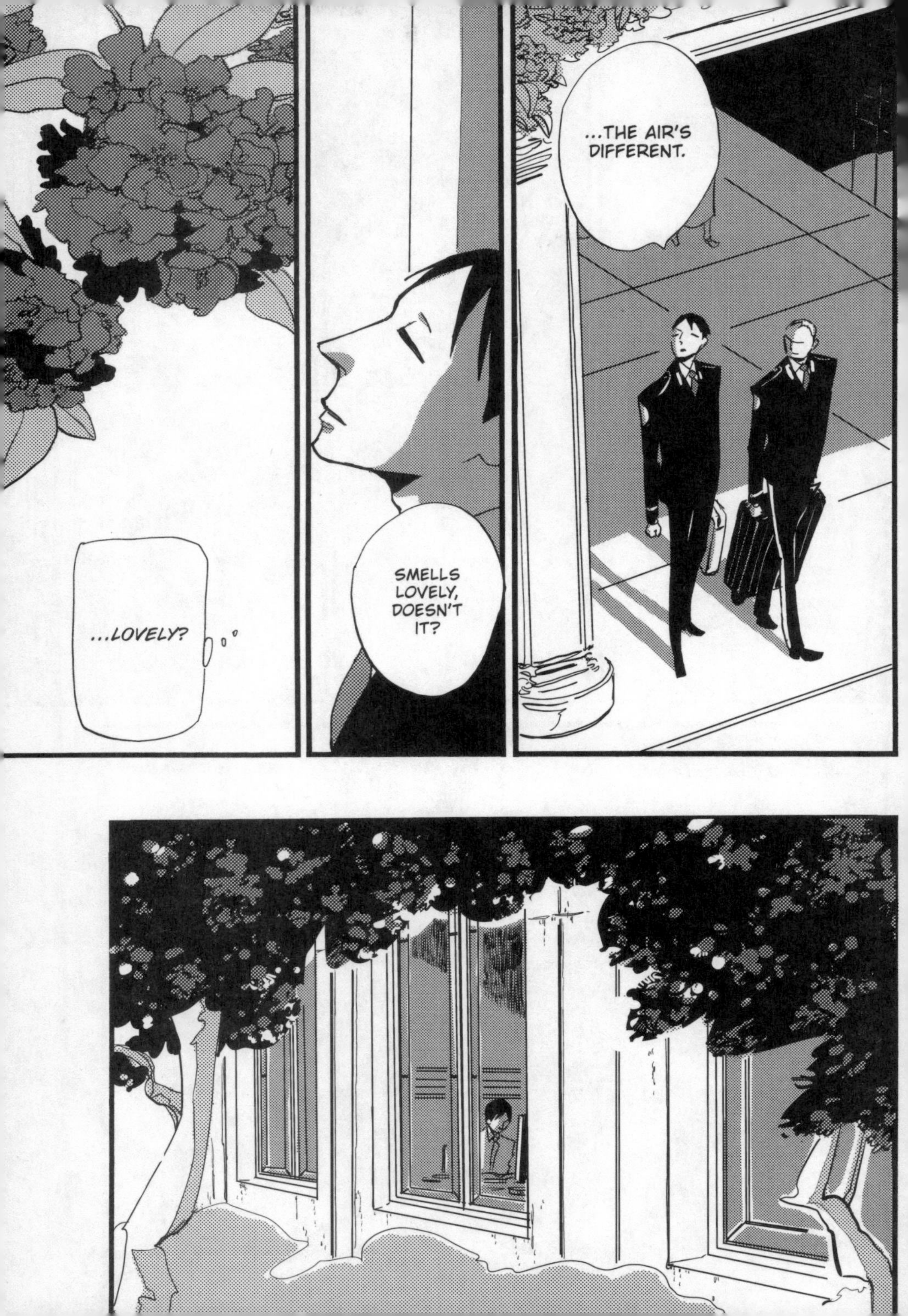
...THE AIR'S DIFFERENT.
SMELLS LOVELY, DOESN'T IT?
...LOVELY?

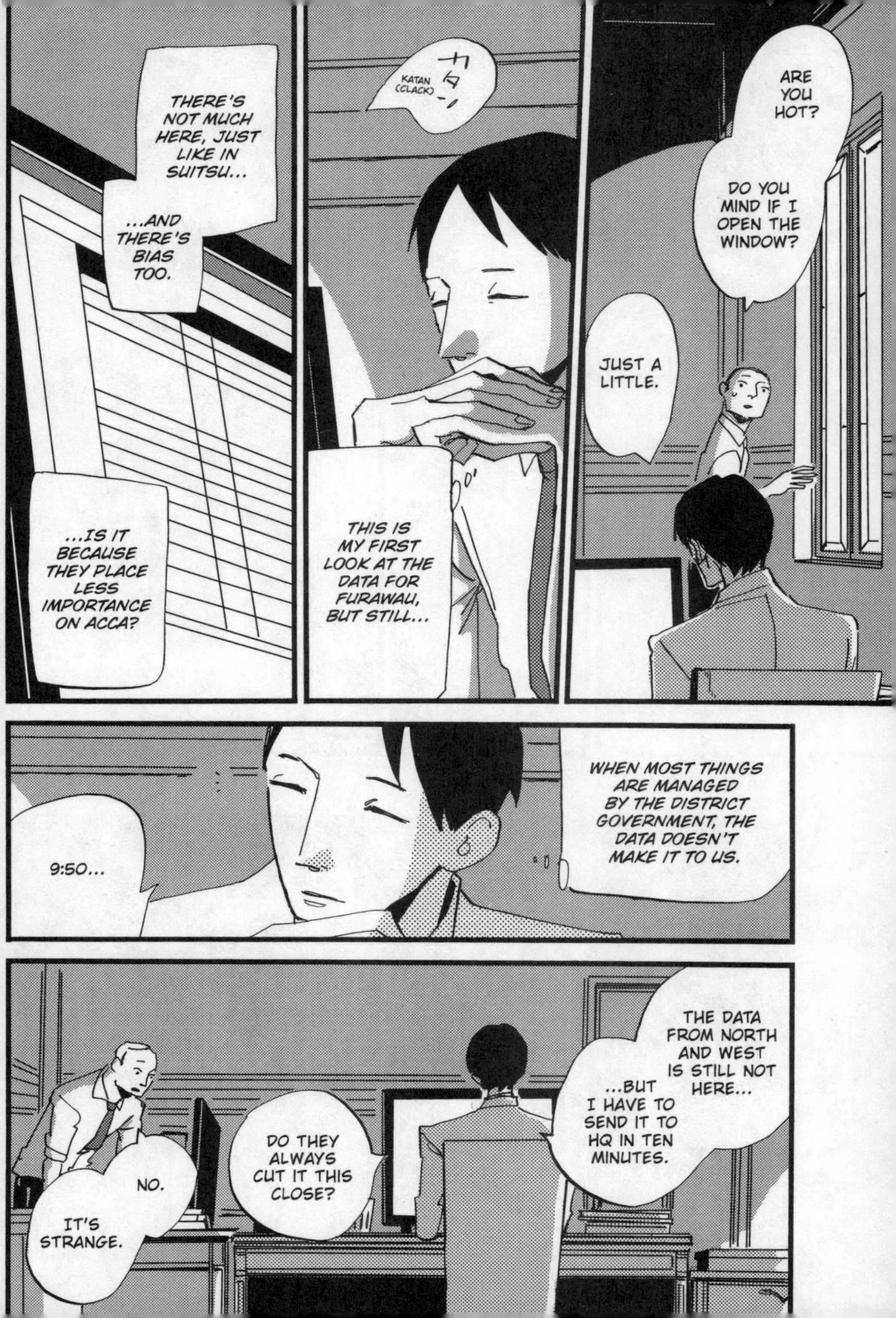

ARE YOU HOT?
DO YOU MIND IF I OPEN THE WINDOW?
JUST A LITTLE.
KATAN (CLACK)
THIS IS MY FIRST LOOK AT THE DATA FOR FURAWAU, BUT STILL...
THERE'S NOT MUCH HERE, JUST LIKE IN SUITSU...
...AND THERE'S BIAS TOO.
...IS IT BECAUSE THEY PLACE LESS IMPORTANCE ON ACCA?
WHEN MOST THINGS ARE MANAGED BY THE DISTRICT GOVERNMENT, THE DATA DOESN'T MAKE IT TO US.
9:50...
THE DATA FROM NORTH AND WEST IS STILL NOT HERE...
...BUT I HAVE TO SEND IT TO HQ IN TEN MINUTES.
DO THEY ALWAYS CUT IT THIS CLOSE?
NO.
IT'S STRANGE.

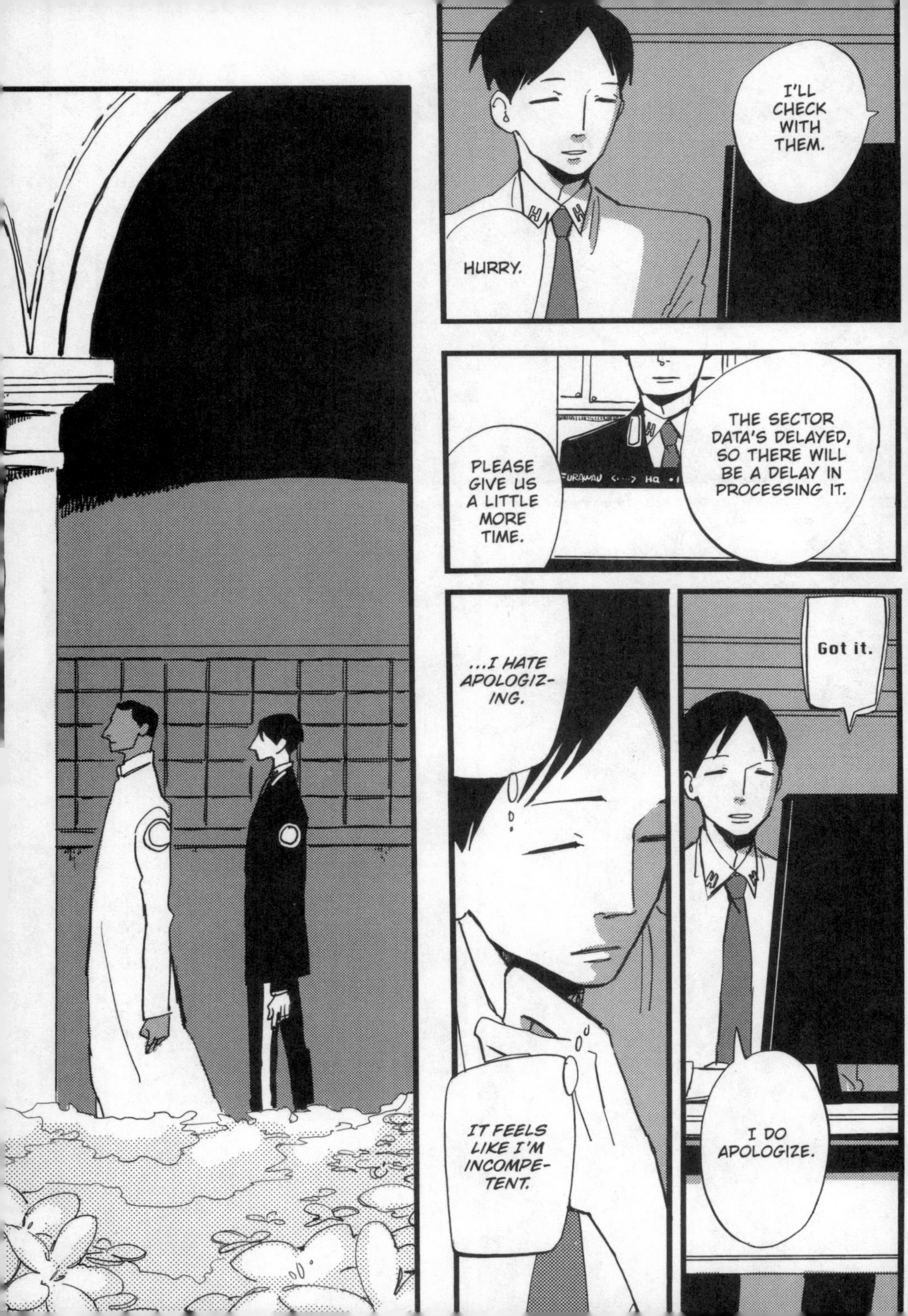
I'LL CHECK WITH THEM.
HURRY.
THE SECTOR DATA'S DELAYED, SO THERE WILL BE A DELAY IN PROCESSING IT.
PLEASE GIVE US A LITTLE MORE TIME.
Got it.
I DO APOLOGIZE.
...I HATE APOLOGIZING.
IT FEELS LIKE I'M INCOMPETENT.

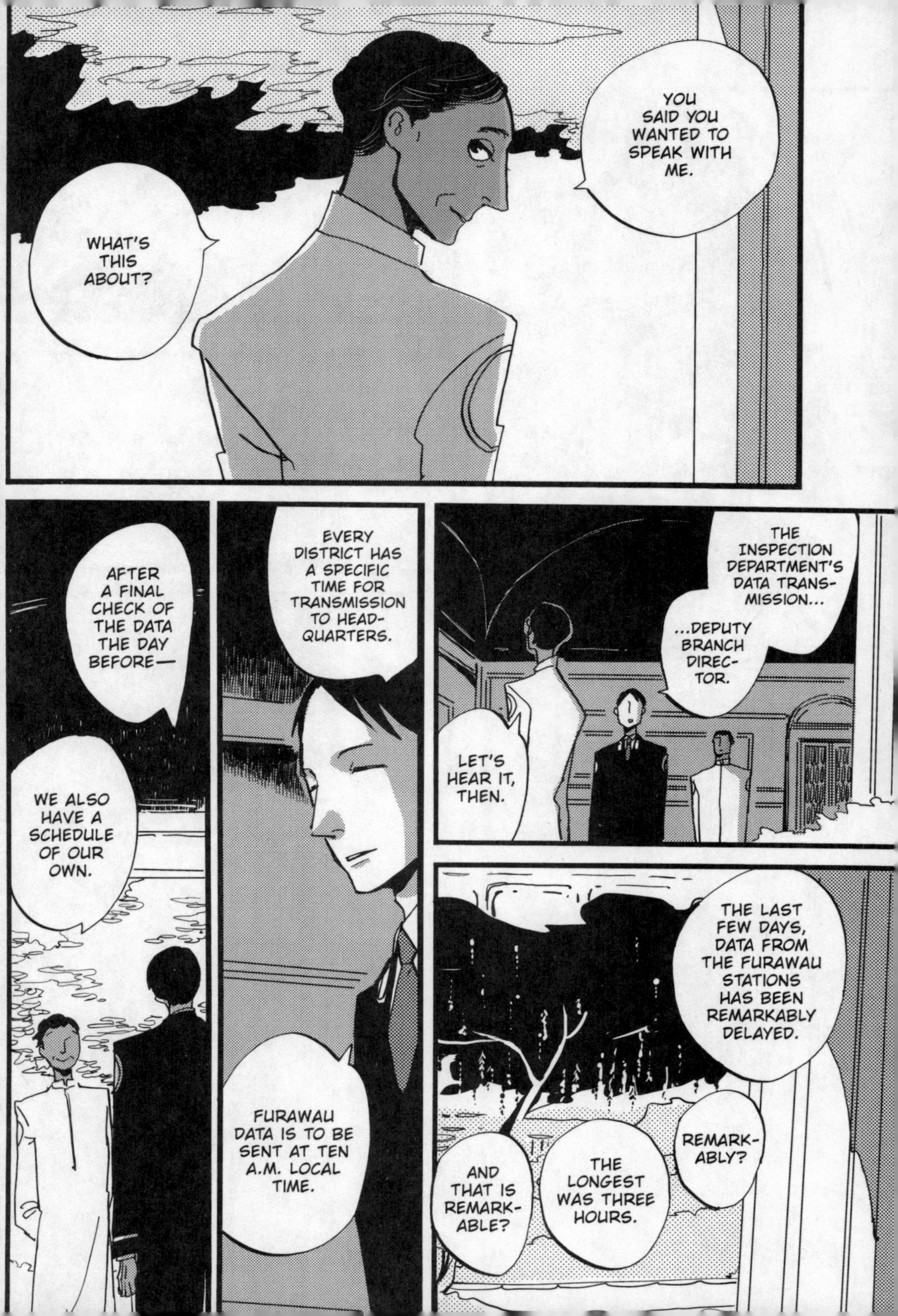
YOU SAID YOU WANTED TO SPEAK WITH ME.
WHAT'S THIS ABOUT?
THE INSPECTION DEPARTMENT'S DATA TRANS-MISSION...
...DEPUTY BRANCH DIREC-TOR.
LET'S HEAR IT, THEN.
THE LAST FEW DAYS, DATA FROM THE FURAWAU STATIONS HAS BEEN REMARKABLY DELAYED.
REMARK-ABLY?
THE LONGEST WAS THREE HOURS.
AND THAT IS REMARK-ABLE?
EVERY DISTRICT HAS A SPECIFIC TIME FOR TRANSMISSION TO HEAD-QUARTERS.
FURAWAU DATA IS TO BE SENT AT TEN A.M. LOCAL TIME.
AFTER A FINAL CHECK OF THE DATA THE DAY BEFORE—
WE ALSO HAVE A SCHEDULE OF OUR OWN.

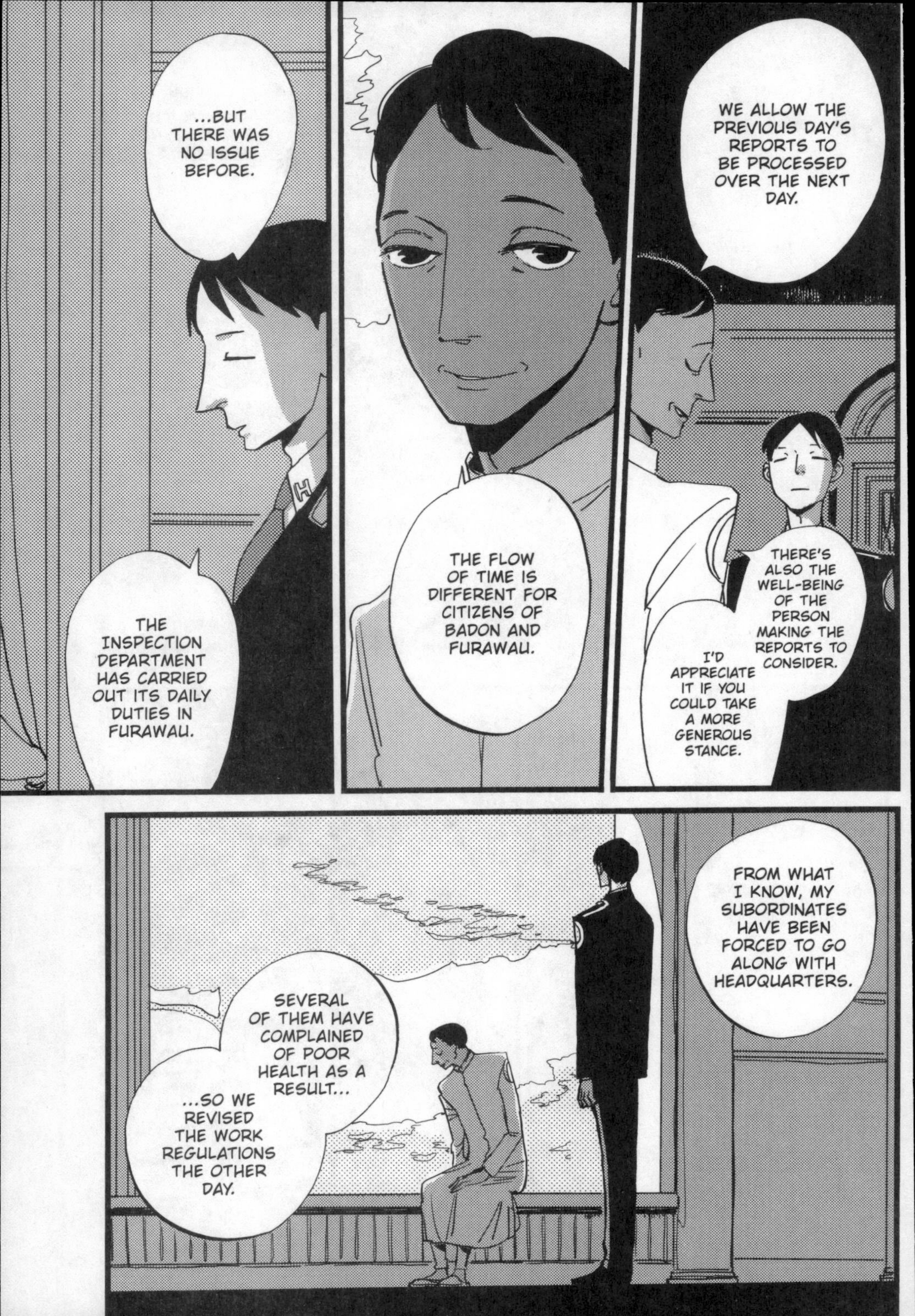
WE ALLOW THE PREVIOUS DAY'S REPORTS TO BE PROCESSED OVER THE NEXT DAY.
THERE'S ALSO THE WELL-BEING OF THE PERSON MAKING THE REPORTS TO CONSIDER.
I'D APPRECIATE IT IF YOU COULD TAKE A MORE GENEROUS STANCE.
THE FLOW OF TIME IS DIFFERENT FOR CITIZENS OF BADON AND FURAWAU.
THE INSPECTION DEPARTMENT HAS CARRIED OUT ITS DAILY DUTIES IN FURAWAU.
...BUT THERE WAS NO ISSUE BEFORE.
FROM WHAT I KNOW, MY SUBORDINATES HAVE BEEN FORCED TO GO ALONG WITH HEADQUARTERS.
SEVERAL OF THEM HAVE COMPLAINED OF POOR HEALTH AS A RESULT...
...SO WE REVISED THE WORK REGULATIONS THE OTHER DAY.

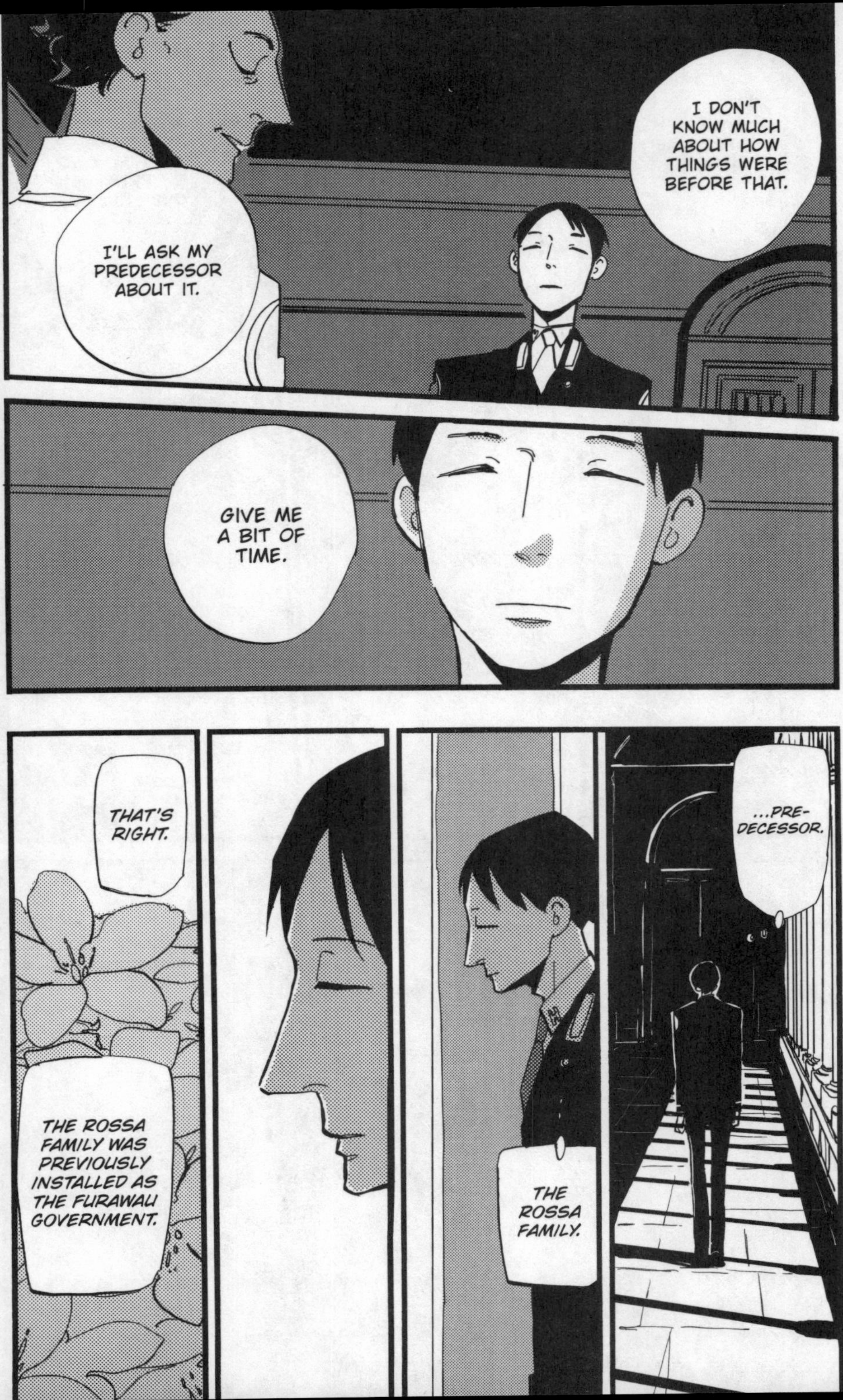
I DON'T KNOW MUCH ABOUT HOW THINGS WERE BEFORE THAT.
I'LL ASK MY PREDECESSOR ABOUT IT.
GIVE ME A BIT OF TIME.
...PRE-DECESSOR.
THE ROSSA FAMILY.
THAT'S RIGHT.
THE ROSSA FAMILY WAS PREVIOUSLY INSTALLED AS THE FURAWAU GOVERNMENT.

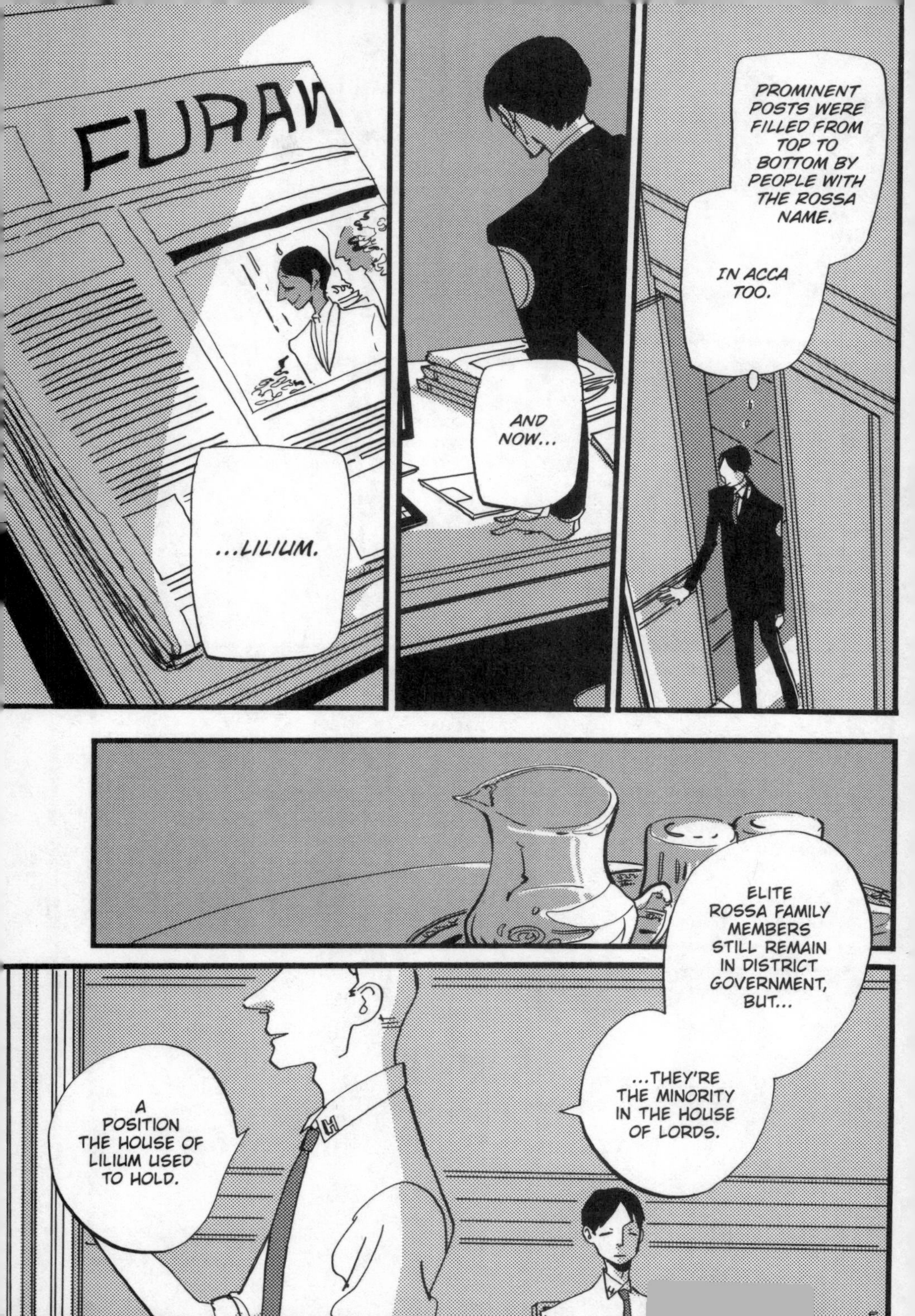
PROMINENT POSTS WERE FILLED FROM TOP TO BOTTOM BY PEOPLE WITH THE ROSSA NAME.
IN ACCA TOO.
AND NOW...
...LILIUM.
FURAN
ELITE ROSSA FAMILY MEMBERS STILL REMAIN IN DISTRICT GOVERNMENT, BUT...
...THEY'RE THE MINORITY IN THE HOUSE OF LORDS.
A POSITION THE HOUSE OF LILIUM USED TO HOLD.

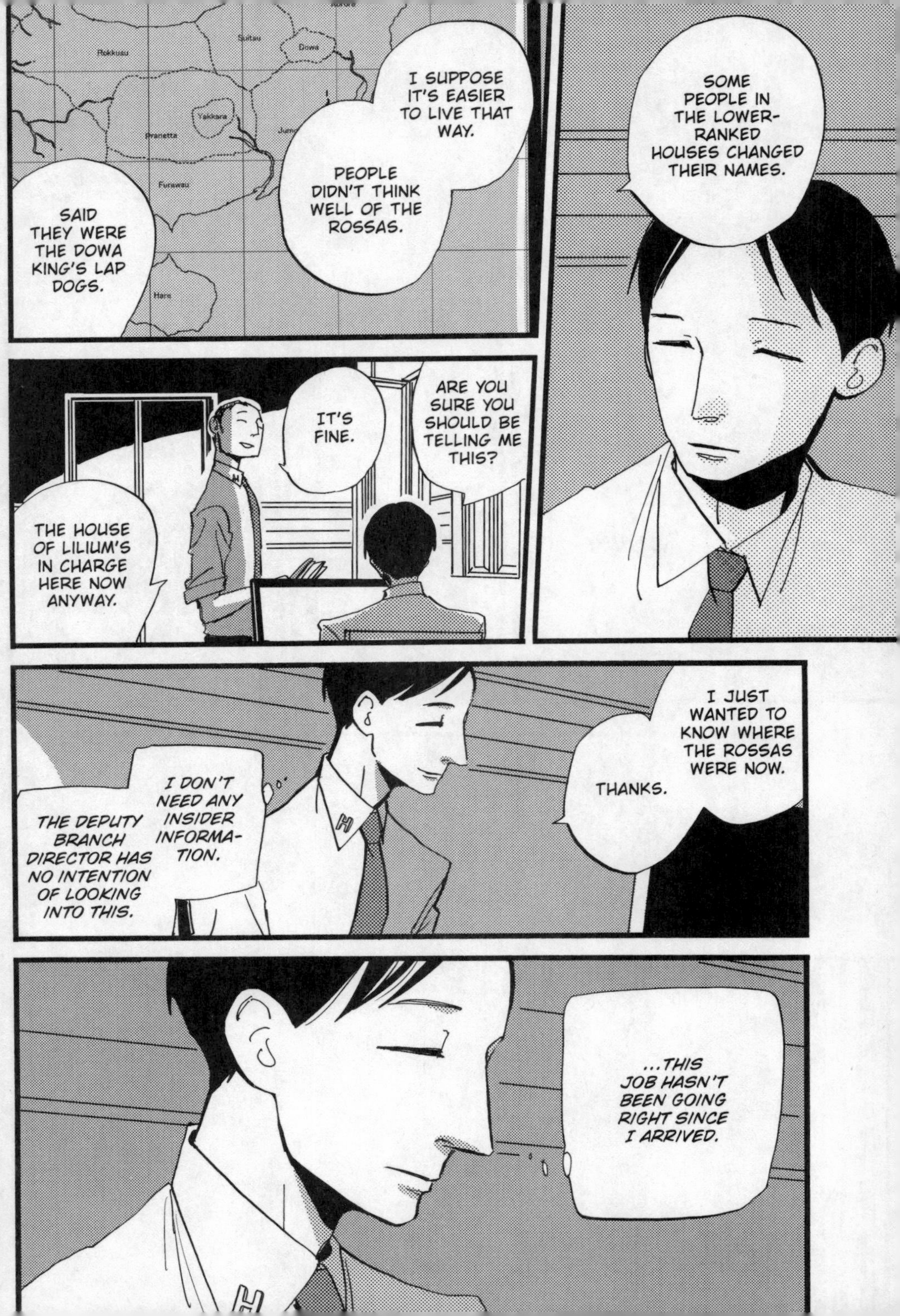
SOME PEOPLE IN THE LOWER-RANKED HOUSES CHANGED THEIR NAMES.
Rokkusu
Suitau
Dowa
Yakkara
Furawau
I SUPPOSE IT'S EASIER TO LIVE THAT WAY.
PEOPLE DIDN'T THINK WELL OF THE ROSSAS.
SAID THEY WERE THE DOWA KING'S LAP DOGS.
ARE YOU SURE YOU SHOULD BE TELLING ME THIS?
IT'S FINE.
THE HOUSE OF LILIUM'S IN CHARGE HERE NOW ANYWAY.
I JUST WANTED TO KNOW WHERE THE ROSSAS WERE NOW.
THANKS.
I DON'T NEED ANY INSIDER INFORMATION.
THE DEPUTY BRANCH DIRECTOR HAS NO INTENTION OF LOOKING INTO THIS.
...THIS JOB HASN'T BEEN GOING RIGHT SINCE I ARRIVED.

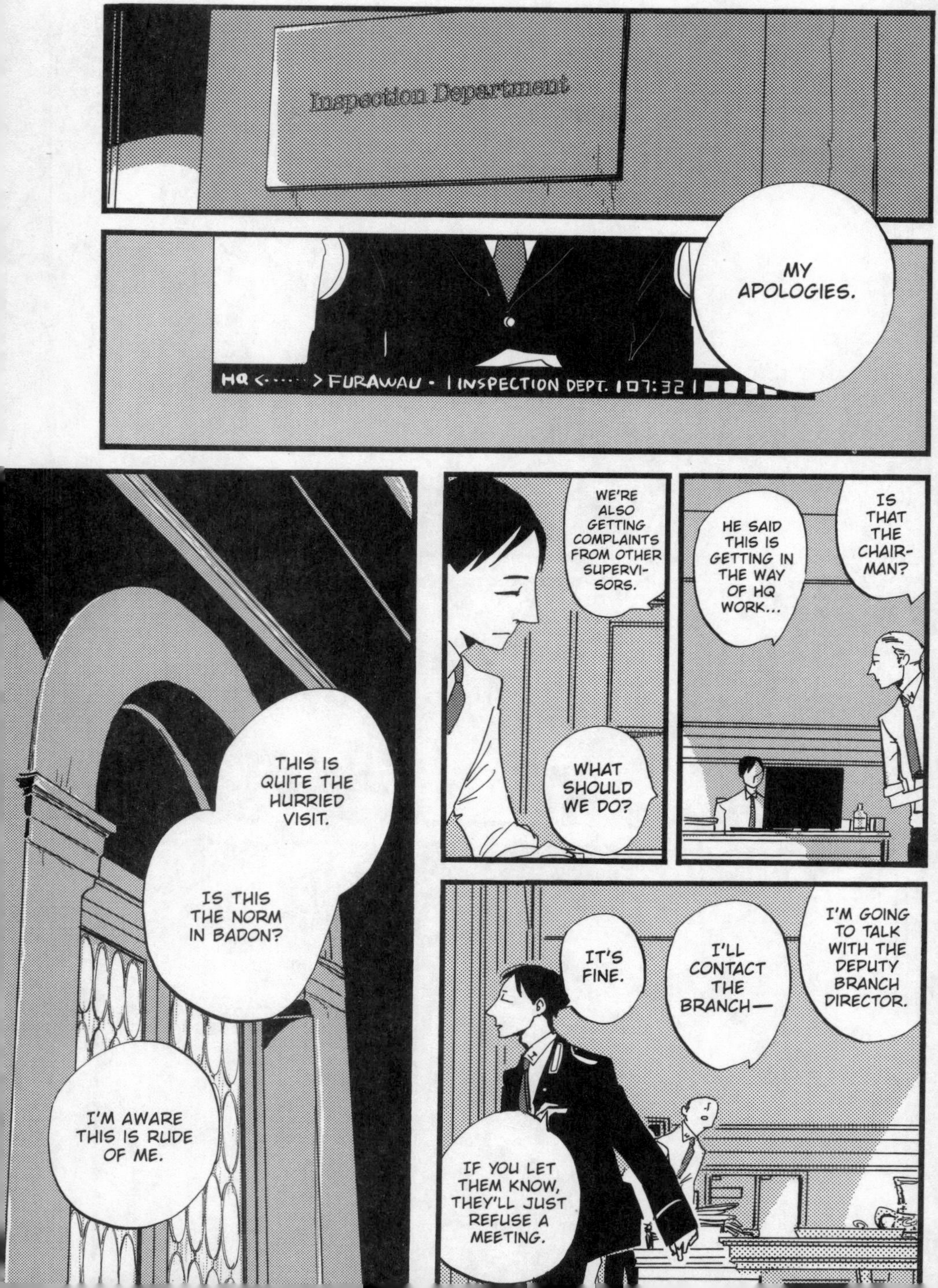
Inspection Department
MY APOLOGIES.
HQ <······> FURAWAU - INSPECTION DEPT. 07:32
IS THAT THE CHAIRMAN?
HE SAID THIS IS GETTING IN THE WAY OF HQ WORK...
WE'RE ALSO GETTING COMPLAINTS FROM OTHER SUPERVISORS.
WHAT SHOULD WE DO?
I'M GOING TO TALK WITH THE DEPUTY BRANCH DIRECTOR.
I'LL CONTACT THE BRANCH—
IT'S FINE.
IF YOU LET THEM KNOW, THEY'LL JUST REFUSE A MEETING.
THIS IS QUITE THE HURRIED VISIT.
IS THIS THE NORM IN BADON?
I'M AWARE THIS IS RUDE OF ME.

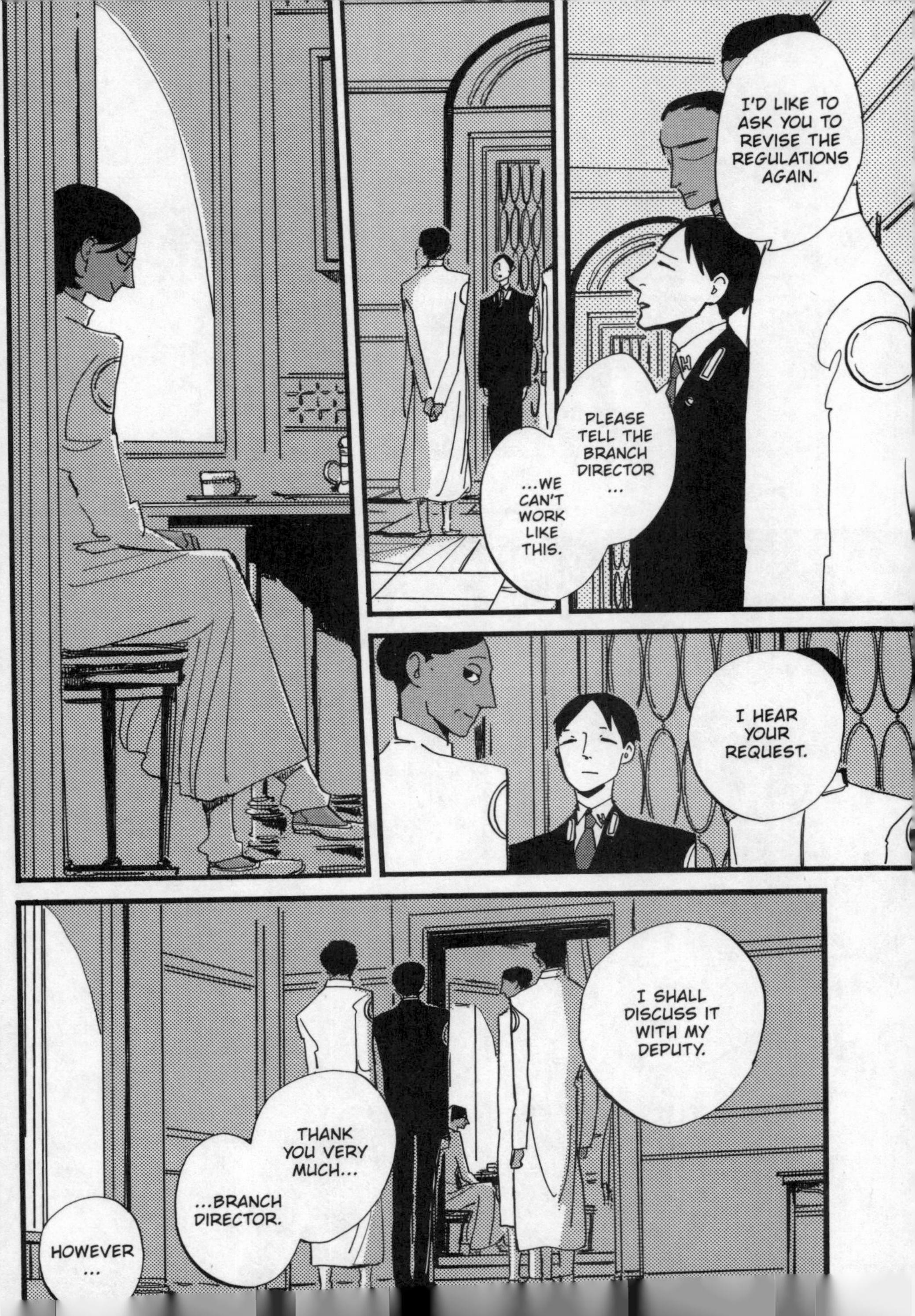
I'D LIKE TO ASK YOU TO REVISE THE REGULATIONS AGAIN.
PLEASE TELL THE BRANCH DIRECTOR ...
...WE CAN'T WORK LIKE THIS.
I HEAR YOUR REQUEST.
I SHALL DISCUSS IT WITH MY DEPUTY.
THANK YOU VERY MUCH...
...BRANCH DIRECTOR.
HOWEVER ...

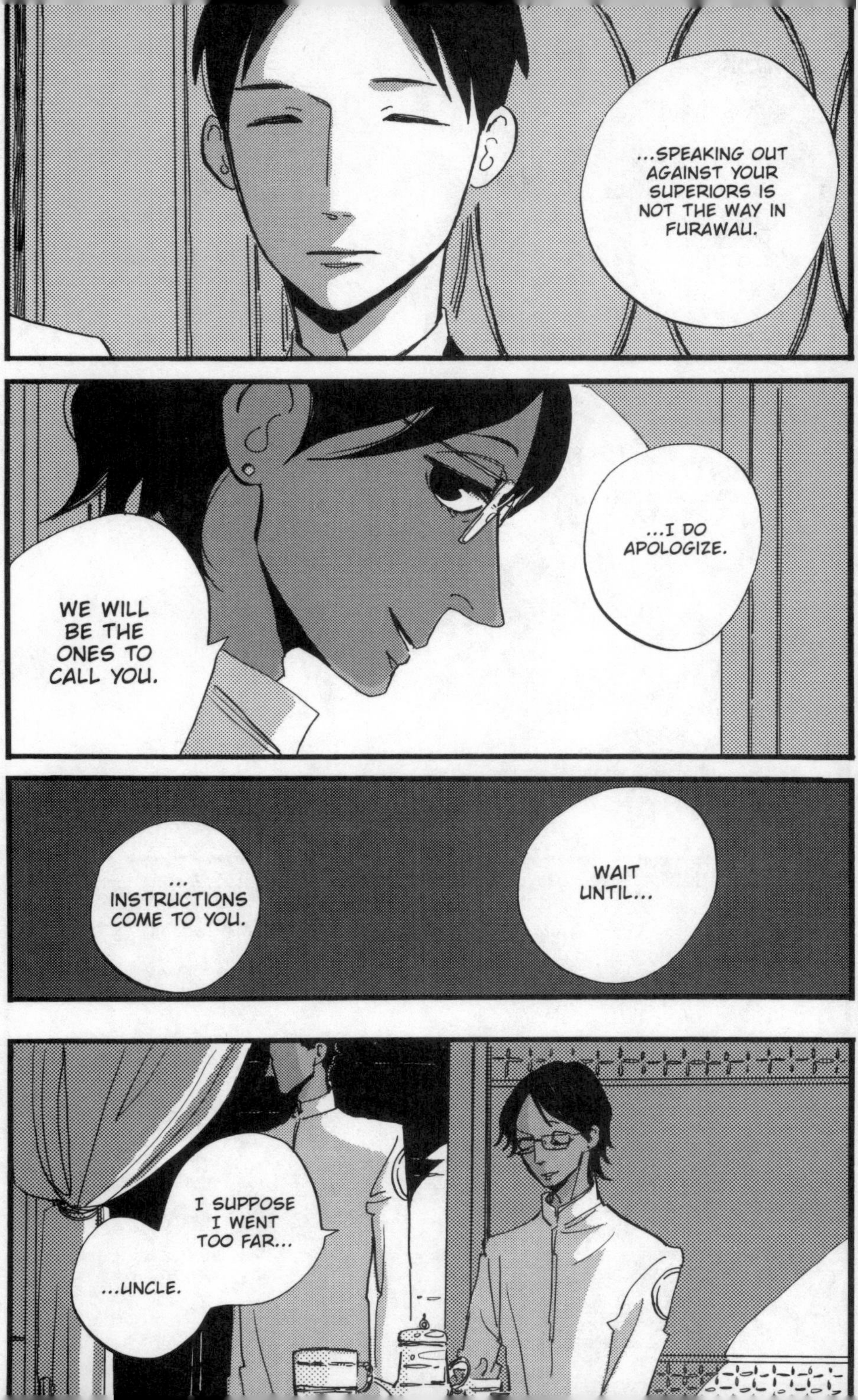
...SPEAKING OUT AGAINST YOUR SUPERIORS IS NOT THE WAY IN FURAWAU.
...I DO APOLOGIZE.
WE WILL BE THE ONES TO CALL YOU.
WAIT UNTIL...
... INSTRUCTIONS COME TO YOU.
I SUPPOSE I WENT TOO FAR...
...UNCLE.

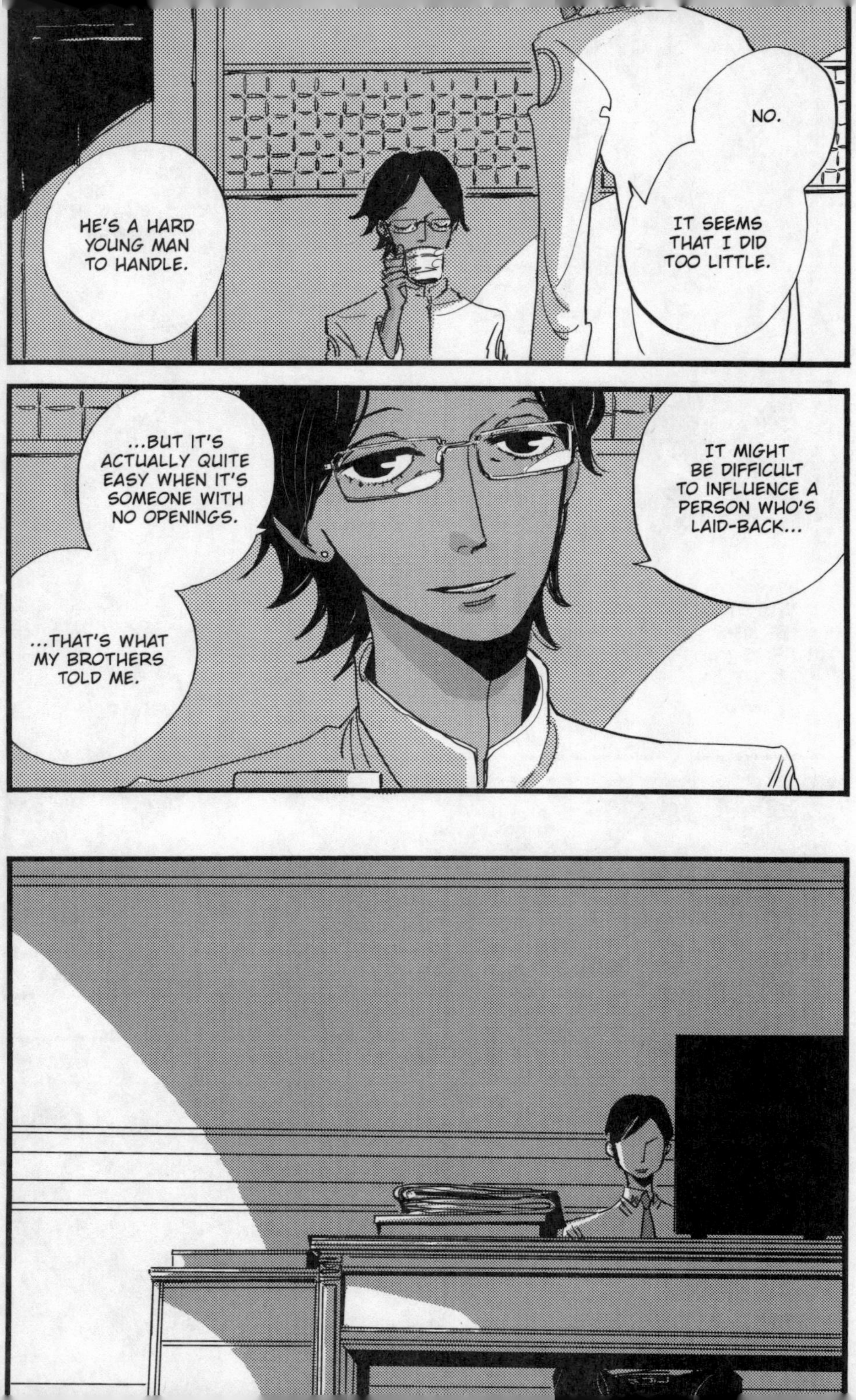
NO.
IT SEEMS THAT I DID TOO LITTLE.
HE'S A HARD YOUNG MAN TO HANDLE.
IT MIGHT BE DIFFICULT TO INFLUENCE A PERSON WHO'S LAID-BACK...
...BUT IT'S ACTUALLY QUITE EASY WHEN IT'S SOMEONE WITH NO OPENINGS.
...THAT'S WHAT MY BROTHERS TOLD ME.

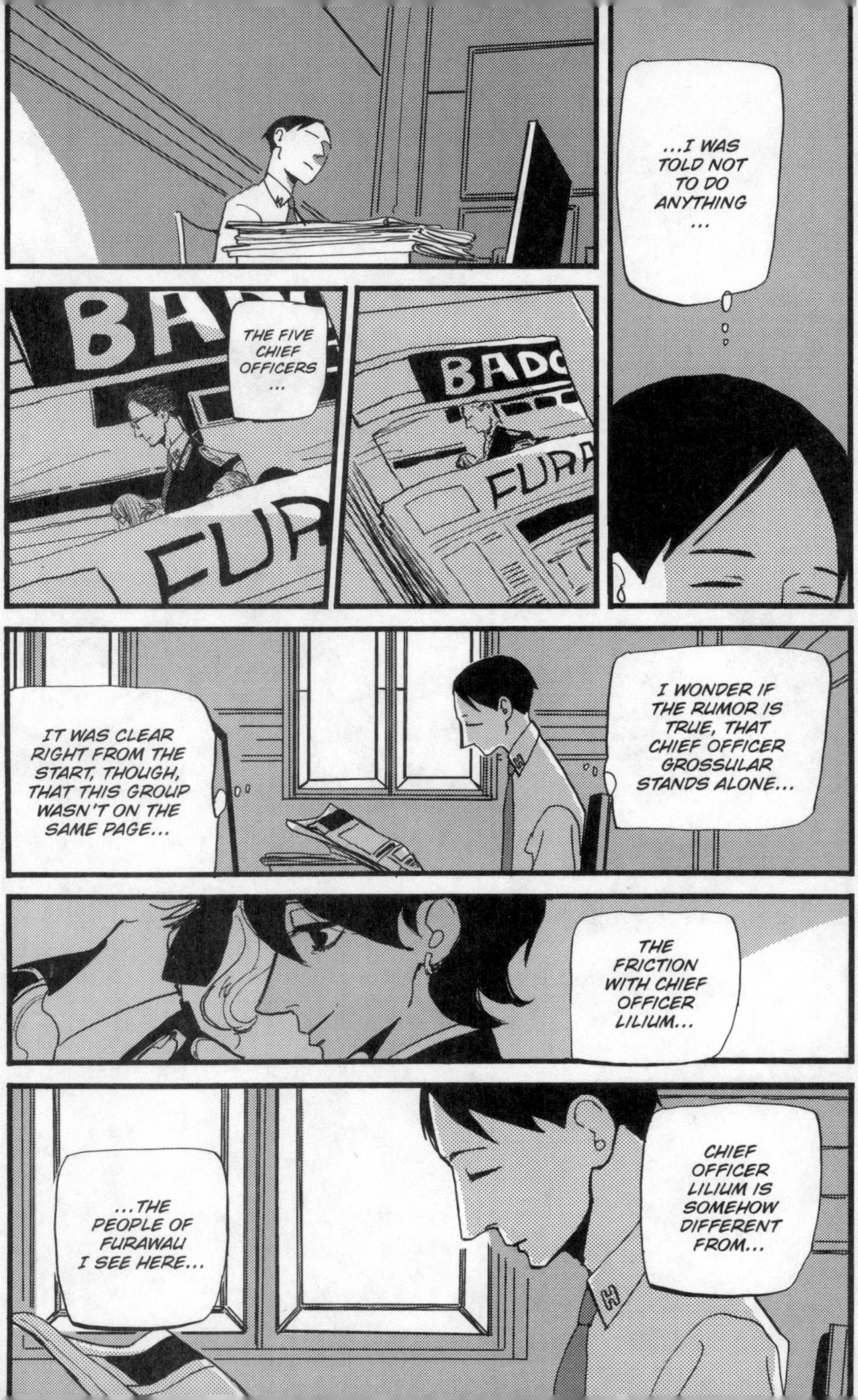
...I WAS TOLD NOT TO DO ANYTHING ...
BADO
FURA
BAD
THE FIVE CHIEF OFFICERS ...
FUR
I WONDER IF THE RUMOR IS TRUE, THAT CHIEF OFFICER GROSSULAR STANDS ALONE...
IT WAS CLEAR RIGHT FROM THE START, THOUGH, THAT THIS GROUP WASN'T ON THE SAME PAGE...
THE FRICTION WITH CHIEF OFFICER LILIUM...
CHIEF OFFICER LILIUM IS SOMEHOW DIFFERENT FROM...
...THE PEOPLE OF FURAWAU I SEE HERE...

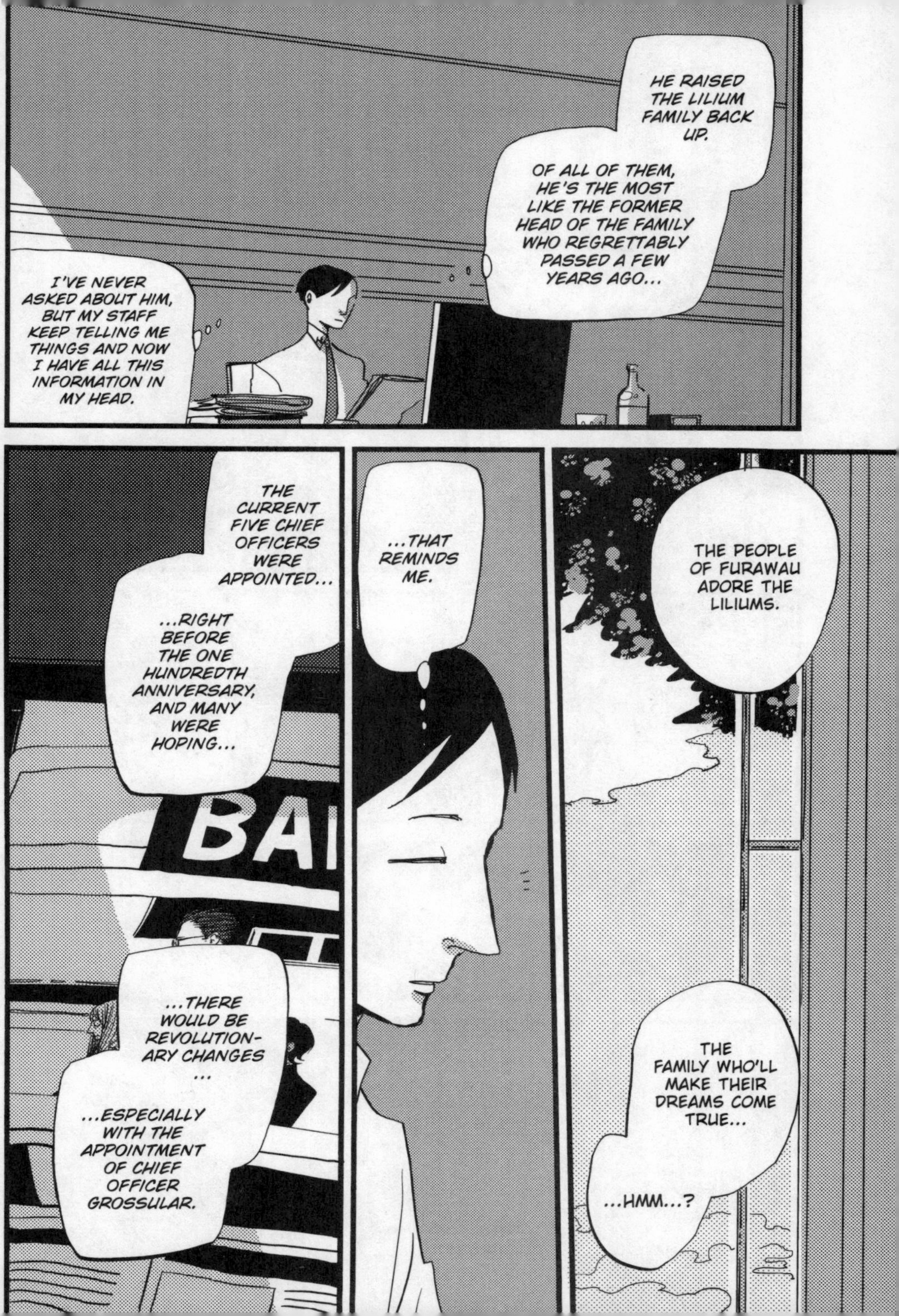
HE RAISED THE LILIUM FAMILY BACK UP.
OF ALL OF THEM, HE'S THE MOST LIKE THE FORMER HEAD OF THE FAMILY WHO REGRETTABLY PASSED A FEW YEARS AGO...
I'VE NEVER ASKED ABOUT HIM, BUT MY STAFF KEEP TELLING ME THINGS AND NOW I HAVE ALL THIS INFORMATION IN MY HEAD.
THE PEOPLE OF FURAWAU ADORE THE LILIUMS.
THE FAMILY WHO'LL MAKE THEIR DREAMS COME TRUE...
...HMM...?
...THAT REMINDS ME.
THE CURRENT FIVE CHIEF OFFICERS WERE APPOINTED...
...RIGHT BEFORE THE ONE HUNDREDTH ANNIVERSARY, AND MANY WERE HOPING...
...THERE WOULD BE REVOLUTIONARY CHANGES...
...ESPECIALLY WITH THE APPOINTMENT OF CHIEF OFFICER GROSSULAR.

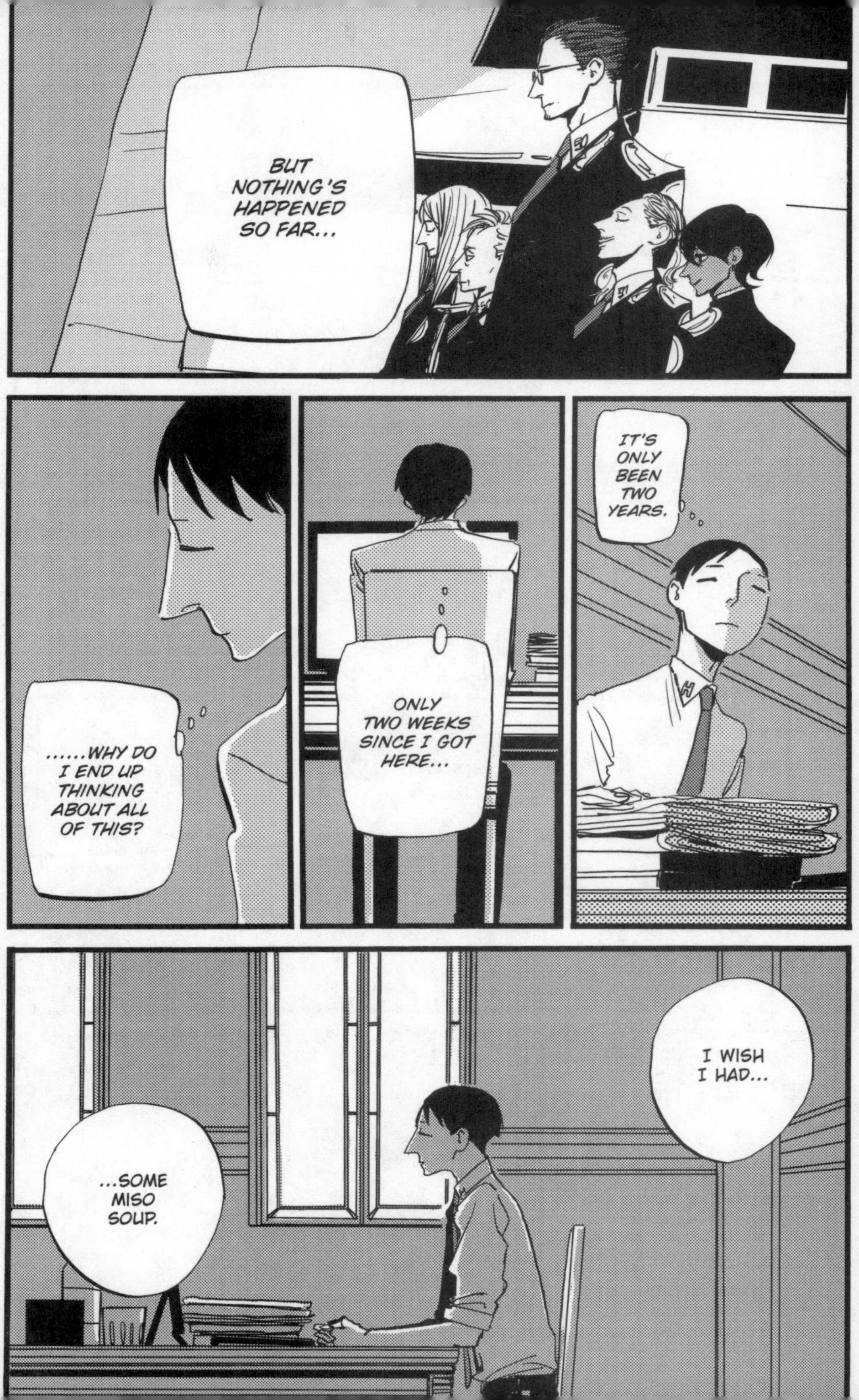
BUT NOTHING'S HAPPENED SO FAR...
IT'S ONLY BEEN TWO YEARS.
ONLY TWO WEEKS SINCE I GOT HERE...
......WHY DO I END UP THINKING ABOUT ALL OF THIS?
I WISH I HAD...
...SOME MISO SOUP.

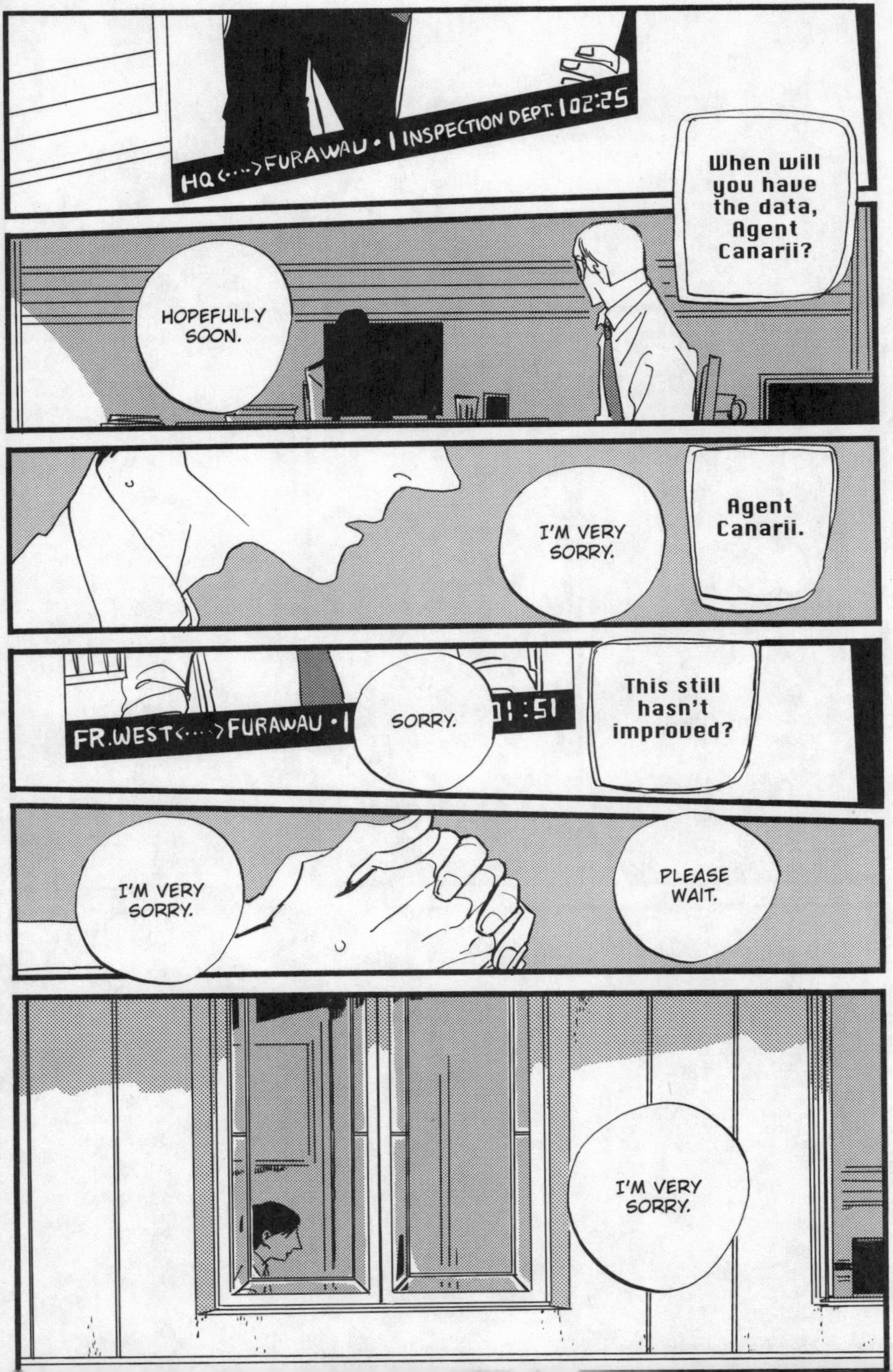
HQ <....> FURAWAU • | INSPECTION DEPT. | 02:25
When will you have the data, Agent Canarii?
HOPEFULLY SOON.
Agent Canarii.
I'M VERY SORRY.
This still hasn't improved?
SORRY.
FR.WEST <....> FURAWAU • |
01:51
PLEASE WAIT.
I'M VERY SORRY.
I'M VERY SORRY.

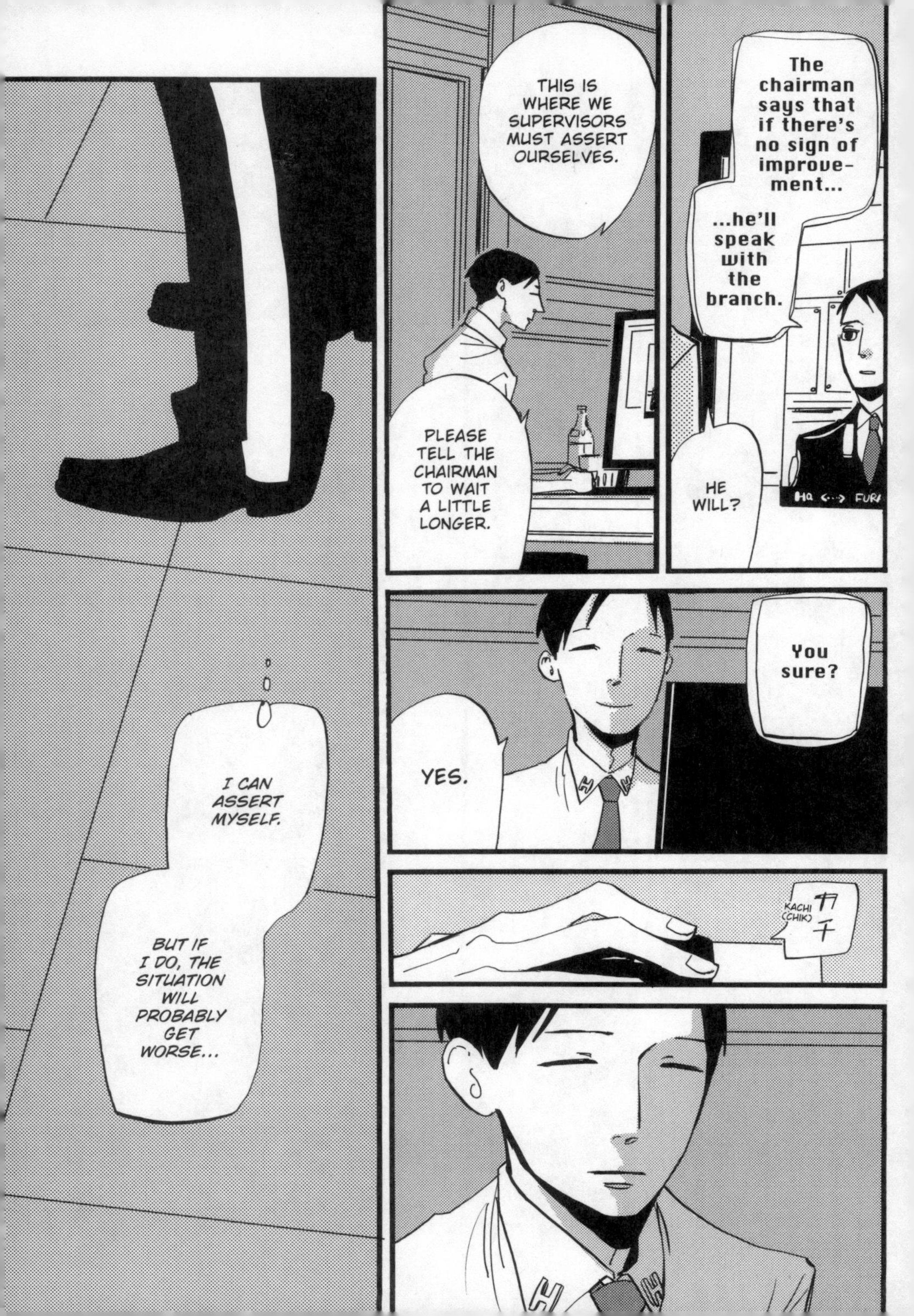
The chairman says that if there's no sign of improvement...
...he'll speak with the branch.
HE WILL?
THIS IS WHERE WE SUPERVISORS MUST ASSERT OURSELVES.
PLEASE TELL THE CHAIRMAN TO WAIT A LITTLE LONGER.
You sure?
YES.
KACHI (CHIK)
I CAN ASSERT MYSELF.
BUT IF I DO, THE SITUATION WILL PROBABLY GET WORSE...

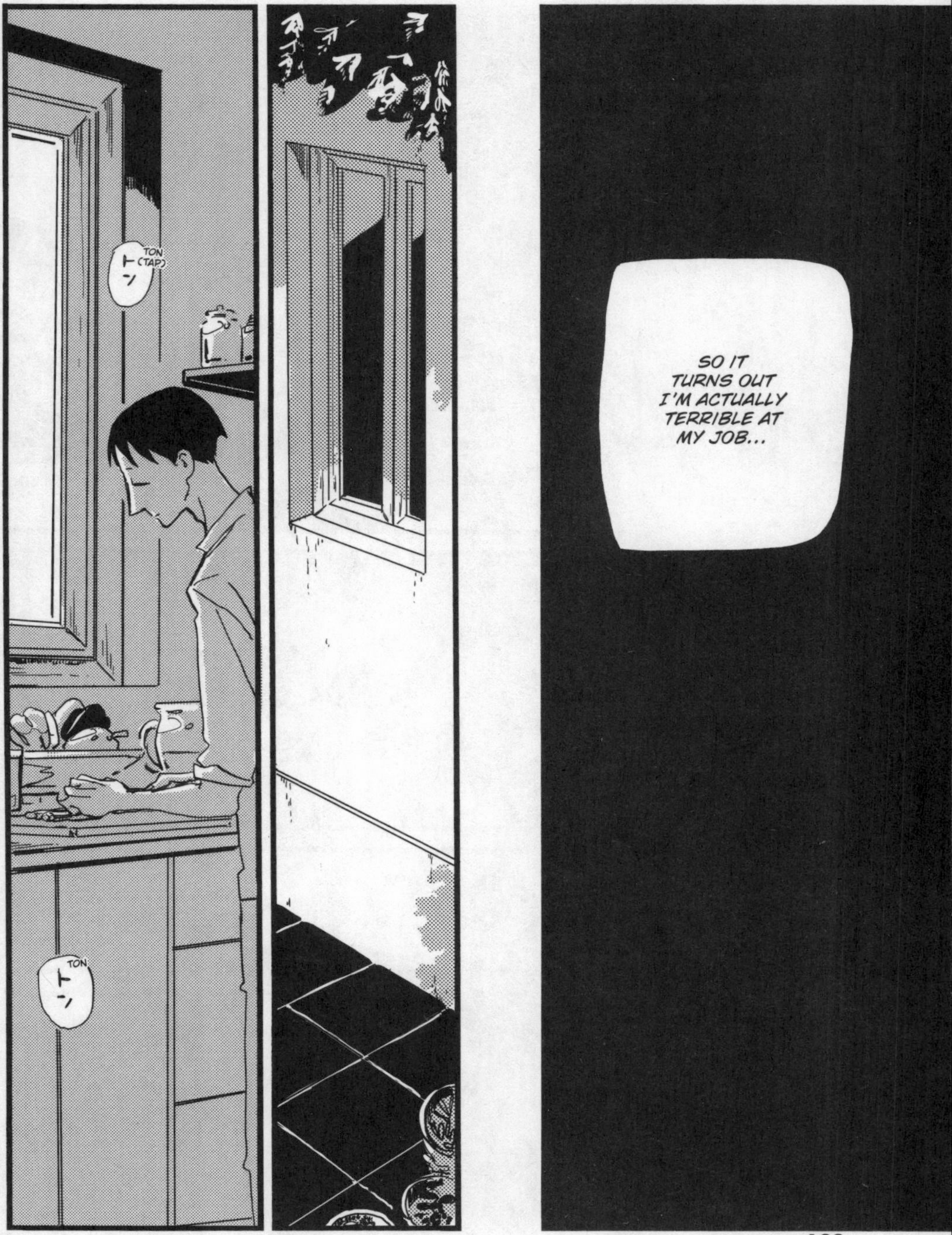
SO IT TURNS OUT I'M ACTUALLY TERRIBLE AT MY JOB...
TON (TAP)
トン
TON
トン

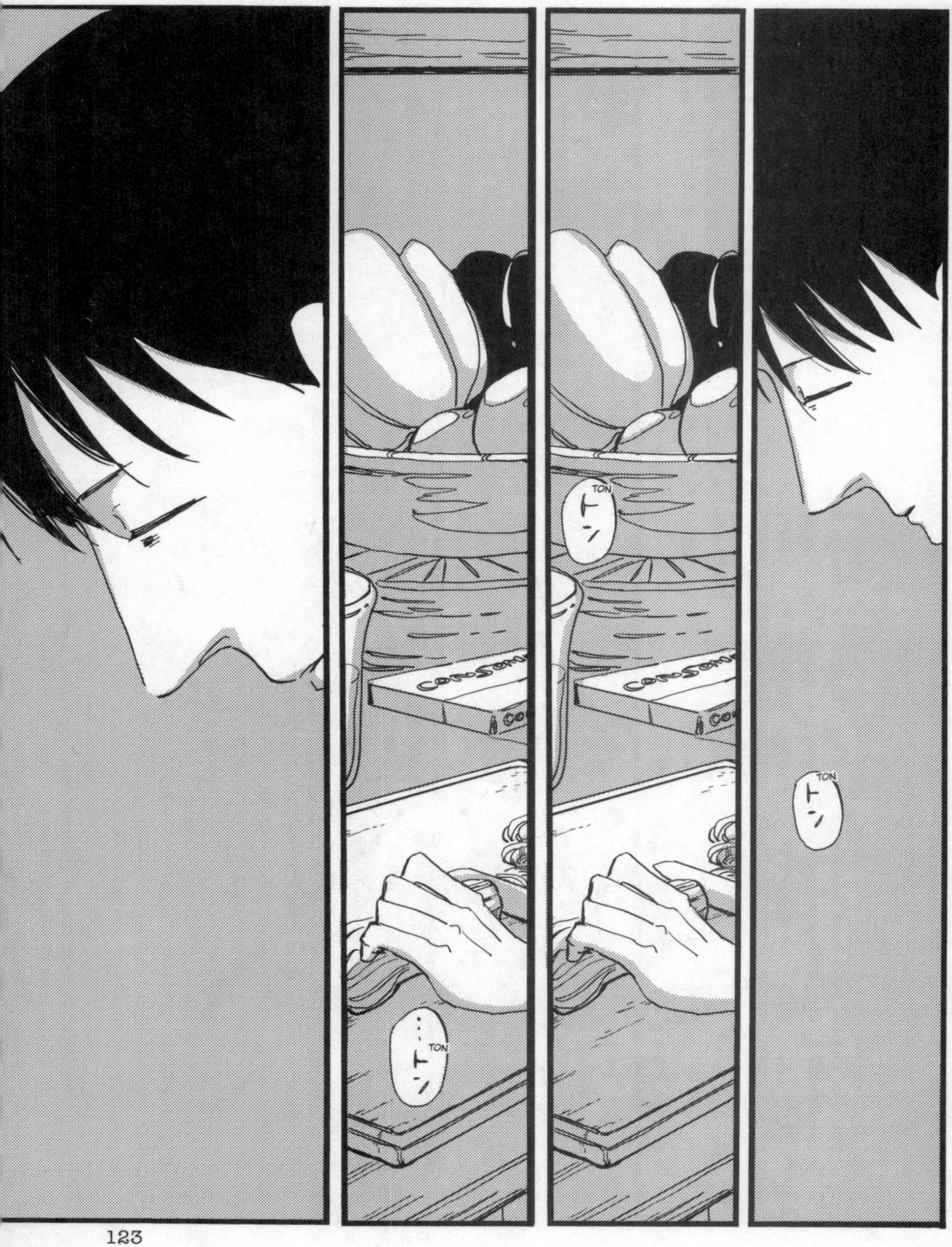

TON トン
TON トン
…TON トン

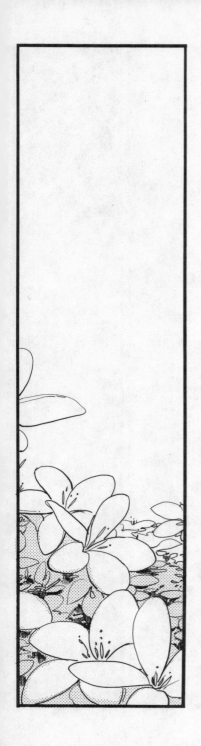

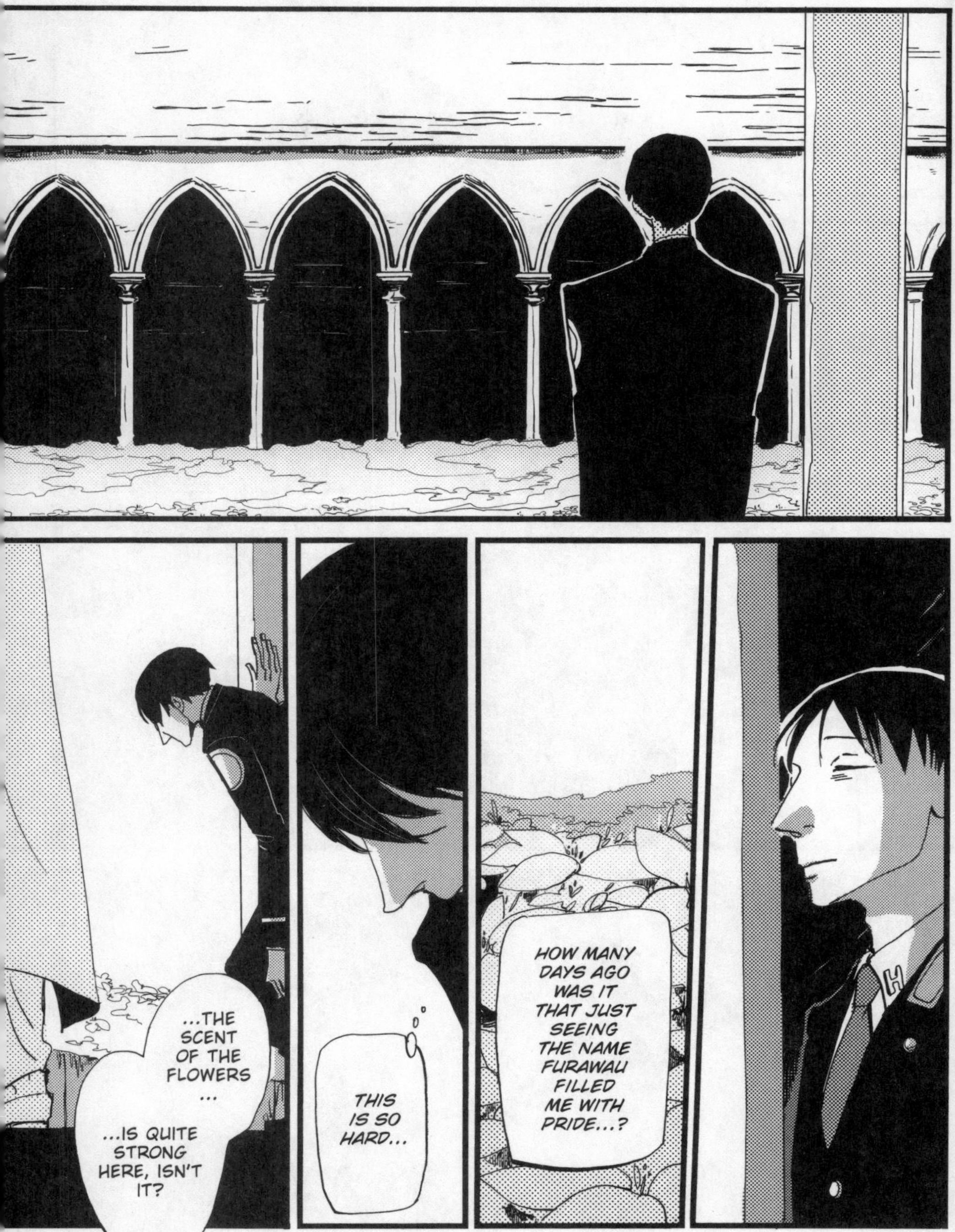
HOW MANY DAYS AGO WAS IT THAT JUST SEEING THE NAME FURAWAU FILLED ME WITH PRIDE...?
THIS IS SO HARD...
...THE SCENT OF THE FLOWERS...
...IS QUITE STRONG HERE, ISN'T IT?

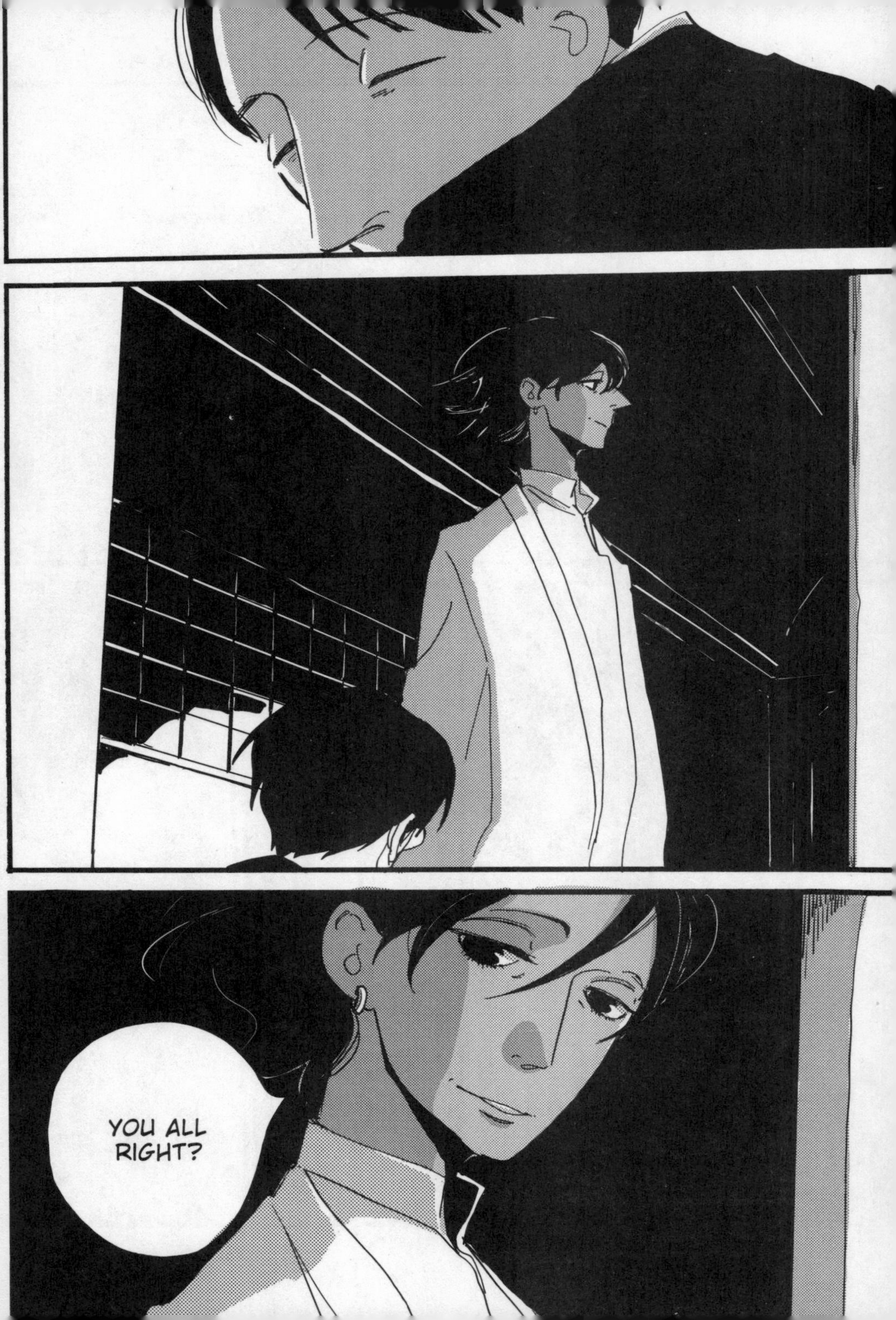
YOU ALL RIGHT?

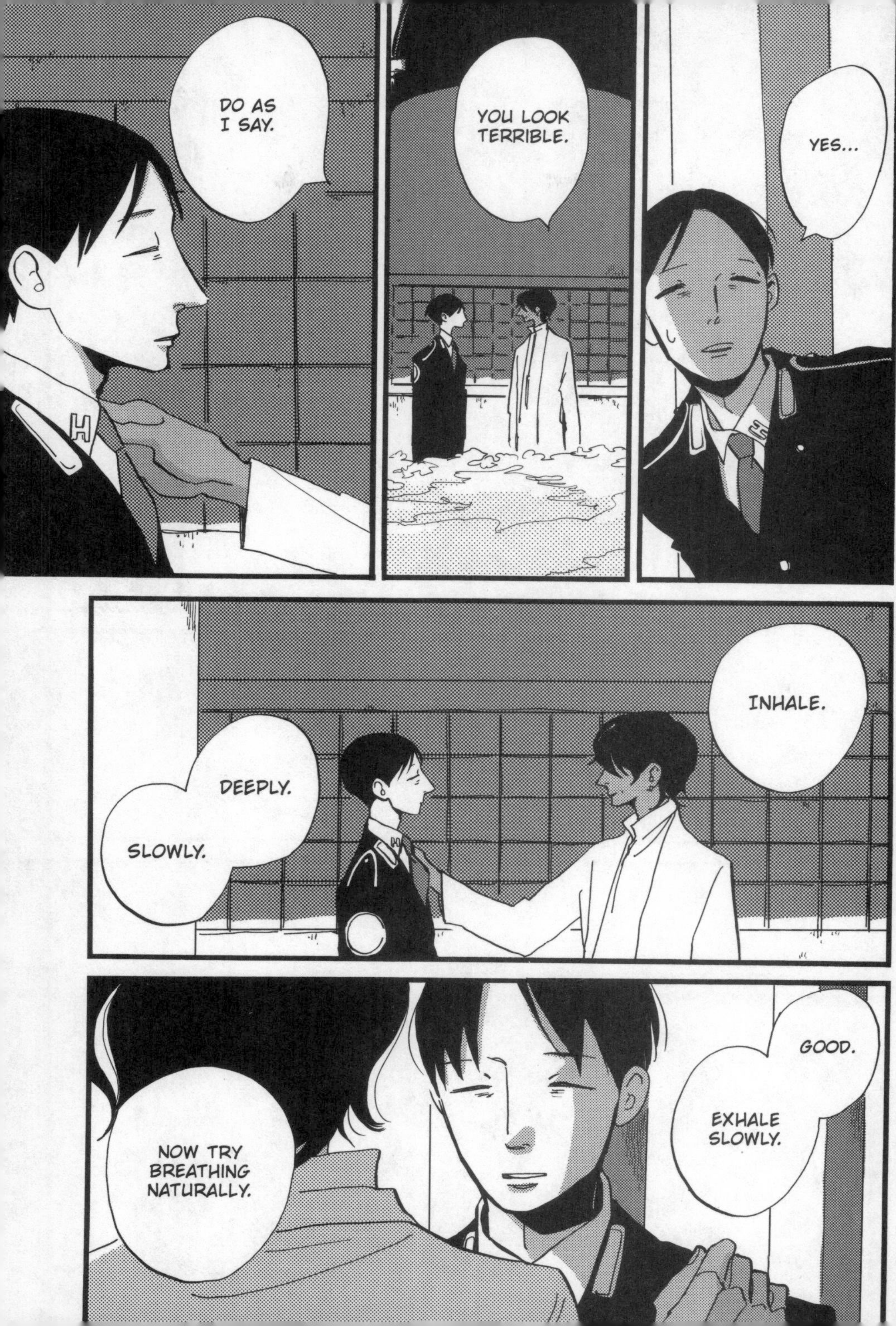
YES...
YOU LOOK TERRIBLE.
DO AS I SAY.
INHALE.
DEEPLY.
SLOWLY.
GOOD.
EXHALE SLOWLY.
NOW TRY BREATHING NATURALLY.

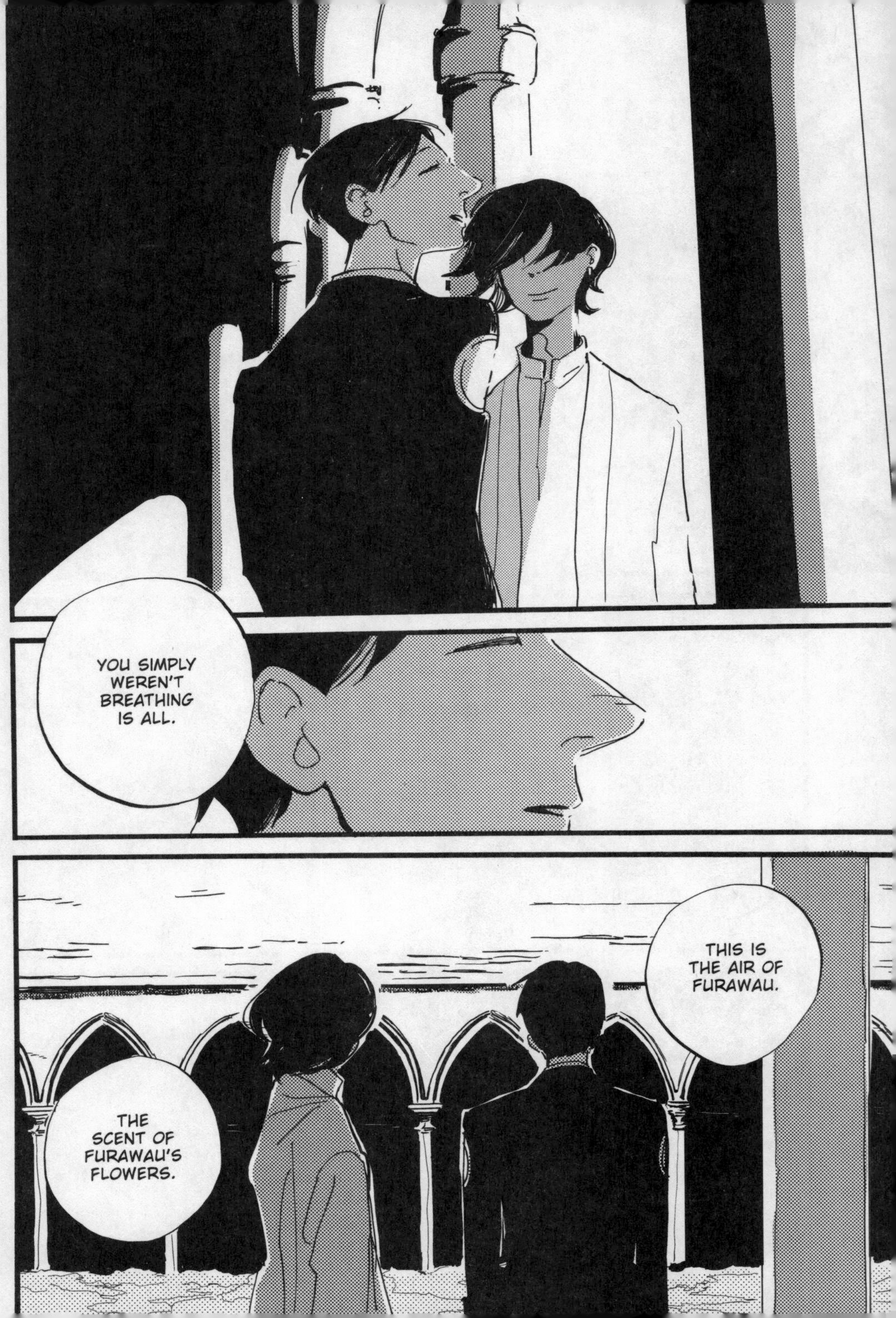
YOU SIMPLY WEREN'T BREATHING IS ALL.
THIS IS THE AIR OF FURAWAU.
THE SCENT OF FURAWAU'S FLOWERS.

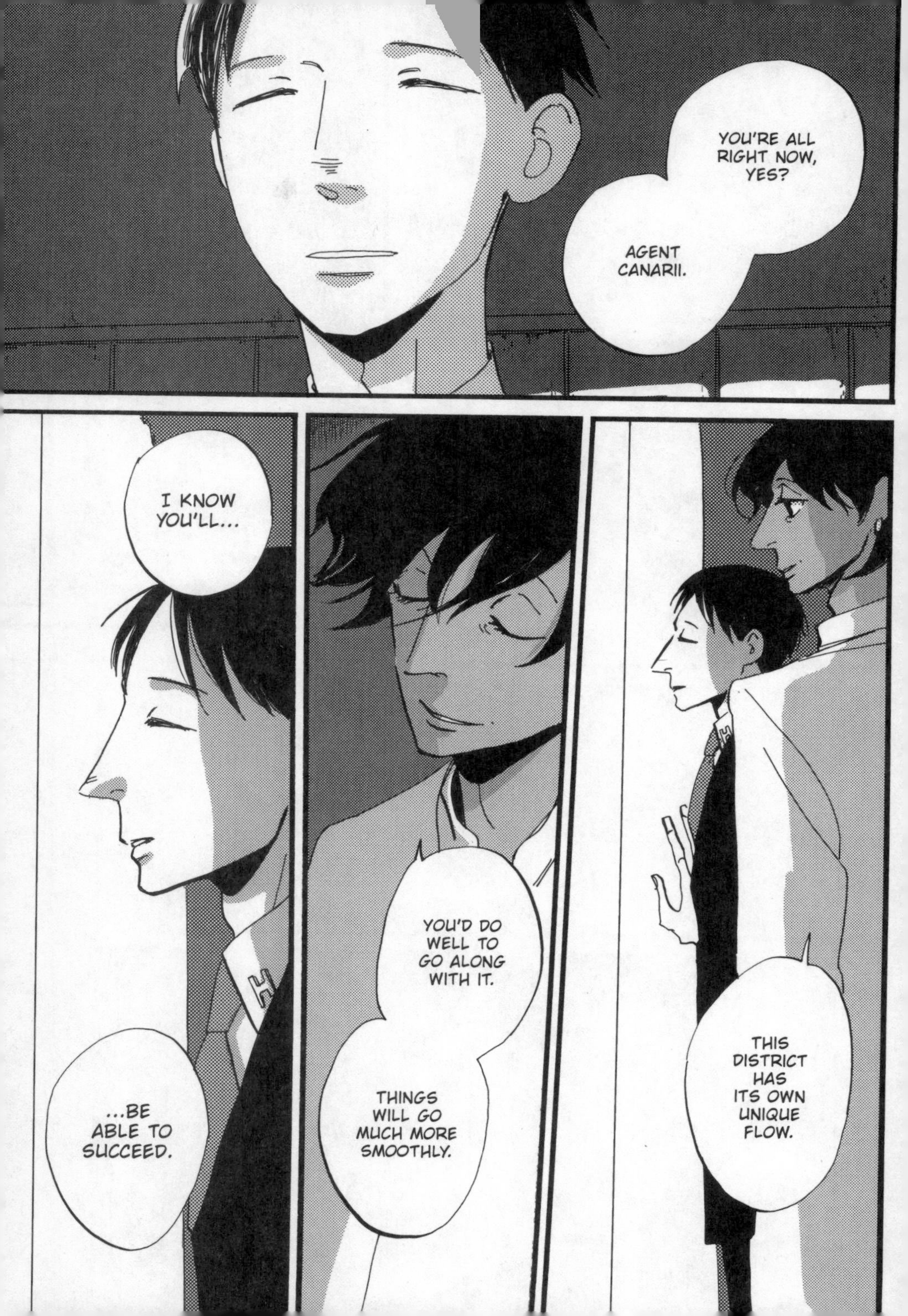
YOU'RE ALL RIGHT NOW, YES?
AGENT CANARII.
THIS DISTRICT HAS ITS OWN UNIQUE FLOW.
YOU'D DO WELL TO GO ALONG WITH IT.
THINGS WILL GO MUCH MORE SMOOTHLY.
I KNOW YOU'LL...
...BE ABLE TO SUCCEED.

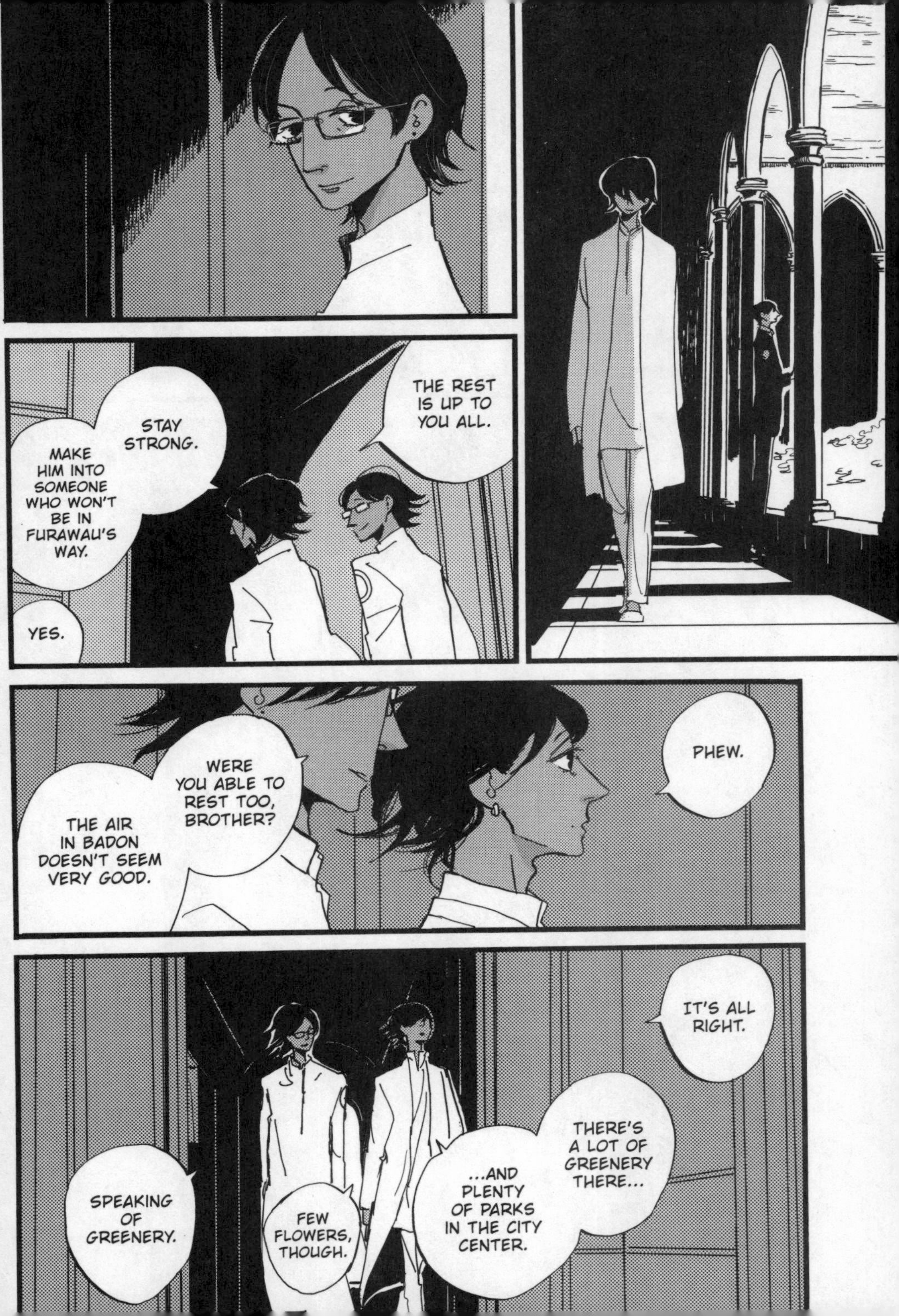
THE REST IS UP TO YOU ALL.
STAY STRONG.
MAKE HIM INTO SOMEONE WHO WON'T BE IN FURAWAU'S WAY.
YES.
PHEW.
WERE YOU ABLE TO REST TOO, BROTHER?
THE AIR IN BADON DOESN'T SEEM VERY GOOD.
IT'S ALL RIGHT.
THERE'S A LOT OF GREENERY THERE...
...AND PLENTY OF PARKS IN THE CITY CENTER.
FEW FLOWERS, THOUGH.
SPEAKING OF GREENERY.

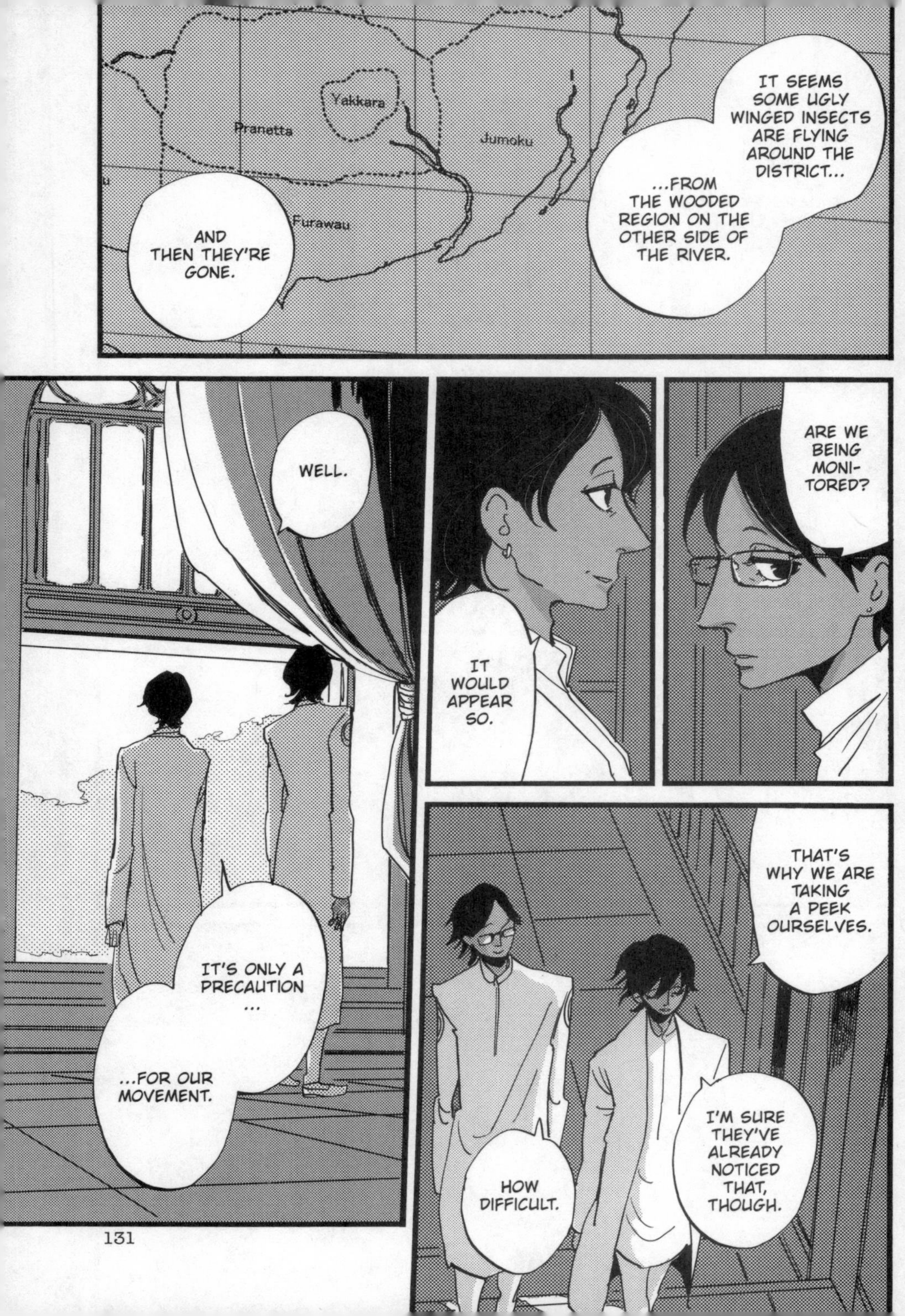
Yakkara
Pranetta
Jumoku
Furawau
IT SEEMS SOME UGLY WINGED INSECTS ARE FLYING AROUND THE DISTRICT...
...FROM THE WOODED REGION ON THE OTHER SIDE OF THE RIVER.
AND THEN THEY'RE GONE.
ARE WE BEING MONI-TORED?
IT WOULD APPEAR SO.
THAT'S WHY WE ARE TAKING A PEEK OURSELVES.
I'M SURE THEY'VE ALREADY NOTICED THAT, THOUGH.
HOW DIFFICULT.
WELL.
IT'S ONLY A PRECAUTION...
...FOR OUR MOVEMENT.

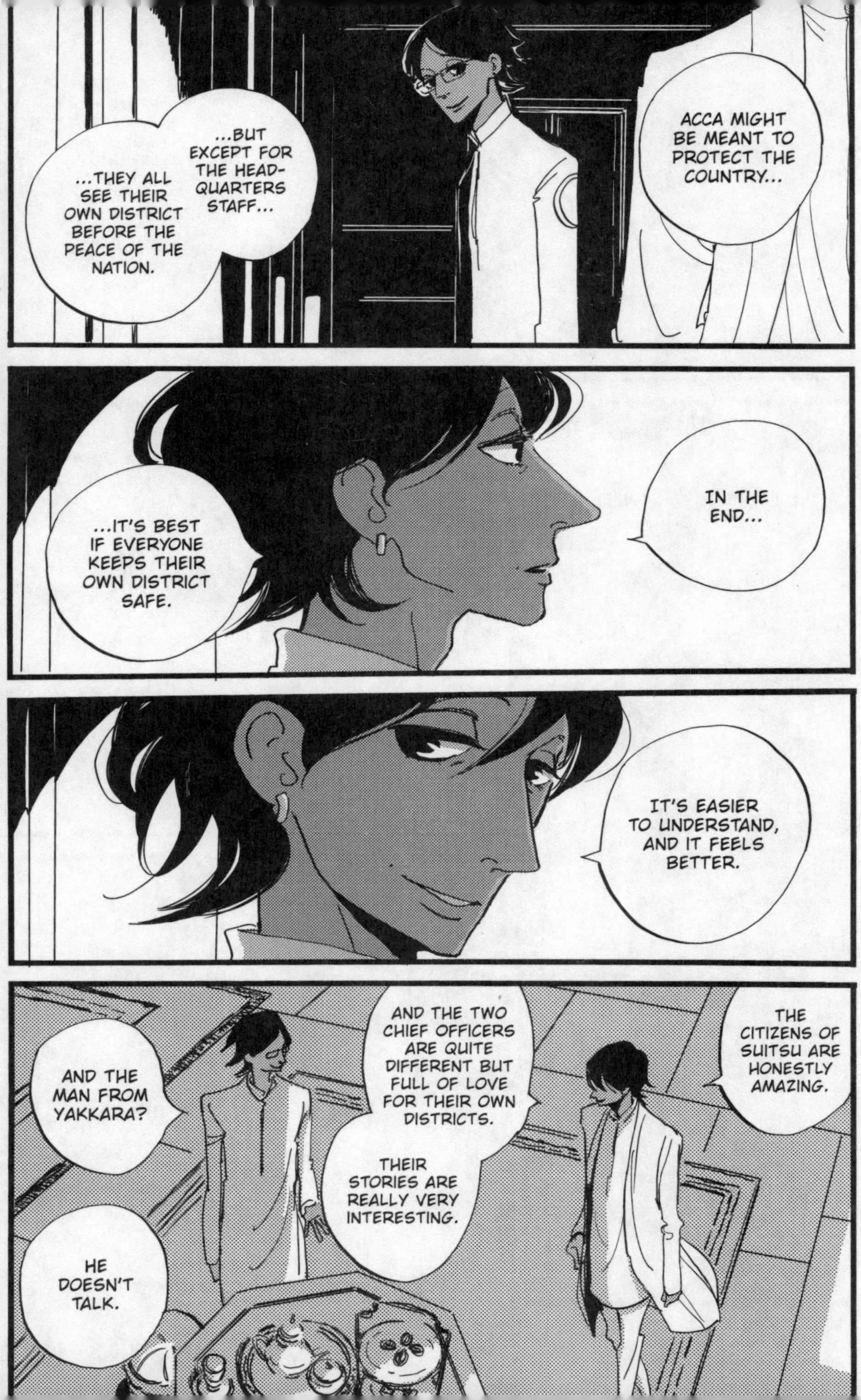
ACCA MIGHT BE MEANT TO PROTECT THE COUNTRY...
...BUT EXCEPT FOR THE HEAD-QUARTERS STAFF...
...THEY ALL SEE THEIR OWN DISTRICT BEFORE THE PEACE OF THE NATION.
IN THE END...
...IT'S BEST IF EVERYONE KEEPS THEIR OWN DISTRICT SAFE.
IT'S EASIER TO UNDERSTAND, AND IT FEELS BETTER.
THE CITIZENS OF SUITSU ARE HONESTLY AMAZING.
AND THE TWO CHIEF OFFICERS ARE QUITE DIFFERENT BUT FULL OF LOVE FOR THEIR OWN DISTRICTS.
THEIR STORIES ARE REALLY VERY INTERESTING.
AND THE MAN FROM YAKKARA?
HE DOESN'T TALK.

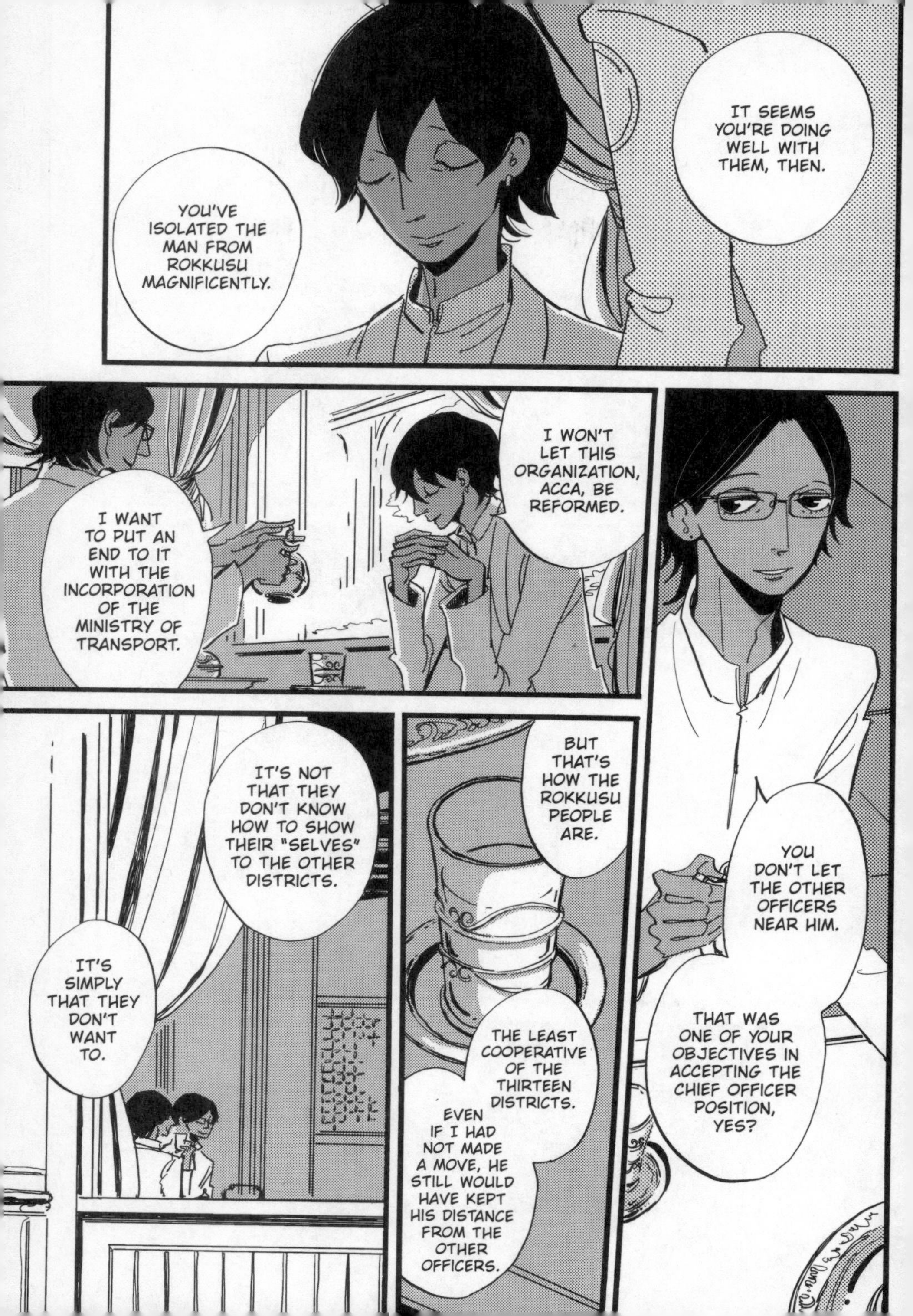
IT SEEMS YOU'RE DOING WELL WITH THEM, THEN.
YOU'VE ISOLATED THE MAN FROM ROKKUSU MAGNIFICENTLY.
YOU DON'T LET THE OTHER OFFICERS NEAR HIM.
THAT WAS ONE OF YOUR OBJECTIVES IN ACCEPTING THE CHIEF OFFICER POSITION, YES?
I WON'T LET THIS ORGANIZATION, ACCA, BE REFORMED.
I WANT TO PUT AN END TO IT WITH THE INCORPORATION OF THE MINISTRY OF TRANSPORT.
BUT THAT'S HOW THE ROKKUSU PEOPLE ARE.
THE LEAST COOPERATIVE OF THE THIRTEEN DISTRICTS.
EVEN IF I HAD NOT MADE A MOVE, HE STILL WOULD HAVE KEPT HIS DISTANCE FROM THE OTHER OFFICERS.
IT'S NOT THAT THEY DON'T KNOW HOW TO SHOW THEIR "SELVES" TO THE OTHER DISTRICTS.
IT'S SIMPLY THAT THEY DON'T WANT TO.

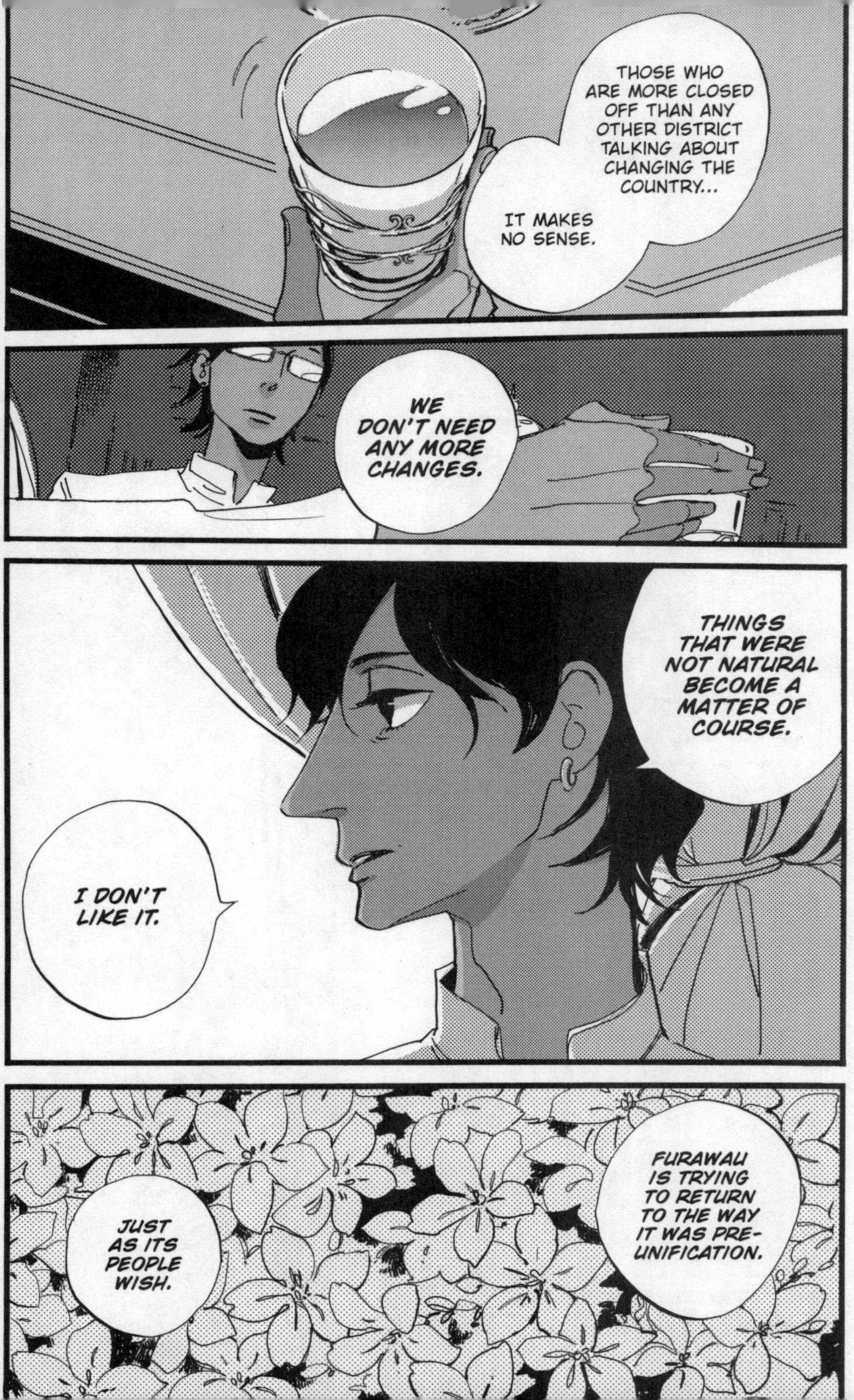
THOSE WHO ARE MORE CLOSED OFF THAN ANY OTHER DISTRICT TALKING ABOUT CHANGING THE COUNTRY...
IT MAKES NO SENSE.
WE DON'T NEED ANY MORE CHANGES.
THINGS THAT WERE NOT NATURAL BECOME A MATTER OF COURSE.
I DON'T LIKE IT.
FURAWAU IS TRYING TO RETURN TO THE WAY IT WAS PRE-UNIFICATION.
JUST AS ITS PEOPLE WISH.

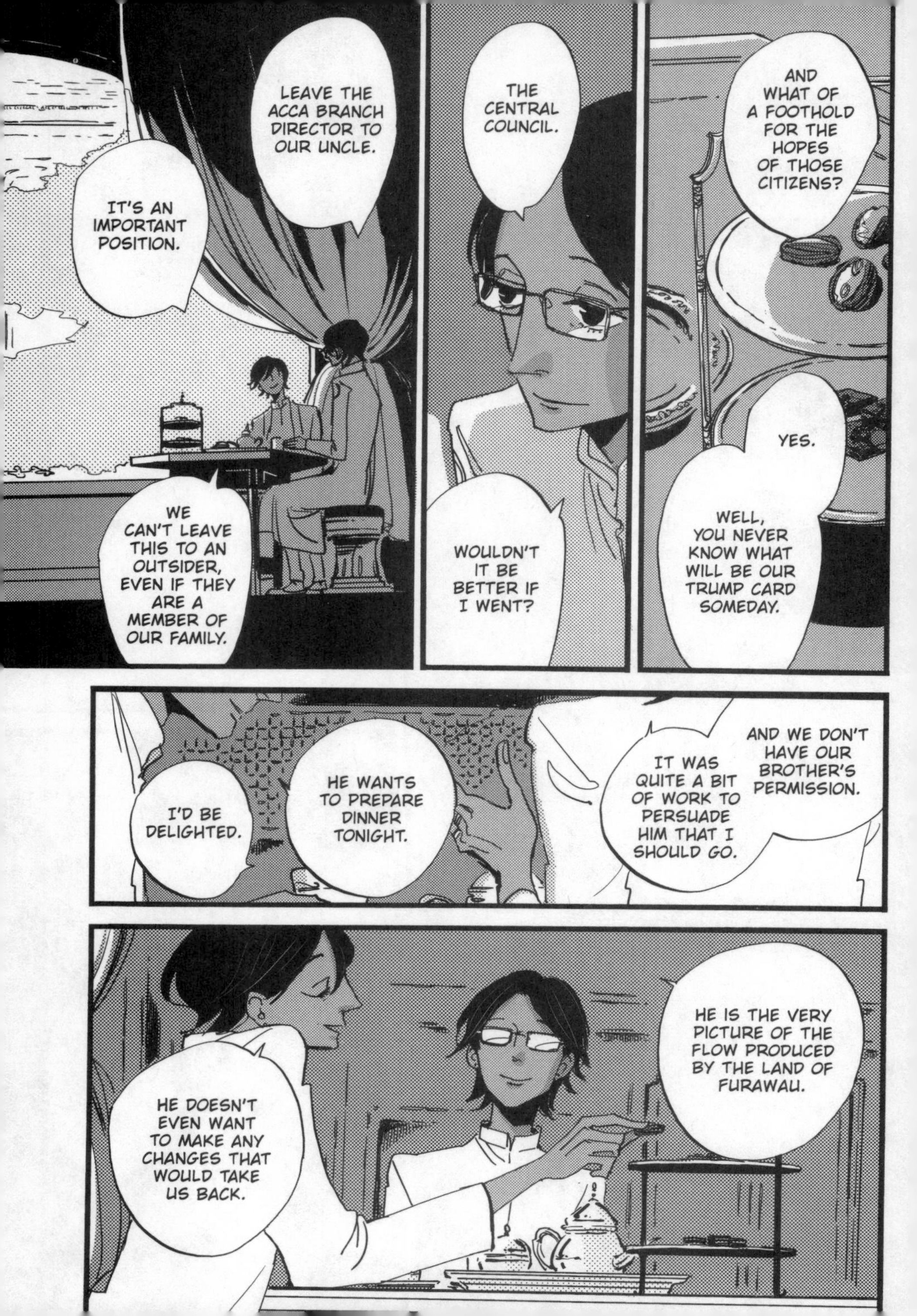
AND WHAT OF A FOOTHOLD FOR THE HOPES OF THOSE CITIZENS?
YES.
WELL, YOU NEVER KNOW WHAT WILL BE OUR TRUMP CARD SOMEDAY.
THE CENTRAL COUNCIL.
WOULDN'T IT BE BETTER IF I WENT?
LEAVE THE ACCA BRANCH DIRECTOR TO OUR UNCLE.
IT'S AN IMPORTANT POSITION.
WE CAN'T LEAVE THIS TO AN OUTSIDER, EVEN IF THEY ARE A MEMBER OF OUR FAMILY.
AND WE DON'T HAVE OUR BROTHER'S PERMISSION.
IT WAS QUITE A BIT OF WORK TO PERSUADE HIM THAT I SHOULD GO.
HE WANTS TO PREPARE DINNER TONIGHT.
I'D BE DELIGHTED.
HE IS THE VERY PICTURE OF THE FLOW PRODUCED BY THE LAND OF FURAWAU.
HE DOESN'T EVEN WANT TO MAKE ANY CHANGES THAT WOULD TAKE US BACK.

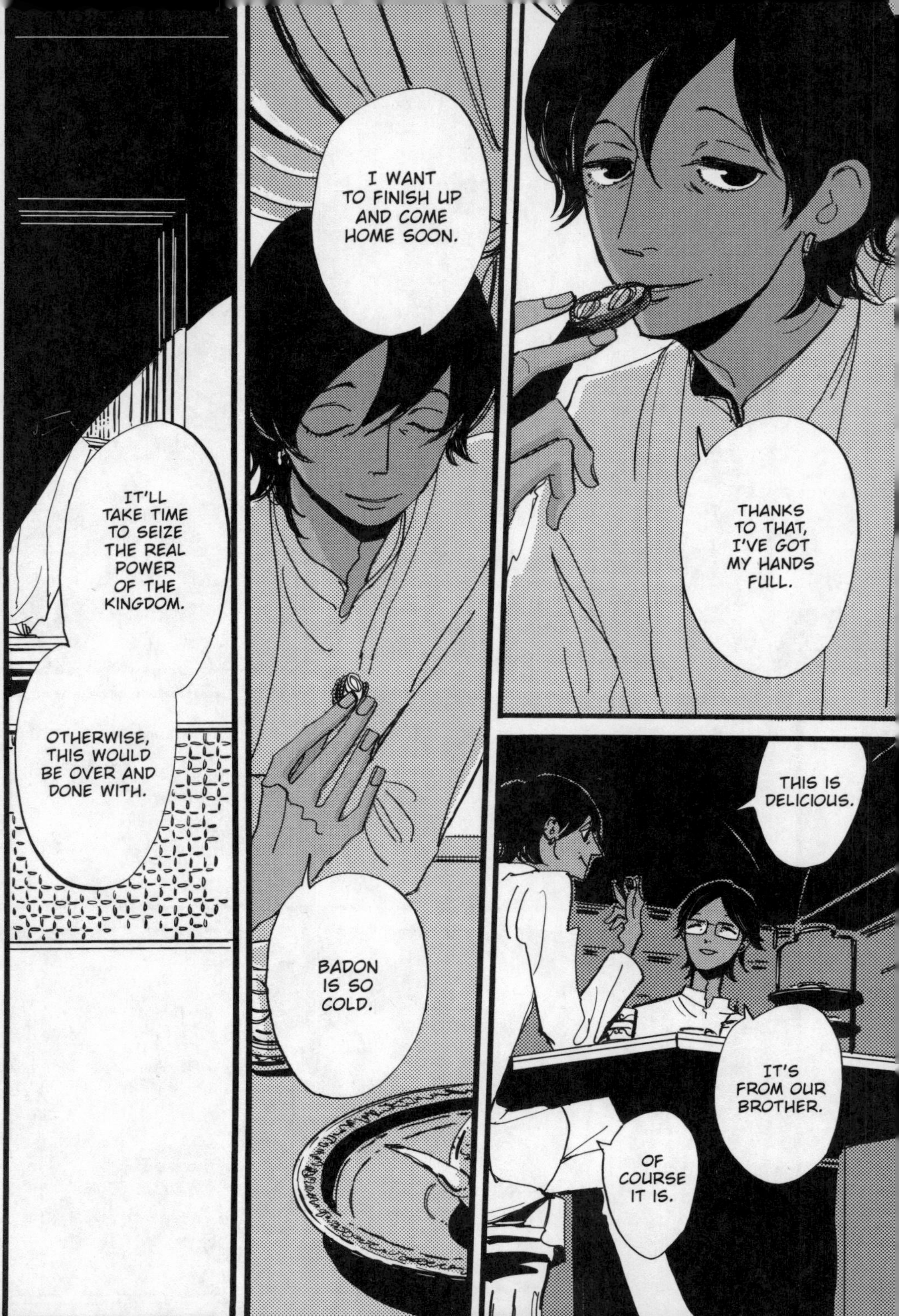
THANKS TO THAT, I'VE GOT MY HANDS FULL.
THIS IS DELICIOUS.
IT'S FROM OUR BROTHER.
OF COURSE IT IS.
I WANT TO FINISH UP AND COME HOME SOON.
BADON IS SO COLD.
IT'LL TAKE TIME TO SEIZE THE REAL POWER OF THE KINGDOM.
OTHERWISE, THIS WOULD BE OVER AND DONE WITH.

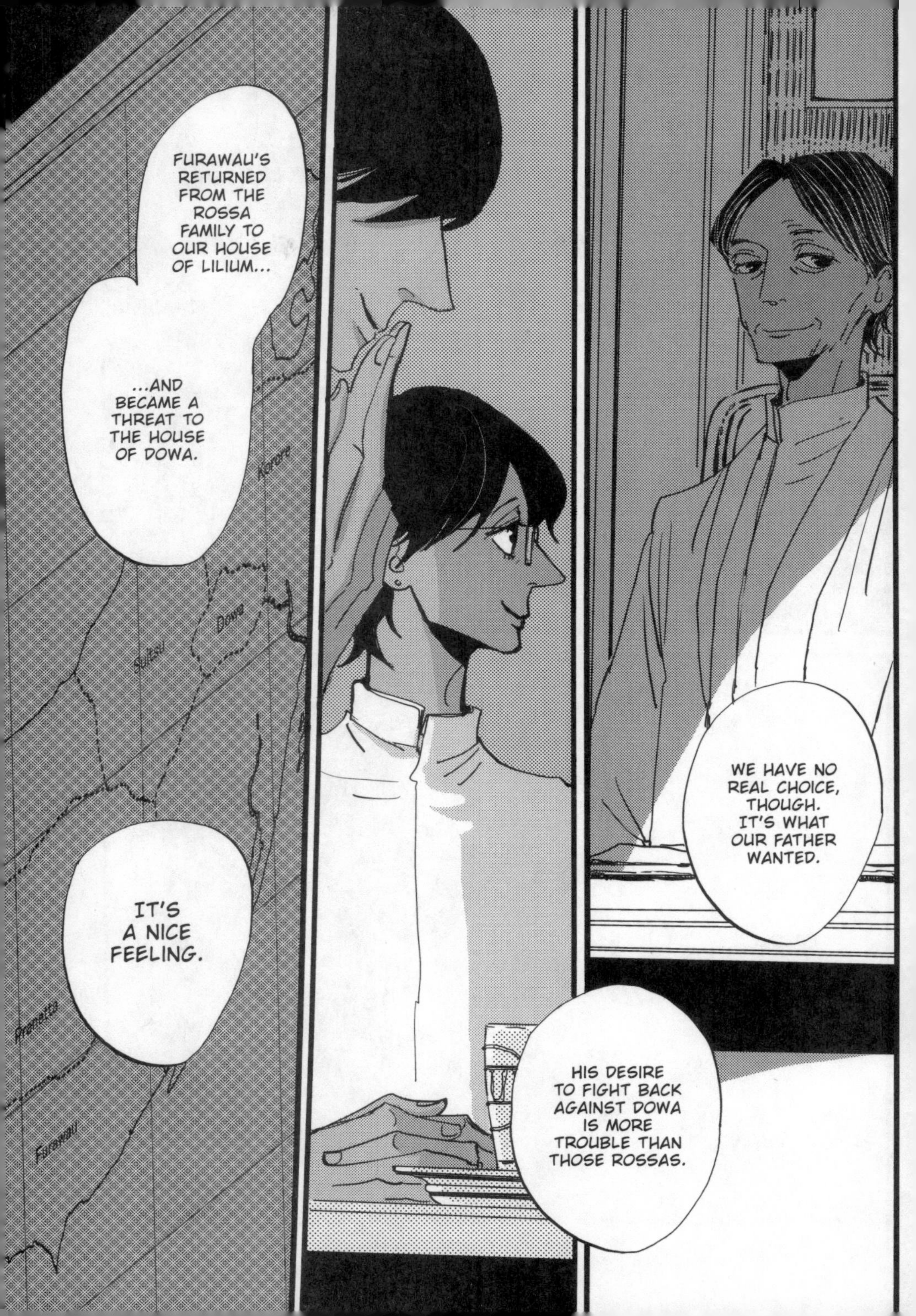
WE HAVE NO REAL CHOICE, THOUGH. IT'S WHAT OUR FATHER WANTED.
HIS DESIRE TO FIGHT BACK AGAINST DOWA IS MORE TROUBLE THAN THOSE ROSSAS.
FURAWAU'S RETURNED FROM THE ROSSA FAMILY TO OUR HOUSE OF LILIUM...
...AND BECAME A THREAT TO THE HOUSE OF DOWA.
IT'S A NICE FEELING.
Korore
Dowa
Furawau

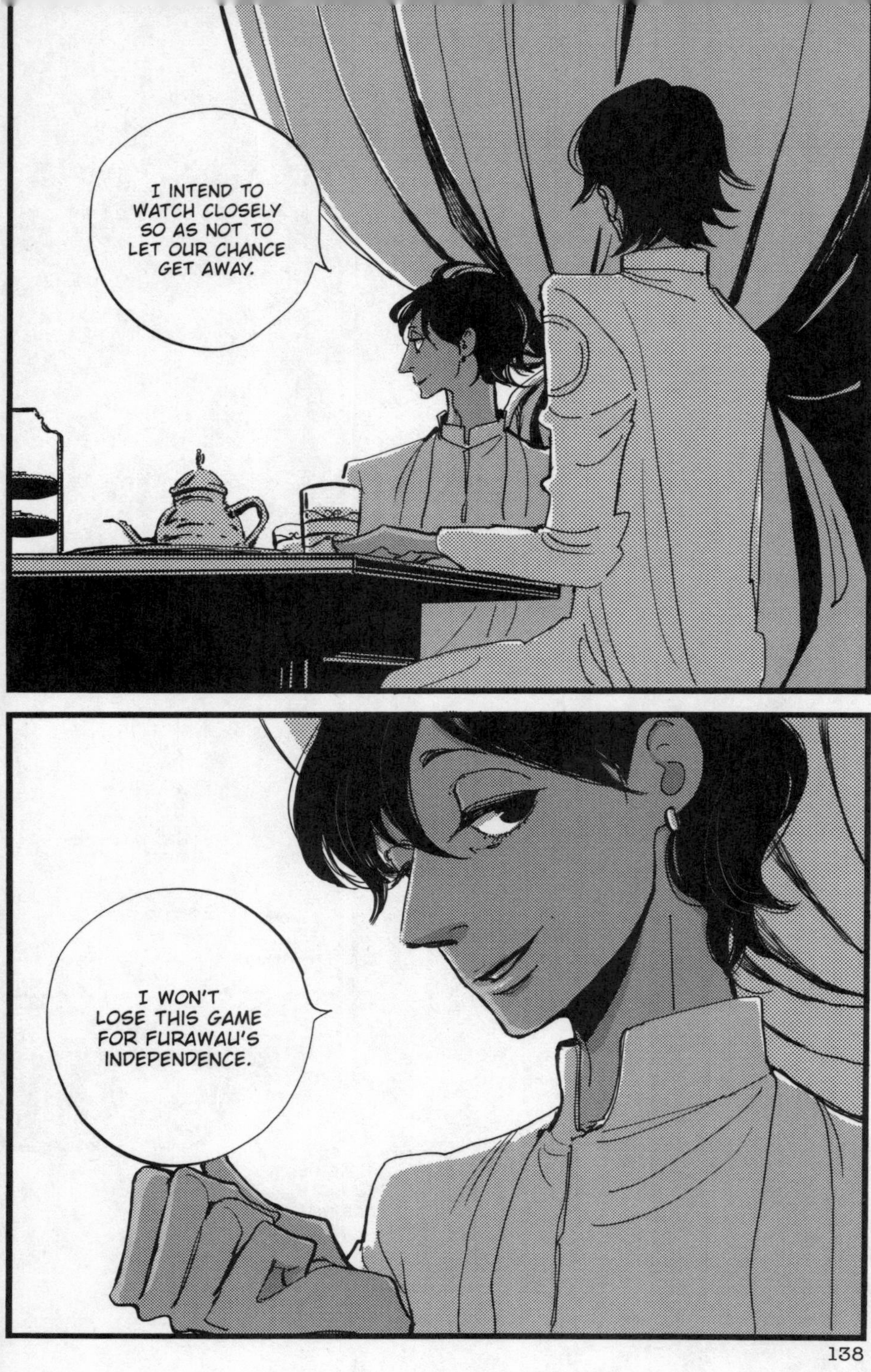
I INTEND TO WATCH CLOSELY SO AS NOT TO LET OUR CHANCE GET AWAY.
I WON'T LOSE THIS GAME FOR FURAWAU'S INDEPENDENCE.

INSPECTION DEPT ACCA 13 TERRITORY

PASS

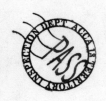

CHAPTER 9

To the Land of Flowers, as Guided

P.S.

CHAPTER 10

Tonight, Pray for

Tomorrow's Sky

P.S.

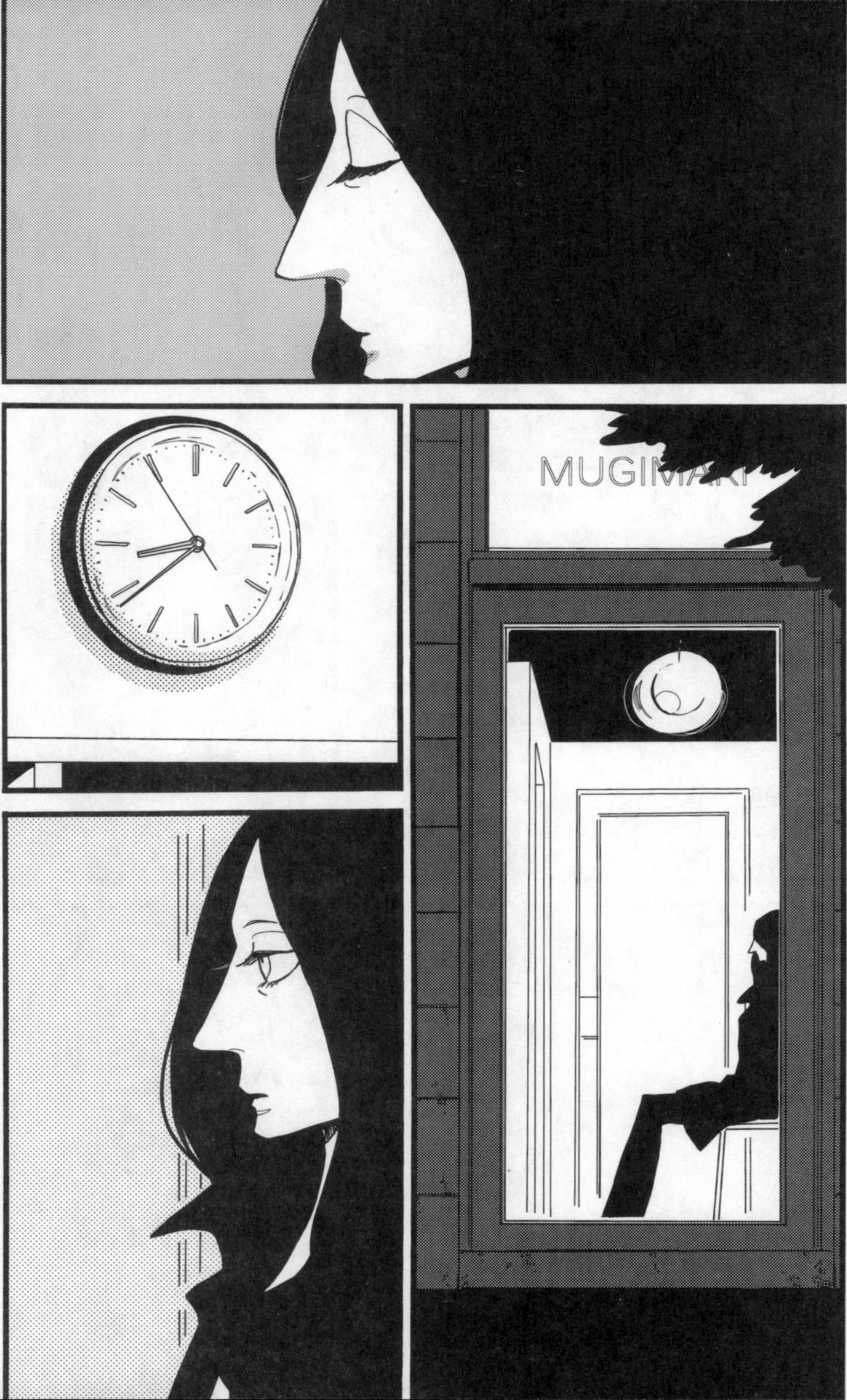
MUGIMAKI

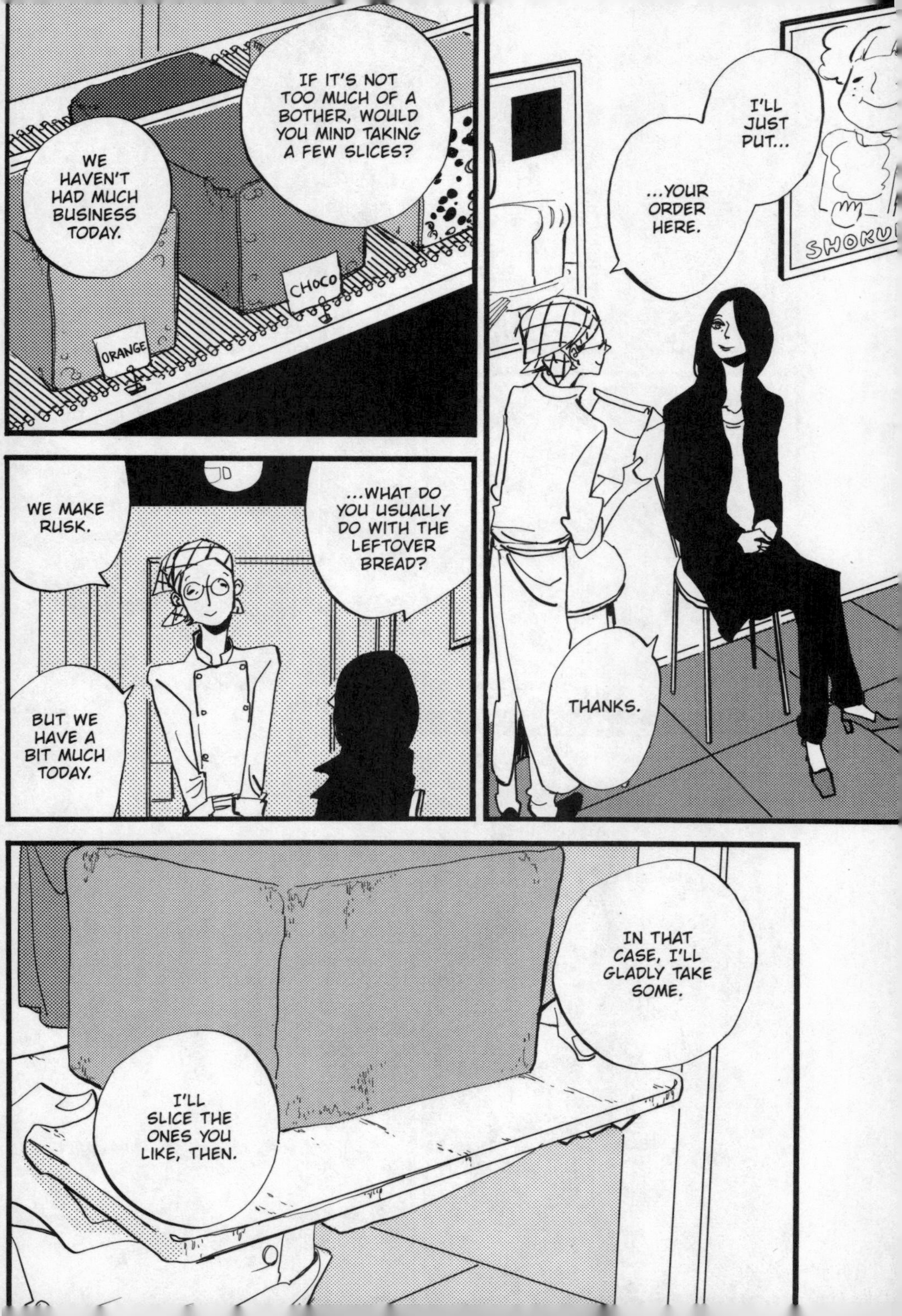
I'LL JUST PUT...
...YOUR ORDER HERE.
THANKS.
IF IT'S NOT TOO MUCH OF A BOTHER, WOULD YOU MIND TAKING A FEW SLICES?
CHOCO
WE HAVEN'T HAD MUCH BUSINESS TODAY.
ORANGE
...WHAT DO YOU USUALLY DO WITH THE LEFTOVER BREAD?
WE MAKE RUSK.
BUT WE HAVE A BIT MUCH TODAY.
IN THAT CASE, I'LL GLADLY TAKE SOME.
I'LL SLICE THE ONES YOU LIKE, THEN.

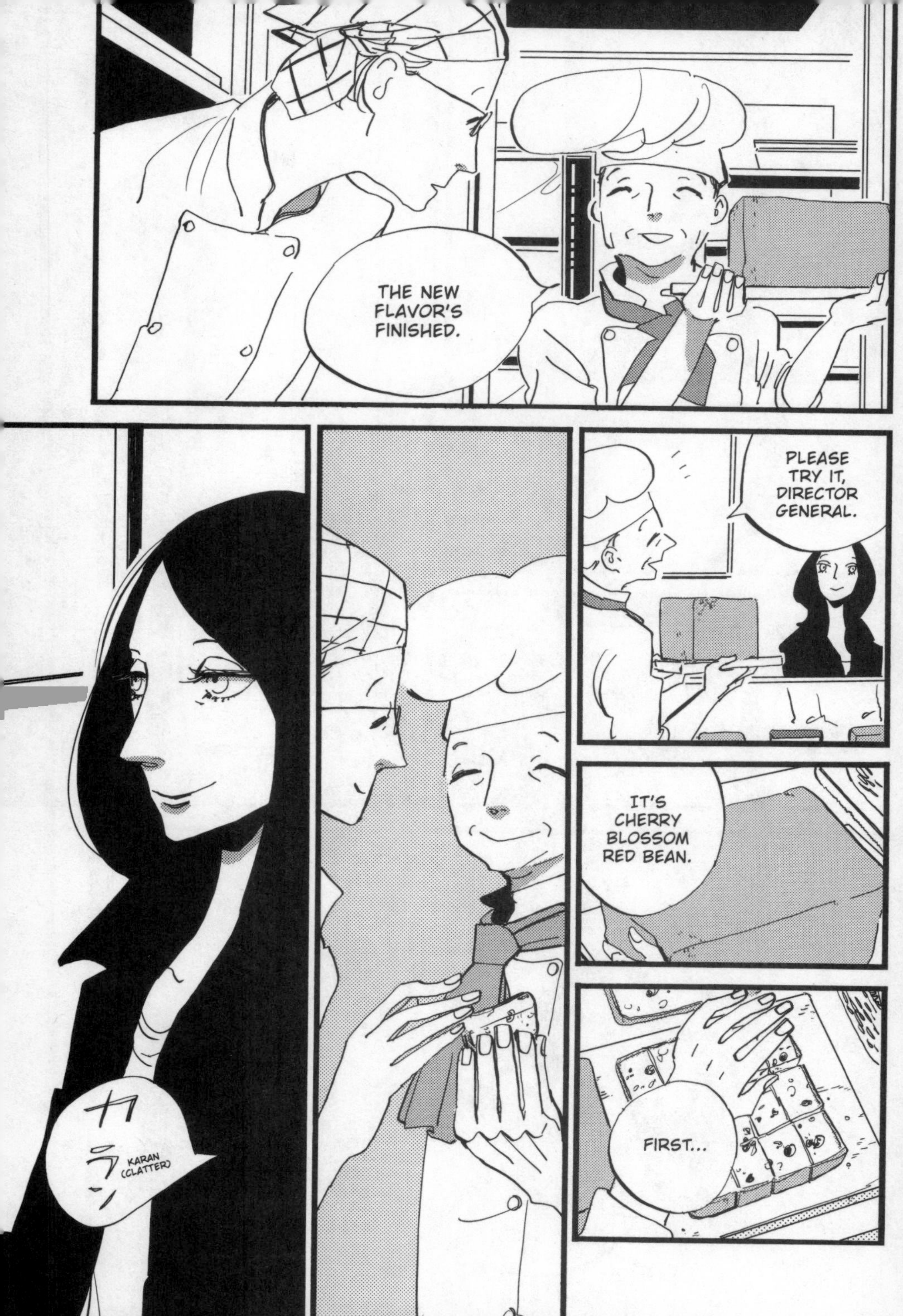
THE NEW FLAVOR'S FINISHED.
PLEASE TRY IT, DIRECTOR GENERAL.
IT'S CHERRY BLOSSOM RED BEAN.
FIRST...
カラン
KARAN (CLATTER)

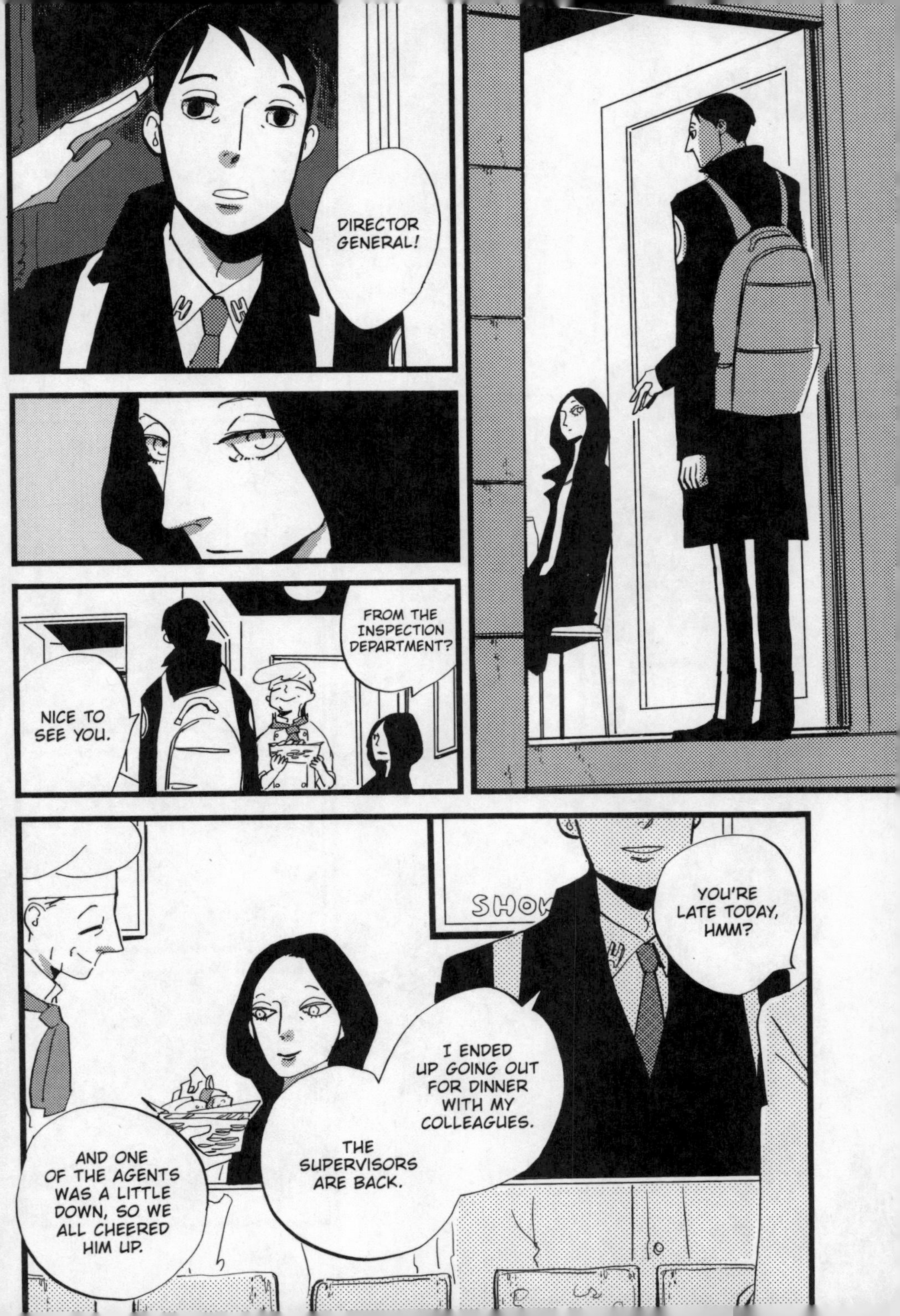
DIRECTOR GENERAL!
FROM THE INSPECTION DEPARTMENT?
NICE TO SEE YOU.
YOU'RE LATE TODAY, HMM?
I ENDED UP GOING OUT FOR DINNER WITH MY COLLEAGUES.
THE SUPERVISORS ARE BACK.
AND ONE OF THE AGENTS WAS A LITTLE DOWN, SO WE ALL CHEERED HIM UP.

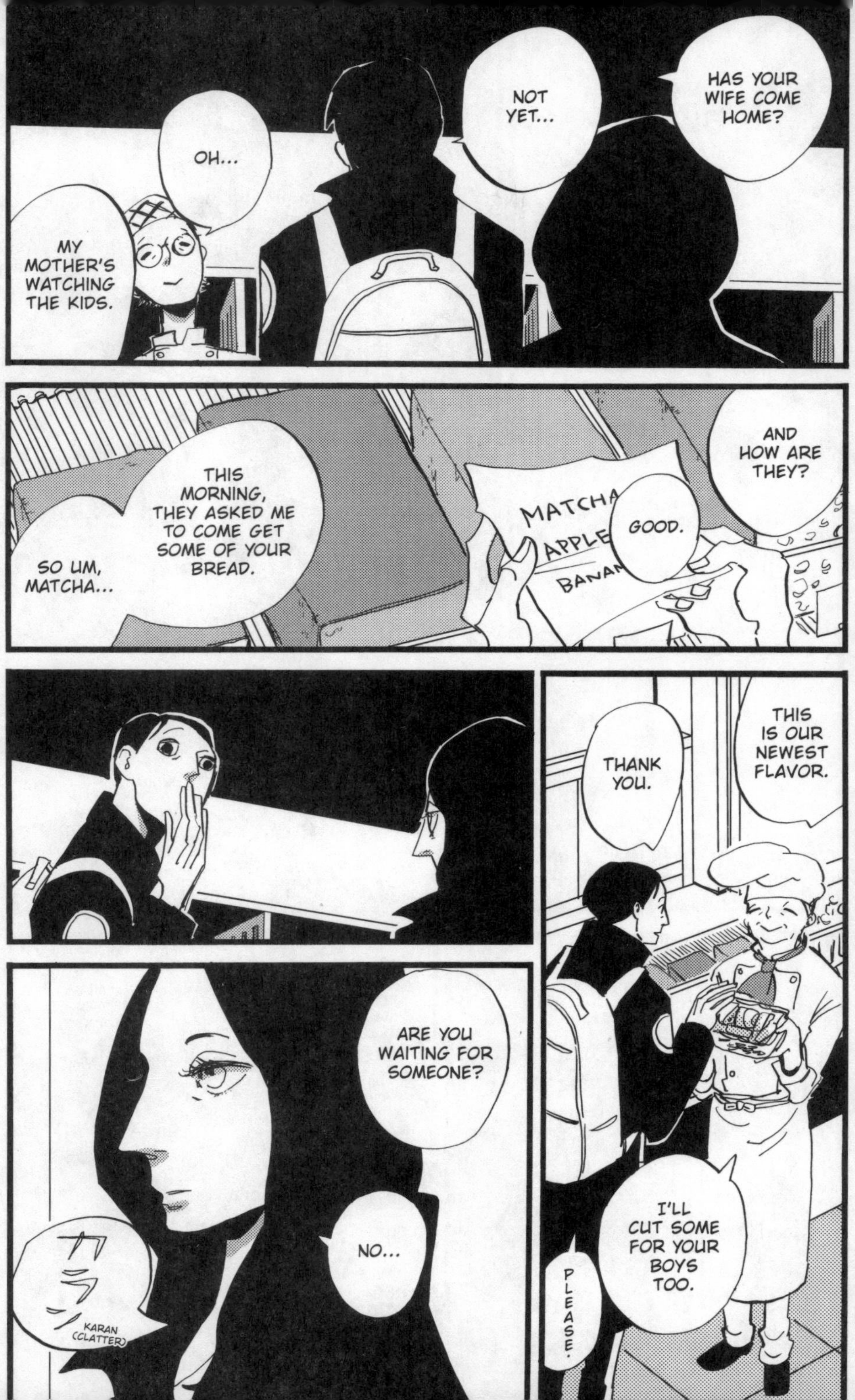
HAS YOUR WIFE COME HOME?
NOT YET...
OH...
MY MOTHER'S WATCHING THE KIDS.
AND HOW ARE THEY?
GOOD.
MATCHA
APPLE
THIS MORNING, THEY ASKED ME TO COME GET SOME OF YOUR BREAD.
SO UM, MATCHA...
THIS IS OUR NEWEST FLAVOR.
THANK YOU.
I'LL CUT SOME FOR YOUR BOYS TOO.
PLEASE.
ARE YOU WAITING FOR SOMEONE?
NO...
カラ
KARAN (CLATTER)

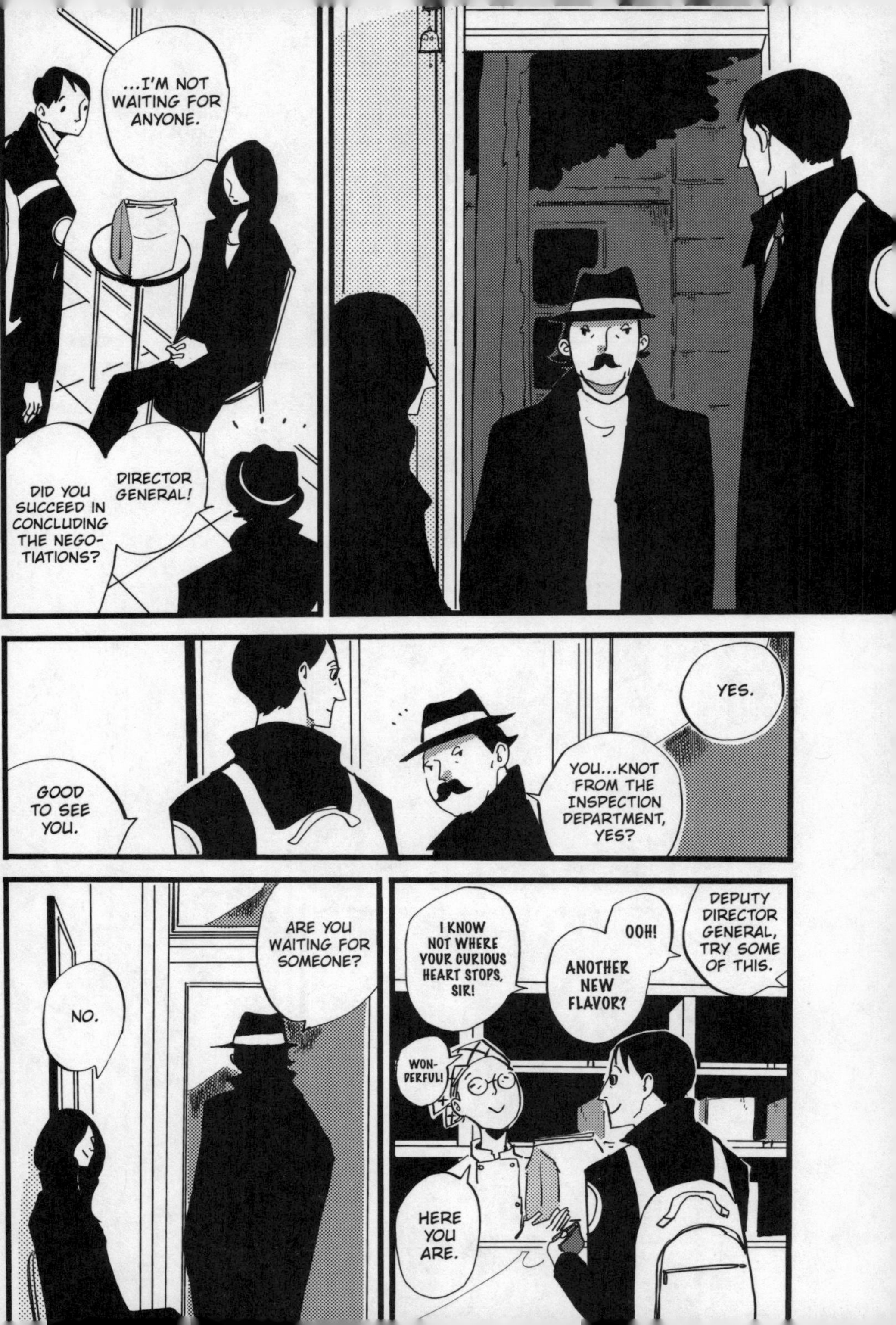
...I'M NOT WAITING FOR ANYONE.
DIRECTOR GENERAL!
DID YOU SUCCEED IN CONCLUDING THE NEGO-TIATIONS?
YES.
YOU...KNOT FROM THE INSPECTION DEPARTMENT, YES?
GOOD TO SEE YOU.
DEPUTY DIRECTOR GENERAL, TRY SOME OF THIS.
OOH!
ANOTHER NEW FLAVOR?
I KNOW NOT WHERE YOUR CURIOUS HEART STOPS, SIR!
WON-DERFUL!
HERE YOU ARE.
ARE YOU WAITING FOR SOMEONE?
NO.

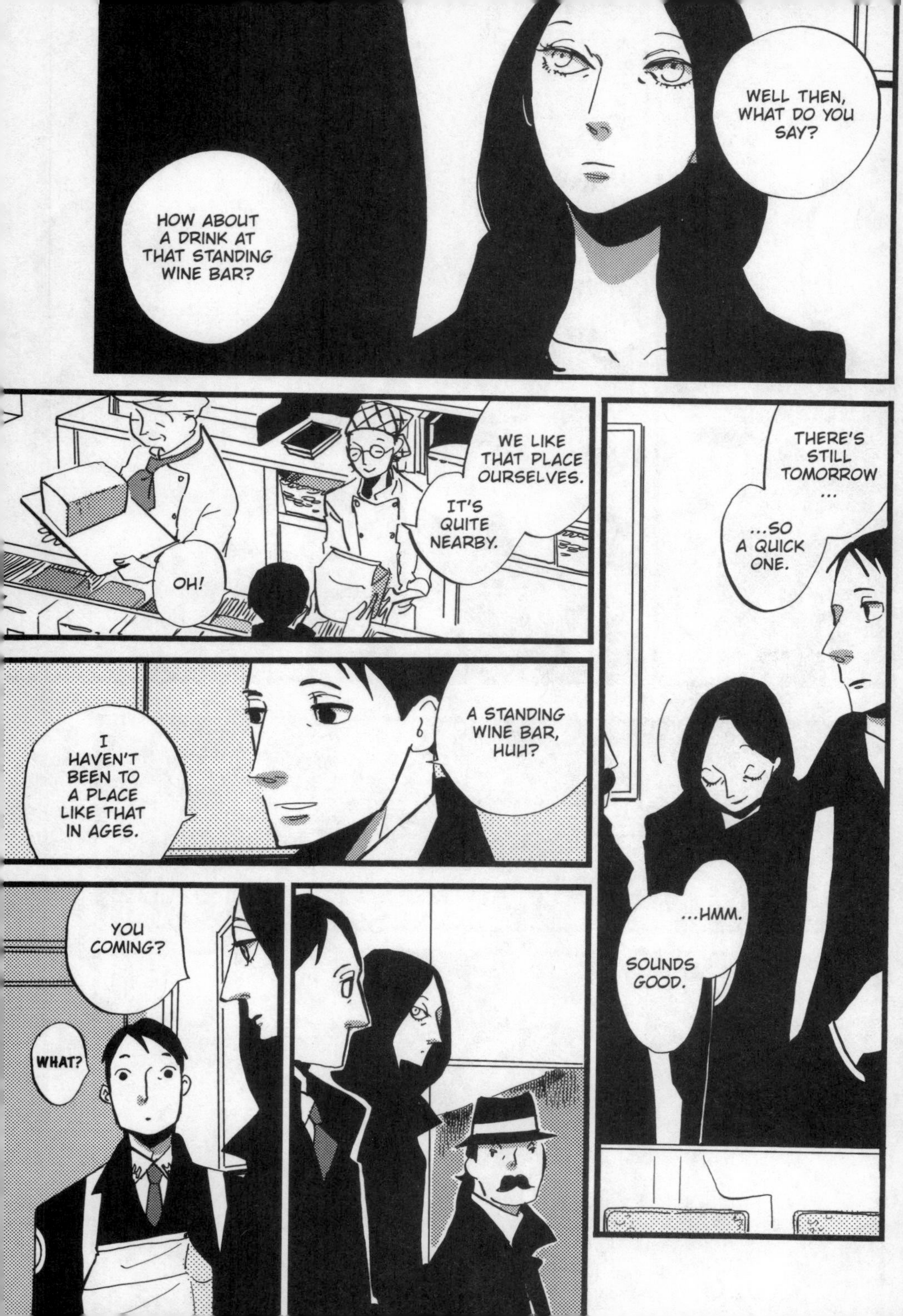
WELL THEN, WHAT DO YOU SAY?
HOW ABOUT A DRINK AT THAT STANDING WINE BAR?
THERE'S STILL TOMORROW ...
...SO A QUICK ONE.
...HMM.
SOUNDS GOOD.
WE LIKE THAT PLACE OURSELVES.
IT'S QUITE NEARBY.
OH!
A STANDING WINE BAR, HUH?
I HAVEN'T BEEN TO A PLACE LIKE THAT IN AGES.
YOU COMING?
WHAT?

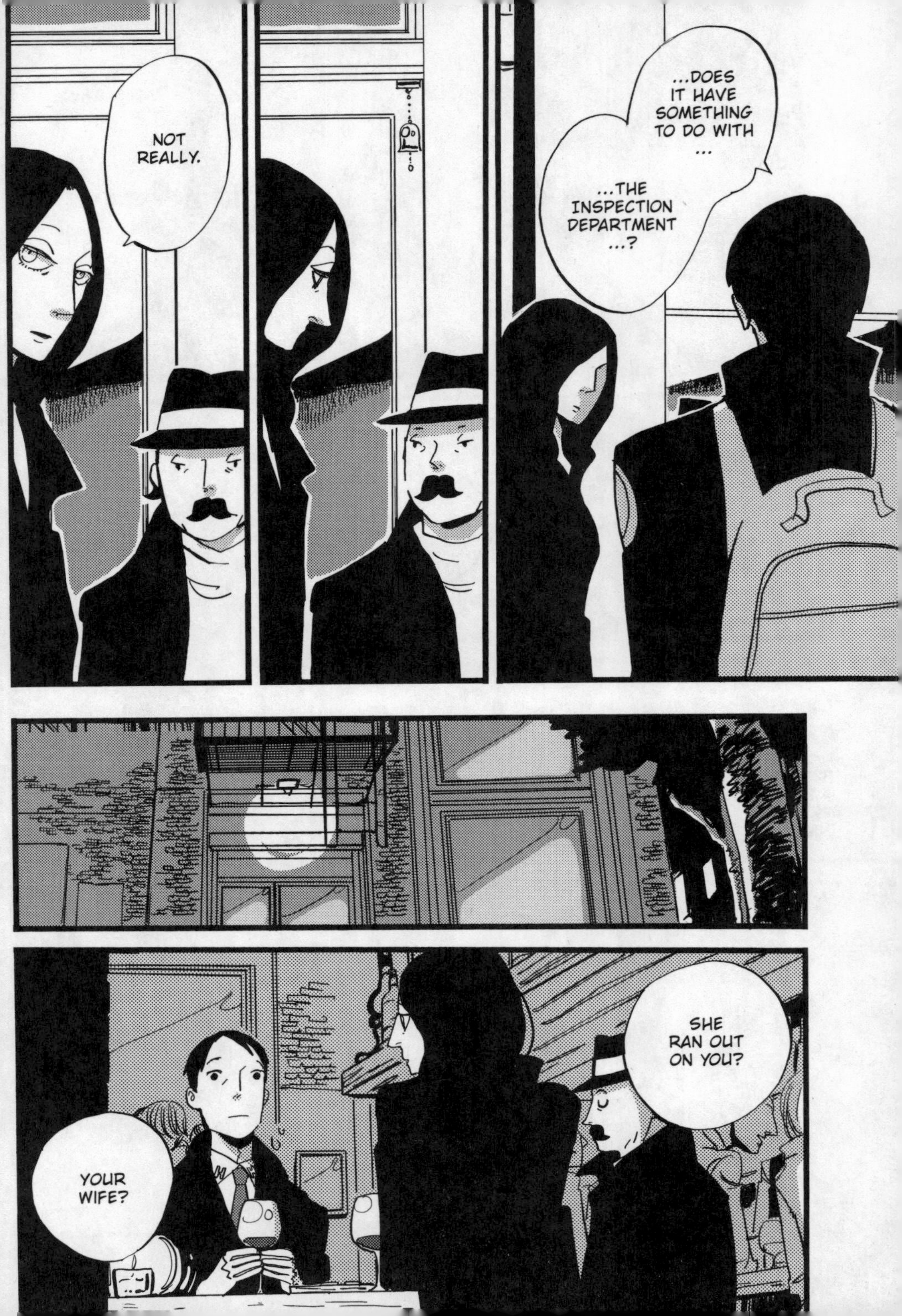
...DOES IT HAVE SOMETHING TO DO WITH ...
...THE INSPECTION DEPARTMENT ...?
NOT REALLY.
SHE RAN OUT ON YOU?
YOUR WIFE?

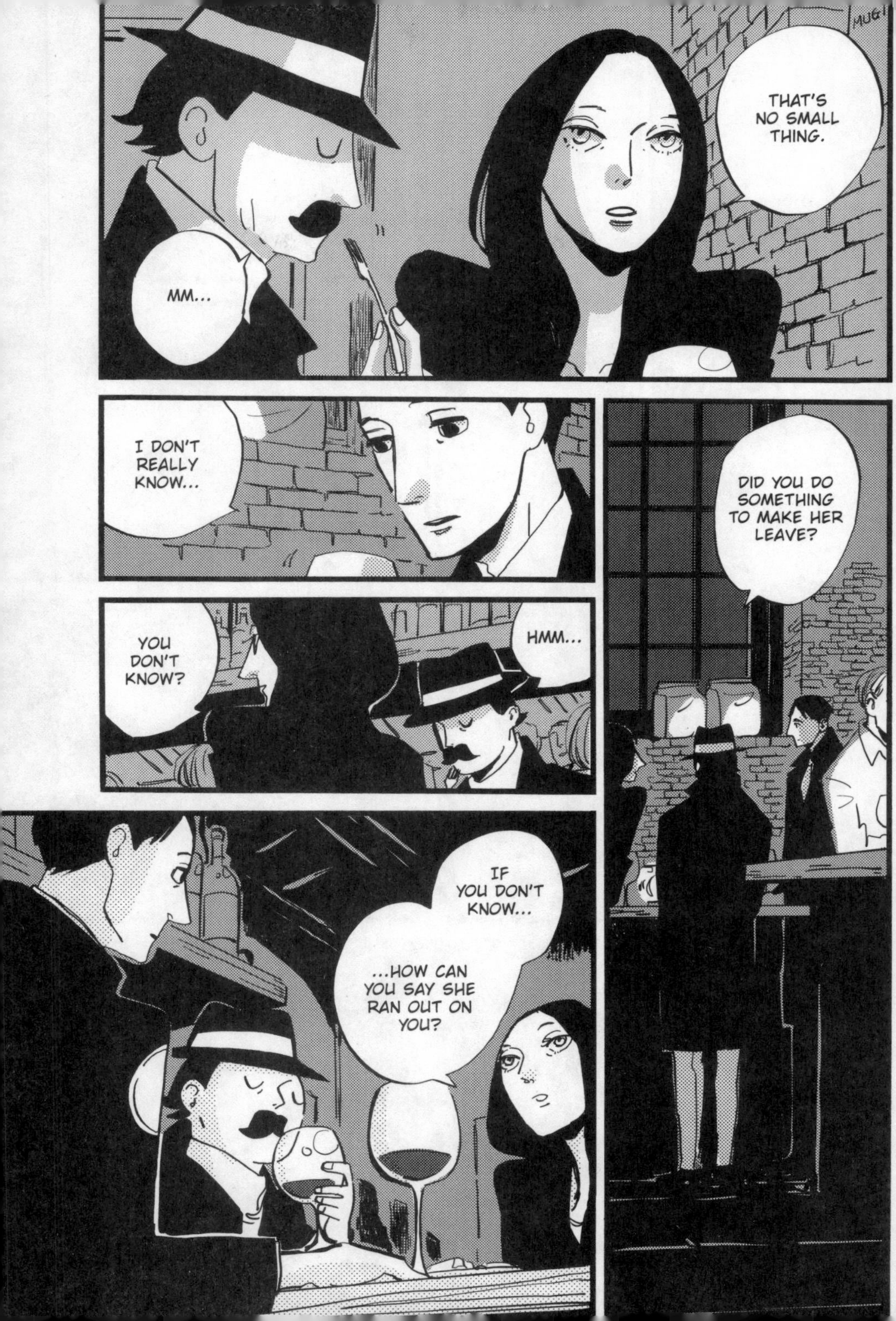
MUGI
THAT'S NO SMALL THING.
MM...
DID YOU DO SOMETHING TO MAKE HER LEAVE?
I DON'T REALLY KNOW...
HMM...
YOU DON'T KNOW?
IF YOU DON'T KNOW...
...HOW CAN YOU SAY SHE RAN OUT ON YOU?

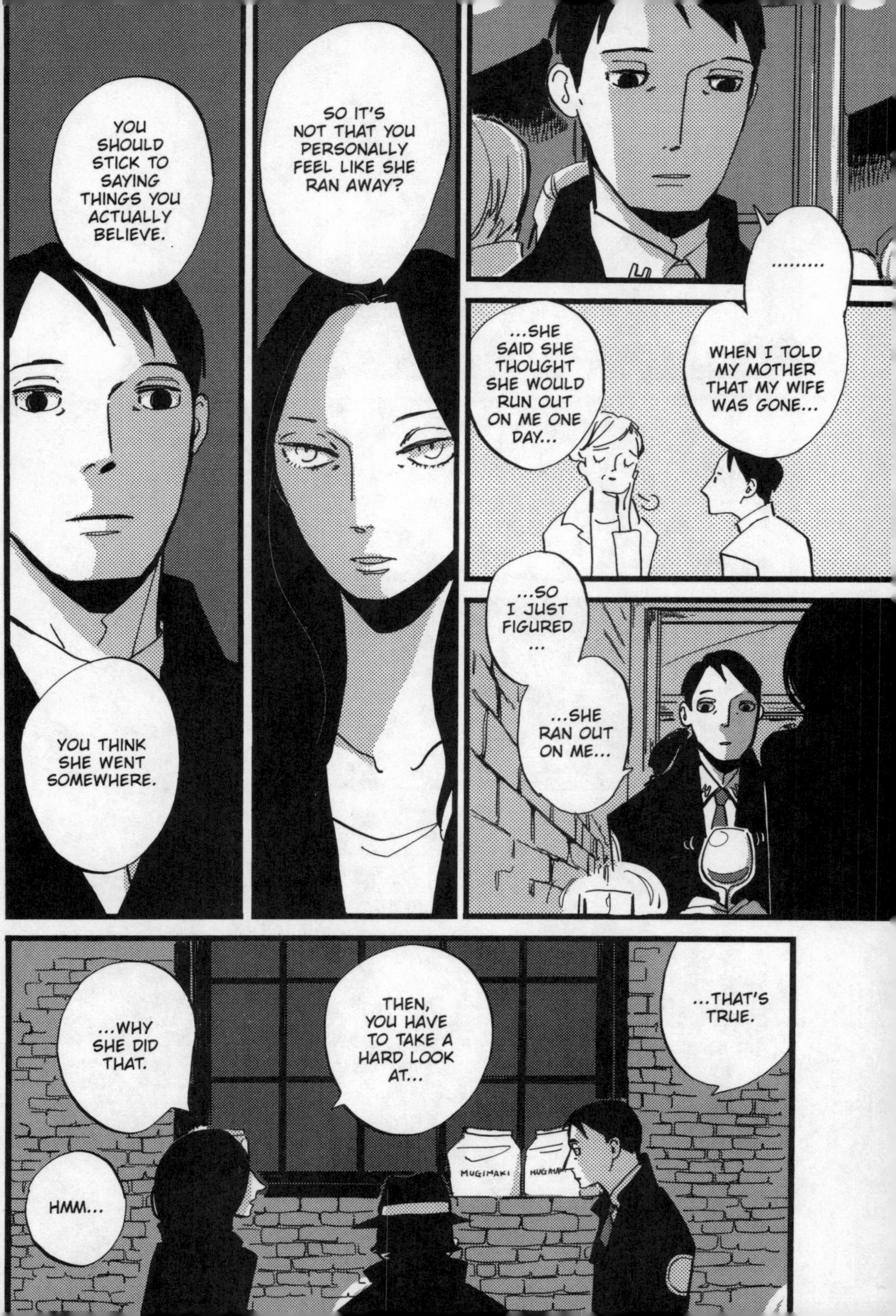
....
WHEN I TOLD MY MOTHER THAT MY WIFE WAS GONE...
...SHE SAID SHE THOUGHT SHE WOULD RUN OUT ON ME ONE DAY...
...SO I JUST FIGURED...
...SHE RAN OUT ON ME...
SO IT'S NOT THAT YOU PERSONALLY FEEL LIKE SHE RAN AWAY?
YOU SHOULD STICK TO SAYING THINGS YOU ACTUALLY BELIEVE.
YOU THINK SHE WENT SOMEWHERE.
...THAT'S TRUE.
THEN, YOU HAVE TO TAKE A HARD LOOK AT...
...WHY SHE DID THAT.
HMM...
MUGIMAKI

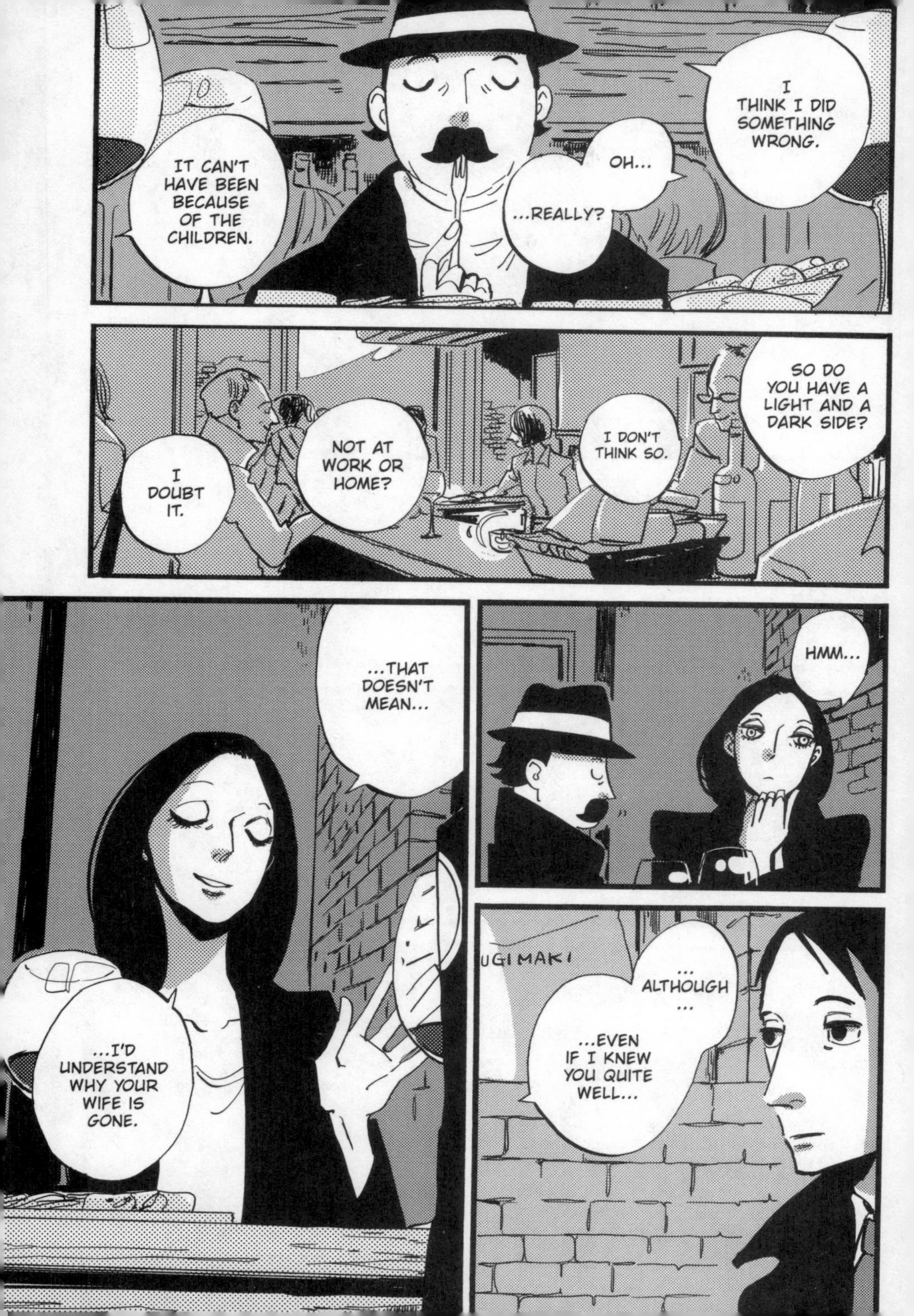
I THINK I DID SOMETHING WRONG.
OH...
...REALLY?
IT CAN'T HAVE BEEN BECAUSE OF THE CHILDREN.
SO DO YOU HAVE A LIGHT AND A DARK SIDE?
I DON'T THINK SO.
NOT AT WORK OR HOME?
I DOUBT IT.
HMM...
... ALTHOUGH ...
...EVEN IF I KNEW YOU QUITE WELL...
...THAT DOESN'T MEAN...
...I'D UNDERSTAND WHY YOUR WIFE IS GONE.

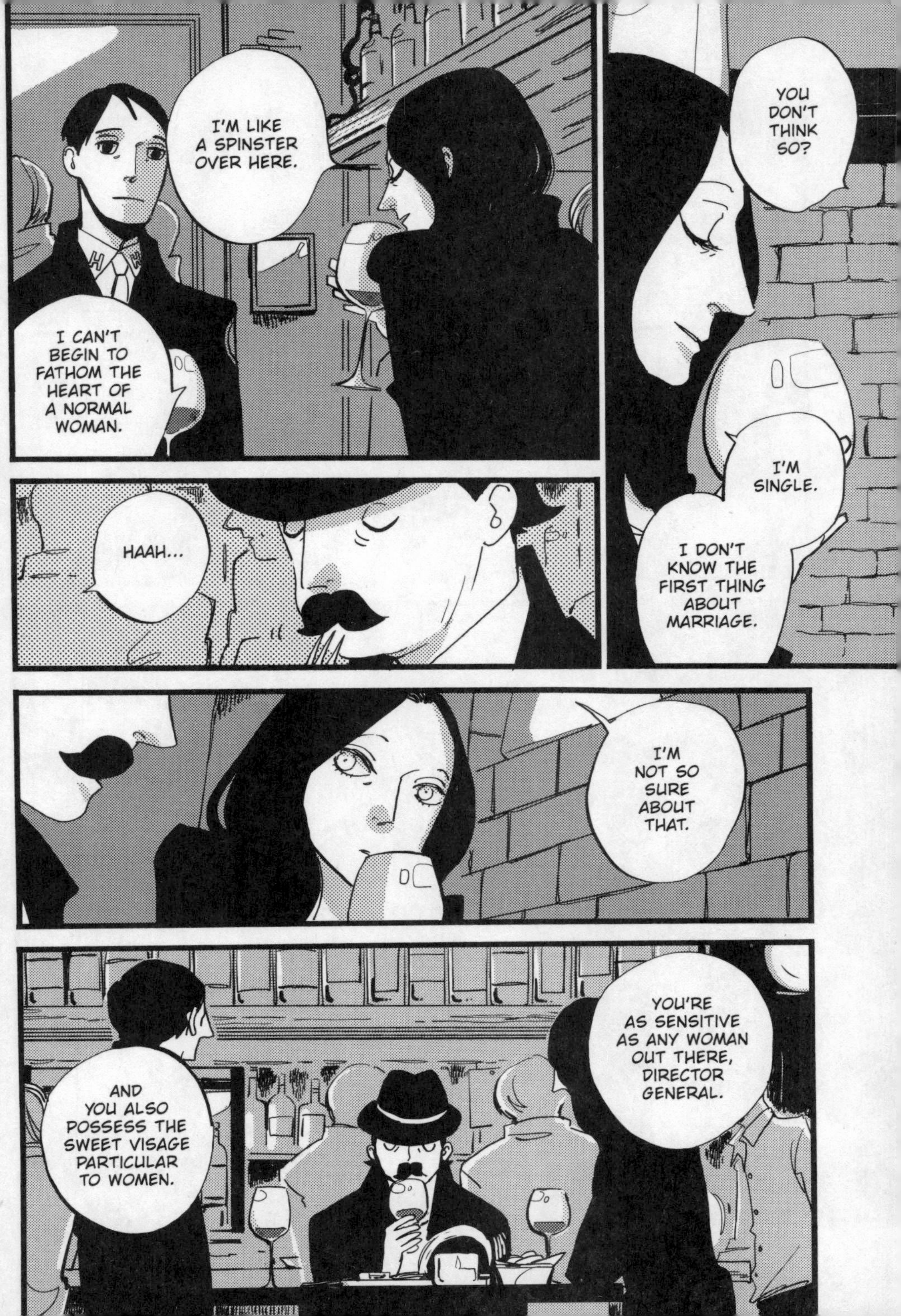
YOU DON'T THINK SO?
I'M SINGLE.
I DON'T KNOW THE FIRST THING ABOUT MARRIAGE.
I'M LIKE A SPINSTER OVER HERE.
I CAN'T BEGIN TO FATHOM THE HEART OF A NORMAL WOMAN.
HAAH...
I'M NOT SO SURE ABOUT THAT.
YOU'RE AS SENSITIVE AS ANY WOMAN OUT THERE, DIRECTOR GENERAL.
AND YOU ALSO POSSESS THE SWEET VISAGE PARTICULAR TO WOMEN.

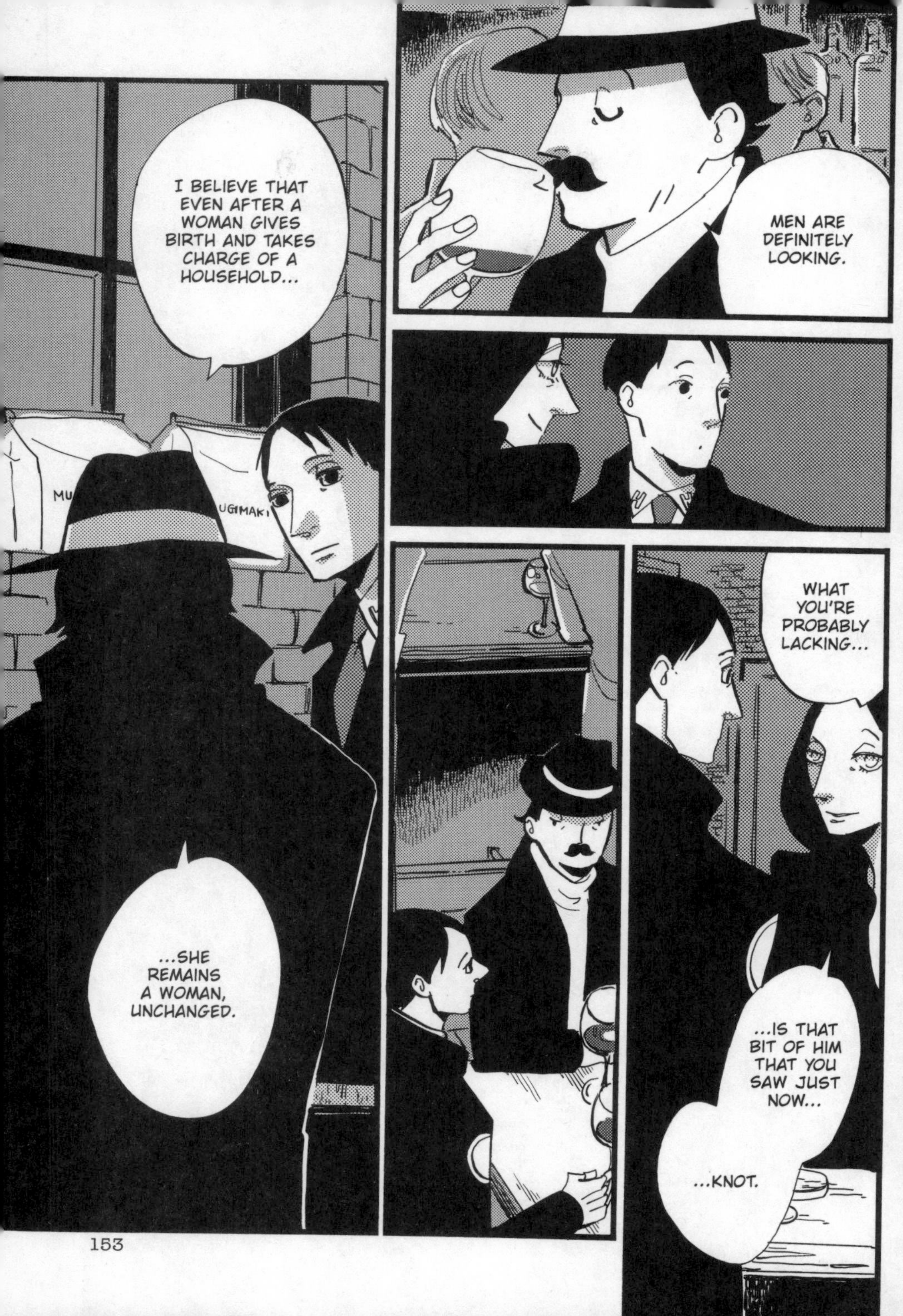
MEN ARE DEFINITELY LOOKING.
WHAT YOU'RE PROBABLY LACKING...
...IS THAT BIT OF HIM THAT YOU SAW JUST NOW...
...KNOT.
I BELIEVE THAT EVEN AFTER A WOMAN GIVES BIRTH AND TAKES CHARGE OF A HOUSEHOLD...
MU
UGIMAKI
...SHE REMAINS A WOMAN, UNCHANGED.

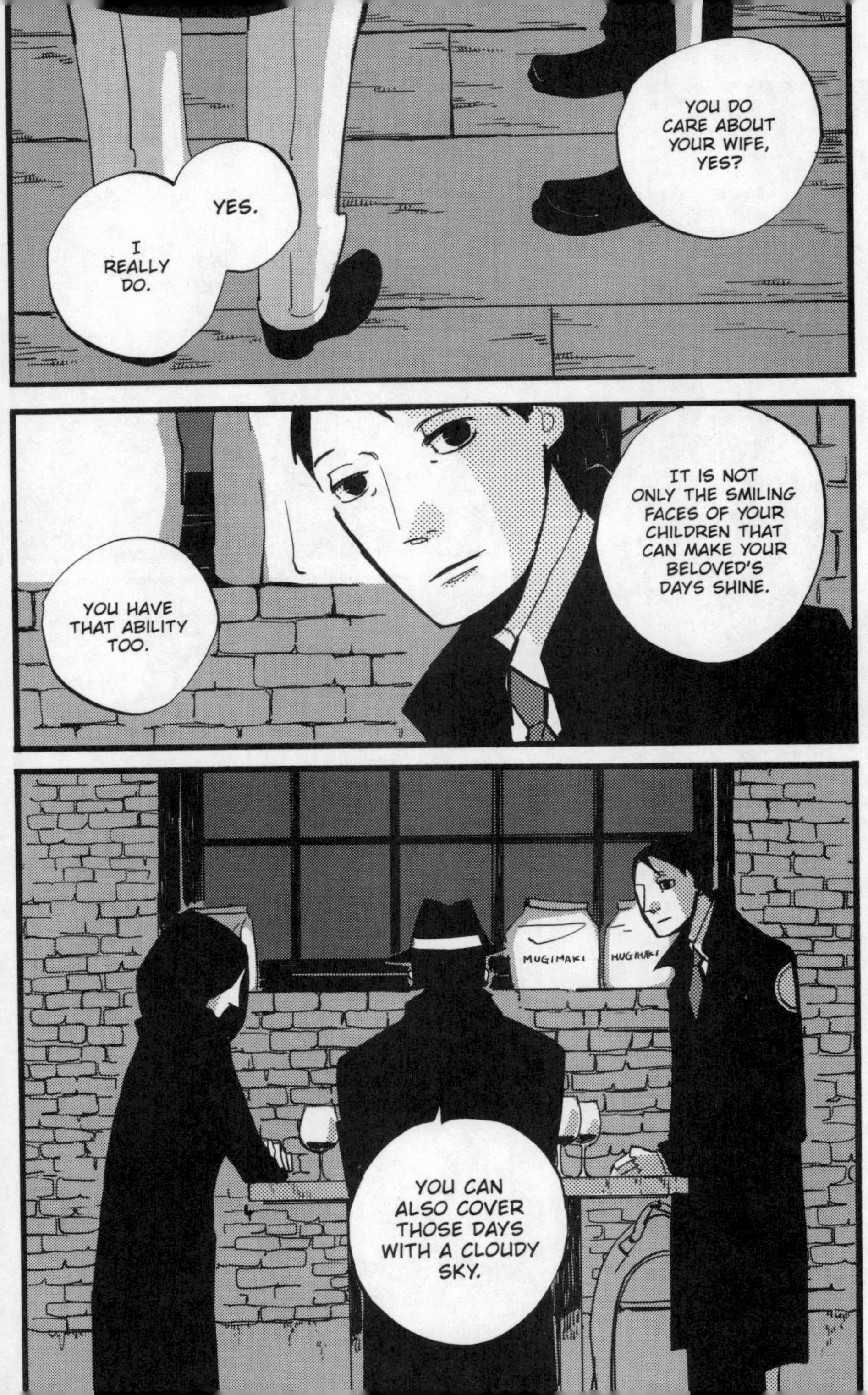
YOU DO CARE ABOUT YOUR WIFE, YES?
YES.
I REALLY DO.
IT IS NOT ONLY THE SMILING FACES OF YOUR CHILDREN THAT CAN MAKE YOUR BELOVED'S DAYS SHINE.
YOU HAVE THAT ABILITY TOO.
MUGIMAKI
MUGIMAKI
YOU CAN ALSO COVER THOSE DAYS WITH A CLOUDY SKY.

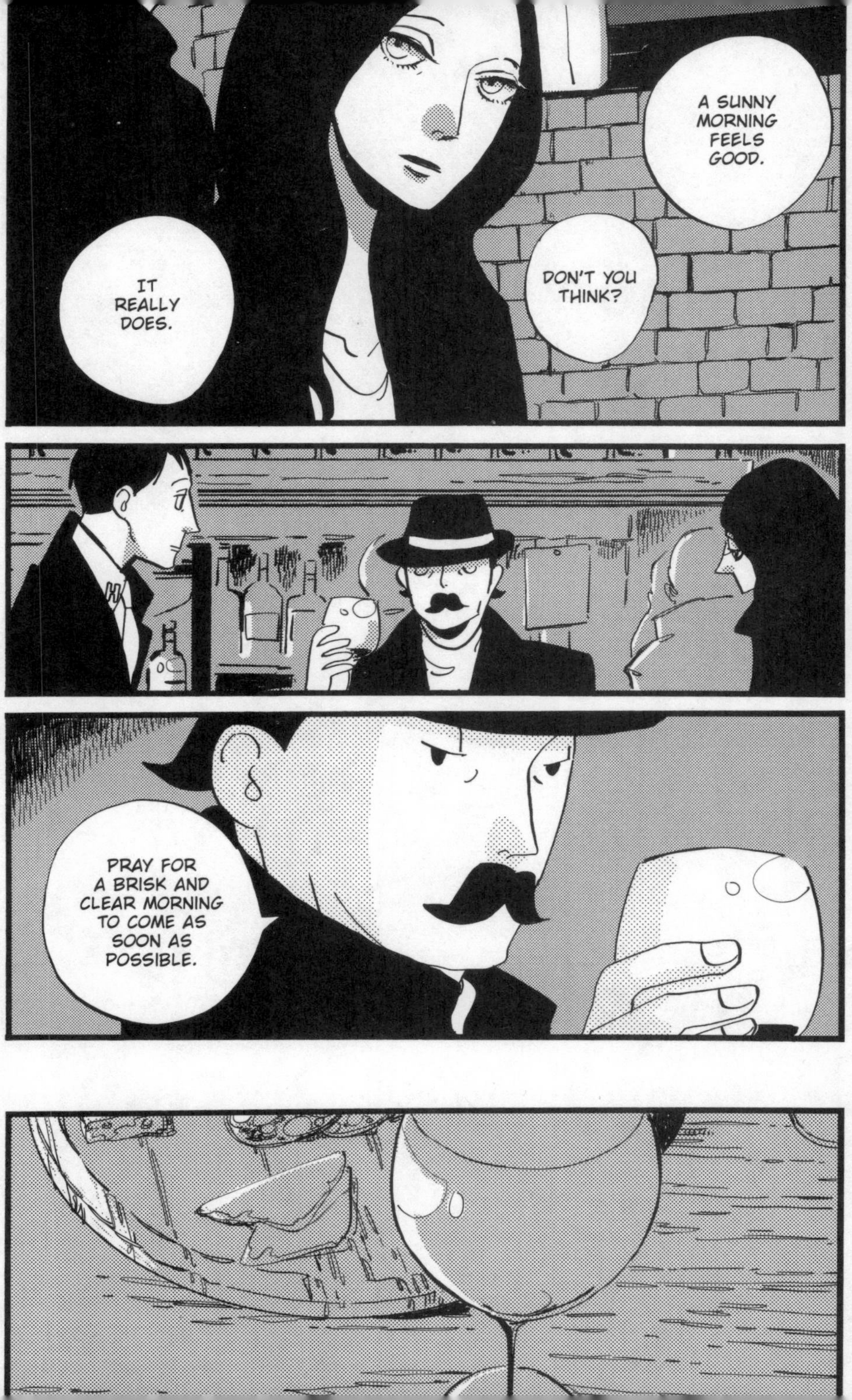
A SUNNY MORNING FEELS GOOD.
DON'T YOU THINK?
IT REALLY DOES.
PRAY FOR A BRISK AND CLEAR MORNING TO COME AS SOON AS POSSIBLE.

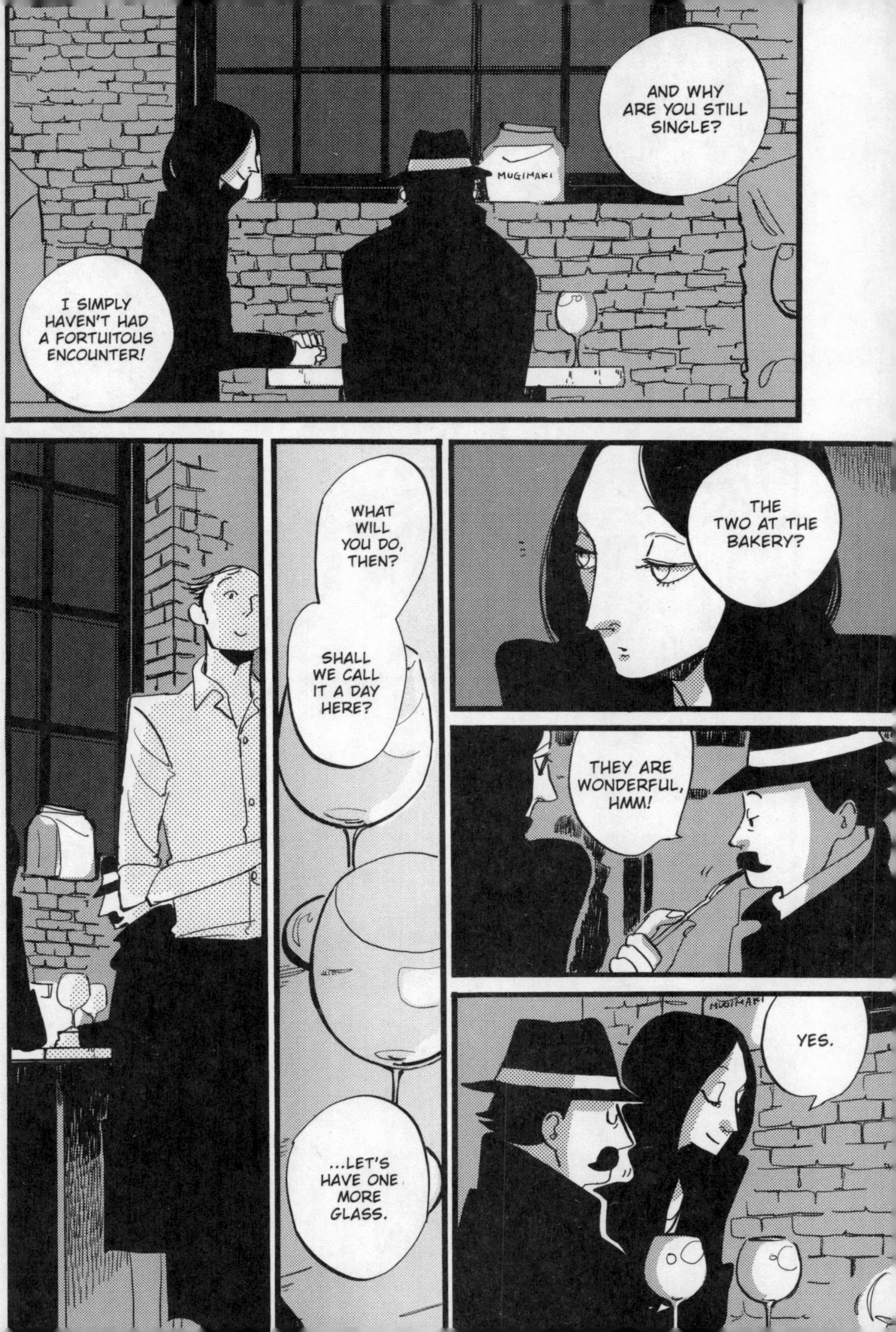
AND WHY ARE YOU STILL SINGLE?
MUGIMAKI
I SIMPLY HAVEN'T HAD A FORTUITOUS ENCOUNTER!
THE TWO AT THE BAKERY?
THEY ARE WONDERFUL, HMM!
MUGIMAKI
YES.
WHAT WILL YOU DO, THEN?
SHALL WE CALL IT A DAY HERE?
...LET'S HAVE ONE MORE GLASS.

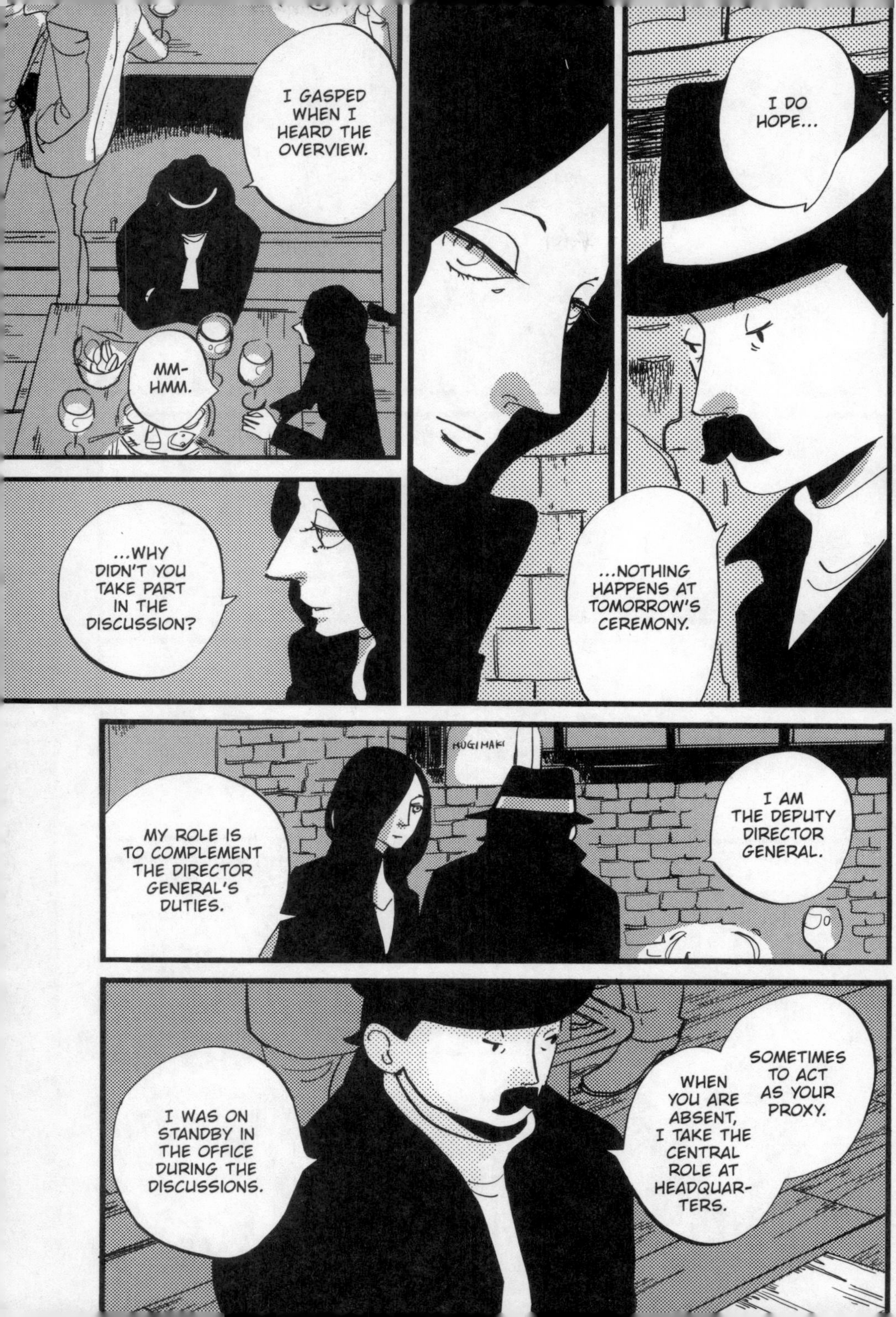
I DO HOPE...
...NOTHING HAPPENS AT TOMORROW'S CEREMONY.
I GASPED WHEN I HEARD THE OVERVIEW.
MM-HMM.
...WHY DIDN'T YOU TAKE PART IN THE DISCUSSION?
MUGIMAKI
I AM THE DEPUTY DIRECTOR GENERAL.
MY ROLE IS TO COMPLEMENT THE DIRECTOR GENERAL'S DUTIES.
SOMETIMES TO ACT AS YOUR PROXY.
WHEN YOU ARE ABSENT, I TAKE THE CENTRAL ROLE AT HEADQUAR-TERS.
I WAS ON STANDBY IN THE OFFICE DURING THE DISCUSSIONS.

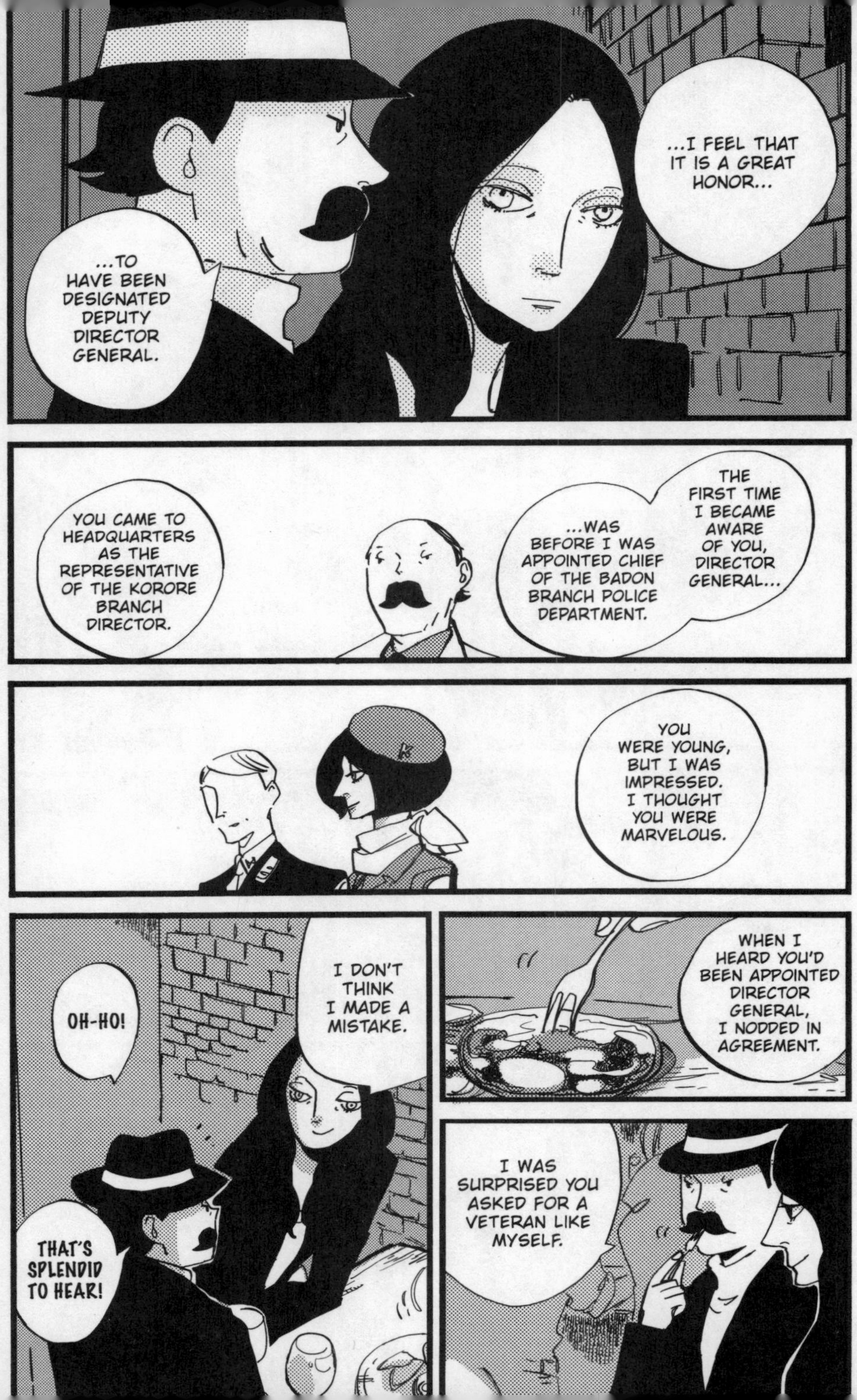
...I FEEL THAT IT IS A GREAT HONOR...
...TO HAVE BEEN DESIGNATED DEPUTY DIRECTOR GENERAL.
THE FIRST TIME I BECAME AWARE OF YOU, DIRECTOR GENERAL...
...WAS BEFORE I WAS APPOINTED CHIEF OF THE BADON BRANCH POLICE DEPARTMENT.
YOU CAME TO HEADQUARTERS AS THE REPRESENTATIVE OF THE KORORE BRANCH DIRECTOR.
YOU WERE YOUNG, BUT I WAS IMPRESSED. I THOUGHT YOU WERE MARVELOUS.
WHEN I HEARD YOU'D BEEN APPOINTED DIRECTOR GENERAL, I NODDED IN AGREEMENT.
I WAS SURPRISED YOU ASKED FOR A VETERAN LIKE MYSELF.
I DON'T THINK I MADE A MISTAKE.
OH-HO!
THAT'S SPLENDID TO HEAR!

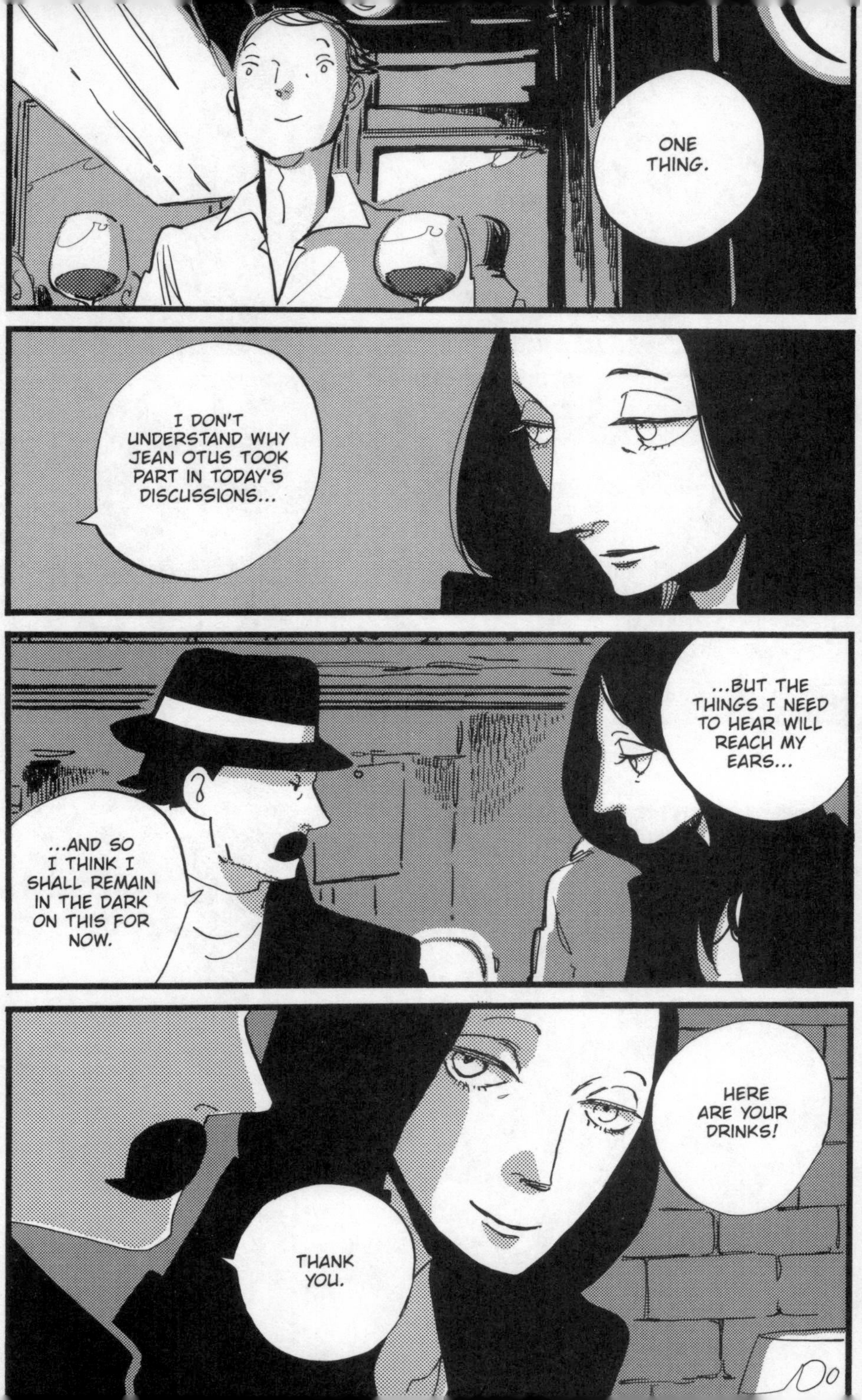
ONE THING.
I DON'T UNDERSTAND WHY JEAN OTUS TOOK PART IN TODAY'S DISCUSSIONS...
...BUT THE THINGS I NEED TO HEAR WILL REACH MY EARS...
...AND SO I THINK I SHALL REMAIN IN THE DARK ON THIS FOR NOW.
HERE ARE YOUR DRINKS!
THANK YOU.

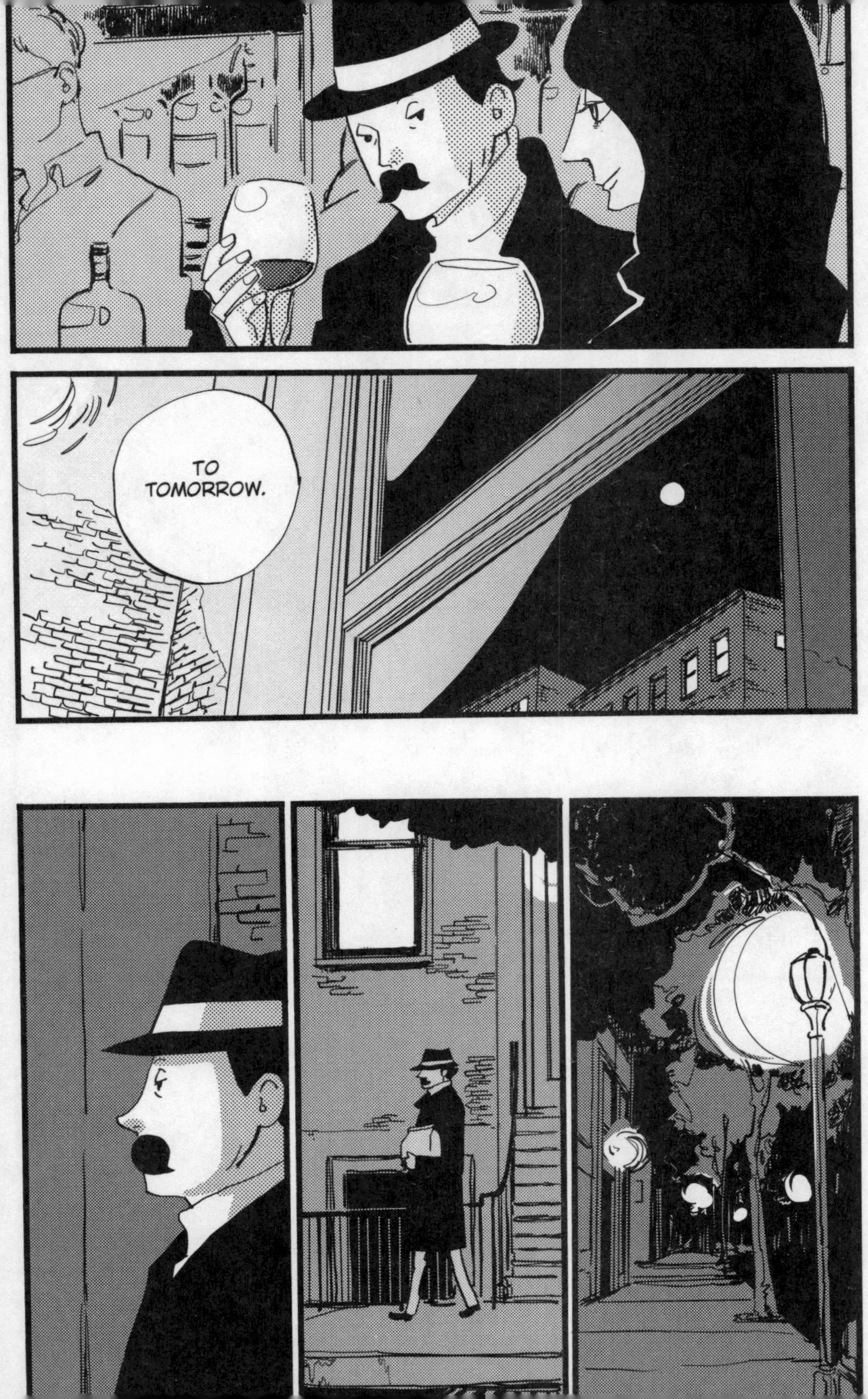
TO TOMORROW.

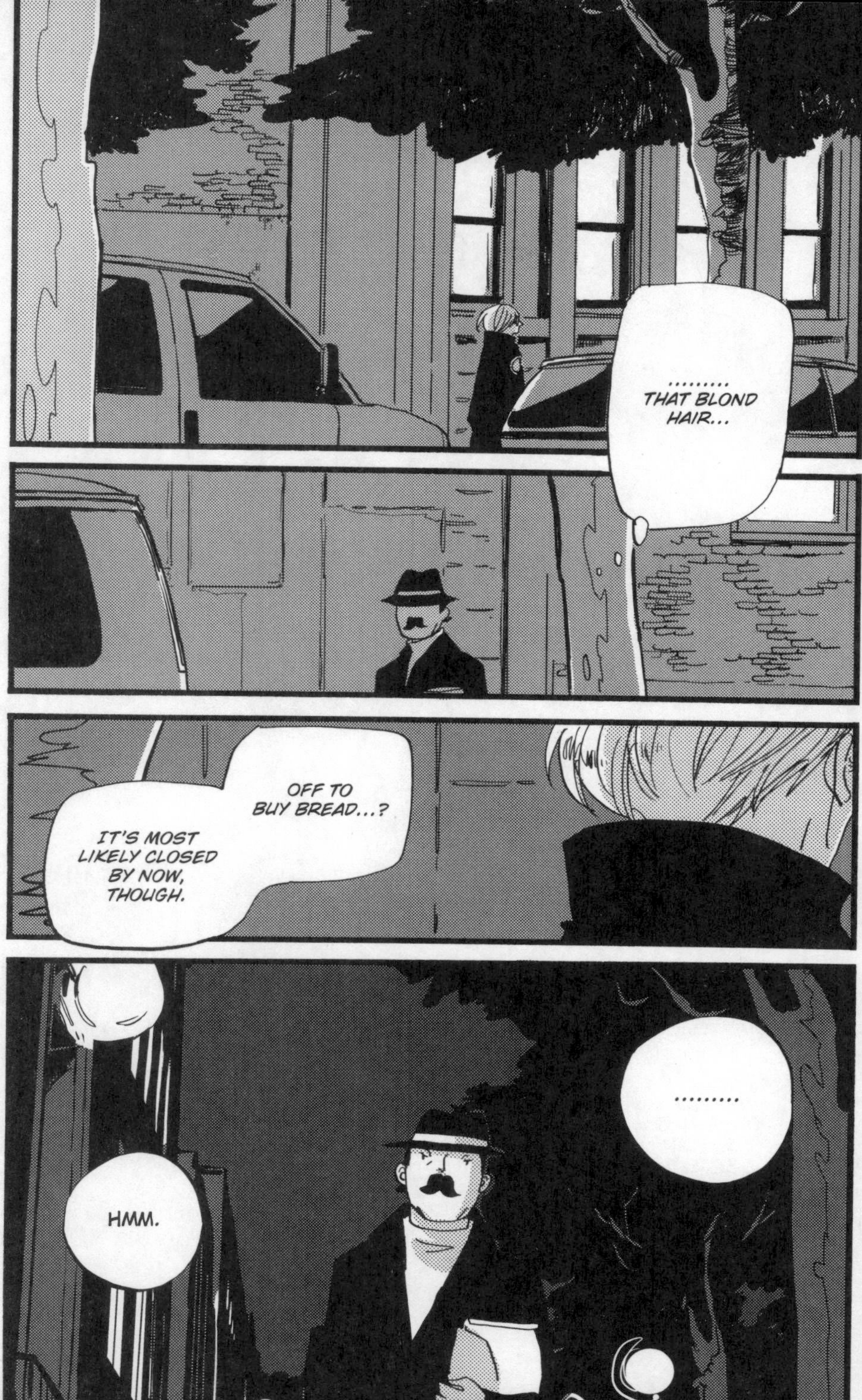
....
THAT BLOND HAIR...
OFF TO BUY BREAD...?
IT'S MOST LIKELY CLOSED BY NOW, THOUGH.
....
HMM.

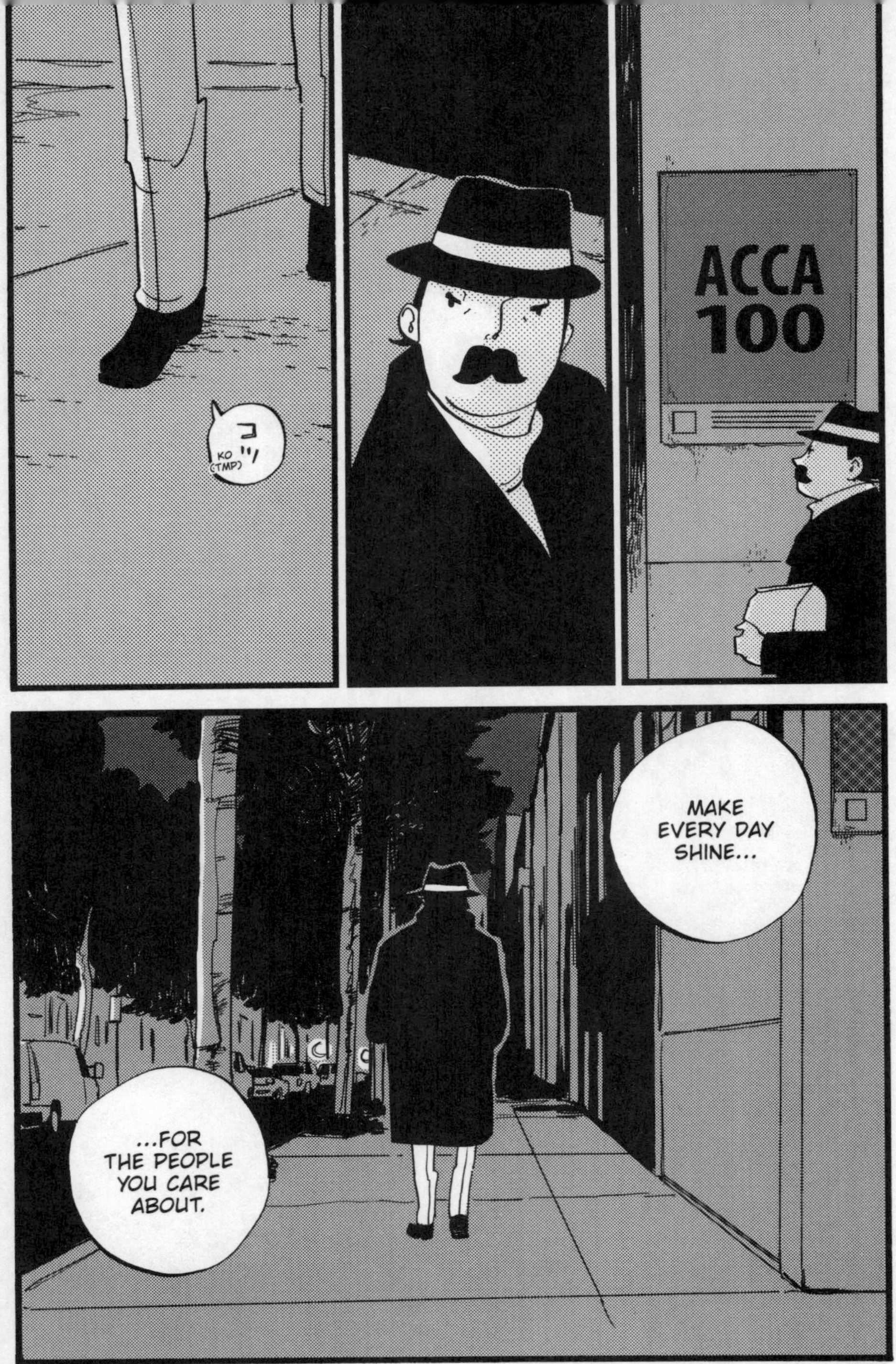
ACCA 100
コツ
KO (TMP)
MAKE EVERY DAY SHINE...
...FOR THE PEOPLE YOU CARE ABOUT.

CHAPTER 10

Tonight, Pray for Tomorrow's Sky

P.S.

INSPECTION DEPT ACCA 13 TERRITORY

PASS

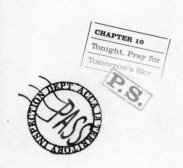

FINAL CHAPTER

The Dinner Party

P.S.

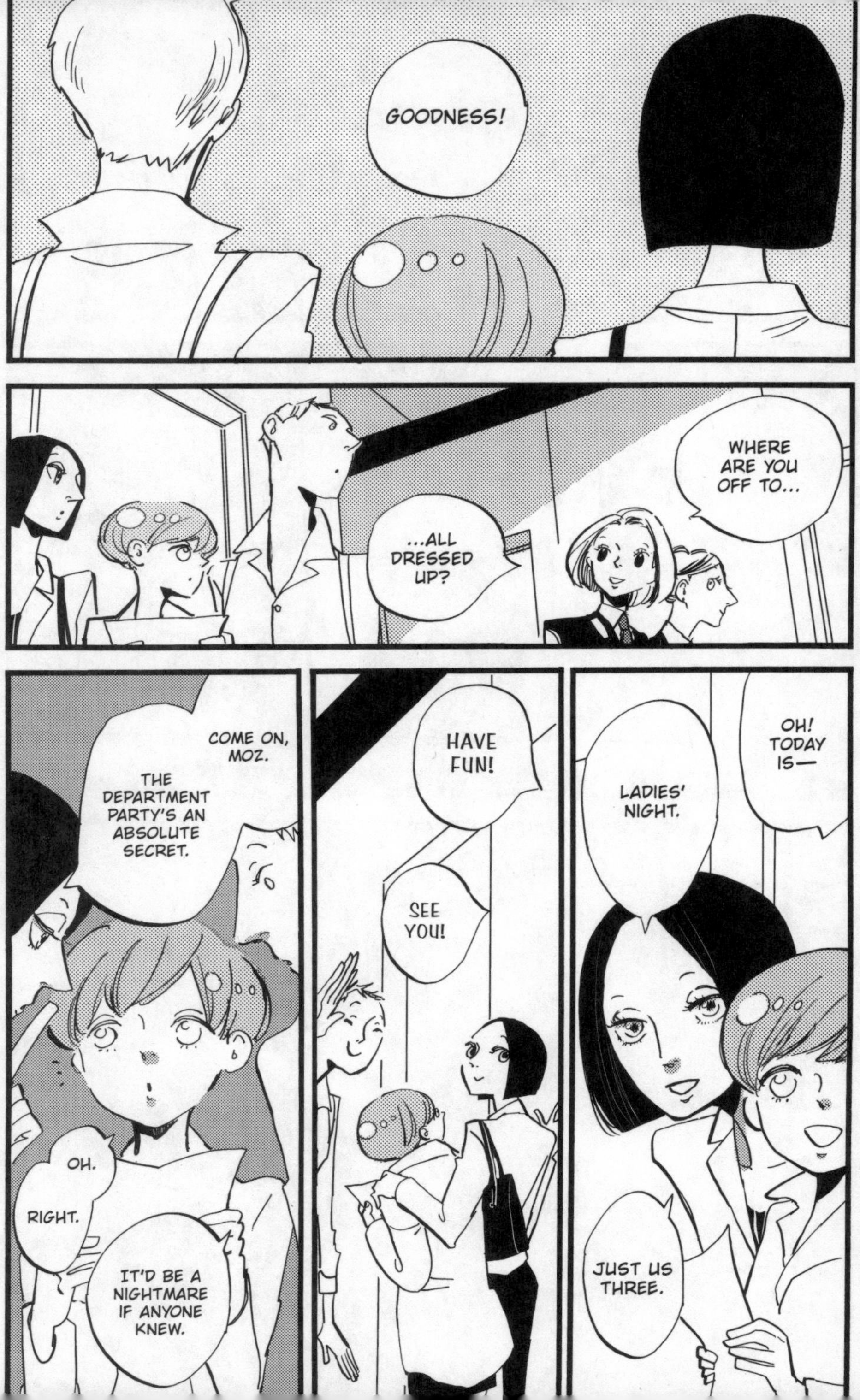
GOODNESS!
WHERE ARE YOU OFF TO...
...ALL DRESSED UP?
OH! TODAY IS—
LADIES' NIGHT.
JUST US THREE.
HAVE FUN!
SEE YOU!
COME ON, MOZ.
THE DEPARTMENT PARTY'S AN ABSOLUTE SECRET.
OH.
RIGHT.
IT'D BE A NIGHTMARE IF ANYONE KNEW.

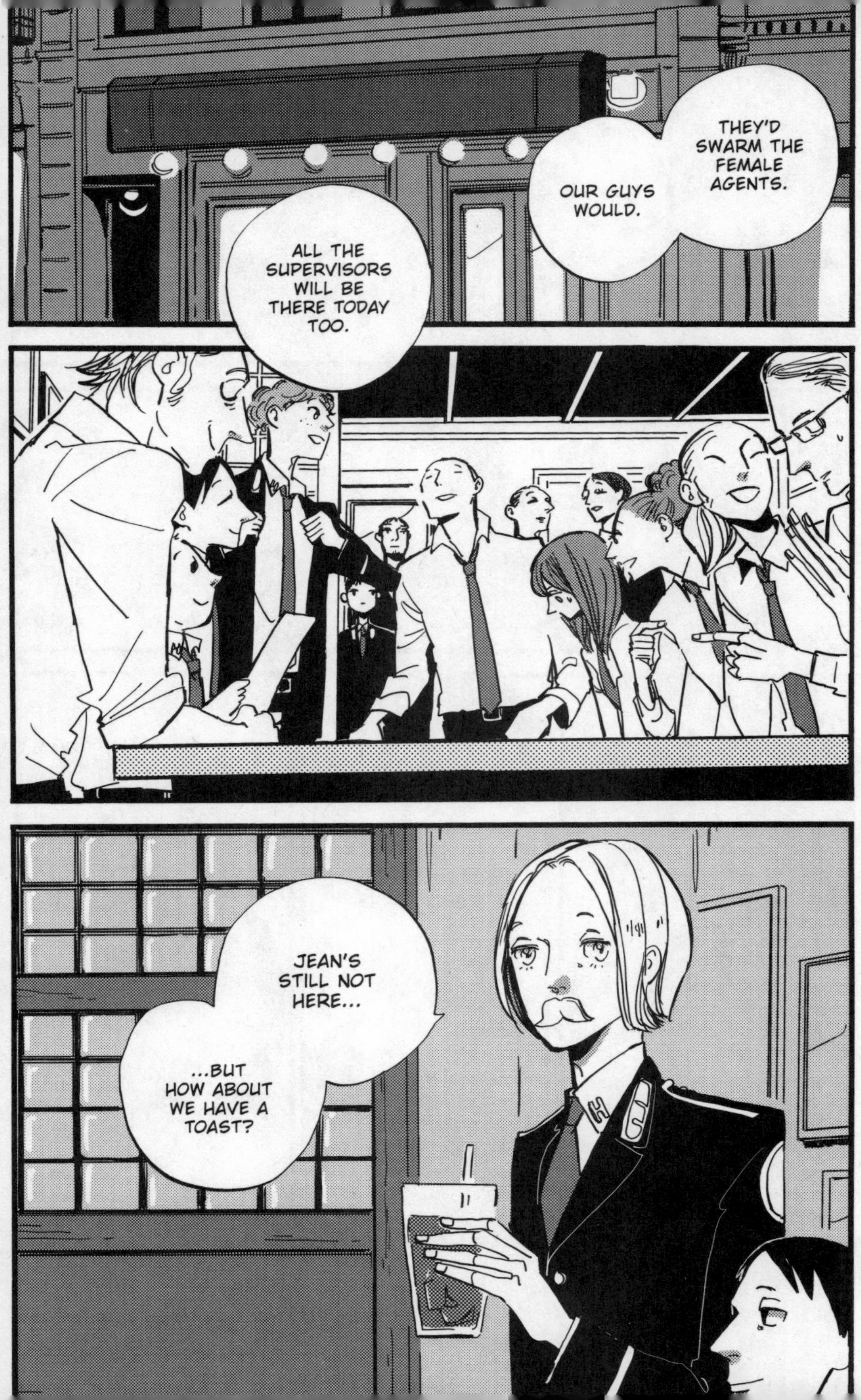
THEY'D SWARM THE FEMALE AGENTS.
OUR GUYS WOULD.
ALL THE SUPERVISORS WILL BE THERE TODAY TOO.
JEAN'S STILL NOT HERE...
...BUT HOW ABOUT WE HAVE A TOAST?

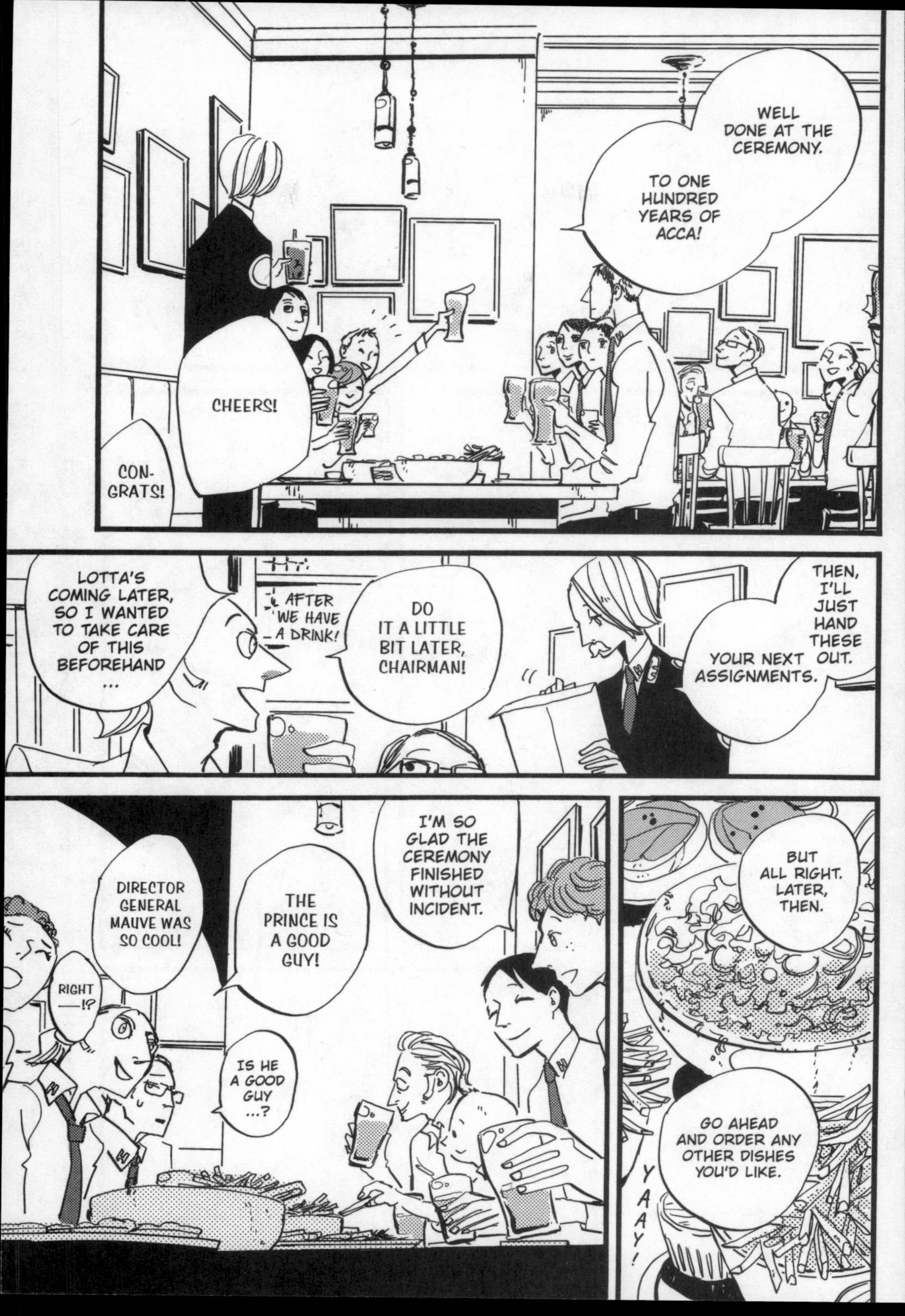
WELL DONE AT THE CEREMONY.
TO ONE HUNDRED YEARS OF ACCA!
CHEERS!
CON-GRATS!
THEN, I'LL JUST HAND THESE OUT.
YOUR NEXT ASSIGNMENTS.
DO IT A LITTLE BIT LATER, CHAIRMAN!
AFTER WE HAVE A DRINK!
LOTTA'S COMING LATER, SO I WANTED TO TAKE CARE OF THIS BEFOREHAND...
BUT ALL RIGHT. LATER, THEN.
GO AHEAD AND ORDER ANY OTHER DISHES YOU'D LIKE.
YAAY!
I'M SO GLAD THE CEREMONY FINISHED WITHOUT INCIDENT.
THE PRINCE IS A GOOD GUY!
DIRECTOR GENERAL MAUVE WAS SO COOL!
RIGHT—!?
IS HE A GOOD GUY...?

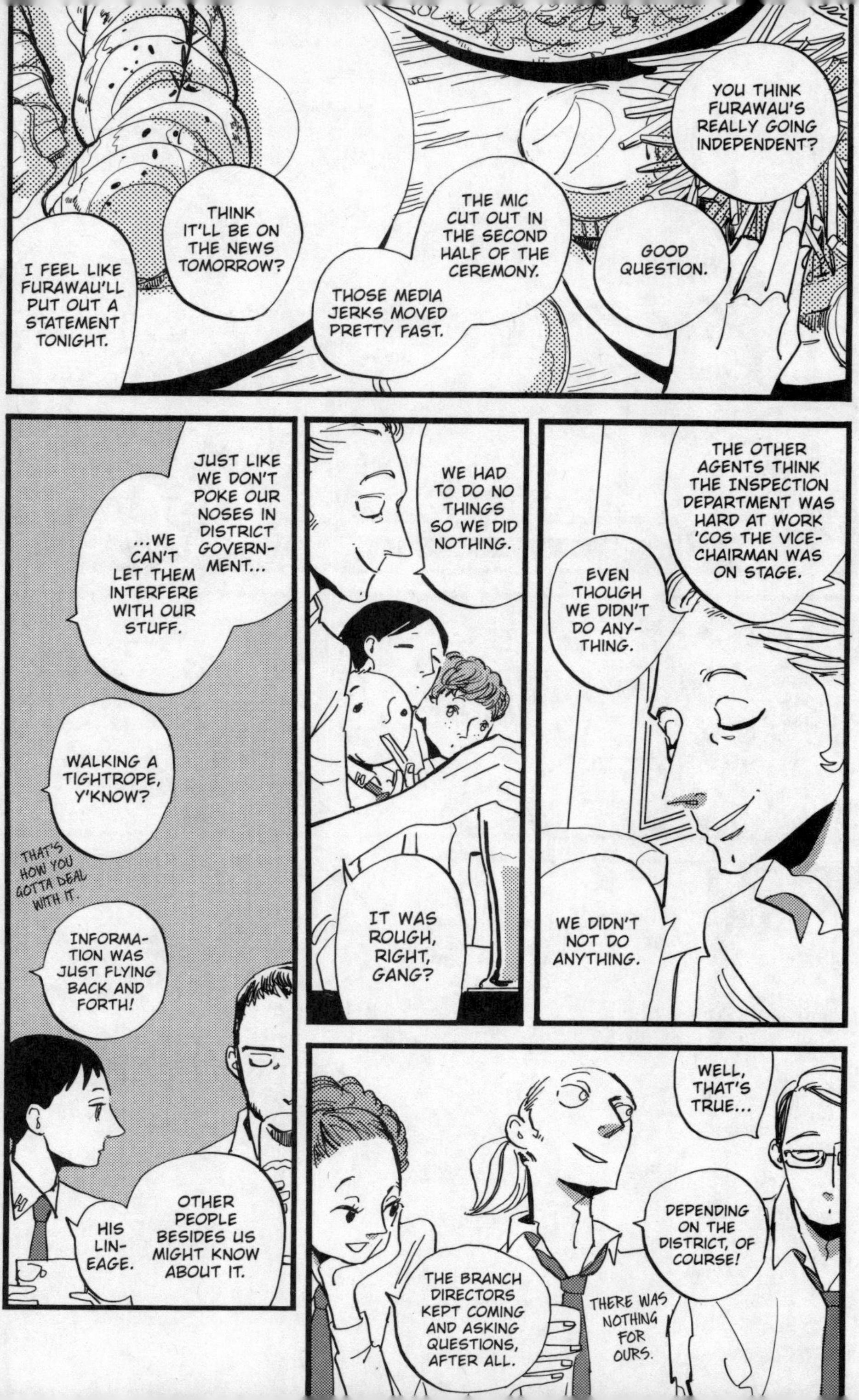
YOU THINK FURAWAU'S REALLY GOING INDEPENDENT?
GOOD QUESTION.
THE MIC CUT OUT IN THE SECOND HALF OF THE CEREMONY.
THOSE MEDIA JERKS MOVED PRETTY FAST.
THINK IT'LL BE ON THE NEWS TOMORROW?
I FEEL LIKE FURAWAU'LL PUT OUT A STATEMENT TONIGHT.
THE OTHER AGENTS THINK THE INSPECTION DEPARTMENT WAS HARD AT WORK 'COS THE VICE-CHAIRMAN WAS ON STAGE.
EVEN THOUGH WE DIDN'T DO ANYTHING.
WE DIDN'T NOT DO ANYTHING.
WE HAD TO DO NO THINGS SO WE DID NOTHING.
IT WAS ROUGH, RIGHT, GANG?
WELL, THAT'S TRUE...
DEPENDING ON THE DISTRICT, OF COURSE!
THERE WAS NOTHING FOR OURS.
THE BRANCH DIRECTORS KEPT COMING AND ASKING QUESTIONS, AFTER ALL.
JUST LIKE WE DON'T POKE OUR NOSES IN DISTRICT GOVERNMENT...
...WE CAN'T LET THEM INTERFERE WITH OUR STUFF.
WALKING A TIGHTROPE, Y'KNOW?
THAT'S HOW YOU GOTTA DEAL WITH IT.
INFORMATION WAS JUST FLYING BACK AND FORTH!
OTHER PEOPLE BESIDES US MIGHT KNOW ABOUT IT.
HIS LINEAGE.

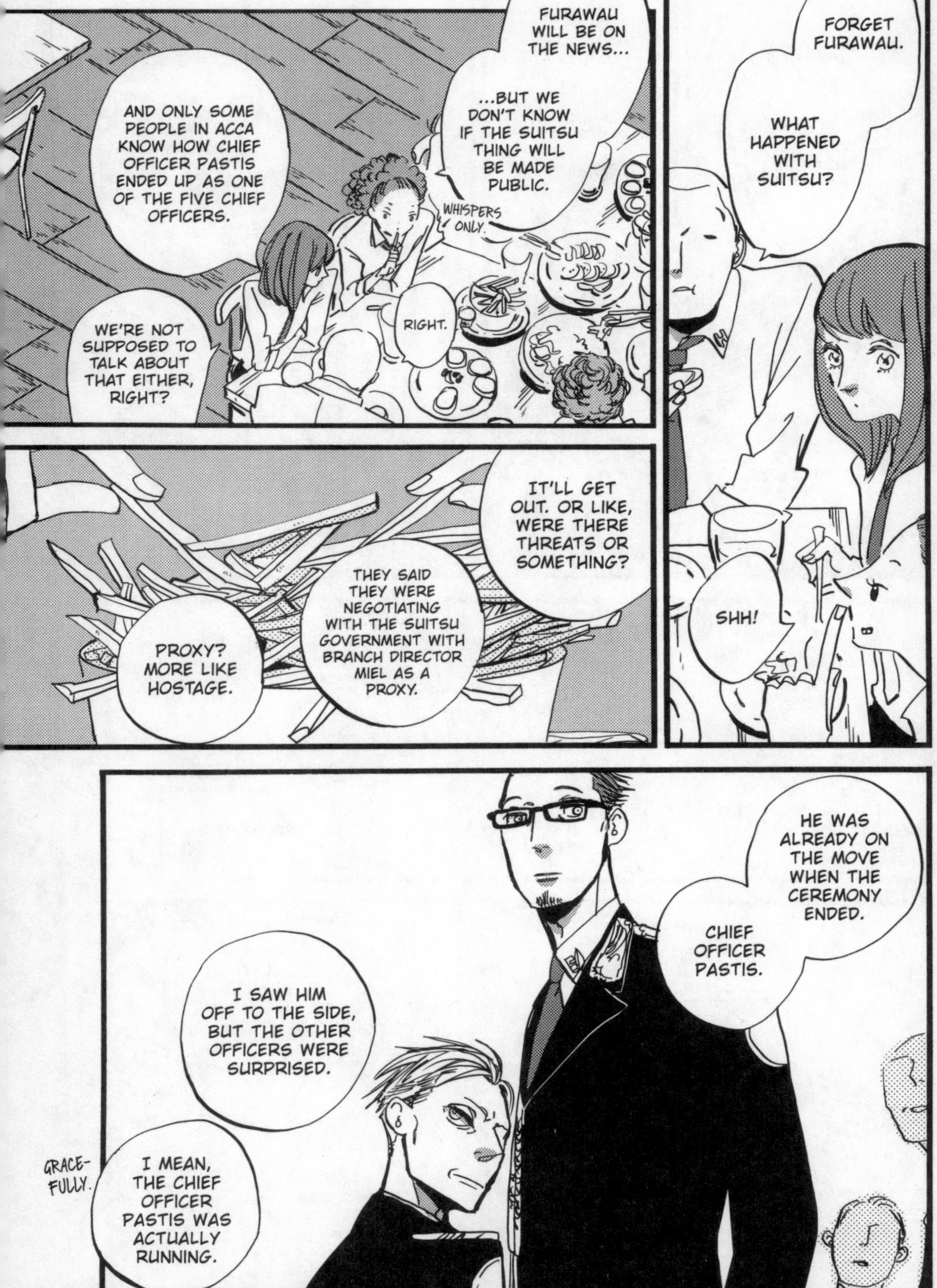
FORGET FURAWAU.
WHAT HAPPENED WITH SUITSU?
SHH!
FURAWAU WILL BE ON THE NEWS...
...BUT WE DON'T KNOW IF THE SUITSU THING WILL BE MADE PUBLIC.
WHISPERS ONLY.
AND ONLY SOME PEOPLE IN ACCA KNOW HOW CHIEF OFFICER PASTIS ENDED UP AS ONE OF THE FIVE CHIEF OFFICERS.
RIGHT.
WE'RE NOT SUPPOSED TO TALK ABOUT THAT EITHER, RIGHT?
IT'LL GET OUT. OR LIKE, WERE THERE THREATS OR SOMETHING?
THEY SAID THEY WERE NEGOTIATING WITH THE SUITSU GOVERNMENT WITH BRANCH DIRECTOR MIEL AS A PROXY.
PROXY? MORE LIKE HOSTAGE.
HE WAS ALREADY ON THE MOVE WHEN THE CEREMONY ENDED.
CHIEF OFFICER PASTIS.
I SAW HIM OFF TO THE SIDE, BUT THE OTHER OFFICERS WERE SURPRISED.
I MEAN, THE CHIEF OFFICER PASTIS WAS ACTUALLY RUNNING.
GRACE-FULLY.

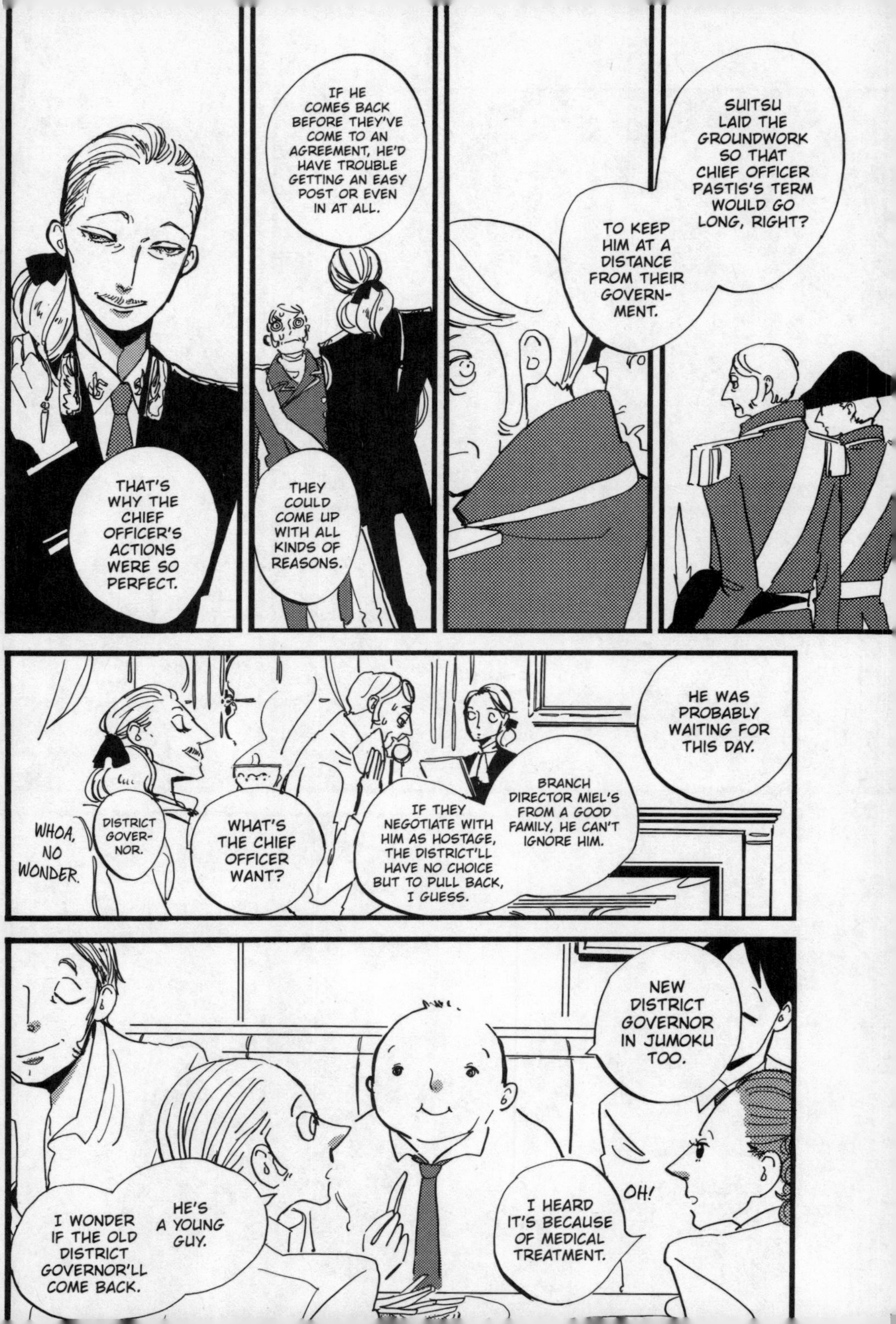
SUITSU LAID THE GROUNDWORK SO THAT CHIEF OFFICER PASTIS'S TERM WOULD GO LONG, RIGHT?
TO KEEP HIM AT A DISTANCE FROM THEIR GOVERNMENT.
IF HE COMES BACK BEFORE THEY'VE COME TO AN AGREEMENT, HE'D HAVE TROUBLE GETTING AN EASY POST OR EVEN IN AT ALL.
THEY COULD COME UP WITH ALL KINDS OF REASONS.
THAT'S WHY THE CHIEF OFFICER'S ACTIONS WERE SO PERFECT.
HE WAS PROBABLY WAITING FOR THIS DAY.
BRANCH DIRECTOR MIEL'S FROM A GOOD FAMILY, HE CAN'T IGNORE HIM.
IF THEY NEGOTIATE WITH HIM AS HOSTAGE, THE DISTRICT'LL HAVE NO CHOICE BUT TO PULL BACK, I GUESS.
WHAT'S THE CHIEF OFFICER WANT?
DISTRICT GOVERNOR.
WHOA, NO WONDER.
NEW DISTRICT GOVERNOR IN JUMOKU TOO.
OH!
I HEARD IT'S BECAUSE OF MEDICAL TREATMENT.
HE'S A YOUNG GUY.
I WONDER IF THE OLD DISTRICT GOVERNOR'LL COME BACK.

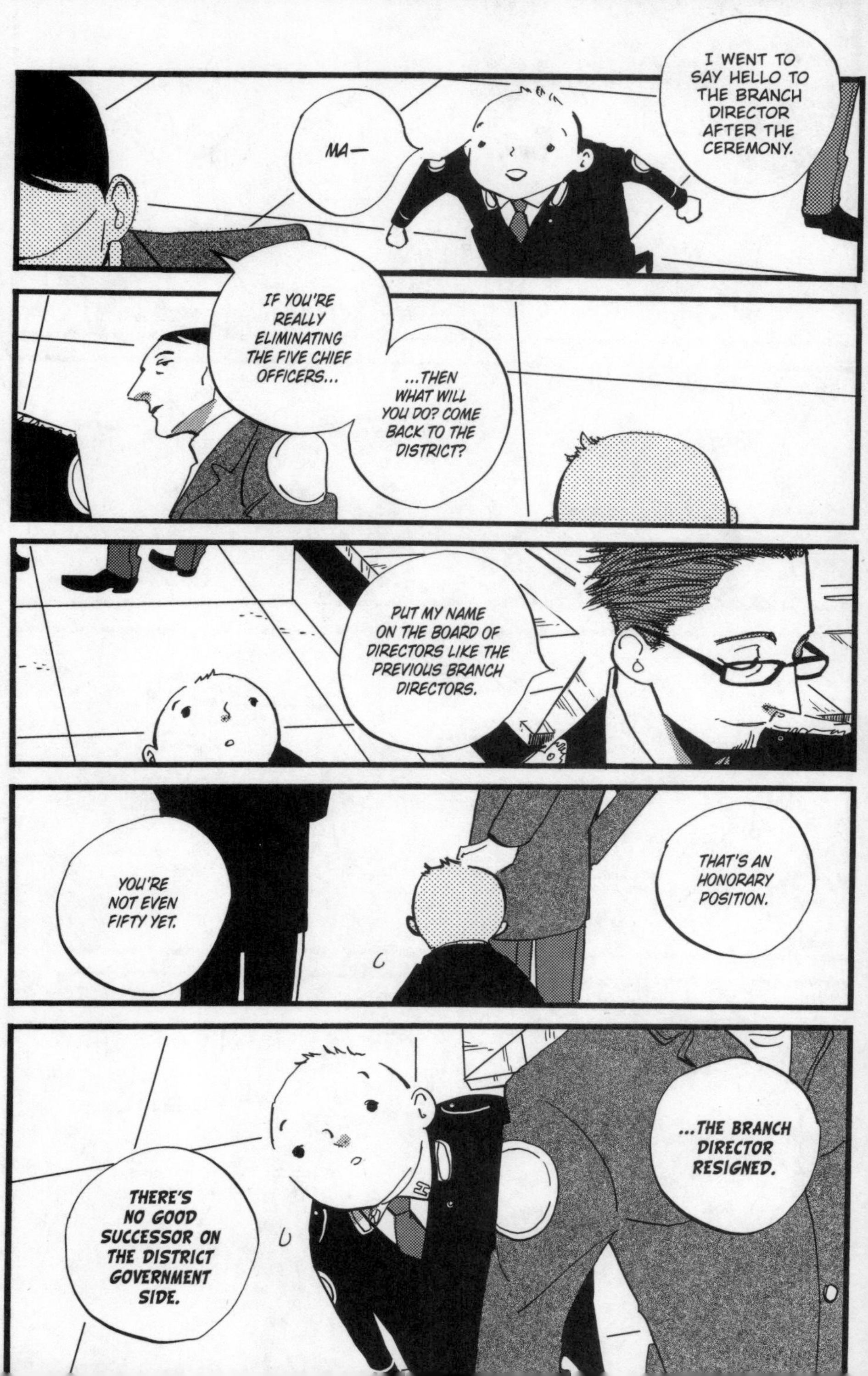

I WENT TO SAY HELLO TO THE BRANCH DIRECTOR AFTER THE CEREMONY.
MA—
IF YOU'RE REALLY ELIMINATING THE FIVE CHIEF OFFICERS...
...THEN WHAT WILL YOU DO? COME BACK TO THE DISTRICT?
PUT MY NAME ON THE BOARD OF DIRECTORS LIKE THE PREVIOUS BRANCH DIRECTORS.
THAT'S AN HONORARY POSITION.
YOU'RE NOT EVEN FIFTY YET.
...THE BRANCH DIRECTOR RESIGNED.
THERE'S NO GOOD SUCCESSOR ON THE DISTRICT GOVERNMENT SIDE.

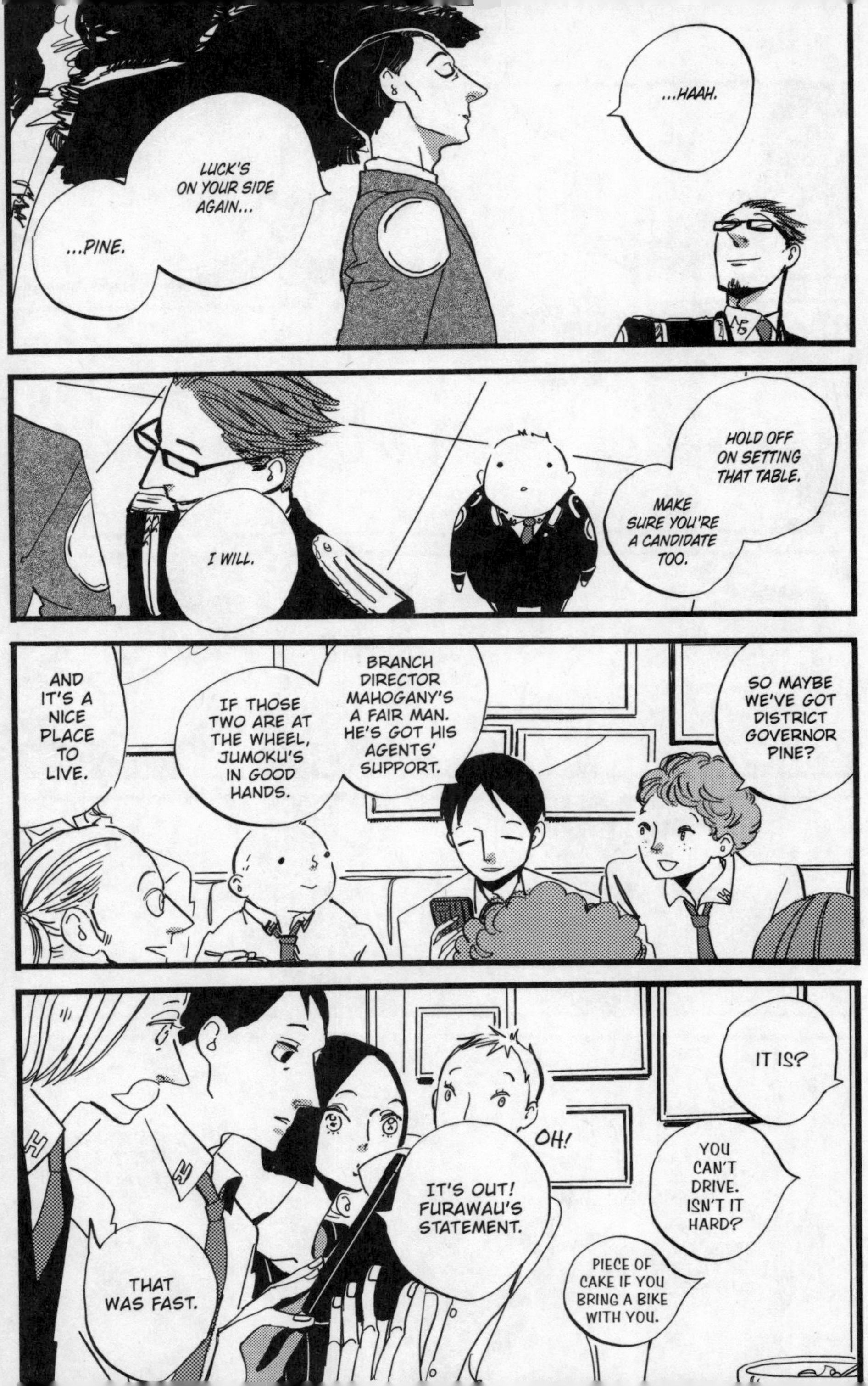
...HAAH.
LUCK'S ON YOUR SIDE AGAIN...
...PINE.
HOLD OFF ON SETTING THAT TABLE.
MAKE SURE YOU'RE A CANDIDATE TOO.
I WILL.
SO MAYBE WE'VE GOT DISTRICT GOVERNOR PINE?
BRANCH DIRECTOR MAHOGANY'S A FAIR MAN. HE'S GOT HIS AGENTS' SUPPORT.
IF THOSE TWO ARE AT THE WHEEL, JUMOKU'S IN GOOD HANDS.
AND IT'S A NICE PLACE TO LIVE.
IT IS?
YOU CAN'T DRIVE. ISN'T IT HARD?
PIECE OF CAKE IF YOU BRING A BIKE WITH YOU.
OH!
IT'S OUT! FURAWAU'S STATEMENT.
THAT WAS FAST.

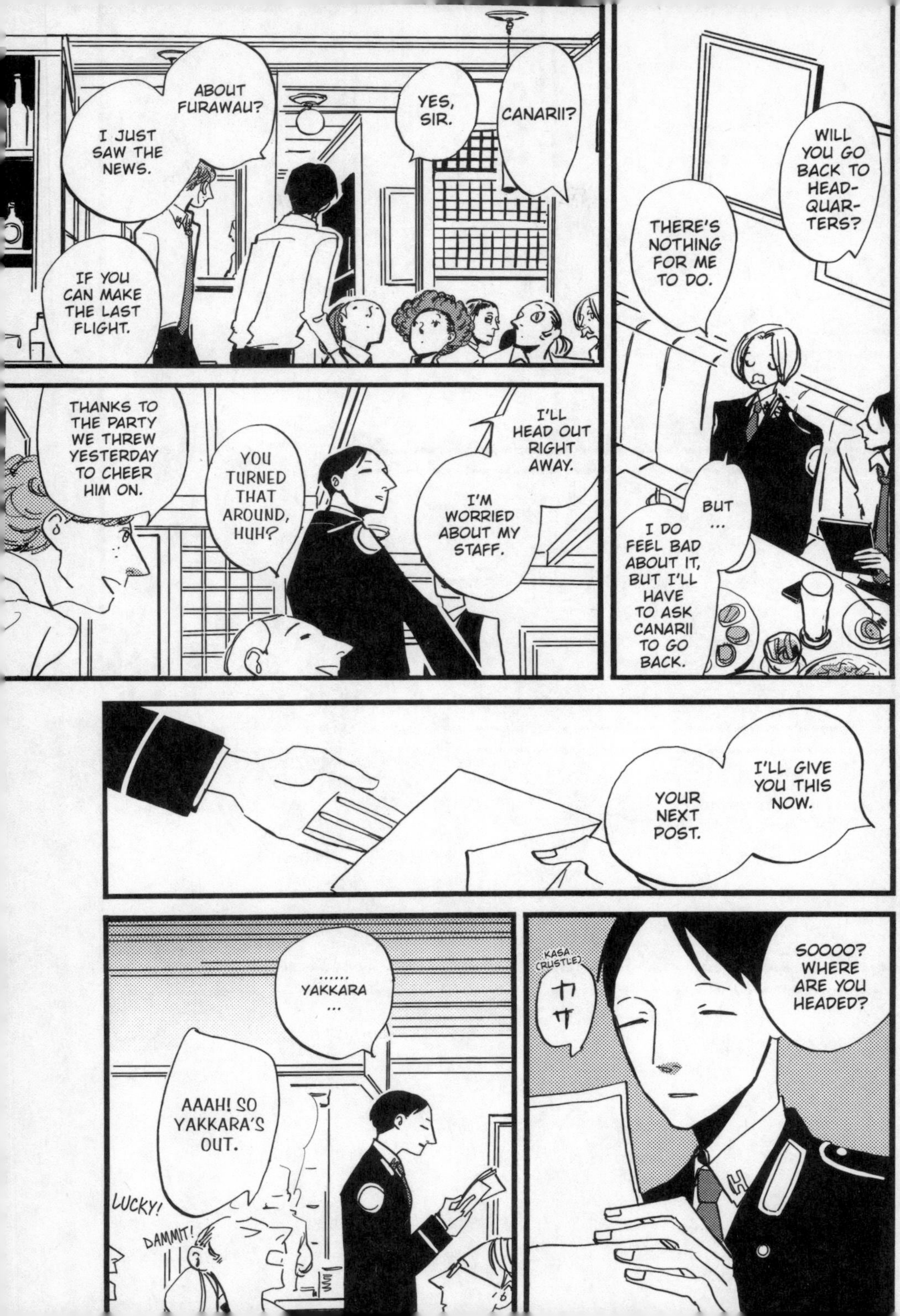
WILL YOU GO BACK TO HEAD-QUARTERS?
THERE'S NOTHING FOR ME TO DO.
BUT ...
I DO FEEL BAD ABOUT IT, BUT I'LL HAVE TO ASK CANARII TO GO BACK.
CANARII?
YES, SIR.
ABOUT FURAWAU?
I JUST SAW THE NEWS.
IF YOU CAN MAKE THE LAST FLIGHT.
I'LL HEAD OUT RIGHT AWAY.
I'M WORRIED ABOUT MY STAFF.
YOU TURNED THAT AROUND, HUH?
THANKS TO THE PARTY WE THREW YESTERDAY TO CHEER HIM ON.
I'LL GIVE YOU THIS NOW.
YOUR NEXT POST.
SOOOO? WHERE ARE YOU HEADED?
KASA (RUSTLE)
カサ
...... YAKKARA ...
AAAH! SO YAKKARA'S OUT.
LUCKY!
DAMMIT!

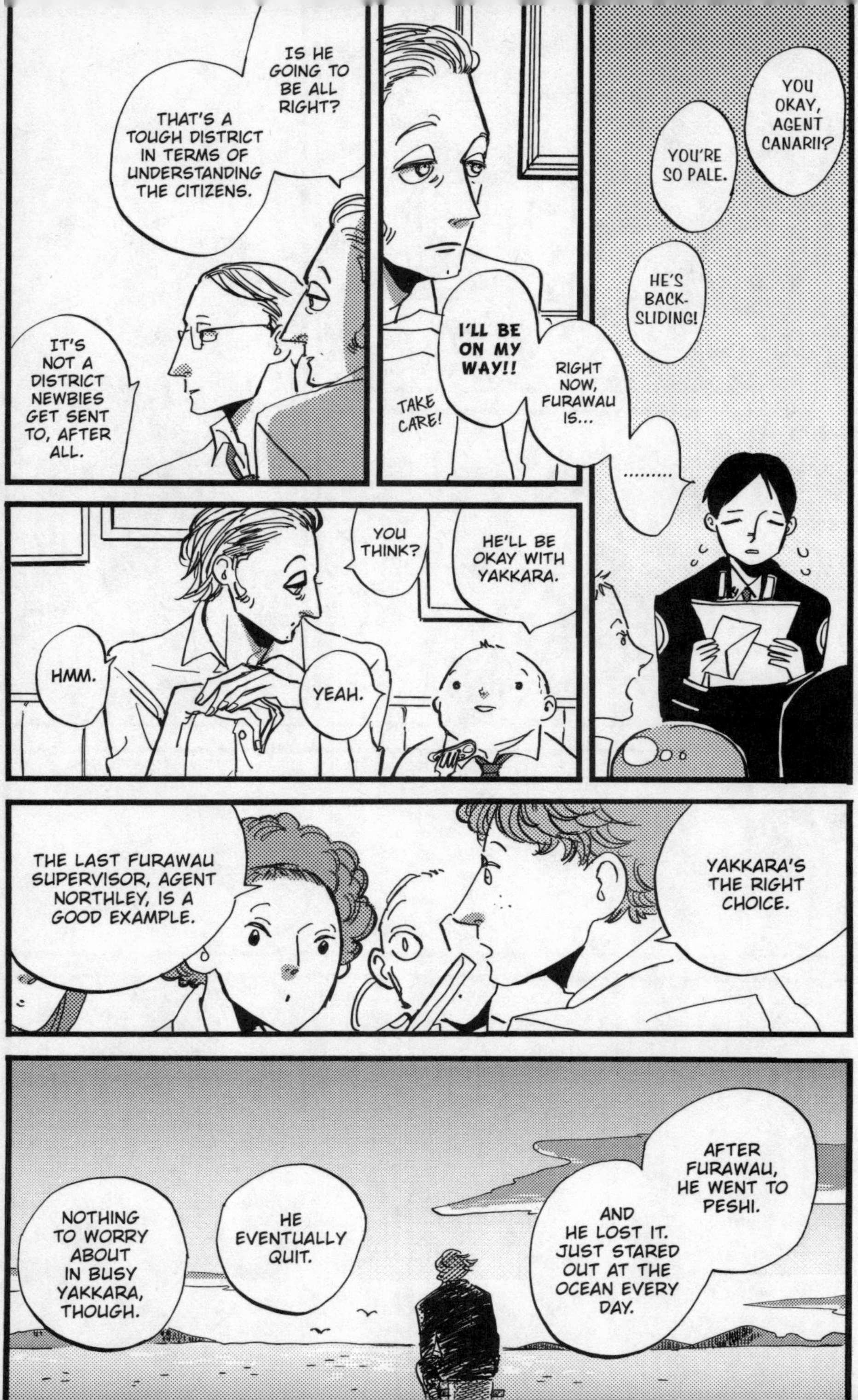
YOU OKAY, AGENT CANARII?
YOU'RE SO PALE.
HE'S BACK-SLIDING!
RIGHT NOW, FURAWAU IS...
....
I'LL BE ON MY WAY!!
TAKE CARE!
IS HE GOING TO BE ALL RIGHT?
THAT'S A TOUGH DISTRICT IN TERMS OF UNDERSTANDING THE CITIZENS.
IT'S NOT A DISTRICT NEWBIES GET SENT TO, AFTER ALL.
HE'LL BE OKAY WITH YAKKARA.
YOU THINK?
YEAH.
HMM.
YAKKARA'S THE RIGHT CHOICE.
THE LAST FURAWAU SUPERVISOR, AGENT NORTHLEY, IS A GOOD EXAMPLE.
AFTER FURAWAU, HE WENT TO PESHI.
AND HE LOST IT. JUST STARED OUT AT THE OCEAN EVERY DAY.
HE EVENTUALLY QUIT.
NOTHING TO WORRY ABOUT IN BUSY YAKKARA, THOUGH.

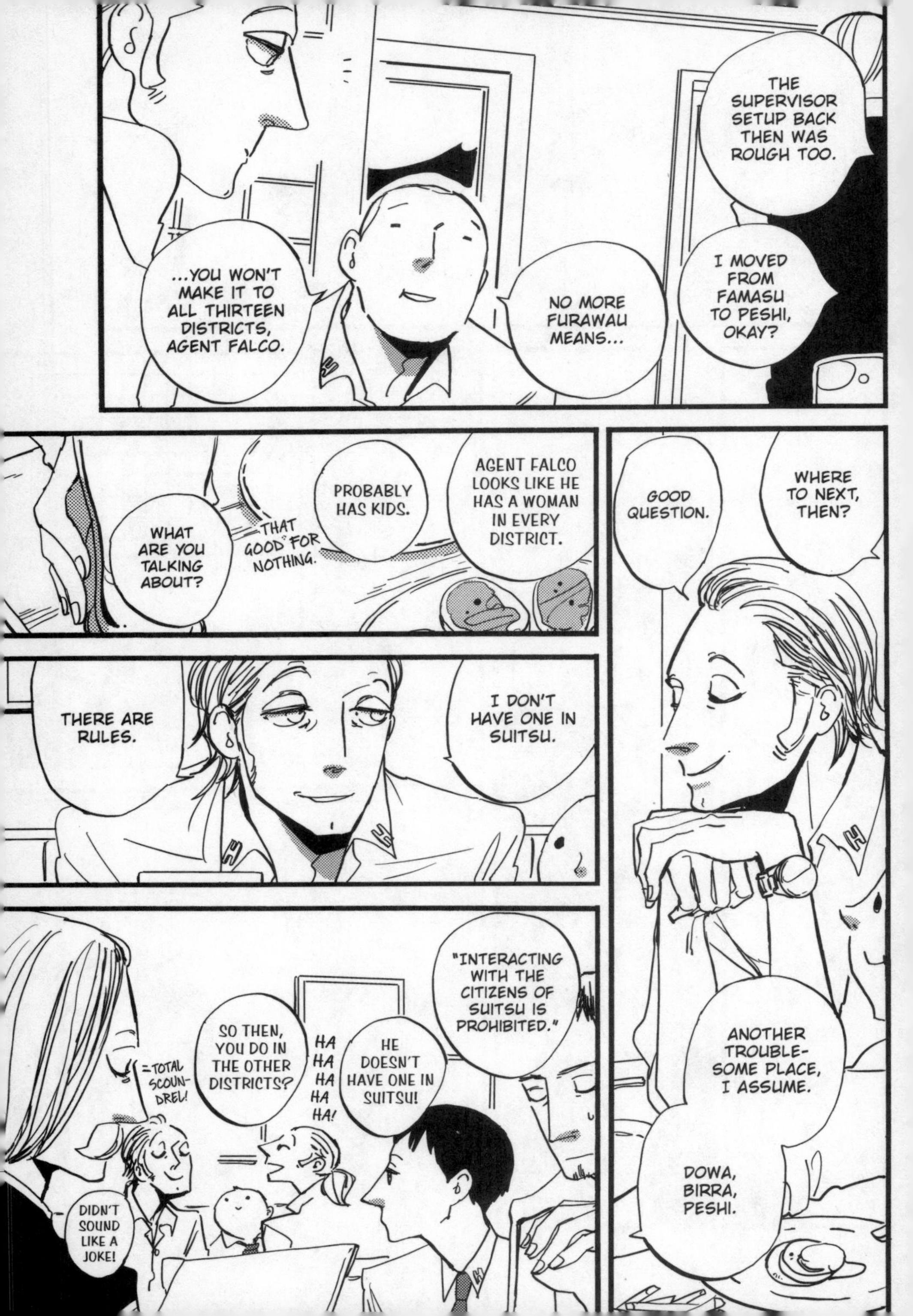
THE SUPERVISOR SETUP BACK THEN WAS ROUGH TOO.
I MOVED FROM FAMASU TO PESHI, OKAY?
NO MORE FURAWAU MEANS...
...YOU WON'T MAKE IT TO ALL THIRTEEN DISTRICTS, AGENT FALCO.
WHERE TO NEXT, THEN?
GOOD QUESTION.
ANOTHER TROUBLE-SOME PLACE, I ASSUME.
DOWA, BIRRA, PESHI.
AGENT FALCO LOOKS LIKE HE HAS A WOMAN IN EVERY DISTRICT.
PROBABLY HAS KIDS.
THAT GOOD FOR NOTHING.
WHAT ARE YOU TALKING ABOUT?
I DON'T HAVE ONE IN SUITSU.
THERE ARE RULES.
"INTERACTING WITH THE CITIZENS OF SUITSU IS PROHIBITED."
HE DOESN'T HAVE ONE IN SUITSU!
HA HA HA HA HA!
SO THEN, YOU DO IN THE OTHER DISTRICTS?
=TOTAL SCOUNDREL!
DIDN'T SOUND LIKE A JOKE!

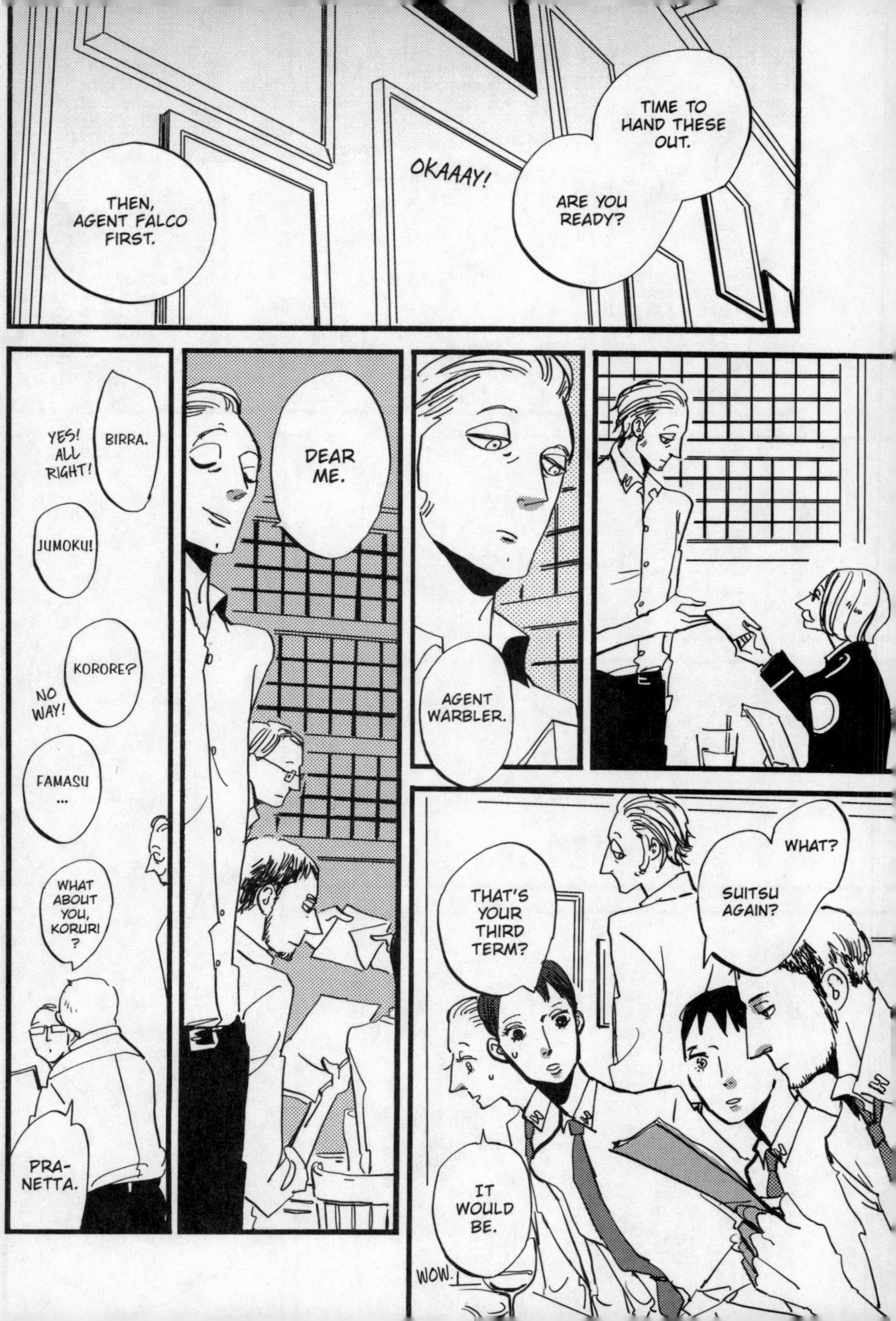
TIME TO HAND THESE OUT.
ARE YOU READY?
OKAAAY!
THEN, AGENT FALCO FIRST.
AGENT WARBLER.
WHAT?
SUITSU AGAIN?
THAT'S YOUR THIRD TERM?
IT WOULD BE.
WOW.
DEAR ME.
BIRRA.
YES! ALL RIGHT!
JUMOKU!
KORORE?
NO WAY!
FAMASU...
WHAT ABOUT YOU, KORURI?
PRA-NETTA.

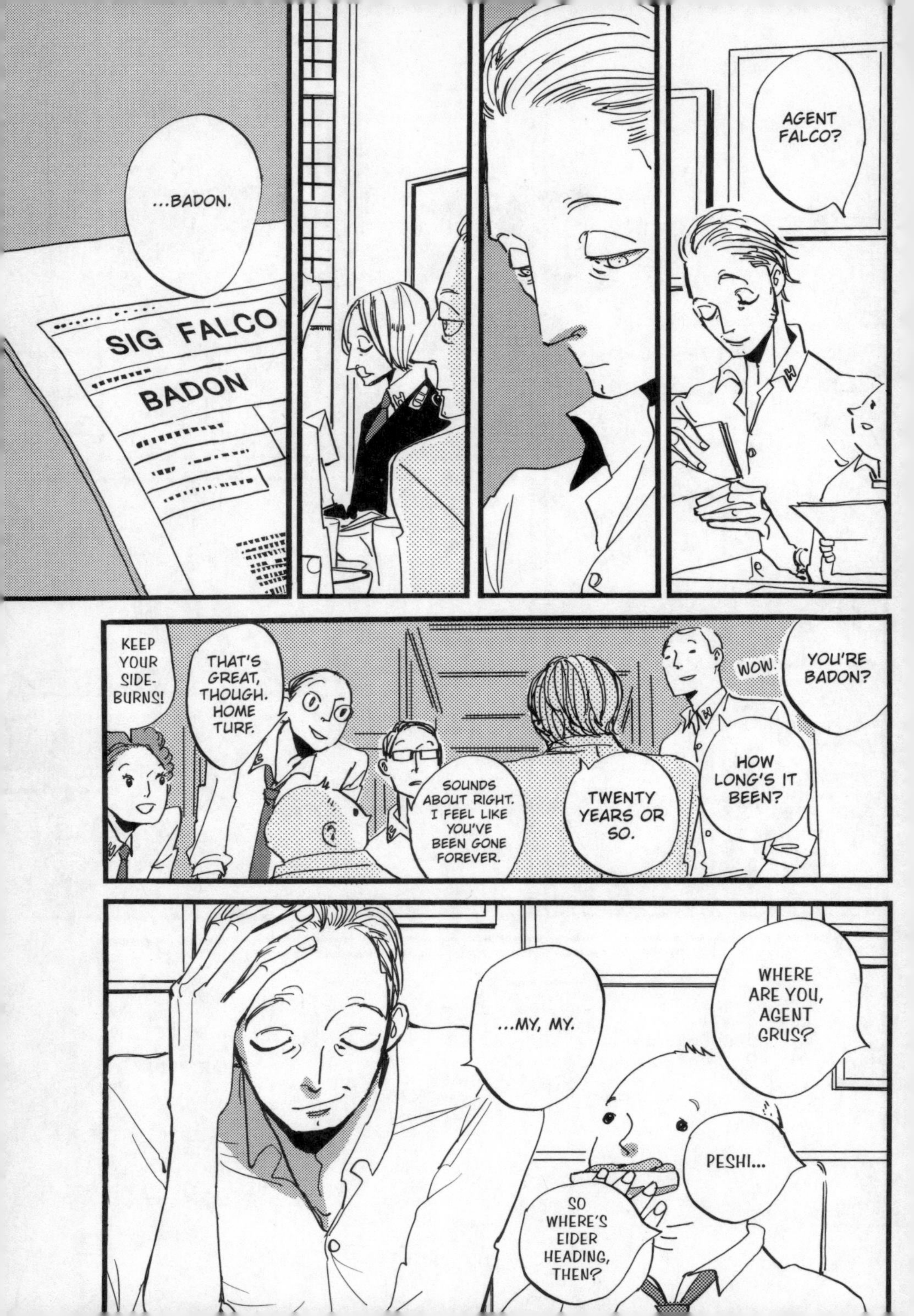
AGENT FALCO?
...BADON.
SIG FALCO
BADON
YOU'RE BADON?
WOW.
HOW LONG'S IT BEEN?
TWENTY YEARS OR SO.
SOUNDS ABOUT RIGHT. I FEEL LIKE YOU'VE BEEN GONE FOREVER.
THAT'S GREAT, THOUGH. HOME TURF.
KEEP YOUR SIDE-BURNS!
WHERE ARE YOU, AGENT GRUS?
...MY, MY.
PESHI...
SO WHERE'S EIDER HEADING, THEN?

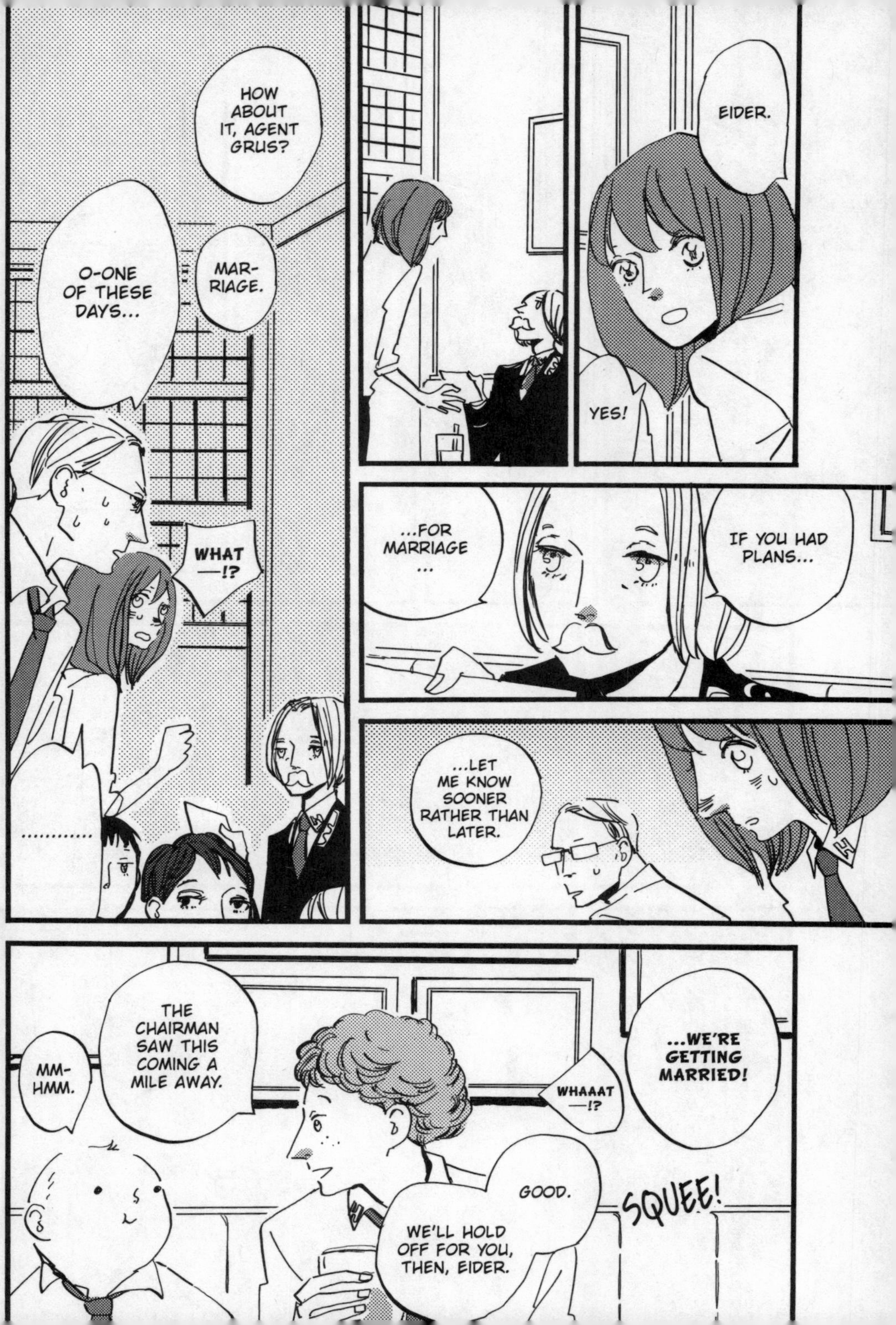
EIDER.
YES!
IF YOU HAD PLANS...
...FOR MARRIAGE...
...LET ME KNOW SOONER RATHER THAN LATER.
HOW ABOUT IT, AGENT GRUS?
MARRIAGE.
O-ONE OF THESE DAYS...
WHAT—!?
....
...WE'RE GETTING MARRIED!
WHAAAT—!?
THE CHAIRMAN SAW THIS COMING A MILE AWAY.
MM-HMM.
SQUEE!
GOOD.
WE'LL HOLD OFF FOR YOU, THEN, EIDER.

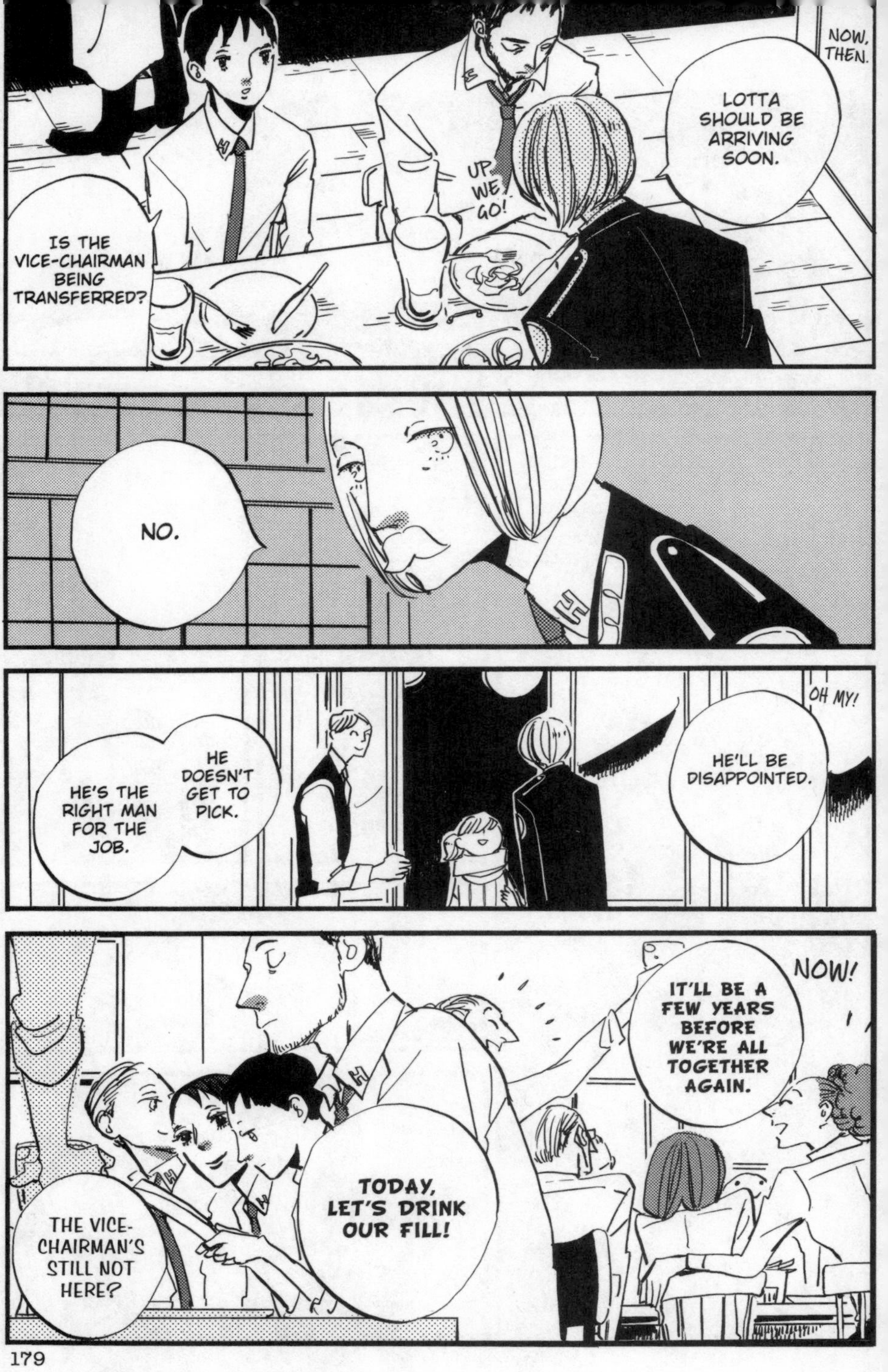
NOW, THEN.
LOTTA SHOULD BE ARRIVING SOON.
UP WE GO!
IS THE VICE-CHAIRMAN BEING TRANSFERRED?
NO.
OH MY!
HE'LL BE DISAPPOINTED.
HE DOESN'T GET TO PICK.
HE'S THE RIGHT MAN FOR THE JOB.
NOW!
IT'LL BE A FEW YEARS BEFORE WE'RE ALL TOGETHER AGAIN.
TODAY, LET'S DRINK OUR FILL!
THE VICE-CHAIRMAN'S STILL NOT HERE?

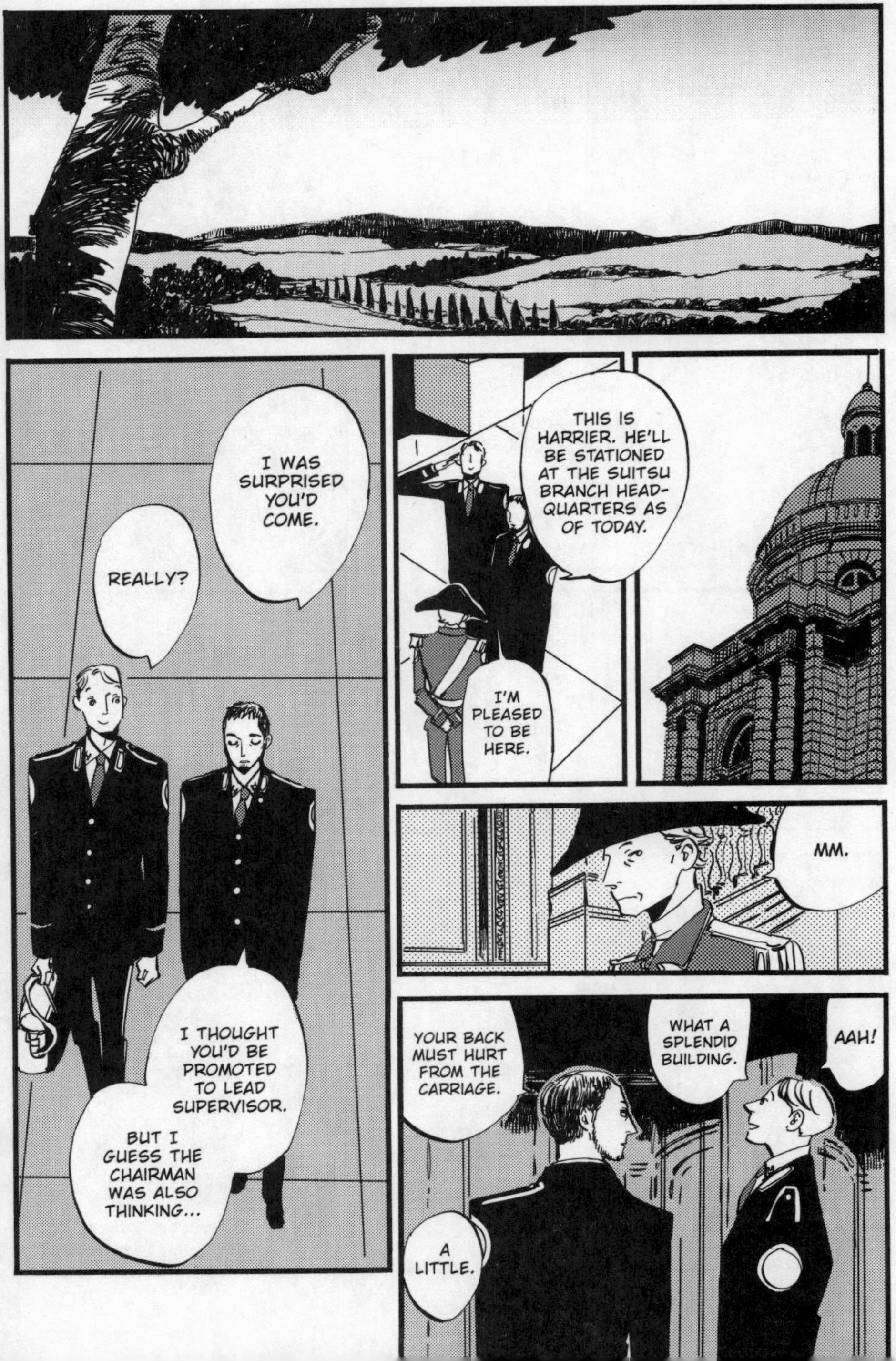
THIS IS HARRIER. HE'LL BE STATIONED AT THE SUITSU BRANCH HEAD-QUARTERS AS OF TODAY.
I'M PLEASED TO BE HERE.
MM.
AAH!
WHAT A SPLENDID BUILDING.
YOUR BACK MUST HURT FROM THE CARRIAGE.
A LITTLE.
I WAS SURPRISED YOU'D COME.
REALLY?
I THOUGHT YOU'D BE PROMOTED TO LEAD SUPERVISOR.
BUT I GUESS THE CHAIRMAN WAS ALSO THINKING...

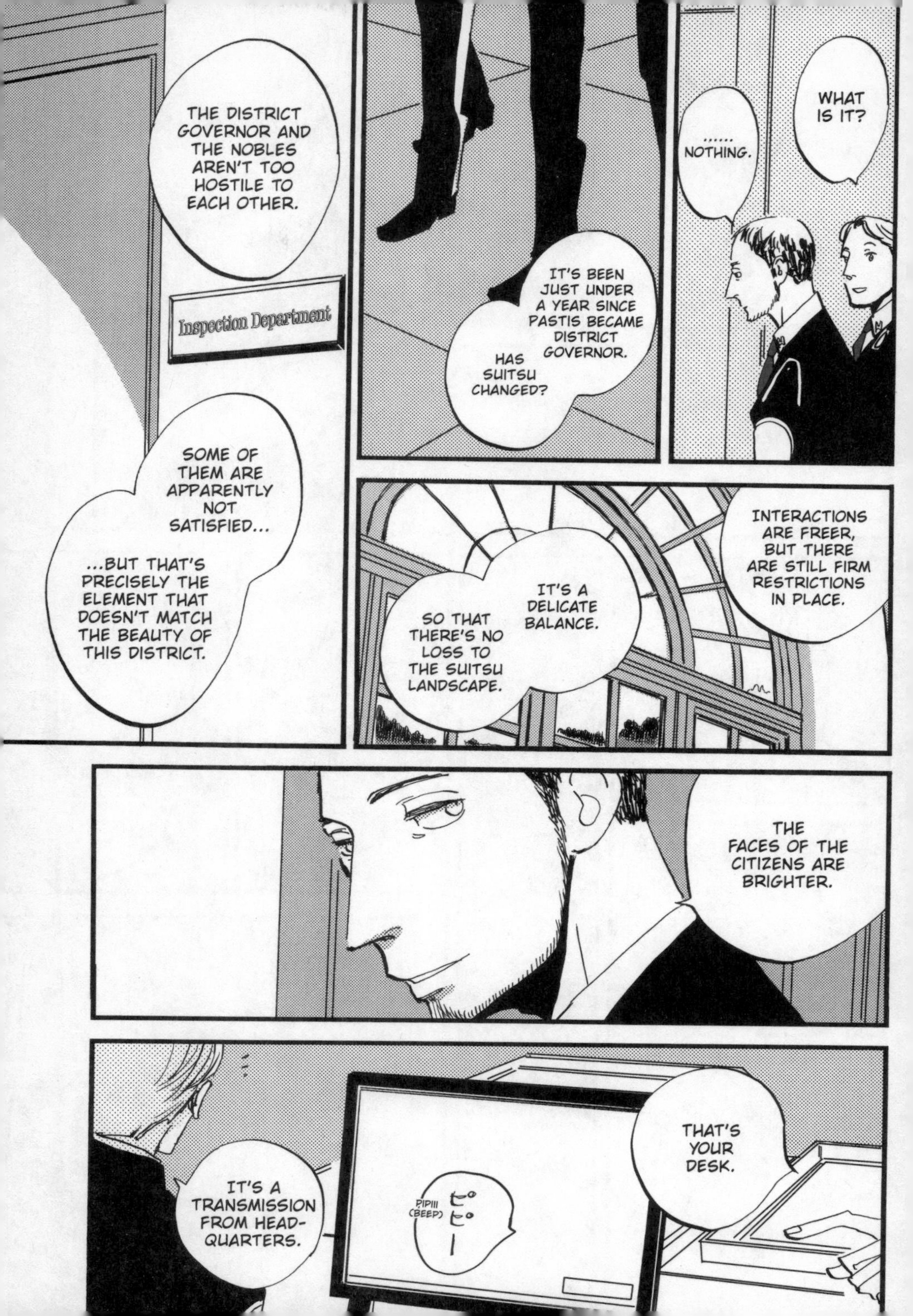
WHAT IS IT?
......
NOTHING.
IT'S BEEN JUST UNDER A YEAR SINCE PASTIS BECAME DISTRICT GOVERNOR.
HAS SUITSU CHANGED?
INTERACTIONS ARE FREER, BUT THERE ARE STILL FIRM RESTRICTIONS IN PLACE.
IT'S A DELICATE BALANCE.
SO THAT THERE'S NO LOSS TO THE SUITSU LANDSCAPE.
THE DISTRICT GOVERNOR AND THE NOBLES AREN'T TOO HOSTILE TO EACH OTHER.
Inspection Department
SOME OF THEM ARE APPARENTLY NOT SATISFIED...
...BUT THAT'S PRECISELY THE ELEMENT THAT DOESN'T MATCH THE BEAUTY OF THIS DISTRICT.
THE FACES OF THE CITIZENS ARE BRIGHTER.
THAT'S YOUR DESK.
ピピー
PIPIII (BEEP)
IT'S A TRANSMISSION FROM HEAD-QUARTERS.

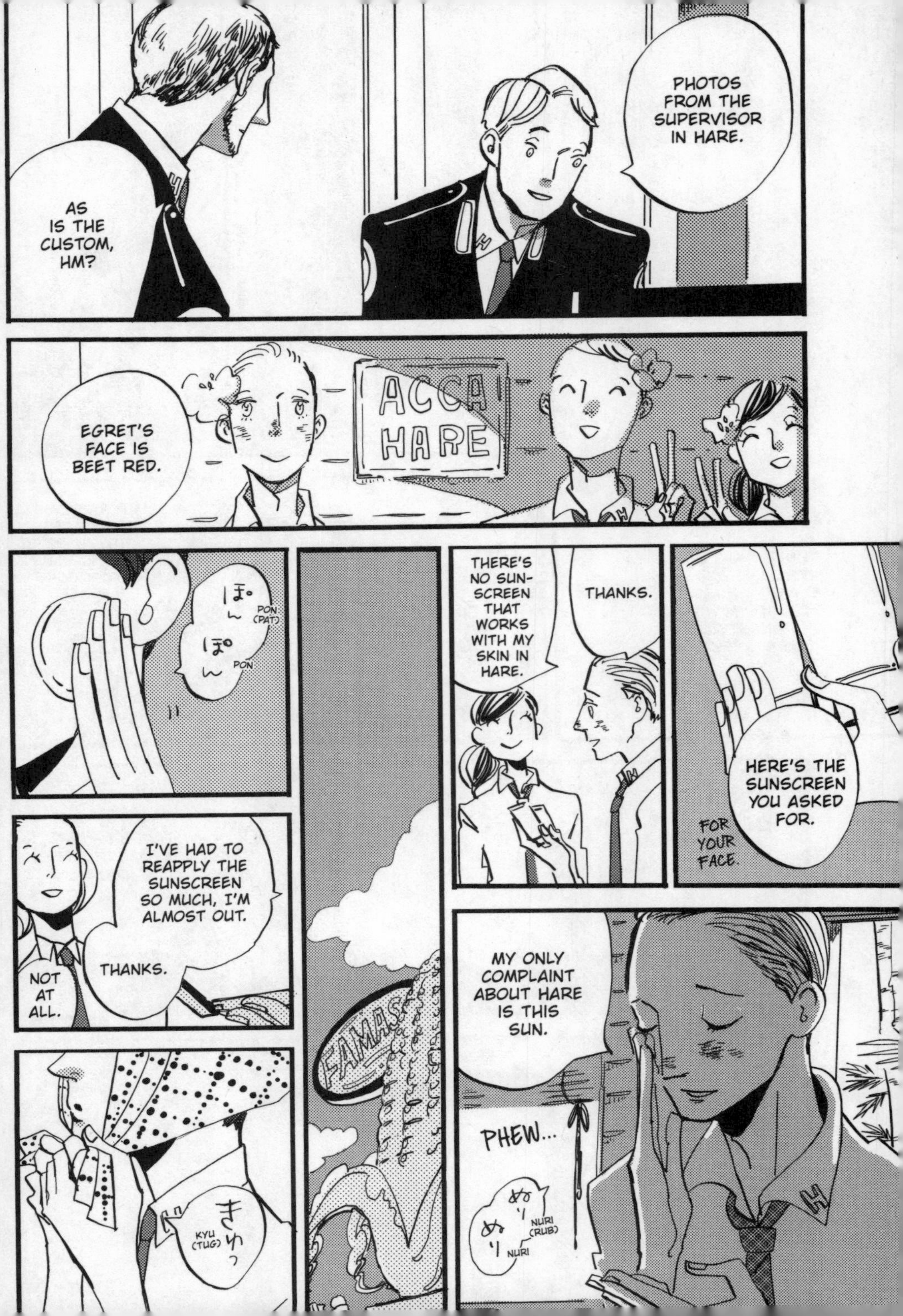
PHOTOS FROM THE SUPERVISOR IN HARE.
AS IS THE CUSTOM, HM?
ACCA HARE
EGRET'S FACE IS BEET RED.
HERE'S THE SUNSCREEN YOU ASKED FOR.
FOR YOUR FACE.
THANKS.
THERE'S NO SUNSCREEN THAT WORKS WITH MY SKIN IN HARE.
MY ONLY COMPLAINT ABOUT HARE IS THIS SUN.
PHEW...
ぬりぬり
NURI (RUB)
NURI
FAMAS
ぽんぽん
PON (PAT)
PON
I'VE HAD TO REAPPLY THE SUNSCREEN SO MUCH, I'M ALMOST OUT.
THANKS.
NOT AT ALL.
きゅっ
KYU (TUG)

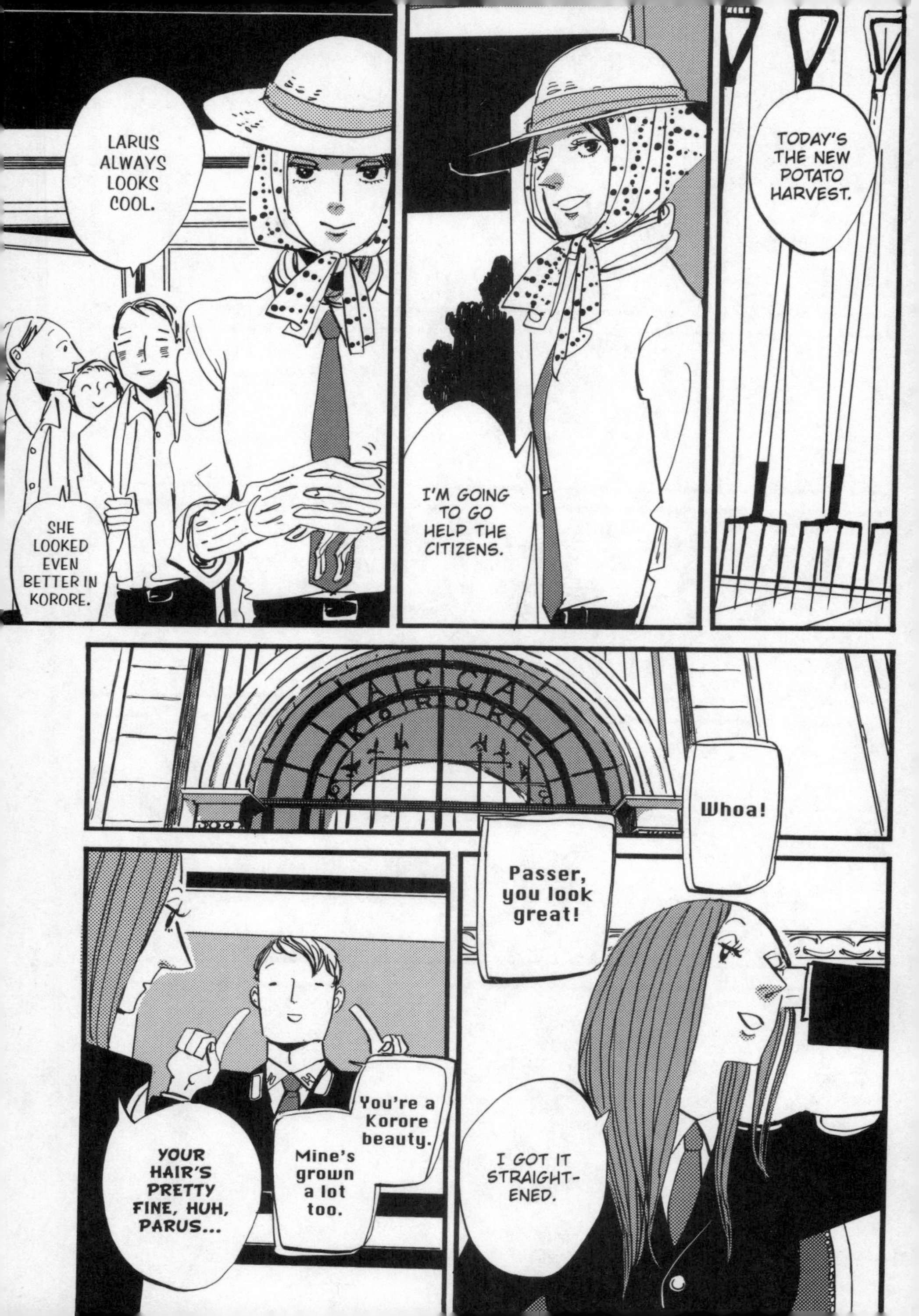
TODAY'S THE NEW POTATO HARVEST.
I'M GOING TO GO HELP THE CITIZENS.
LARUS ALWAYS LOOKS COOL.
SHE LOOKED EVEN BETTER IN KORORE.
Whoa!
Passer, you look great!
I GOT IT STRAIGHT-ENED.
You're a Korore beauty.
Mine's grown a lot too.
YOUR HAIR'S PRETTY FINE, HUH, PARUS...

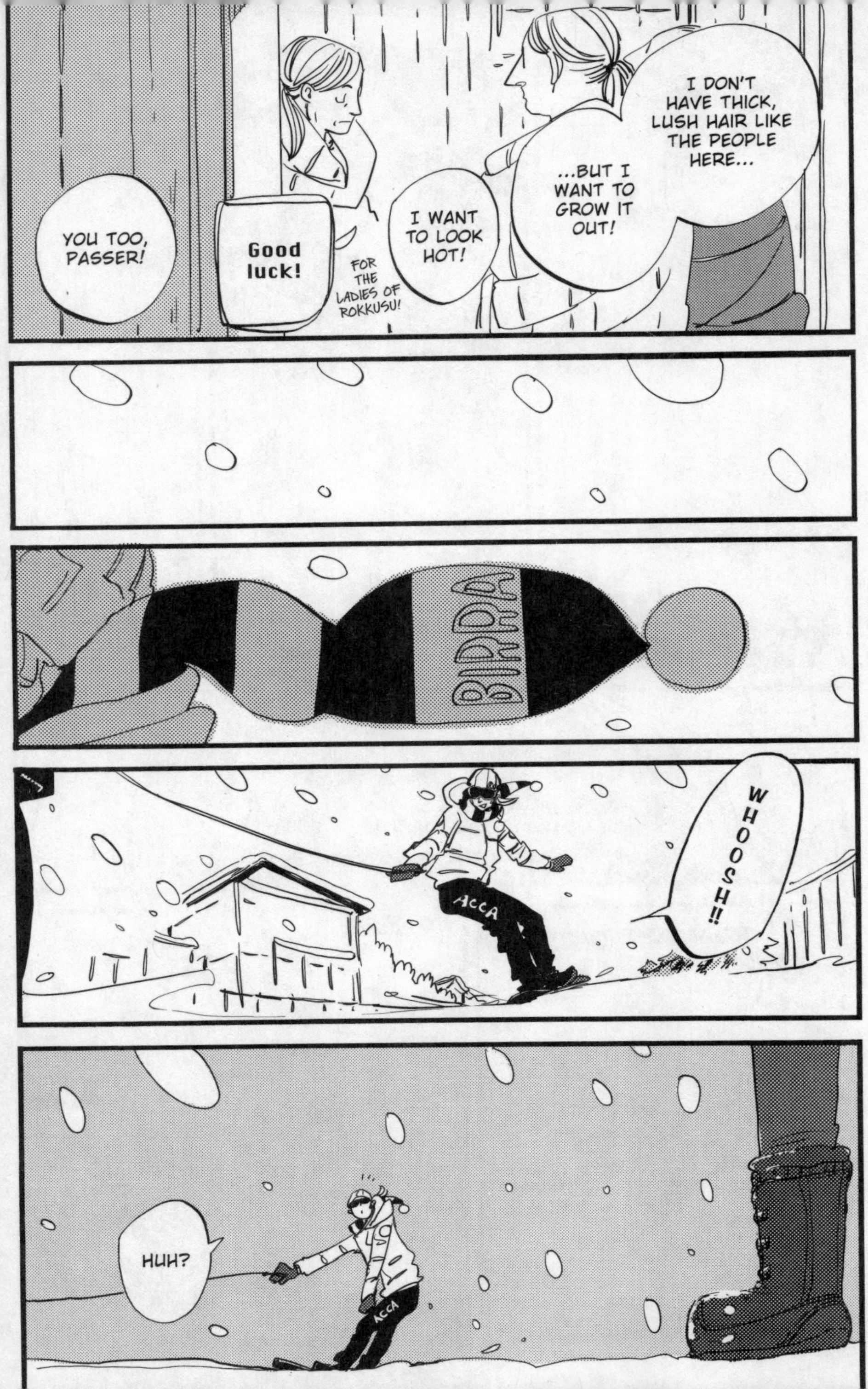
I DON'T HAVE THICK, LUSH HAIR LIKE THE PEOPLE HERE...
...BUT I WANT TO GROW IT OUT!
I WANT TO LOOK HOT!
FOR THE LADIES OF ROKKUSU!
Good luck!
YOU TOO, PASSER!
BIRRA
WHOOSH!!
ACCA
HUH?
ACCA

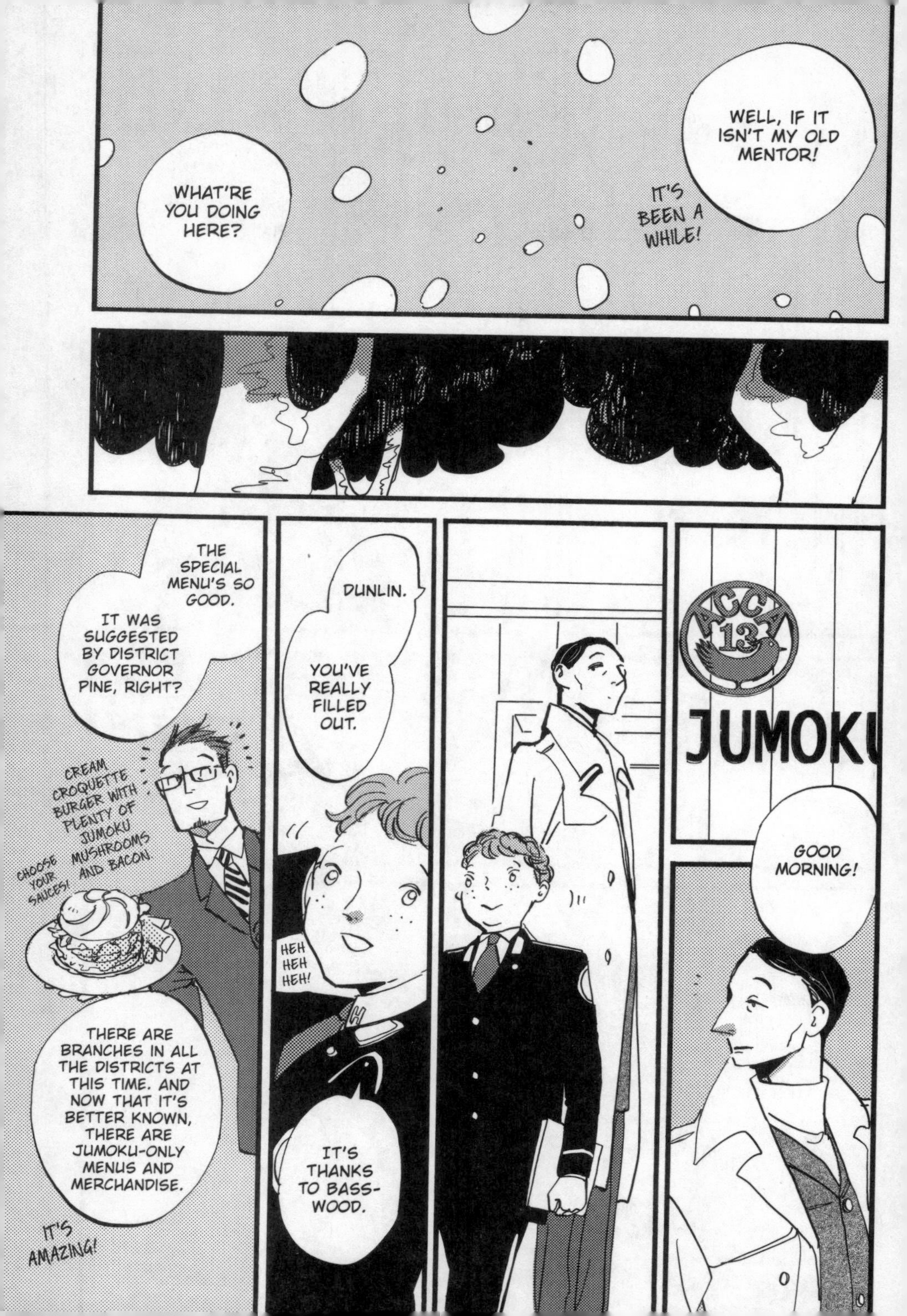
WELL, IF IT ISN'T MY OLD MENTOR!
IT'S BEEN A WHILE!
WHAT'RE YOU DOING HERE?
ACCA 13
JUMOKU
GOOD MORNING!
DUNLIN.
YOU'VE REALLY FILLED OUT.
HEH HEH HEH!
IT'S THANKS TO BASSWOOD.
THE SPECIAL MENU'S SO GOOD.
IT WAS SUGGESTED BY DISTRICT GOVERNOR PINE, RIGHT?
CREAM CROQUETTE BURGER WITH PLENTY OF JUMOKU MUSHROOMS AND BACON
CHOOSE YOUR SAUCES!
THERE ARE BRANCHES IN ALL THE DISTRICTS AT THIS TIME. AND NOW THAT IT'S BETTER KNOWN, THERE ARE JUMOKU-ONLY MENUS AND MERCHANDISE.
IT'S AMAZING!

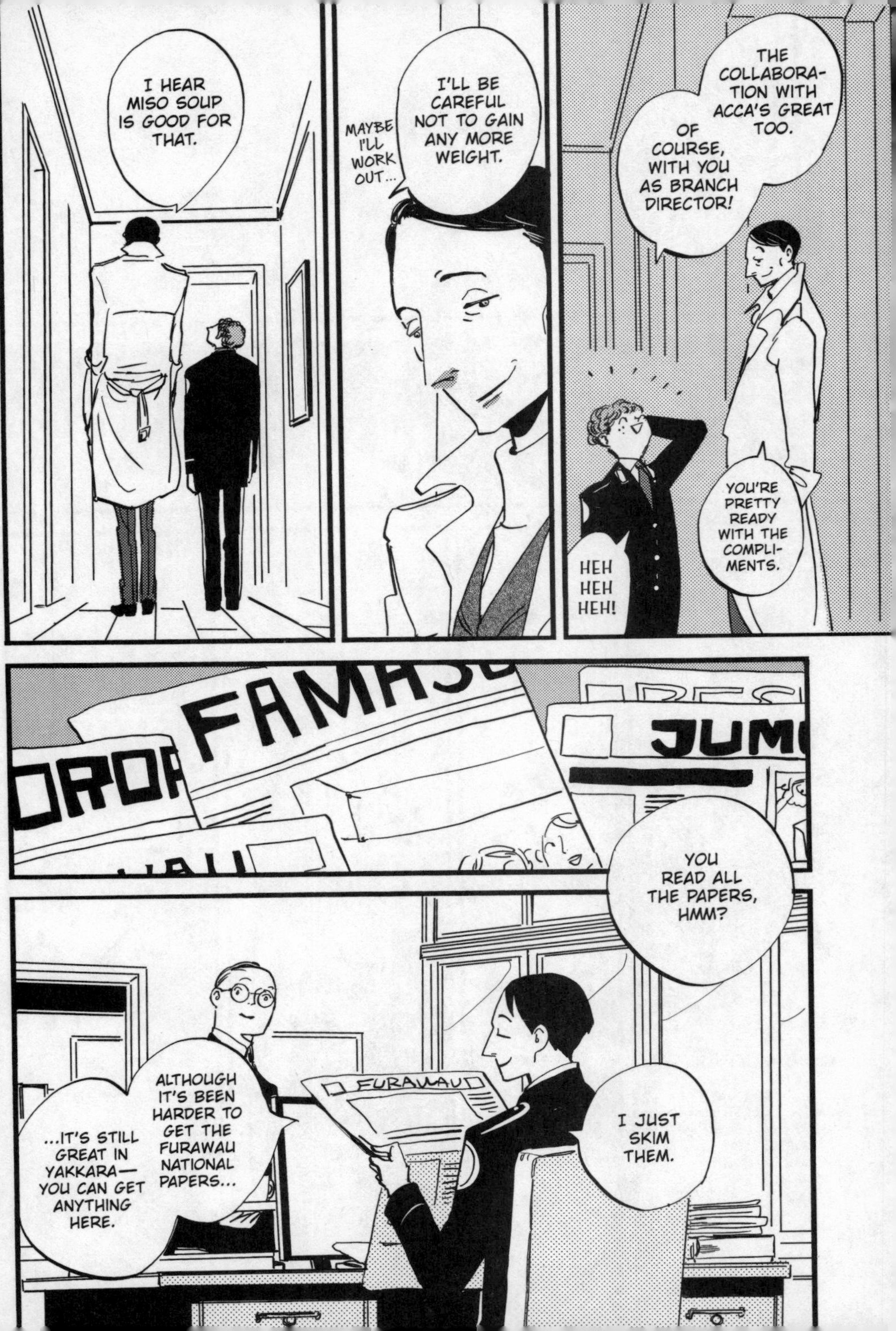
THE COLLABORATION WITH ACCA'S GREAT TOO.
OF COURSE, WITH YOU AS BRANCH DIRECTOR!
YOU'RE PRETTY READY WITH THE COMPLIMENTS.
HEH HEH HEH!
I'LL BE CAREFUL NOT TO GAIN ANY MORE WEIGHT.
MAYBE I'LL WORK OUT...
I HEAR MISO SOUP IS GOOD FOR THAT.
YOU READ ALL THE PAPERS, HMM?
I JUST SKIM THEM.
FURAWAU
ALTHOUGH IT'S BEEN HARDER TO GET THE FURAWAU NATIONAL PAPERS...
...IT'S STILL GREAT IN YAKKARA— YOU CAN GET ANYTHING HERE.

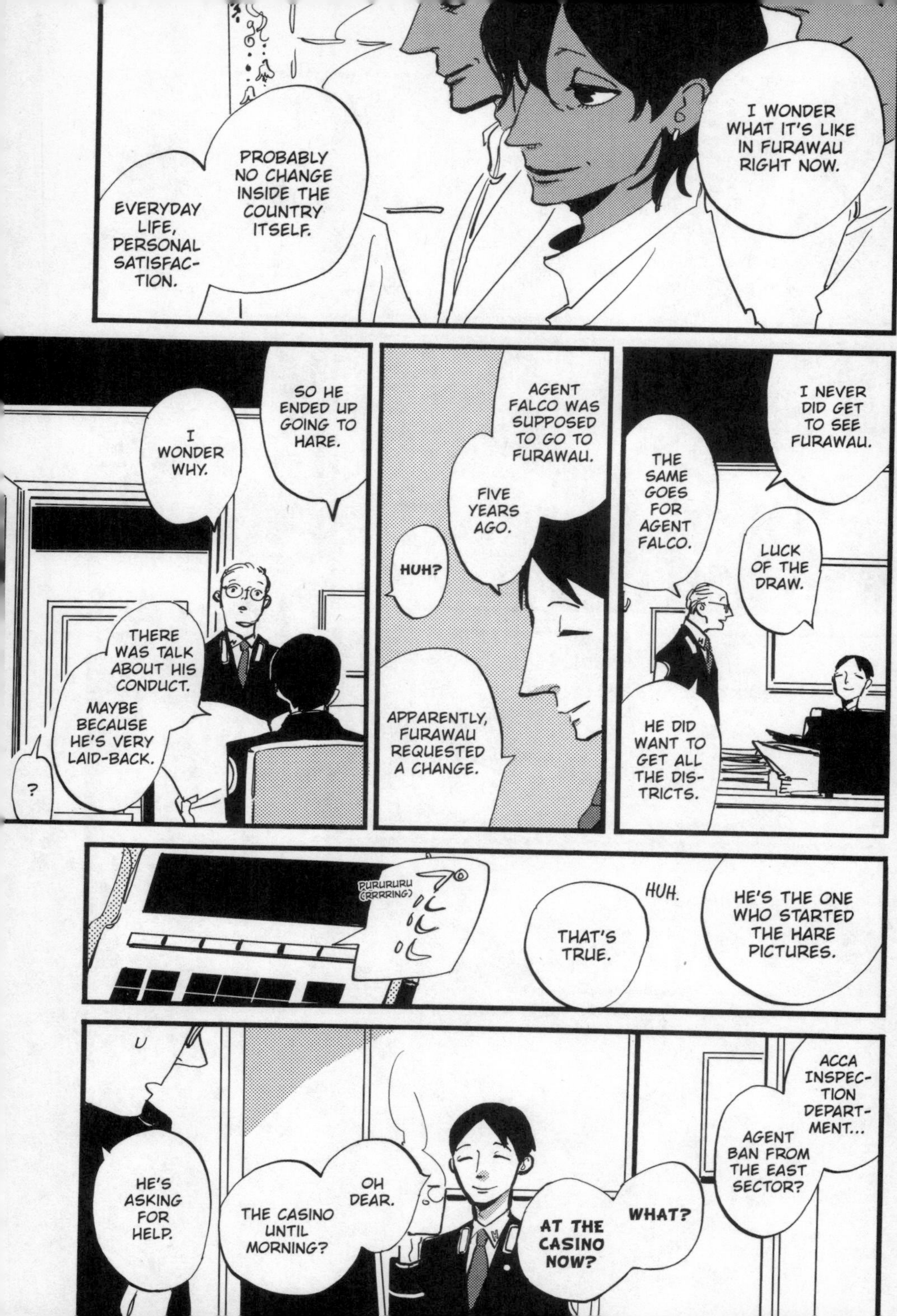
I WONDER WHAT IT'S LIKE IN FURAWAU RIGHT NOW.
PROBABLY NO CHANGE INSIDE THE COUNTRY ITSELF.
EVERYDAY LIFE, PERSONAL SATISFACTION.
I NEVER DID GET TO SEE FURAWAU.
THE SAME GOES FOR AGENT FALCO.
LUCK OF THE DRAW.
HE DID WANT TO GET ALL THE DISTRICTS.
AGENT FALCO WAS SUPPOSED TO GO TO FURAWAU.
FIVE YEARS AGO.
HUH?
APPARENTLY, FURAWAU REQUESTED A CHANGE.
SO HE ENDED UP GOING TO HARE.
I WONDER WHY.
THERE WAS TALK ABOUT HIS CONDUCT.
MAYBE BECAUSE HE'S VERY LAID-BACK.
?
HE'S THE ONE WHO STARTED THE HARE PICTURES.
HUH.
THAT'S TRUE.
PURURURU (RRRRING)
ACCA INSPECTION DEPARTMENT...
AGENT BAN FROM THE EAST SECTOR?
WHAT?
AT THE CASINO NOW?
OH DEAR.
THE CASINO UNTIL MORNING?
HE'S ASKING FOR HELP.

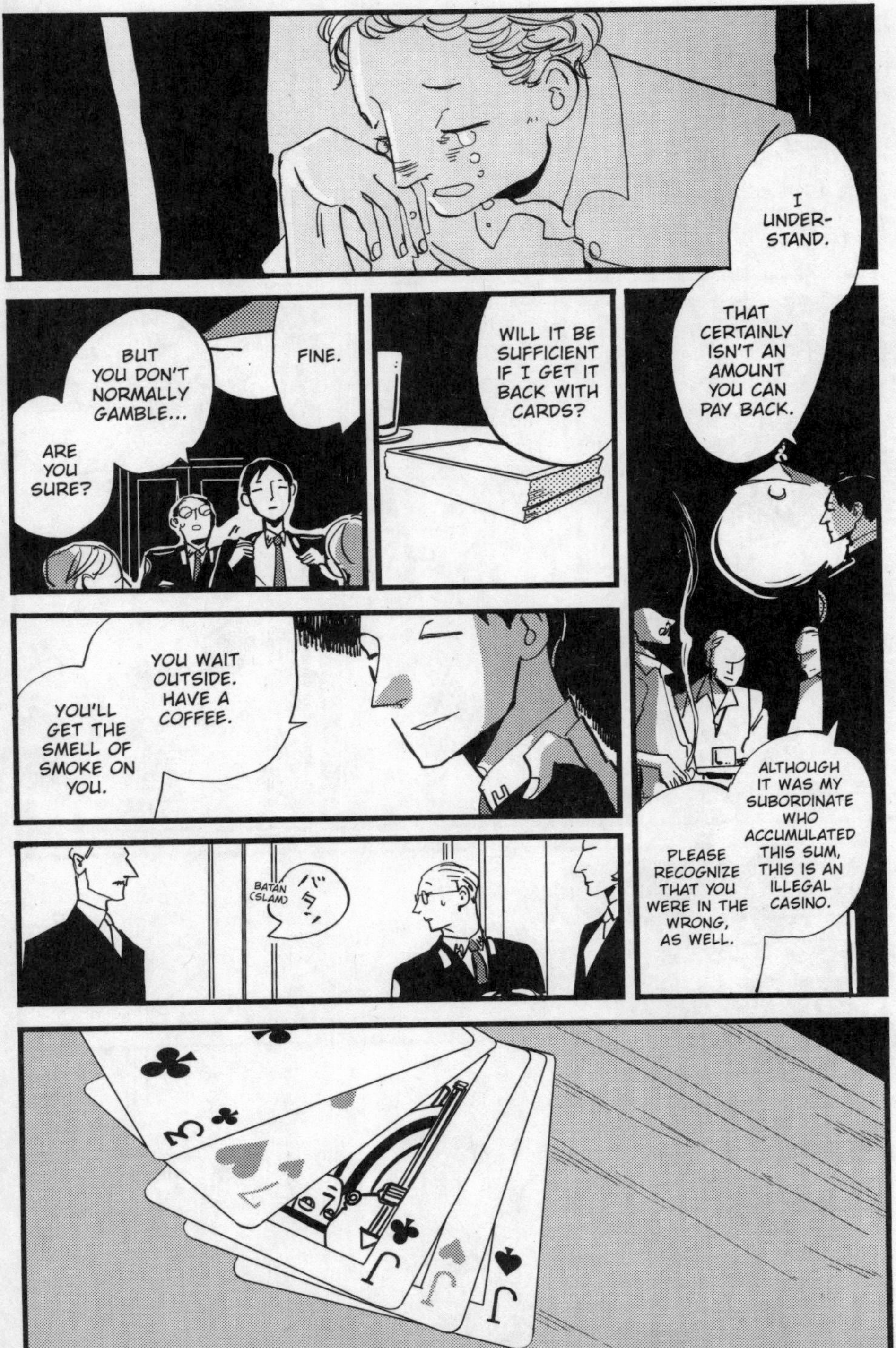
I UNDERSTAND.
THAT CERTAINLY ISN'T AN AMOUNT YOU CAN PAY BACK.
ALTHOUGH IT WAS MY SUBORDINATE WHO ACCUMULATED THIS SUM, THIS IS AN ILLEGAL CASINO.
PLEASE RECOGNIZE THAT YOU WERE IN THE WRONG, AS WELL.
WILL IT BE SUFFICIENT IF I GET IT BACK WITH CARDS?
FINE.
BUT YOU DON'T NORMALLY GAMBLE...
ARE YOU SURE?
YOU WAIT OUTSIDE. HAVE A COFFEE.
YOU'LL GET THE SMELL OF SMOKE ON YOU.
BATAN (SLAM)
バタン

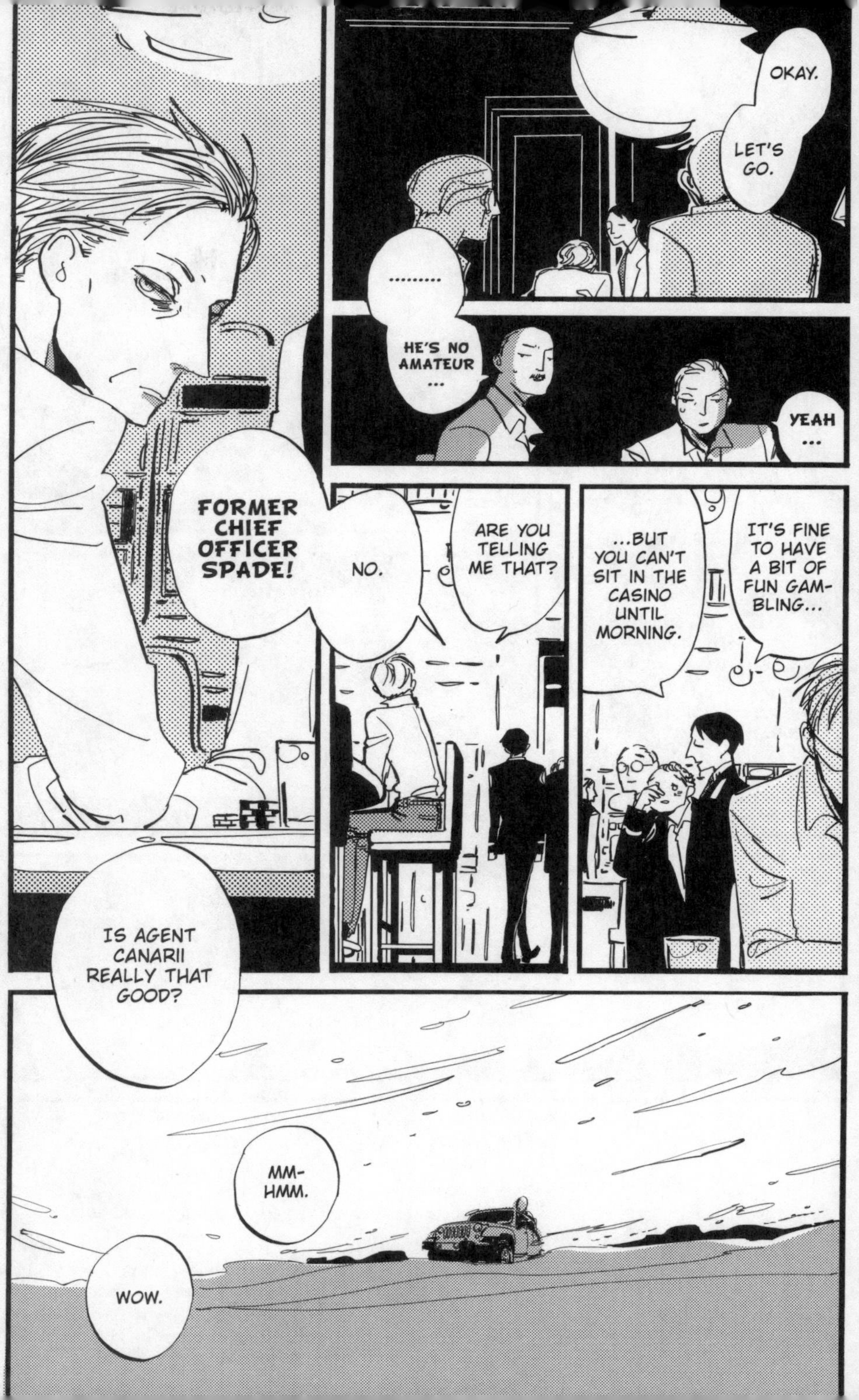
OKAY.
LET'S GO.
....
HE'S NO AMATEUR ...
YEAH ...
IT'S FINE TO HAVE A BIT OF FUN GAMBLING...
...BUT YOU CAN'T SIT IN THE CASINO UNTIL MORNING.
ARE YOU TELLING ME THAT?
NO.
FORMER CHIEF OFFICER SPADE!
IS AGENT CANARII REALLY THAT GOOD?
MM-HMM.
WOW.

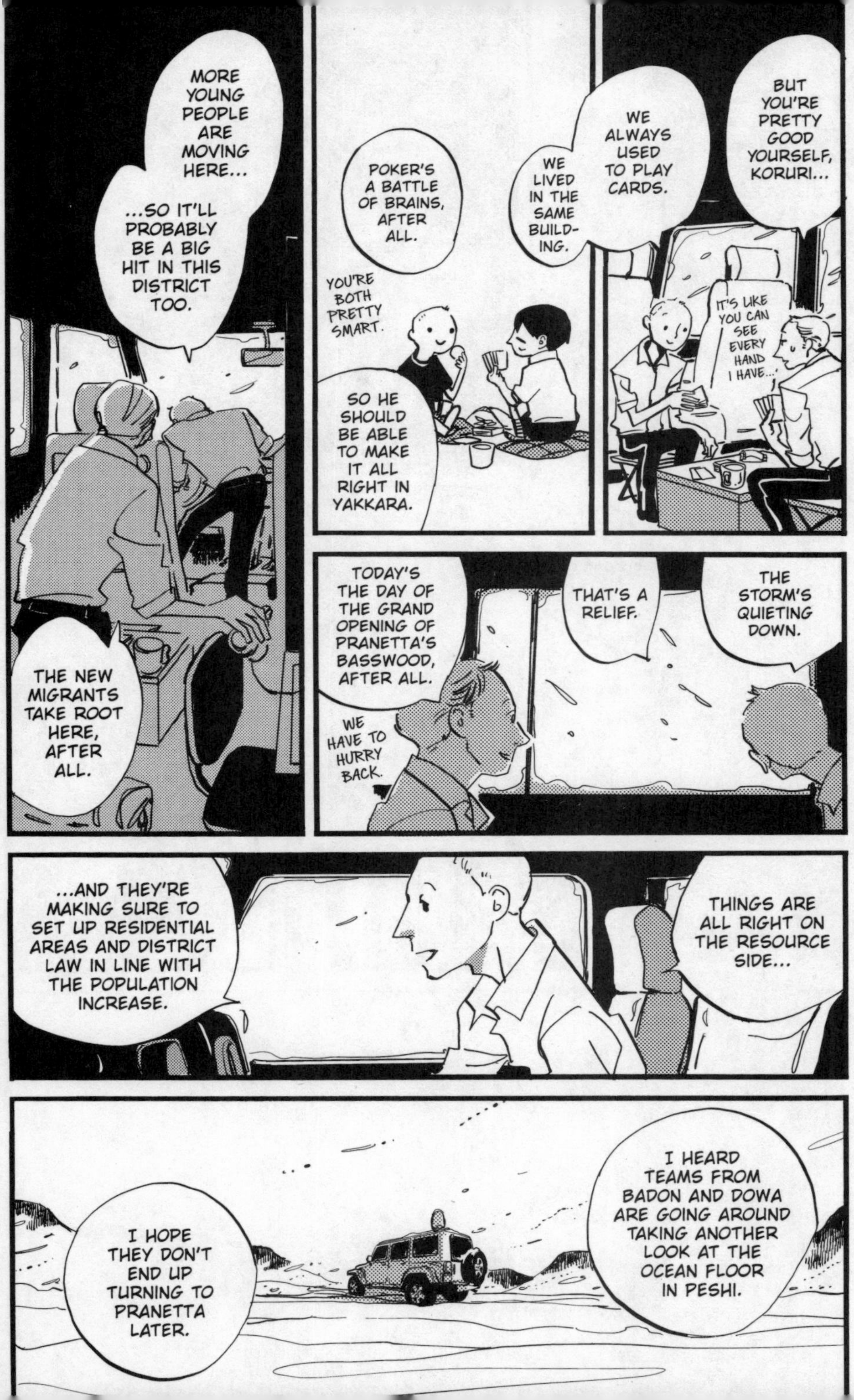
BUT YOU'RE PRETTY GOOD YOURSELF, KORURI...
IT'S LIKE YOU CAN SEE EVERY HAND I HAVE...
WE ALWAYS USED TO PLAY CARDS.
WE LIVED IN THE SAME BUILD-ING.
POKER'S A BATTLE OF BRAINS, AFTER ALL.
YOU'RE BOTH PRETTY SMART.
SO HE SHOULD BE ABLE TO MAKE IT ALL RIGHT IN YAKKARA.
THE STORM'S QUIETING DOWN.
THAT'S A RELIEF.
TODAY'S THE DAY OF THE GRAND OPENING OF PRANETTA'S BASSWOOD, AFTER ALL.
WE HAVE TO HURRY BACK.
MORE YOUNG PEOPLE ARE MOVING HERE...
...SO IT'LL PROBABLY BE A BIG HIT IN THIS DISTRICT TOO.
THE NEW MIGRANTS TAKE ROOT HERE, AFTER ALL.
THINGS ARE ALL RIGHT ON THE RESOURCE SIDE...
...AND THEY'RE MAKING SURE TO SET UP RESIDENTIAL AREAS AND DISTRICT LAW IN LINE WITH THE POPULATION INCREASE.
I HEARD TEAMS FROM BADON AND DOWA ARE GOING AROUND TAKING ANOTHER LOOK AT THE OCEAN FLOOR IN PESHI.
I HOPE THEY DON'T END UP TURNING TO PRANETTA LATER.

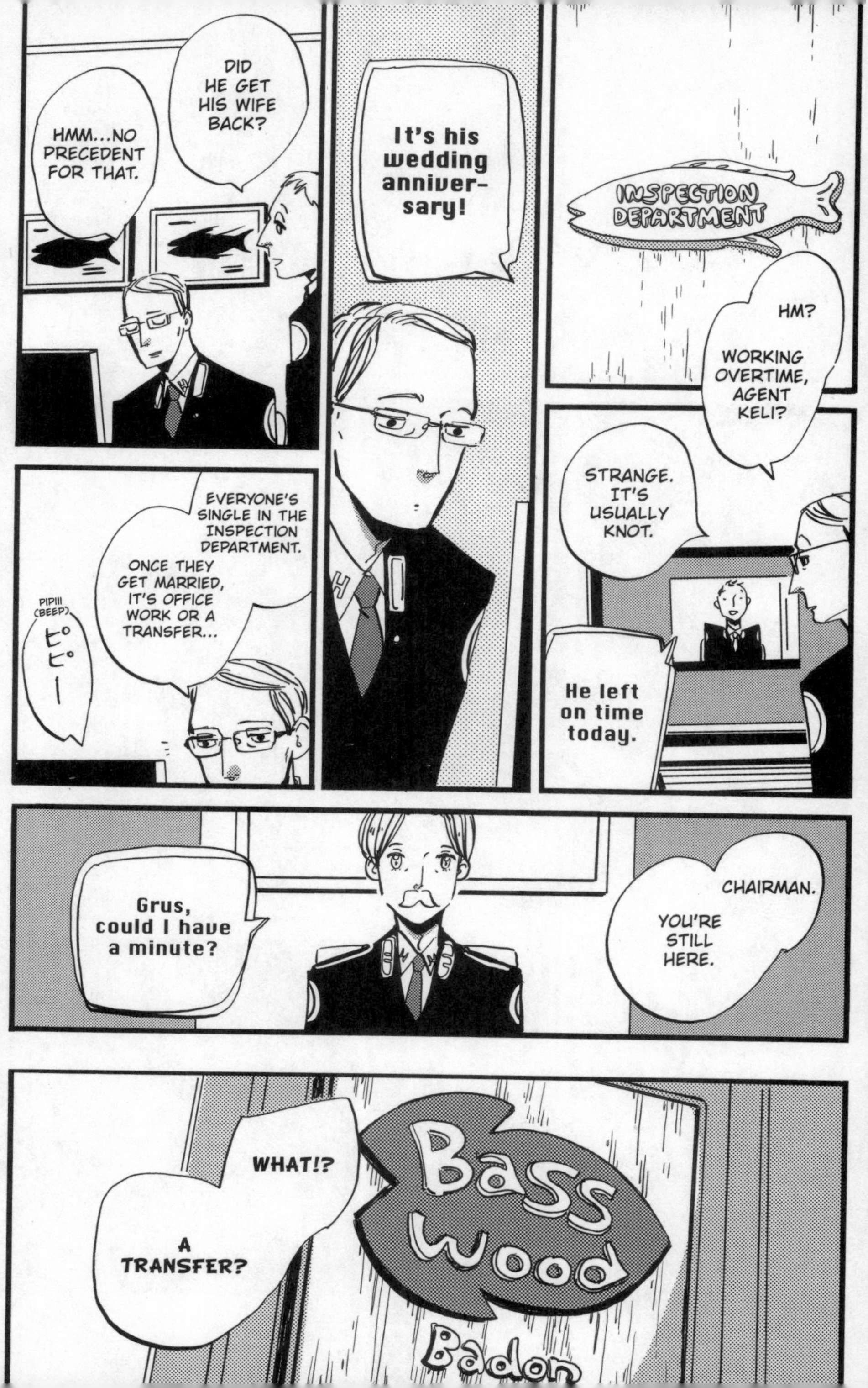

INSPECTION DEPARTMENT
HM?
WORKING OVERTIME, AGENT KELI?
STRANGE. IT'S USUALLY KNOT.
He left on time today.
It's his wedding anniver-sary!
DID HE GET HIS WIFE BACK?
HMM...NO PRECEDENT FOR THAT.
EVERYONE'S SINGLE IN THE INSPECTION DEPARTMENT.
ONCE THEY GET MARRIED, IT'S OFFICE WORK OR A TRANSFER...
PIPIII (BEEP)
ピピー
CHAIRMAN.
YOU'RE STILL HERE.
Grus, could I have a minute?
Bass wood
Badon
WHAT!?
A TRANSFER?

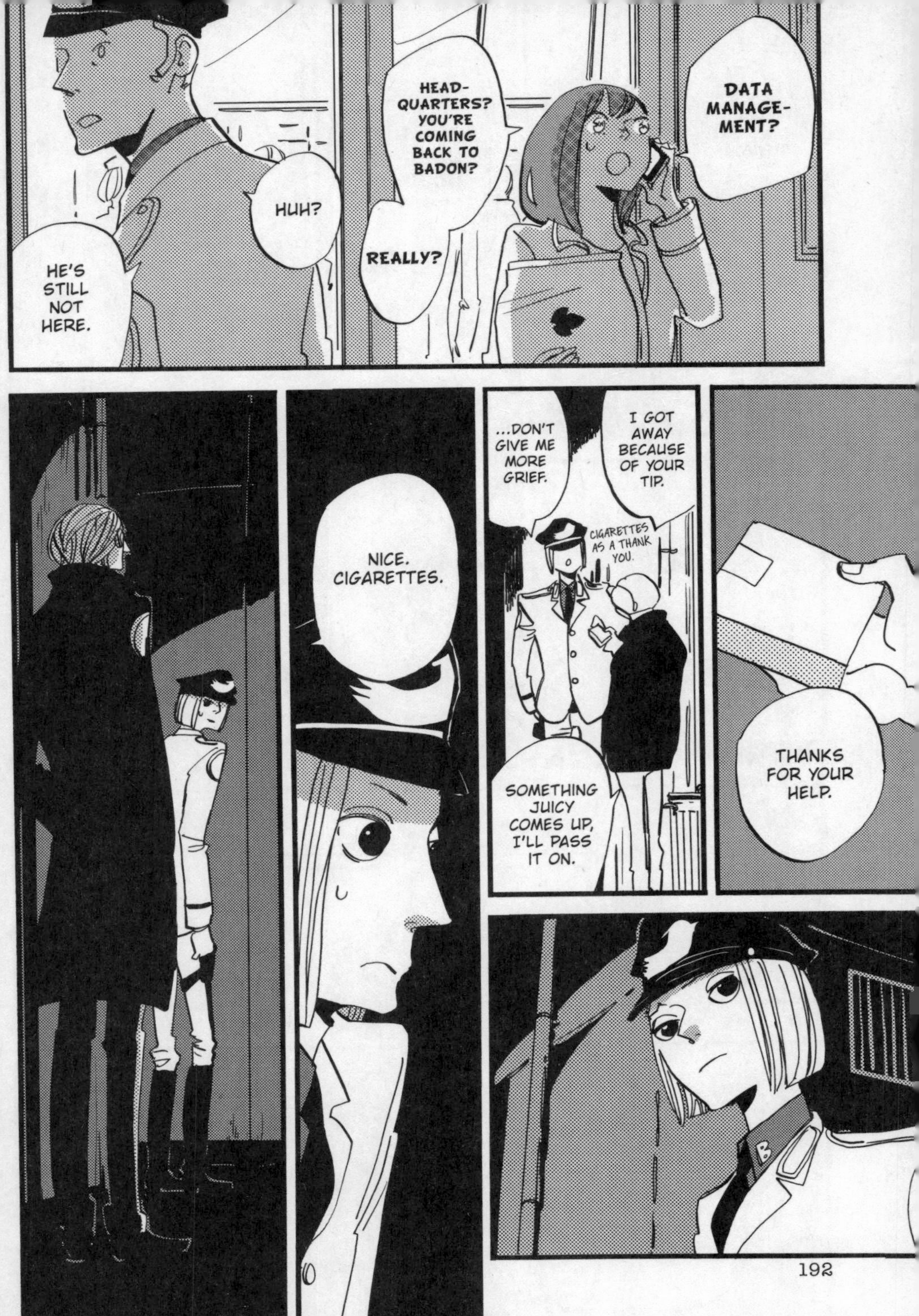
DATA MANAGE-MENT?
HEAD-QUARTERS? YOU'RE COMING BACK TO BADON?
REALLY?
HUH?
HE'S STILL NOT HERE.
THANKS FOR YOUR HELP.
I GOT AWAY BECAUSE OF YOUR TIP.
...DON'T GIVE ME MORE GRIEF.
CIGARETTES AS A THANK YOU.
SOMETHING JUICY COMES UP, I'LL PASS IT ON.
NICE. CIGARETTES.

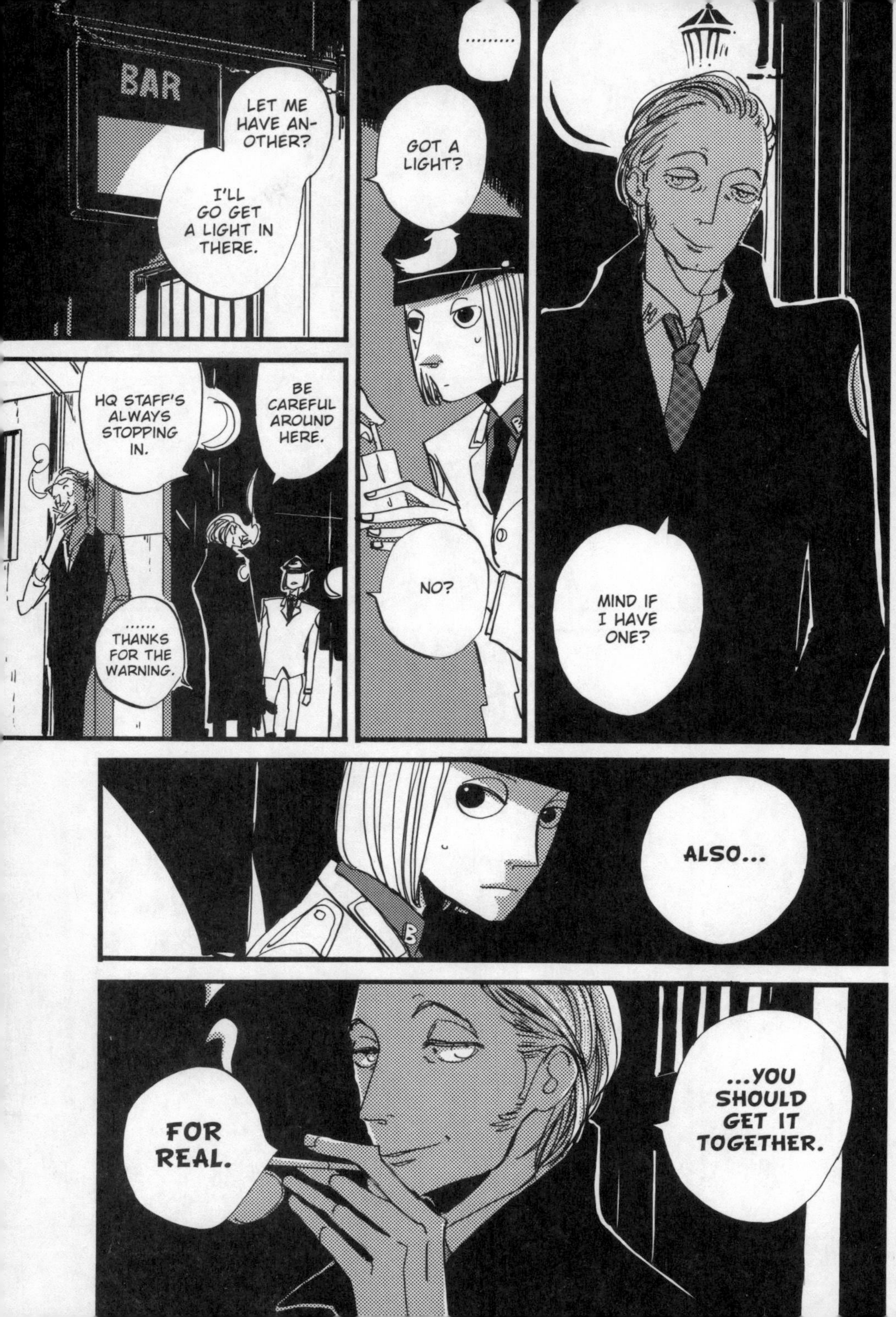
MIND IF I HAVE ONE?
....
GOT A LIGHT?
NO?
LET ME HAVE AN-OTHER?
I'LL GO GET A LIGHT IN THERE.
BAR
BE CAREFUL AROUND HERE.
HQ STAFF'S ALWAYS STOPPING IN.
...... THANKS FOR THE WARNING.
ALSO...
...YOU SHOULD GET IT TOGETHER.
FOR REAL.

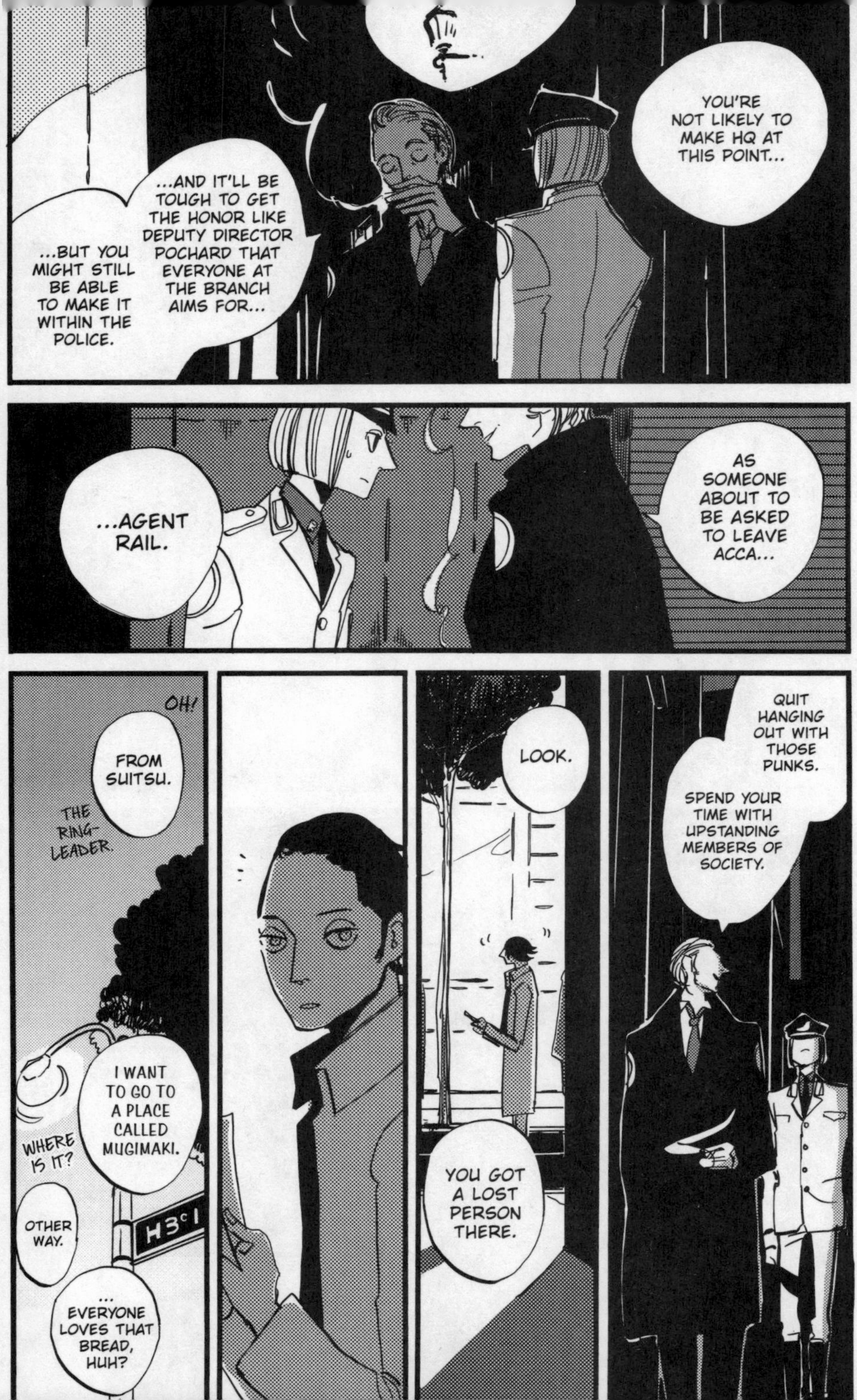
YOU'RE NOT LIKELY TO MAKE HQ AT THIS POINT...
...AND IT'LL BE TOUGH TO GET THE HONOR LIKE DEPUTY DIRECTOR POCHARD THAT EVERYONE AT THE BRANCH AIMS FOR...
...BUT YOU MIGHT STILL BE ABLE TO MAKE IT WITHIN THE POLICE.
AS SOMEONE ABOUT TO BE ASKED TO LEAVE ACCA...
...AGENT RAIL.
QUIT HANGING OUT WITH THOSE PUNKS.
SPEND YOUR TIME WITH UPSTANDING MEMBERS OF SOCIETY.
LOOK.
YOU GOT A LOST PERSON THERE.
OH!
FROM SUITSU.
THE RING-LEADER.
I WANT TO GO TO A PLACE CALLED MUGIMAKI.
WHERE IS IT?
OTHER WAY.
...EVERYONE LOVES THAT BREAD, HUH?

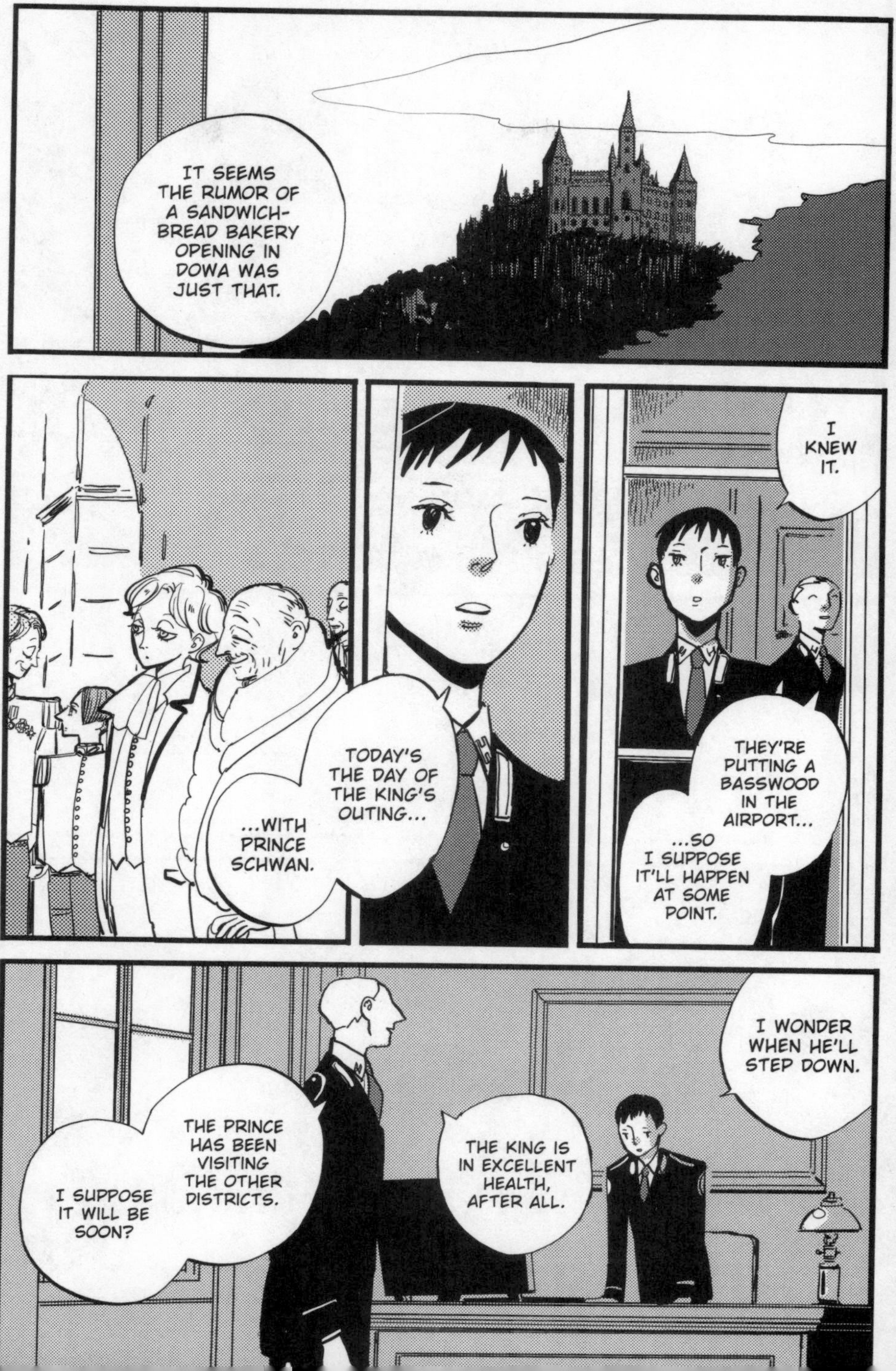
IT SEEMS THE RUMOR OF A SANDWICH-BREAD BAKERY OPENING IN DOWA WAS JUST THAT.
I KNEW IT.
THEY'RE PUTTING A BASSWOOD IN THE AIRPORT...
...SO I SUPPOSE IT'LL HAPPEN AT SOME POINT.
TODAY'S THE DAY OF THE KING'S OUTING...
...WITH PRINCE SCHWAN.
I WONDER WHEN HE'LL STEP DOWN.
THE KING IS IN EXCELLENT HEALTH, AFTER ALL.
THE PRINCE HAS BEEN VISITING THE OTHER DISTRICTS.
I SUPPOSE IT WILL BE SOON?

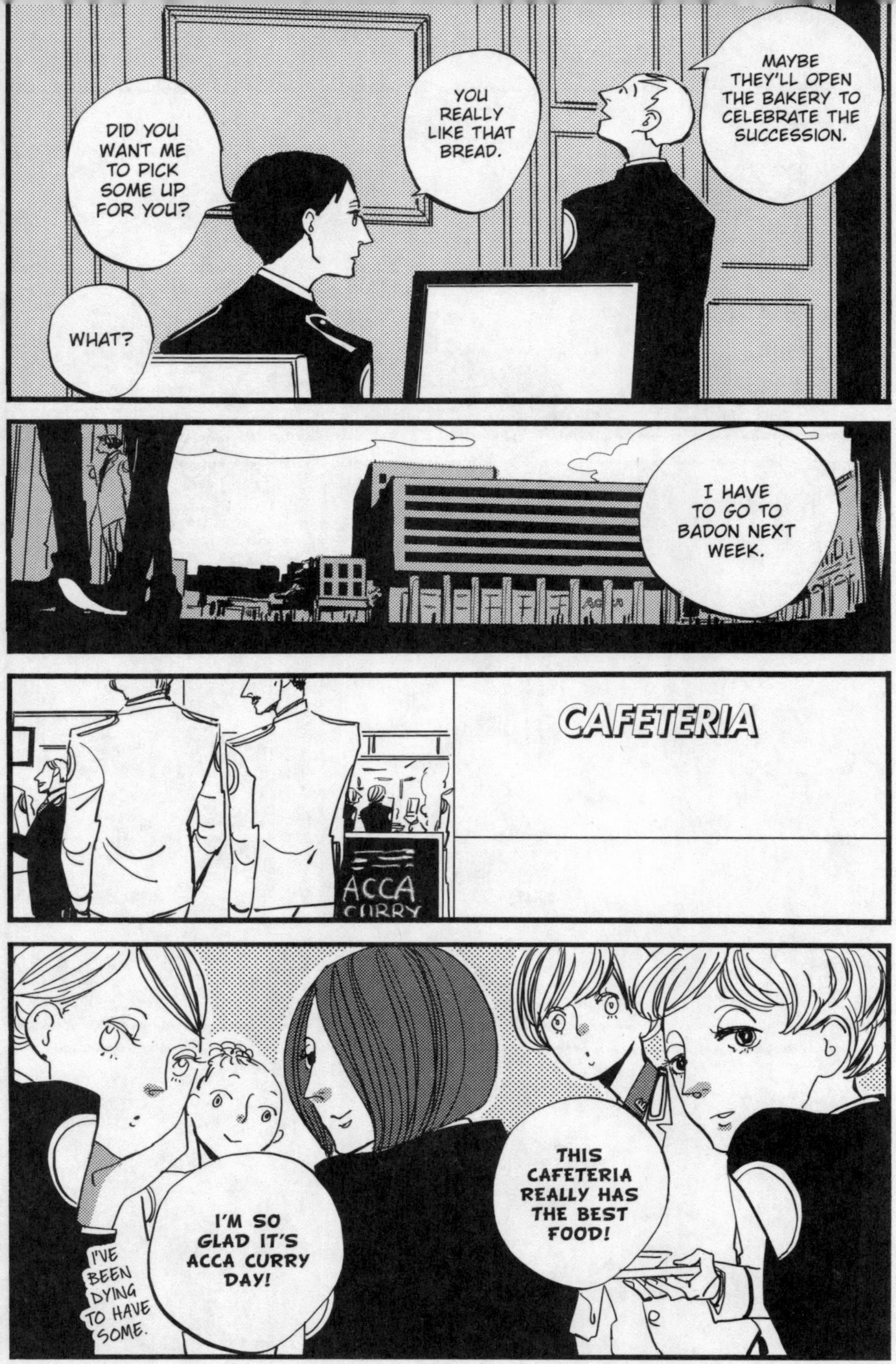
MAYBE THEY'LL OPEN THE BAKERY TO CELEBRATE THE SUCCESSION.
YOU REALLY LIKE THAT BREAD.
DID YOU WANT ME TO PICK SOME UP FOR YOU?
WHAT?
I HAVE TO GO TO BADON NEXT WEEK.
CAFETERIA
ACCA CURRY
THIS CAFETERIA REALLY HAS THE BEST FOOD!
I'M SO GLAD IT'S ACCA CURRY DAY!
I'VE BEEN DYING TO HAVE SOME.

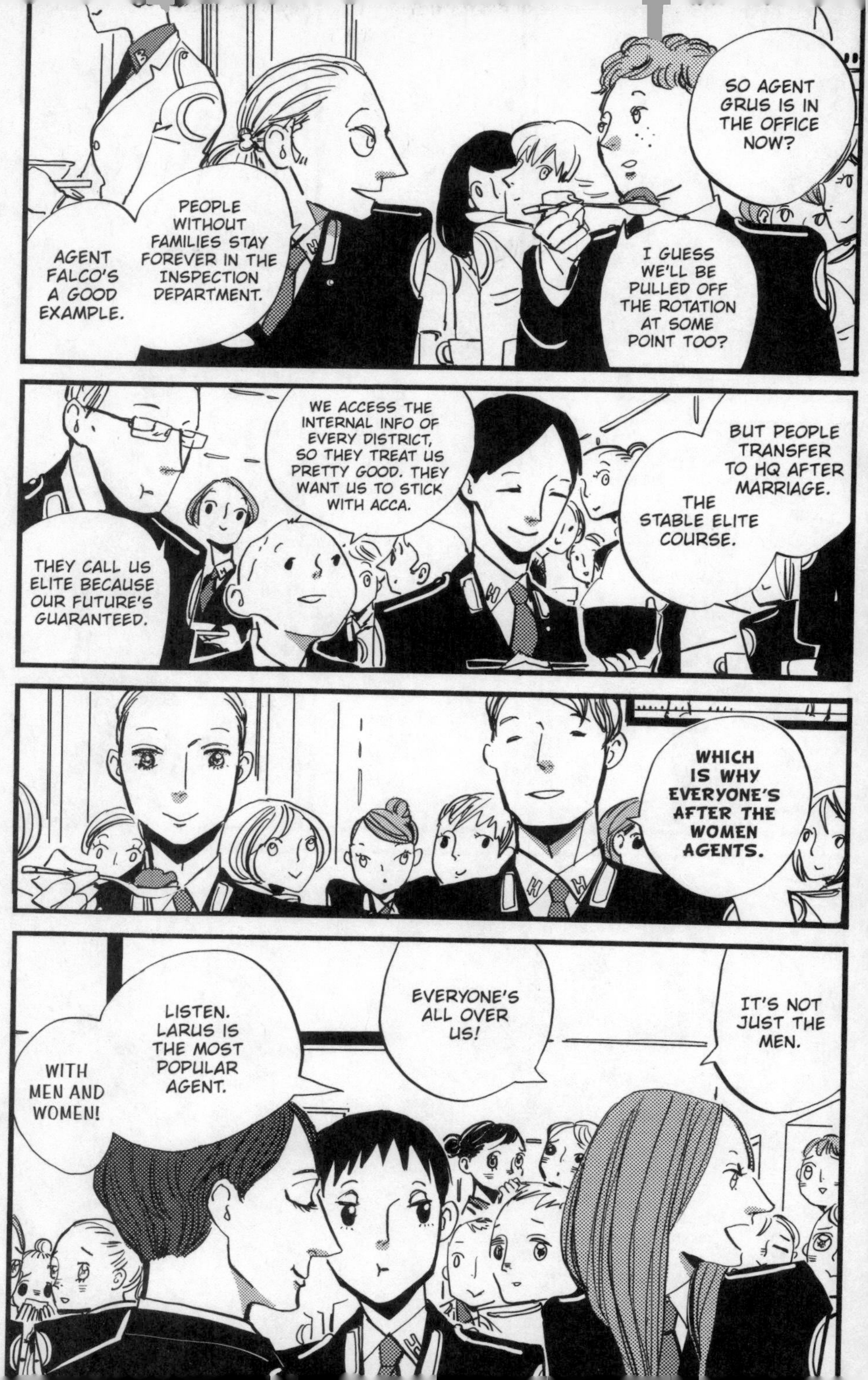
SO AGENT GRUS IS IN THE OFFICE NOW?
I GUESS WE'LL BE PULLED OFF THE ROTATION AT SOME POINT TOO?
PEOPLE WITHOUT FAMILIES STAY FOREVER IN THE INSPECTION DEPARTMENT.
AGENT FALCO'S A GOOD EXAMPLE.
BUT PEOPLE TRANSFER TO HQ AFTER MARRIAGE.
THE STABLE ELITE COURSE.
WE ACCESS THE INTERNAL INFO OF EVERY DISTRICT, SO THEY TREAT US PRETTY GOOD. THEY WANT US TO STICK WITH ACCA.
THEY CALL US ELITE BECAUSE OUR FUTURE'S GUARANTEED.
WHICH IS WHY EVERYONE'S AFTER THE WOMEN AGENTS.
IT'S NOT JUST THE MEN.
EVERYONE'S ALL OVER US!
LISTEN. LARUS IS THE MOST POPULAR AGENT.
WITH MEN AND WOMEN!

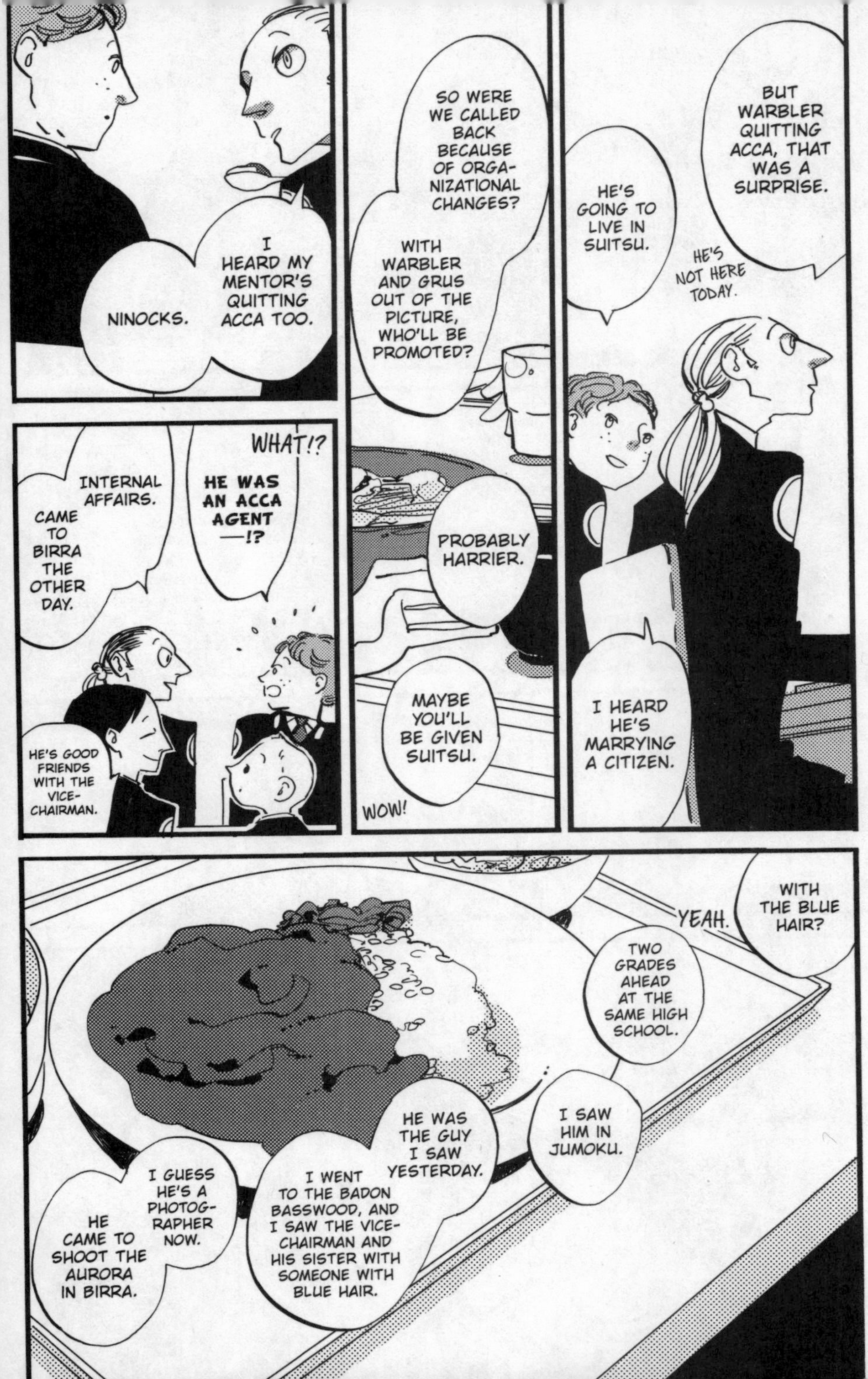
BUT WARBLER QUITTING ACCA, THAT WAS A SURPRISE.
HE'S NOT HERE TODAY.
HE'S GOING TO LIVE IN SUITSU.
I HEARD HE'S MARRYING A CITIZEN.
SO WERE WE CALLED BACK BECAUSE OF ORGANIZATIONAL CHANGES?
WITH WARBLER AND GRUS OUT OF THE PICTURE, WHO'LL BE PROMOTED?
PROBABLY HARRIER.
MAYBE YOU'LL BE GIVEN SUITSU.
WOW!
I HEARD MY MENTOR'S QUITTING ACCA TOO.
NINOCKS.
WHAT!?
HE WAS AN ACCA AGENT—!?
INTERNAL AFFAIRS.
CAME TO BIRRA THE OTHER DAY.
HE'S GOOD FRIENDS WITH THE VICE-CHAIRMAN.
WITH THE BLUE HAIR?
YEAH.
TWO GRADES AHEAD AT THE SAME HIGH SCHOOL.
I SAW HIM IN JUMOKU.
HE WAS THE GUY I SAW YESTERDAY.
I WENT TO THE BADON BASSWOOD, AND I SAW THE VICE-CHAIRMAN AND HIS SISTER WITH SOMEONE WITH BLUE HAIR.
I GUESS HE'S A PHOTOGRAPHER NOW.
HE CAME TO SHOOT THE AURORA IN BIRRA.

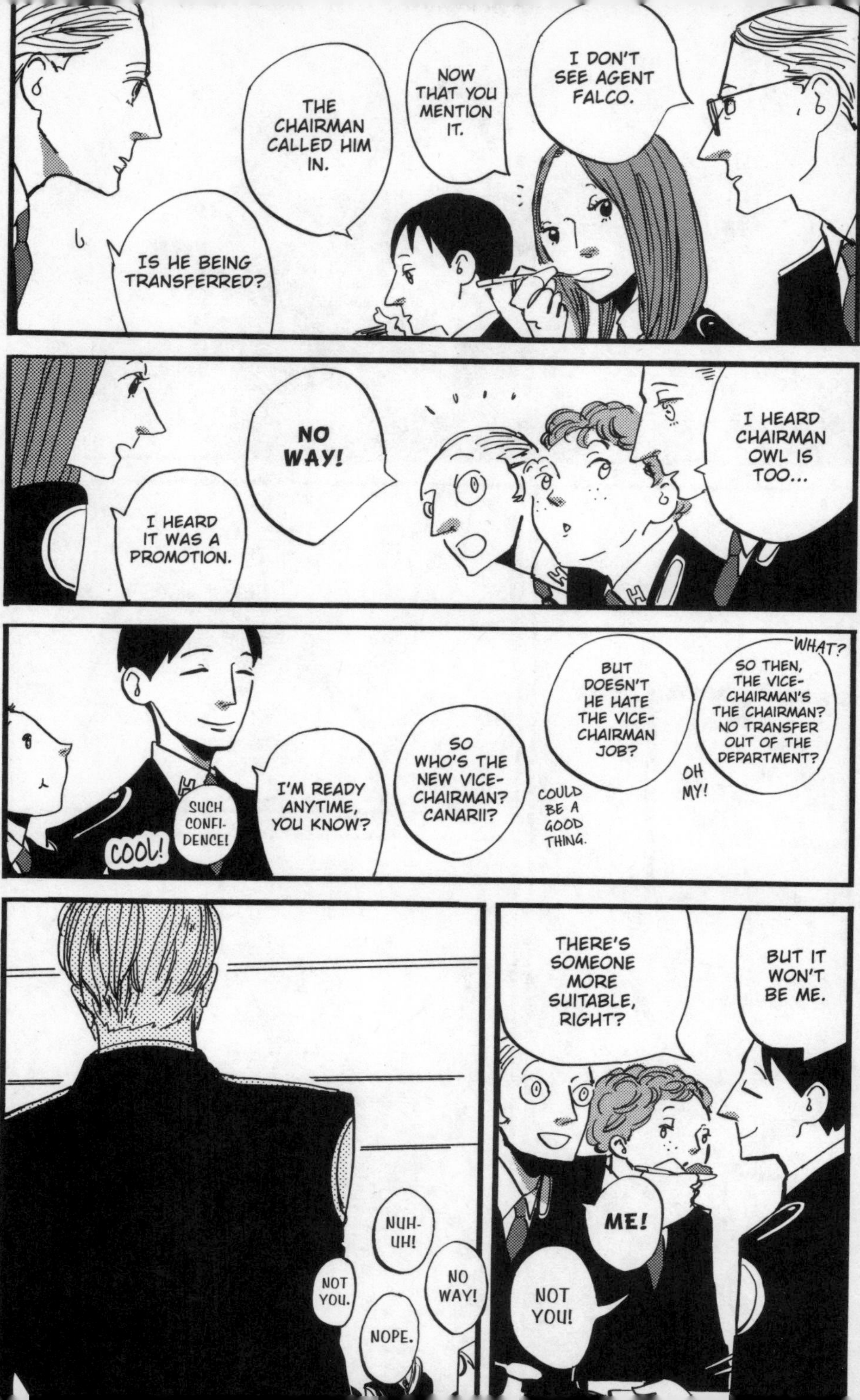
I DON'T SEE AGENT FALCO.
NOW THAT YOU MENTION IT.
THE CHAIRMAN CALLED HIM IN.
IS HE BEING TRANSFERRED?
I HEARD CHAIRMAN OWL IS TOO...
NO WAY!
I HEARD IT WAS A PROMOTION.
WHAT?
SO THEN, THE VICE-CHAIRMAN'S THE CHAIRMAN? NO TRANSFER OUT OF THE DEPARTMENT?
OH MY!
BUT DOESN'T HE HATE THE VICE-CHAIRMAN JOB?
COULD BE A GOOD THING.
SO WHO'S THE NEW VICE-CHAIRMAN? CANARII?
I'M READY ANYTIME, YOU KNOW?
SUCH CONFIDENCE!
COOL!
BUT IT WON'T BE ME.
THERE'S SOMEONE MORE SUITABLE, RIGHT?
ME!
NOT YOU!
NUH-UH!
NO WAY!
NOT YOU.
NOPE.

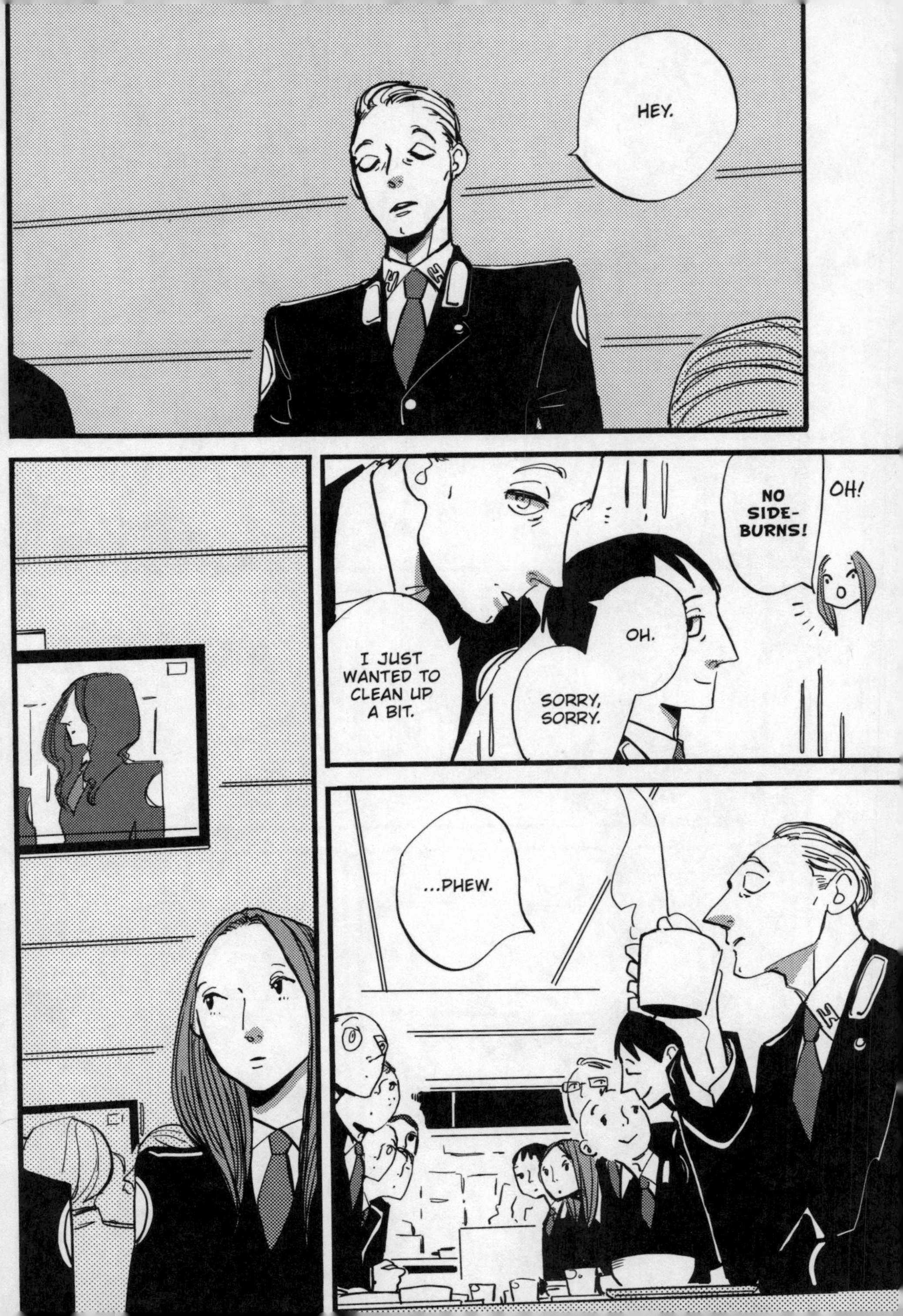
HEY.
OH!
NO SIDE-BURNS!
OH.
SORRY, SORRY.
I JUST WANTED TO CLEAN UP A BIT.
...PHEW.

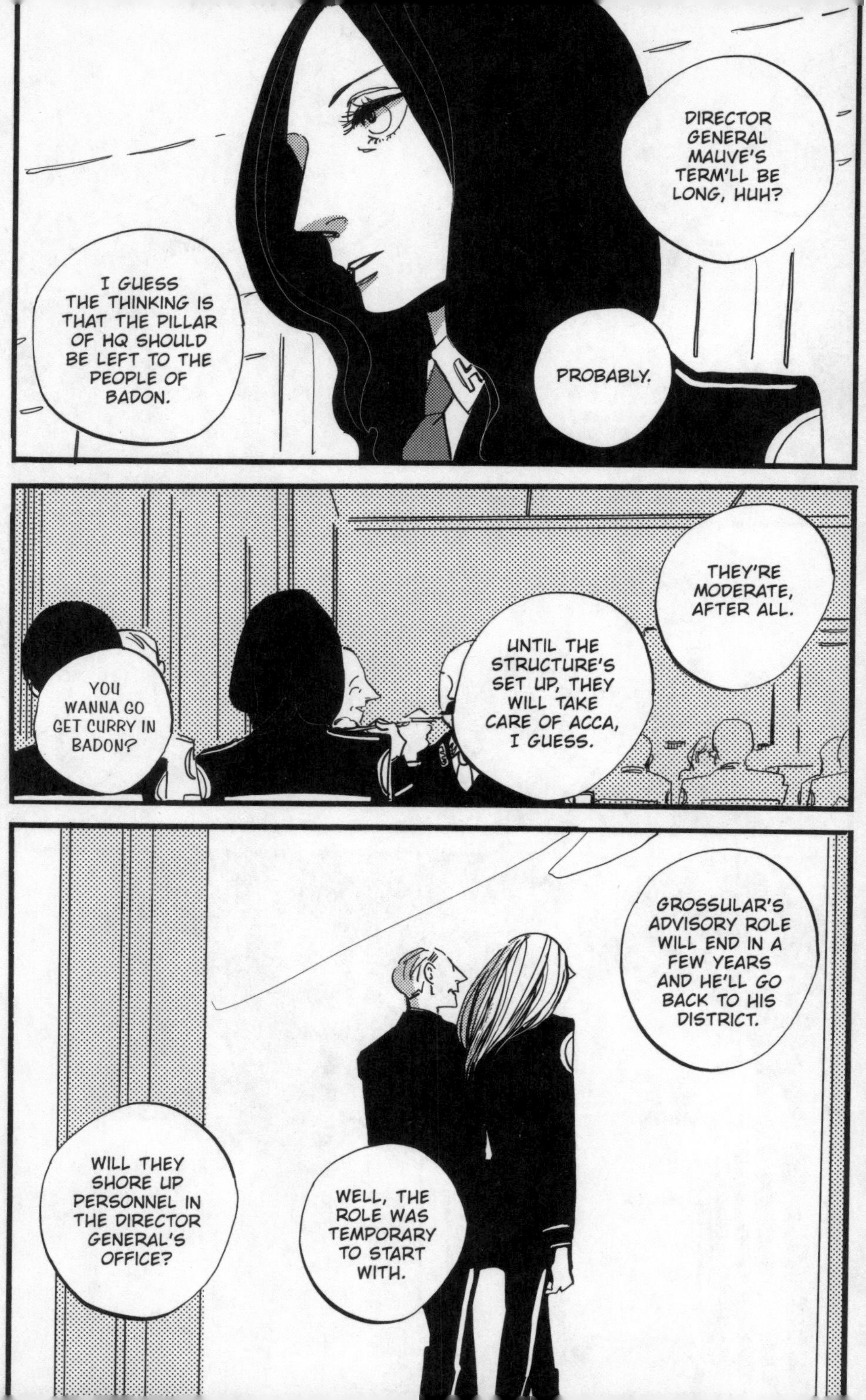
DIRECTOR GENERAL MAUVE'S TERM'LL BE LONG, HUH?
PROBABLY.
I GUESS THE THINKING IS THAT THE PILLAR OF HQ SHOULD BE LEFT TO THE PEOPLE OF BADON.
THEY'RE MODERATE, AFTER ALL.
UNTIL THE STRUCTURE'S SET UP, THEY WILL TAKE CARE OF ACCA, I GUESS.
YOU WANNA GO GET CURRY IN BADON?
GROSSULAR'S ADVISORY ROLE WILL END IN A FEW YEARS AND HE'LL GO BACK TO HIS DISTRICT.
WELL, THE ROLE WAS TEMPORARY TO START WITH.
WILL THEY SHORE UP PERSONNEL IN THE DIRECTOR GENERAL'S OFFICE?

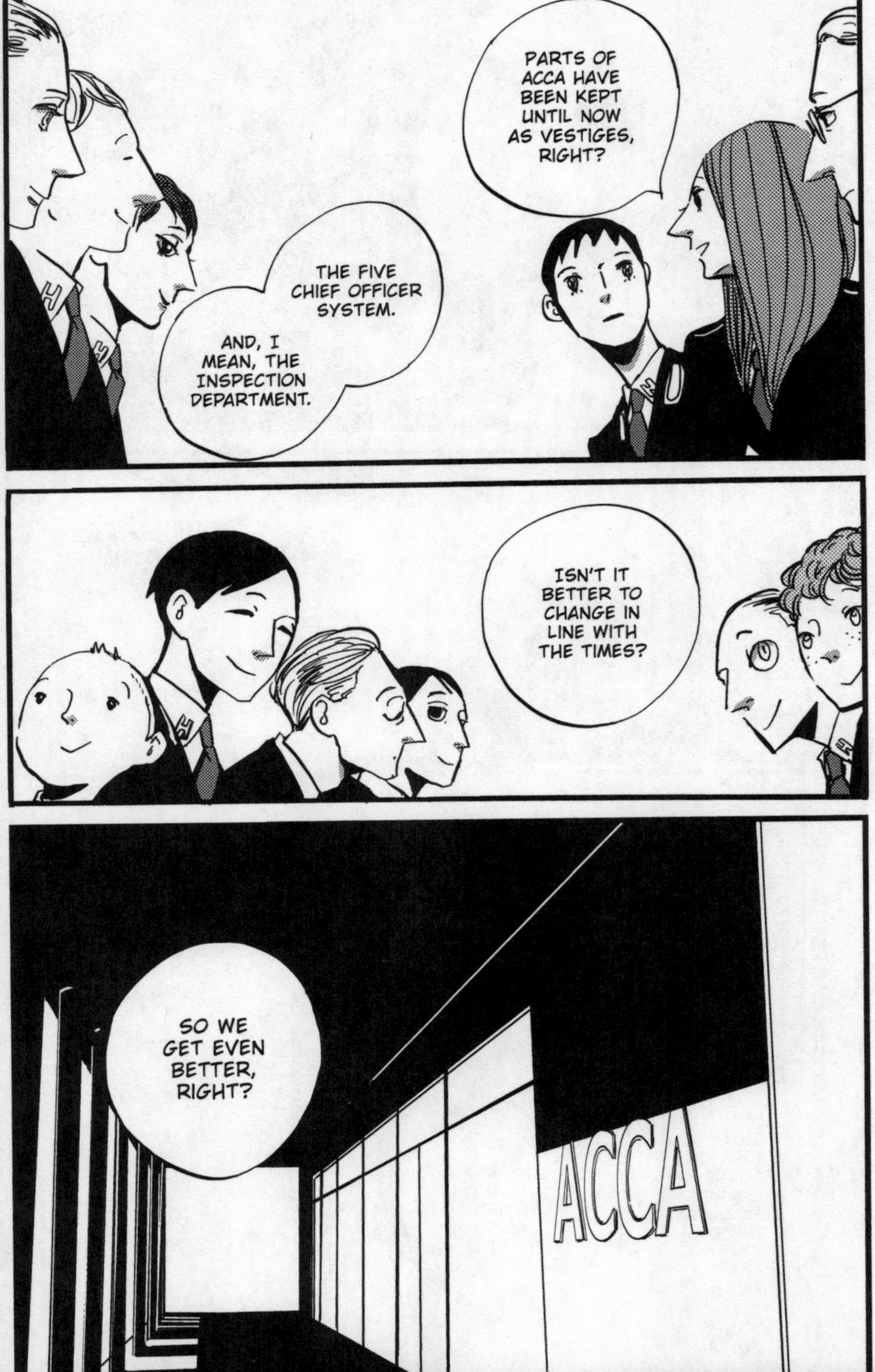
PARTS OF ACCA HAVE BEEN KEPT UNTIL NOW AS VESTIGES, RIGHT?
THE FIVE CHIEF OFFICER SYSTEM.
AND, I MEAN, THE INSPECTION DEPARTMENT.
ISN'T IT BETTER TO CHANGE IN LINE WITH THE TIMES?
SO WE GET EVEN BETTER, RIGHT?
ACCA

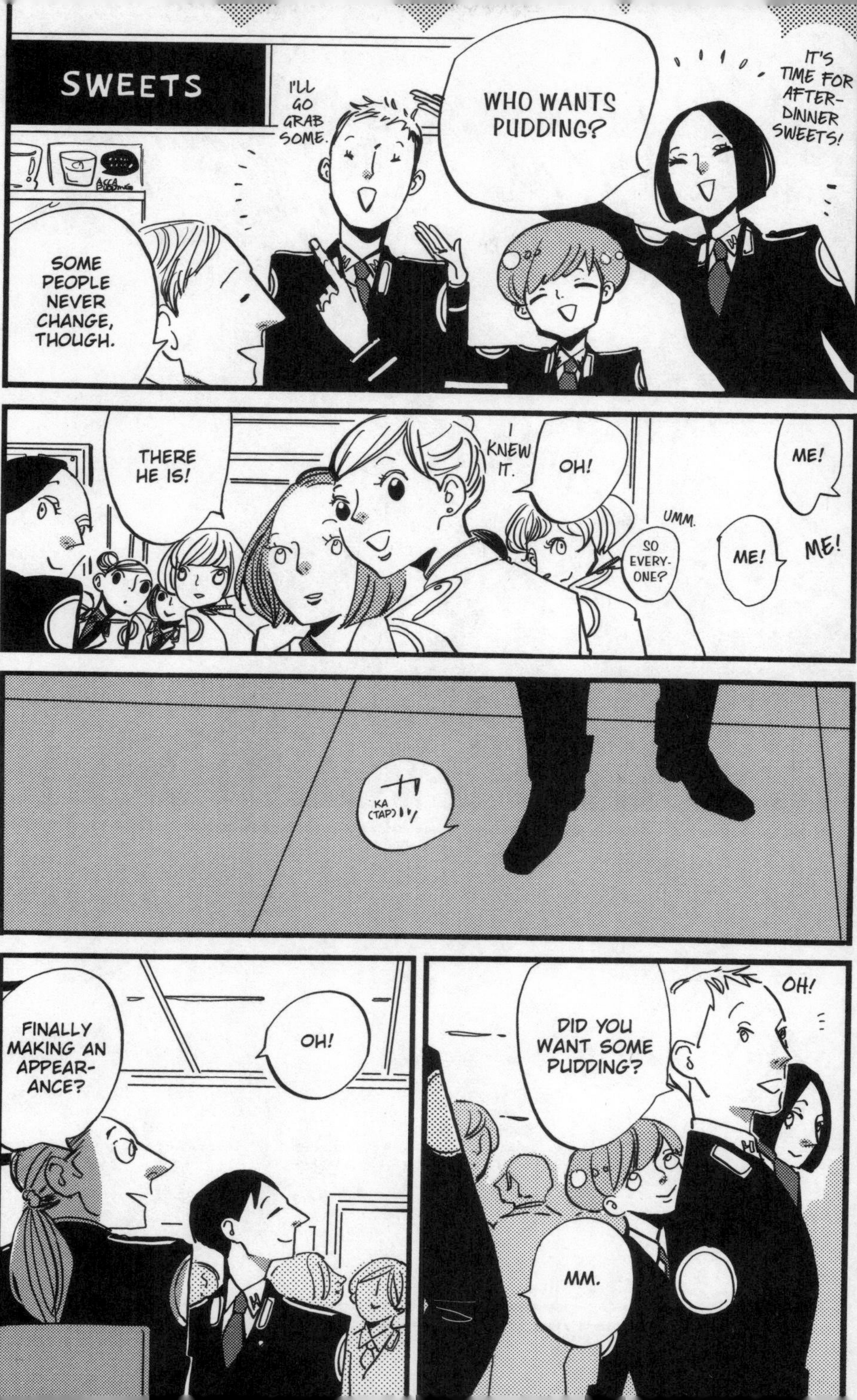
IT'S TIME FOR AFTER-DINNER SWEETS!
WHO WANTS PUDDING?
I'LL GO GRAB SOME.
SWEETS
SOME PEOPLE NEVER CHANGE, THOUGH.
ME!
ME!
ME!
UMM.
SO EVERY-ONE?
OH!
I KNEW IT.
THERE HE IS!
KA (TAP)
OH!
DID YOU WANT SOME PUDDING?
MM.
OH!
FINALLY MAKING AN APPEAR-ANCE?

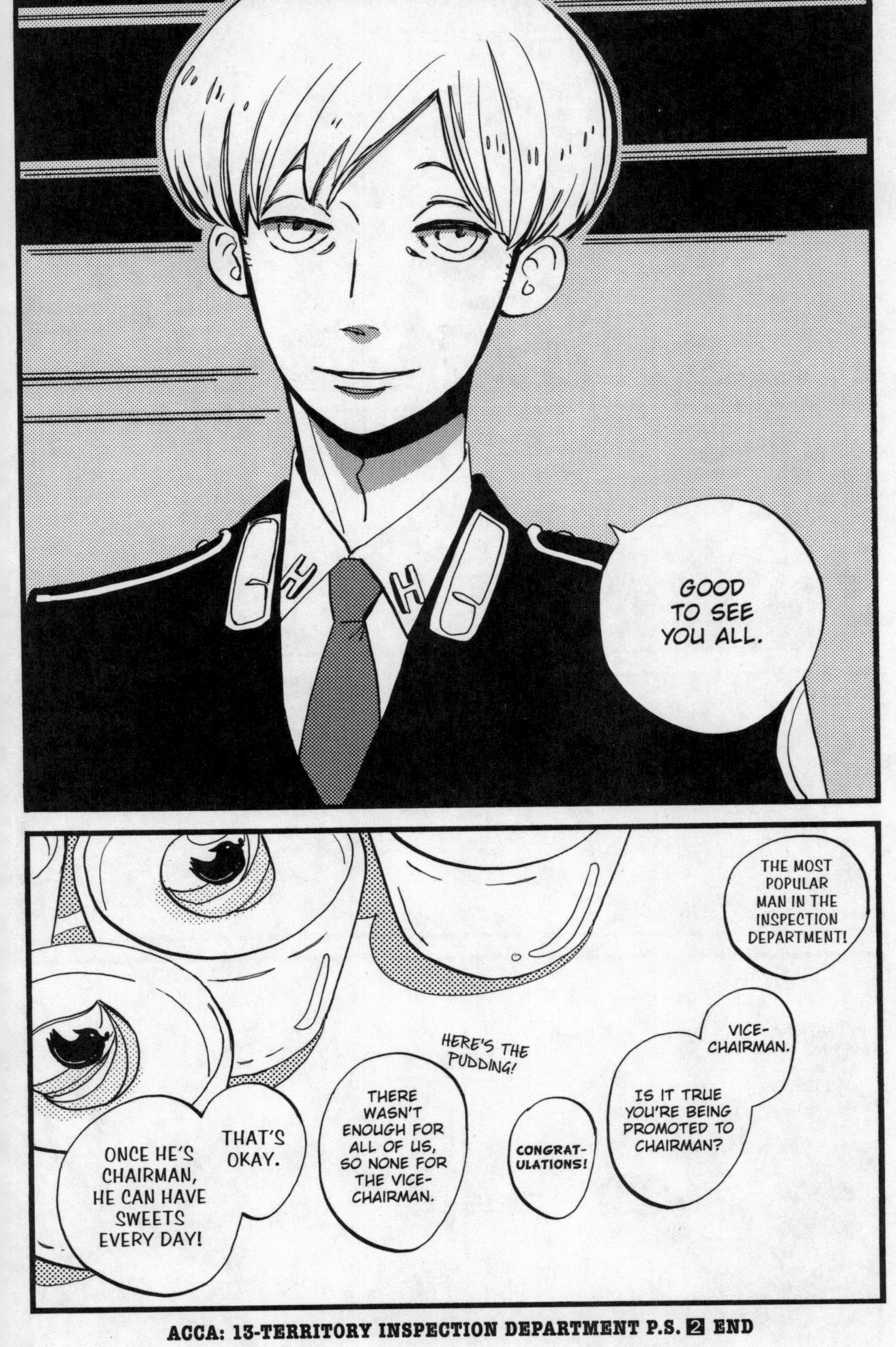
GOOD TO SEE YOU ALL.
THE MOST POPULAR MAN IN THE INSPECTION DEPARTMENT!
VICE-CHAIRMAN.
IS IT TRUE YOU'RE BEING PROMOTED TO CHAIRMAN?
CONGRAT-ULATIONS!
HERE'S THE PUDDING!
THERE WASN'T ENOUGH FOR ALL OF US, SO NONE FOR THE VICE-CHAIRMAN.
THAT'S OKAY.
ONCE HE'S CHAIRMAN, HE CAN HAVE SWEETS EVERY DAY!

ACCA: 13-TERRITORY INSPECTION DEPARTMENT P.S. 2 END

ACCA
13
TERRITORY
INSPECTION
DEPARTMENT
DEPT ACCA 13 TERRITORY INSPECTION
PASS
P.S.

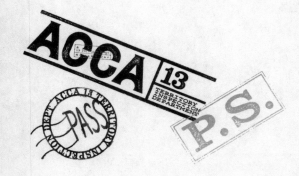

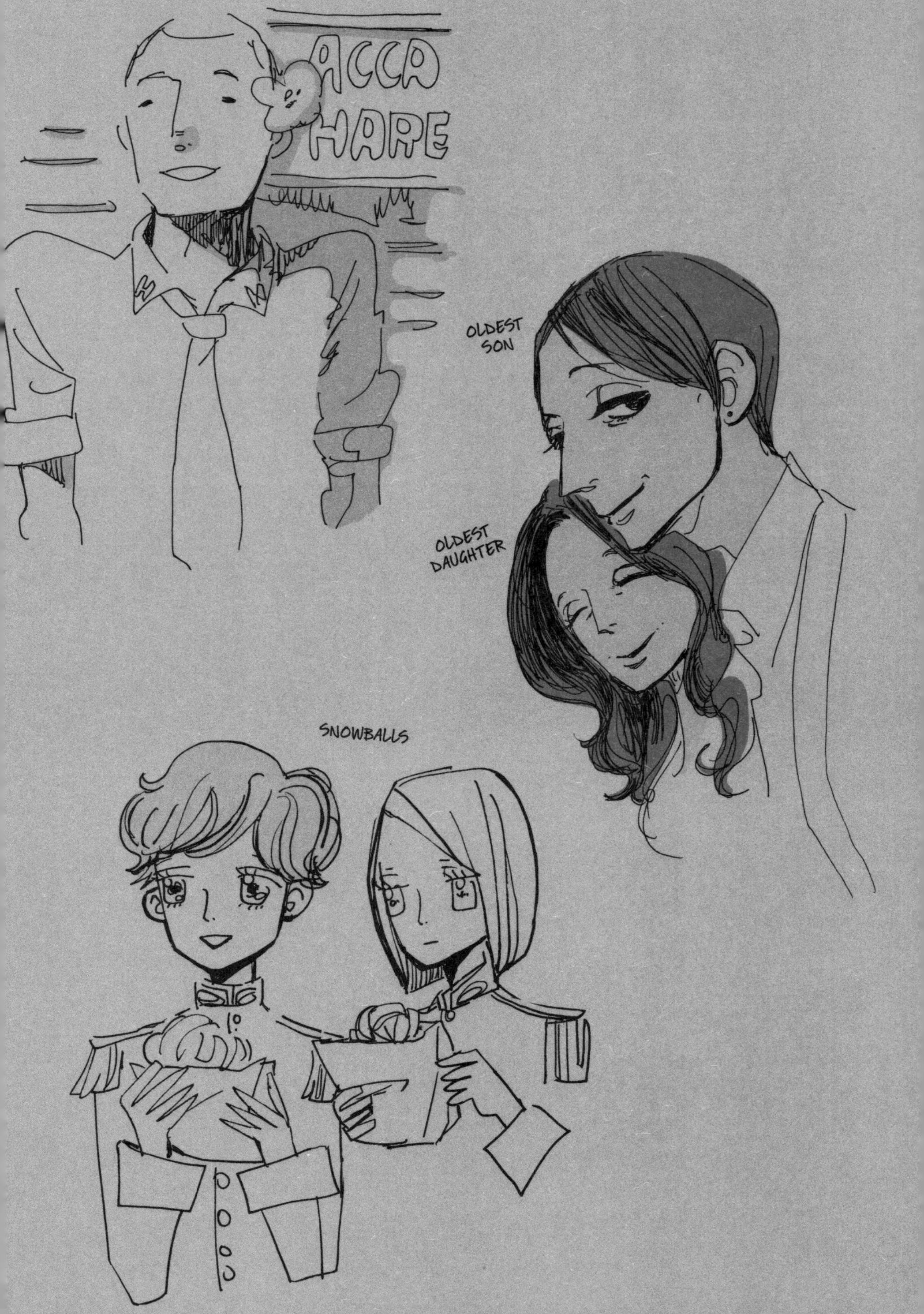
ACCA
HARE
OLDEST SON
OLDEST DAUGHTER
SNOWBALLS

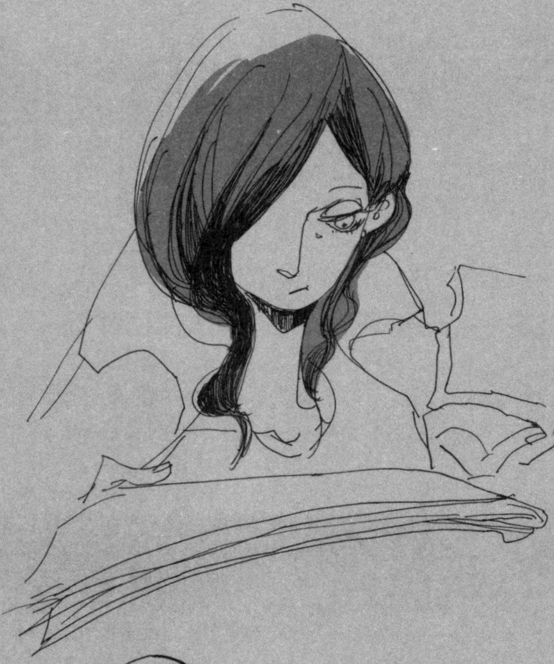
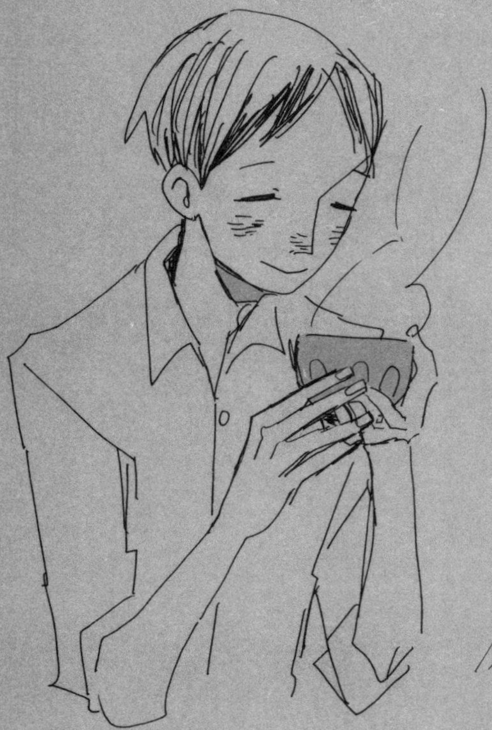
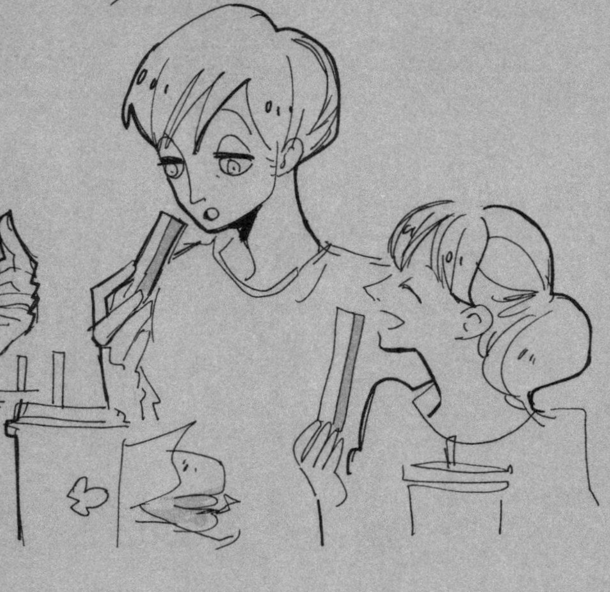
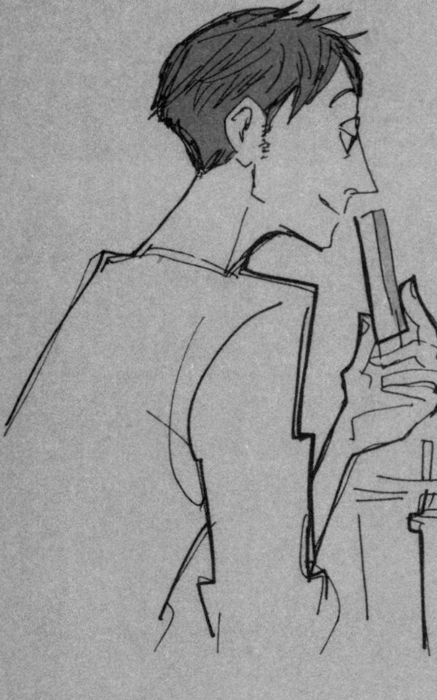

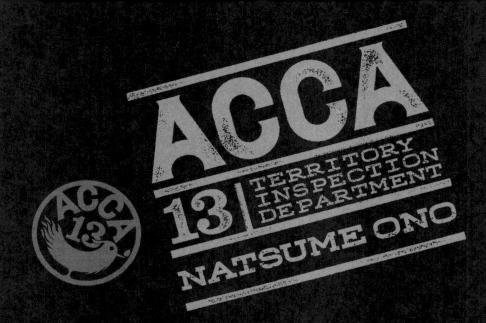

Complete in six volumes!
On sale now to rave reviews!!

With the world divided up into thirteen districts, ACCA is the massive organization that unifies them all. ACCA Headquarters Inspection Department Vice-Chairman Jean Otus—also known as "Jean the cigarette peddler"—is a pretty shrewd man. But he finds himself caught in a web of intrigue as rumors spread within the organization of a coup d'état. Words, eyes, invitations follow him everywhere. The secret machinations of the entire world reach out to trap Jean!!

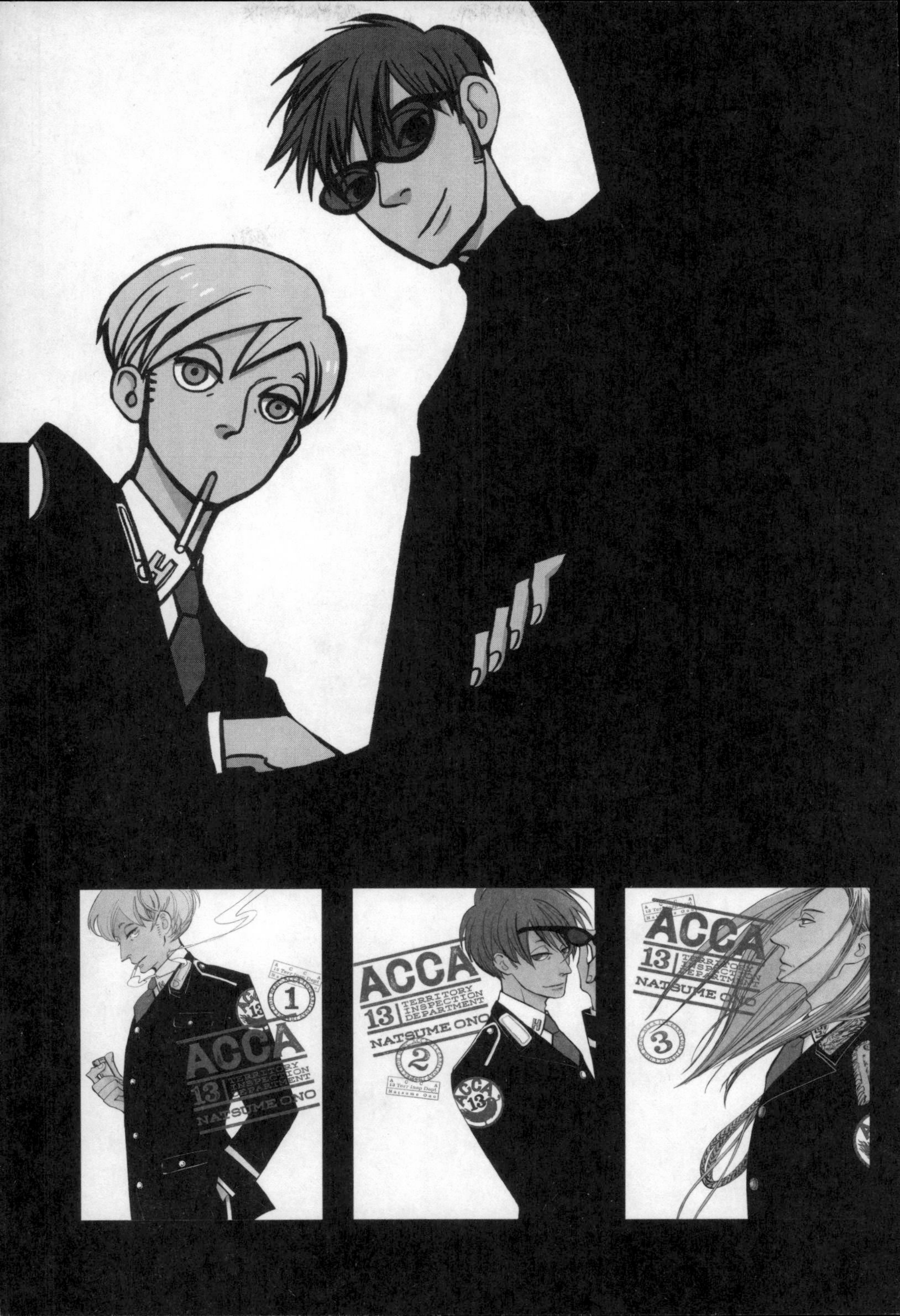
ACCA
13
TERRITORY INSPECTION DEPARTMENT
NATSUME ONO
3
ACCA
13
TERRITORY INSPECTION DEPARTMENT
NATSUME ONO
2
13 Terr Insp Dept
Natsume Ono
1
ACCA
13
TERRITORY INSPECTION DEPARTMENT
NATSUME ONO

VOLUMES 1-6 **IN STORES NOW!**

VOLUMES 1-13 AVAILABLE DIGITALLY!

Toilet-bound Hanako-Kun

At Kamome Academy, rumors abound about the school's Seven Mysteries, one of which is Hanako-san. Said to occupy the third stall of the third floor girls' bathroom in the old school building, Hanako-san grants any wish when summoned. Nene Yashiro, an occult-loving high school girl who dreams of romance, ventures into this haunted bathroom...but the Hanako-san she meets there is nothing like she imagined! Kamome Academy's

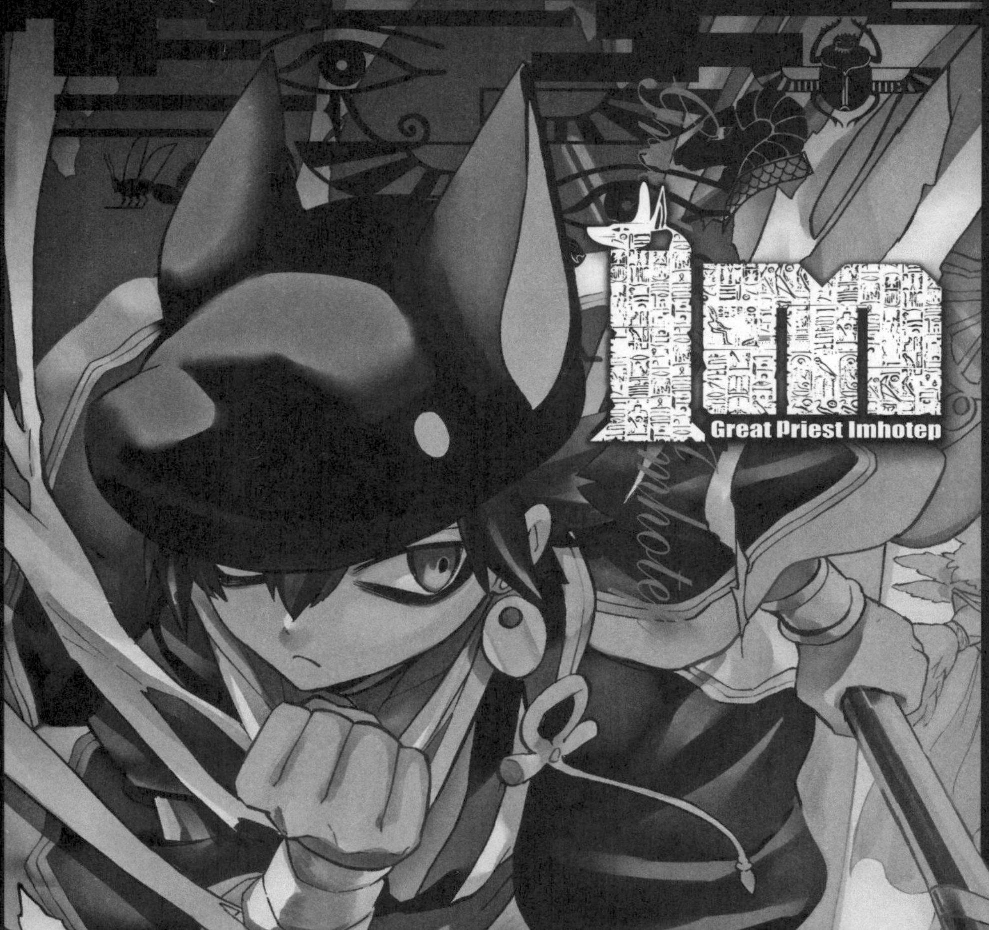
Im
Great Priest Imhotep
VOLUMES 1-6
IN STORES NOW!
VOLUMES 1-11 AVAILABLE DIGITALLY!

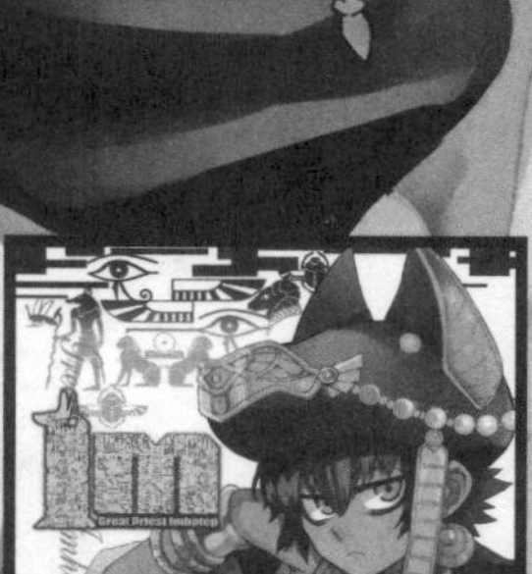
Im
Great Priest Imhotep
1
MAKOTO MORISHITA

From the sands of ancient Egypt to the streets of modern Japan, being displaced by thousands of miles and years won't distract the newly resurrected Great Priest Imhotep from his hunt for the Magai, devious beings who impersonate the gods and have an appetite for destruction! When schoolgirl Hinome crosses paths with this illustrious ancient, is her loner lifestyle about to change for the better...or the worse?!

For more information
visit www.yenpress.com

Yen Press

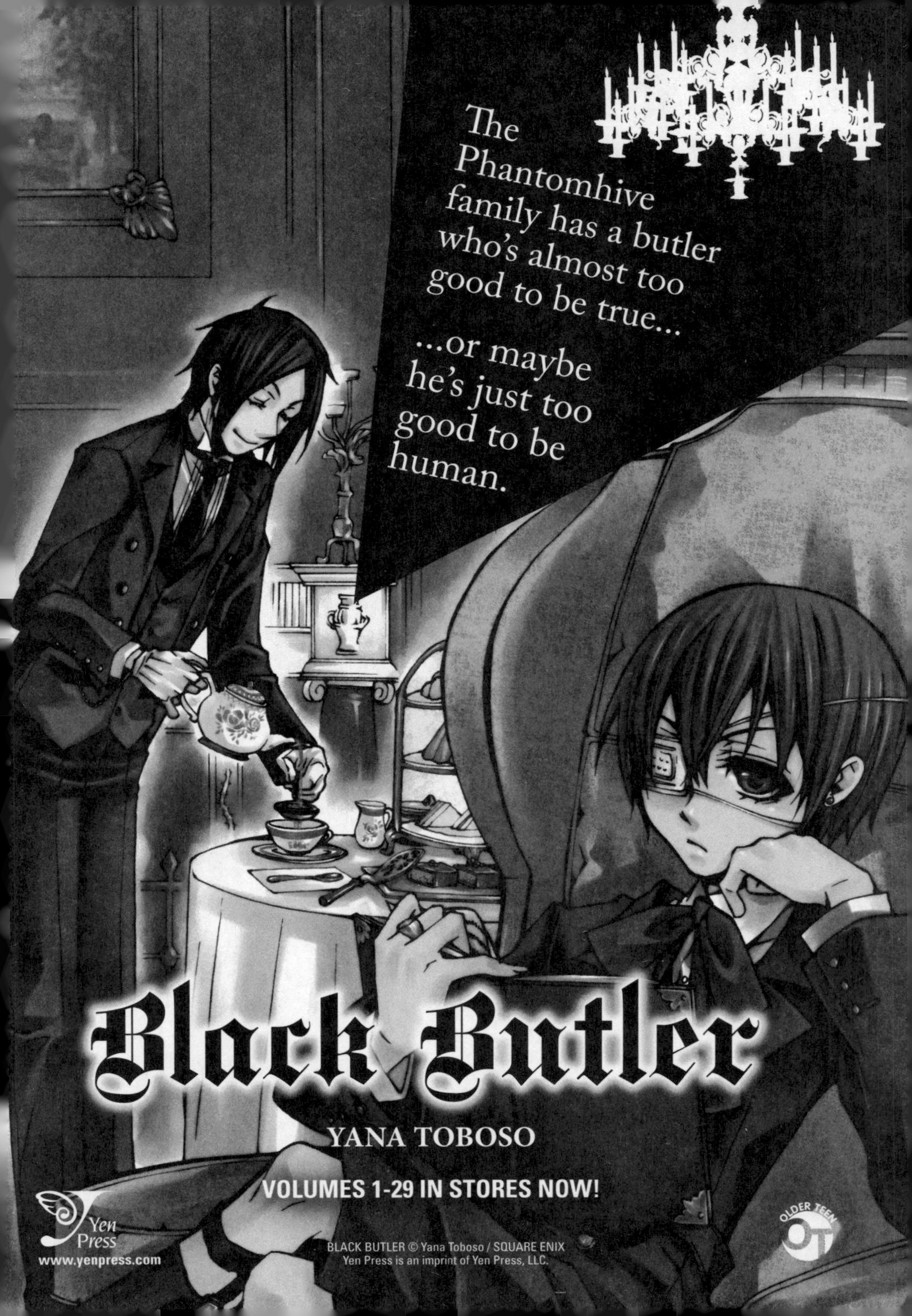
The Phantomhive family has a butler who's almost too good to be true...
...or maybe he's just too good to be human.
Black Butler
YANA TOBOSO
VOLUMES 1-29 IN STORES NOW!
Yen Press
www.yenpress.com
BLACK BUTLER © Yana Toboso / SQUARE ENIX
Yen Press is an imprint of Yen Press, LLC.
OLDER TEEN
OT

Translation: JOCELYNE ALLEN   **Lettering: LYS BLAKESLEE**

ACCA JUSAN-KU KANSATSU-KA P.S. Volume 2 ©2017 Natsume Ono/Square Enix Co., Ltd. First published in Japan in 2017 by Square Enix Co., Ltd. English translation rights arranged with Square Enix Co., Ltd. and Yen Press, LLC through Tuttle-Mori Agency, Inc.

English translation ©2020 by Square Enix Co., Ltd.

Yen Press
150 West 30th Street, 19th Floor
New York, NY 10001

Visit us at yenpress.com
facebook.com/yenpress
twitter.com/yenpress
yenpress.tumblr.com
instagram.com/yenpress

First Yen Press Edition: December 2020

Yen Press is an imprint of Yen Press, LLC.
The Yen Press name and logo are trademarks of
Yen Press, LLC.

The publisher is not responsible for websites (or their content) that are not owned by the publisher.

Library of Congress Control Number: 2020940349

ISBNs: 978-1-9753-1740-9 (paperback)
       978-1-9753-1741-6 (ebook)

10 9 8 7 6 5 4 3 2 1

WOR

Printed in the United States of America